This book belongs to:

_____

SPERA

ASCENSION of the STARLESS™

Volume One

JOSH TIERNEY

MILONOGIANNIS • ATELIER SENTÔ • LEE • SOURYA • SEICHE

Published by
ARCHAIA™

S P E R A
ASCENSION
of the STARLESS™

Written by
JOSH TIERNEY

Illustrated by
GIANNIS MILONOGIANNIS
ATELIER SENTÔ
MINDY LEE
SOURYA SIHACHAKR
VALENTIN SEICHE

Character Designs and Cover Art by
AFU CHAN

Design by
KELSEY DIETERICH

Edited by
REBECCA TAYLOR

ARCHAIA™

ROSS RICHIE CEO & Founder • MARK SMYLIE Founder of Archaia • MATT GAGNON Editor-in-Chief • STEPHEN CHRISTY President of Development • FILIP SABLIK VP of Publishing & Marketing
LANCE KREITER VP of Licensing & Merchandising • PHIL BARBARO VP of Finance • BRYCE CARLSON Managing Editor • MEL CAYLO Marketing Manager • SCOTT NEWMAN Production Design Manager
IRENE BRADISH Operations Manager • CHRISTINE DINH Brand Communications Manager • DAFNA PLEBAN Editor • SHANNON WATTERS Editor • ERIC HARBURN Editor • REBECCA TAYLOR Editor
IAN BRILL Editor • CHRIS ROSA Assistant Editor • ALEX GALER Assistant Editor • WHITNEY LEOPARD Assistant Editor • JASMINE AMIRI Assistant Editor • CAMERON CHITTOCK Assistant Editor
KELSEY DIETERICH Production Designer • EMI YONEMURA BROWN Production Designer • DEVIN FUNCHES E-Commerce & Inventory Coordinator • ANDY LIEGL Event Coordinator • BRIANNA HART Administrative Coordinator
AARON FERRARA Operations Assistant • JOSÉ MEZA Sales Assistant • MICHELLE ANKLEY Sales Assistant • ELIZABETH LOUGHRIDGE Accounting Assistant • STEPHANIE HOCUTT PR Assistant

SPERA: ASCENSION OF THE STARLESS Volume One, October 2014. Published by Archaia, a division of Boom Entertainment, Inc.

BOOM! Studios, 5670 Wilshire Boulevard, Suite 450, Los Angeles, CA 90036-5679.

Printed in China. First Printing. ISBN: 978-1-60886-414-0, eISBN: 978-1-61398-268-6

Table of Contents

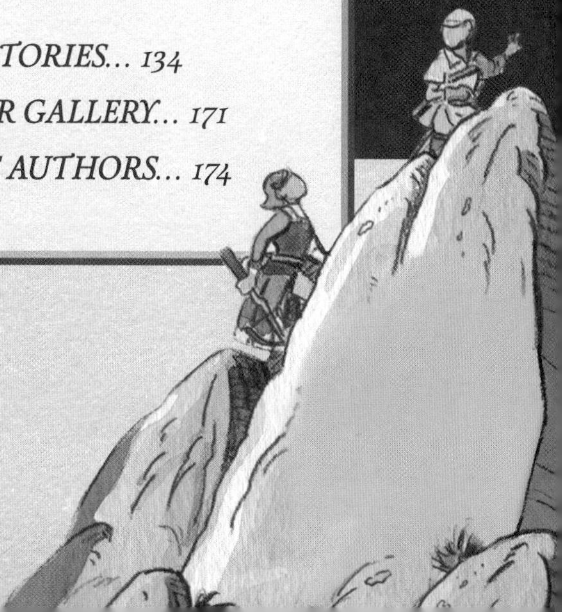

CHAPTER ONE

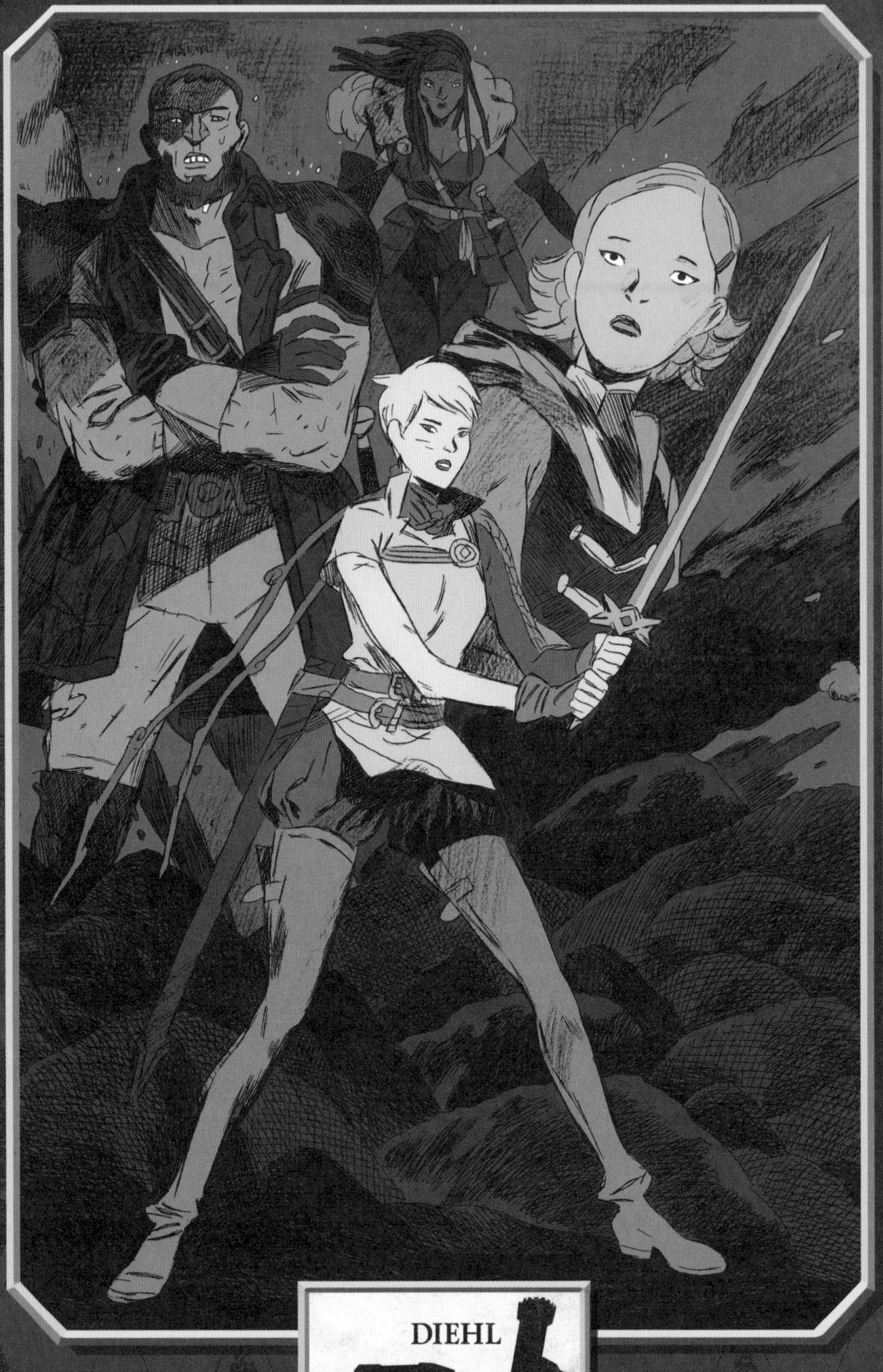
DIEHL

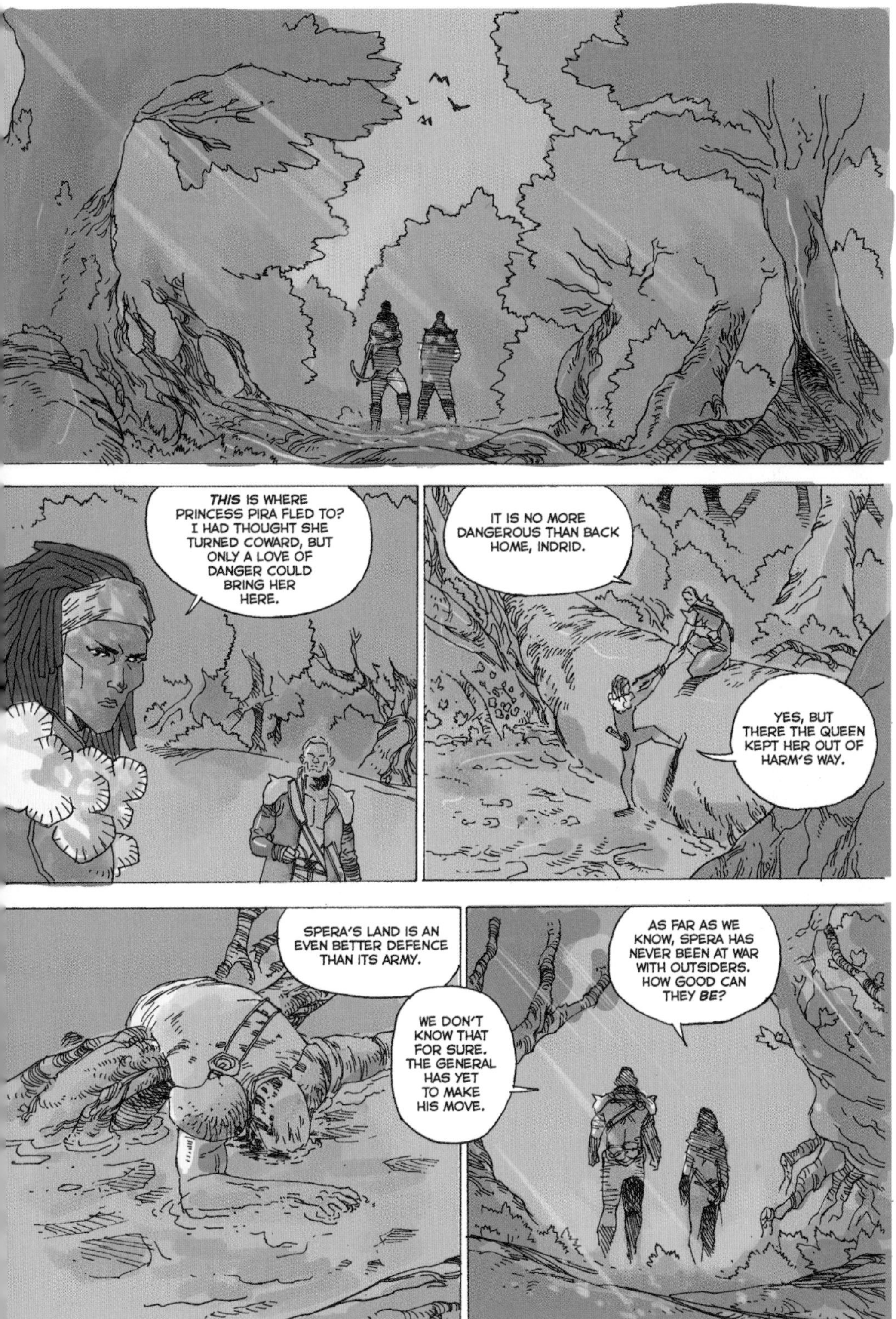
THIS IS WHERE PRINCESS PIRA FLED TO? I HAD THOUGHT SHE TURNED COWARD, BUT ONLY A LOVE OF DANGER COULD BRING HER HERE.
IT IS NO MORE DANGEROUS THAN BACK HOME, INDRID.
YES, BUT THERE THE QUEEN KEPT HER OUT OF HARM'S WAY.
SPERA'S LAND IS AN EVEN BETTER DEFENCE THAN ITS ARMY.
WE DON'T KNOW THAT FOR SURE. THE GENERAL HAS YET TO MAKE HIS MOVE.
AS FAR AS WE KNOW, SPERA HAS NEVER BEEN AT WAR WITH OUTSIDERS. HOW GOOD CAN THEY *BE*?

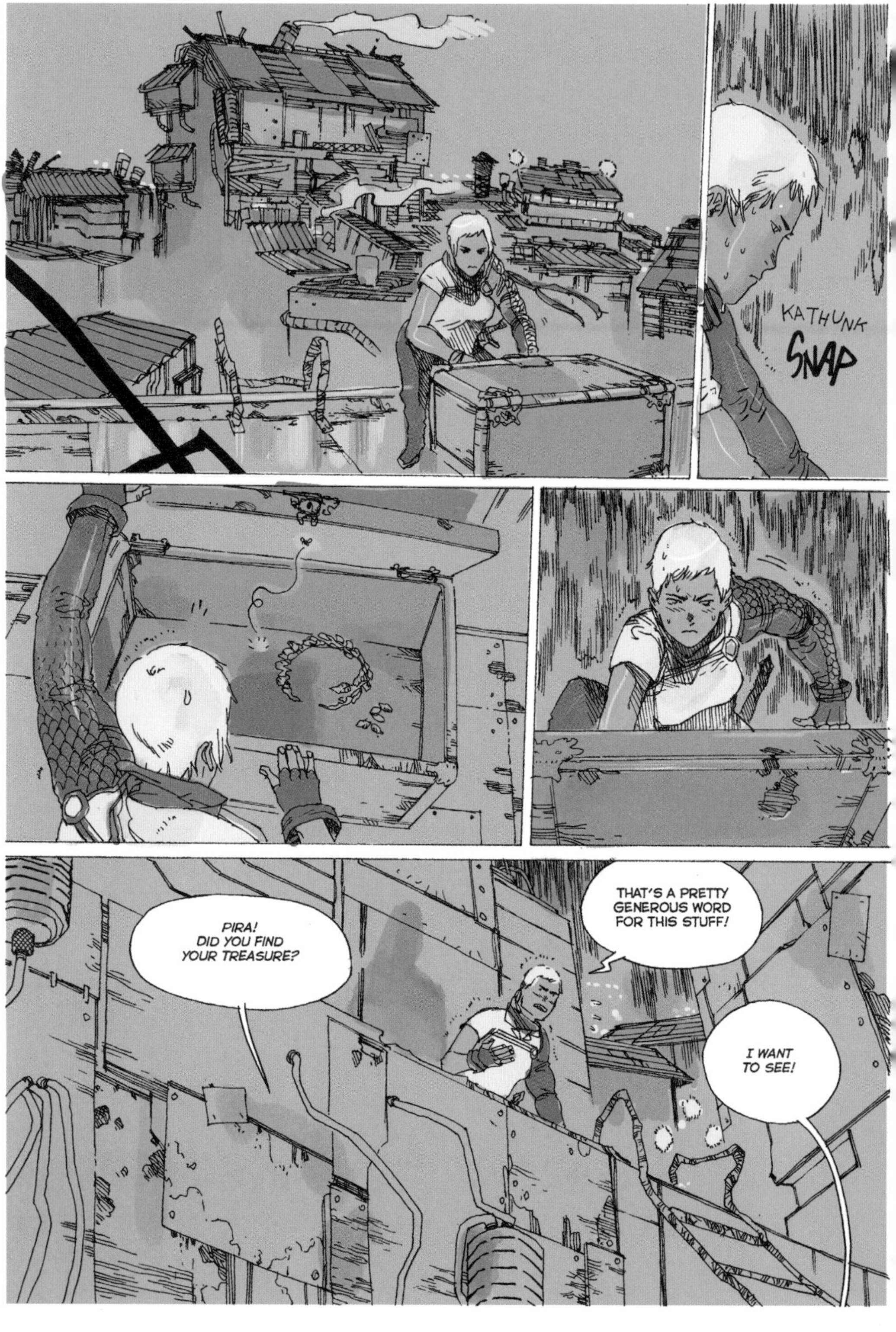
KATHUNK
SNAP
PIRA! DID YOU FIND YOUR TREASURE?
THAT'S A PRETTY GENEROUS WORD FOR THIS STUFF!
I WANT TO SEE!

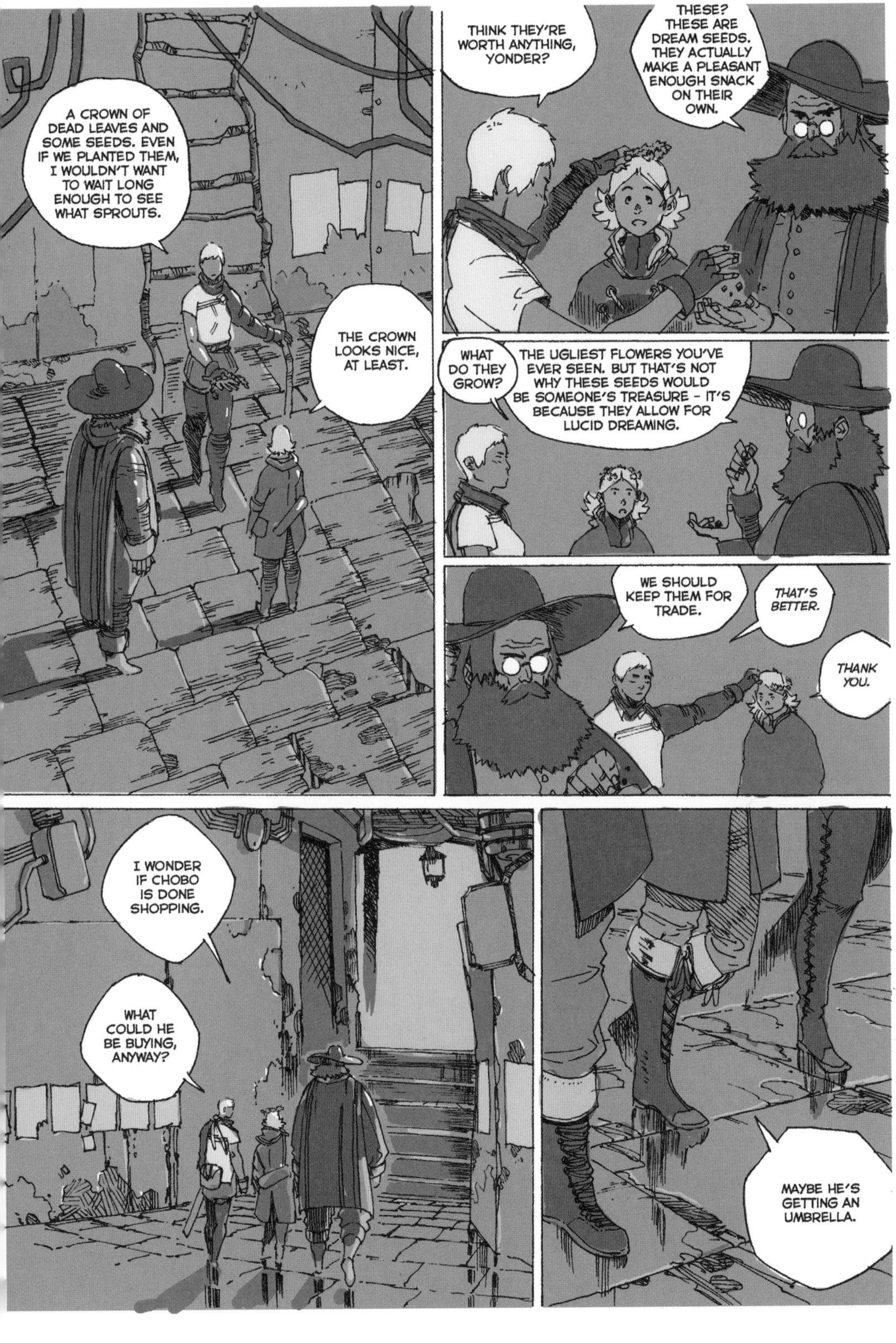
A CROWN OF DEAD LEAVES AND SOME SEEDS. EVEN IF WE PLANTED THEM, I WOULDN'T WANT TO WAIT LONG ENOUGH TO SEE WHAT SPROUTS.
THE CROWN LOOKS NICE, AT LEAST.
THINK THEY'RE WORTH ANYTHING, YONDER?
THESE? THESE ARE DREAM SEEDS. THEY ACTUALLY MAKE A PLEASANT ENOUGH SNACK ON THEIR OWN.
WHAT DO THEY GROW?
THE UGLIEST FLOWERS YOU'VE EVER SEEN. BUT THAT'S NOT WHY THESE SEEDS WOULD BE SOMEONE'S TREASURE - IT'S BECAUSE THEY ALLOW FOR LUCID DREAMING.
WE SHOULD KEEP THEM FOR TRADE.
THAT'S BETTER.
THANK YOU.
I WONDER IF CHOBO IS DONE SHOPPING.
WHAT COULD HE BE BUYING, ANYWAY?
MAYBE HE'S GETTING AN UMBRELLA.

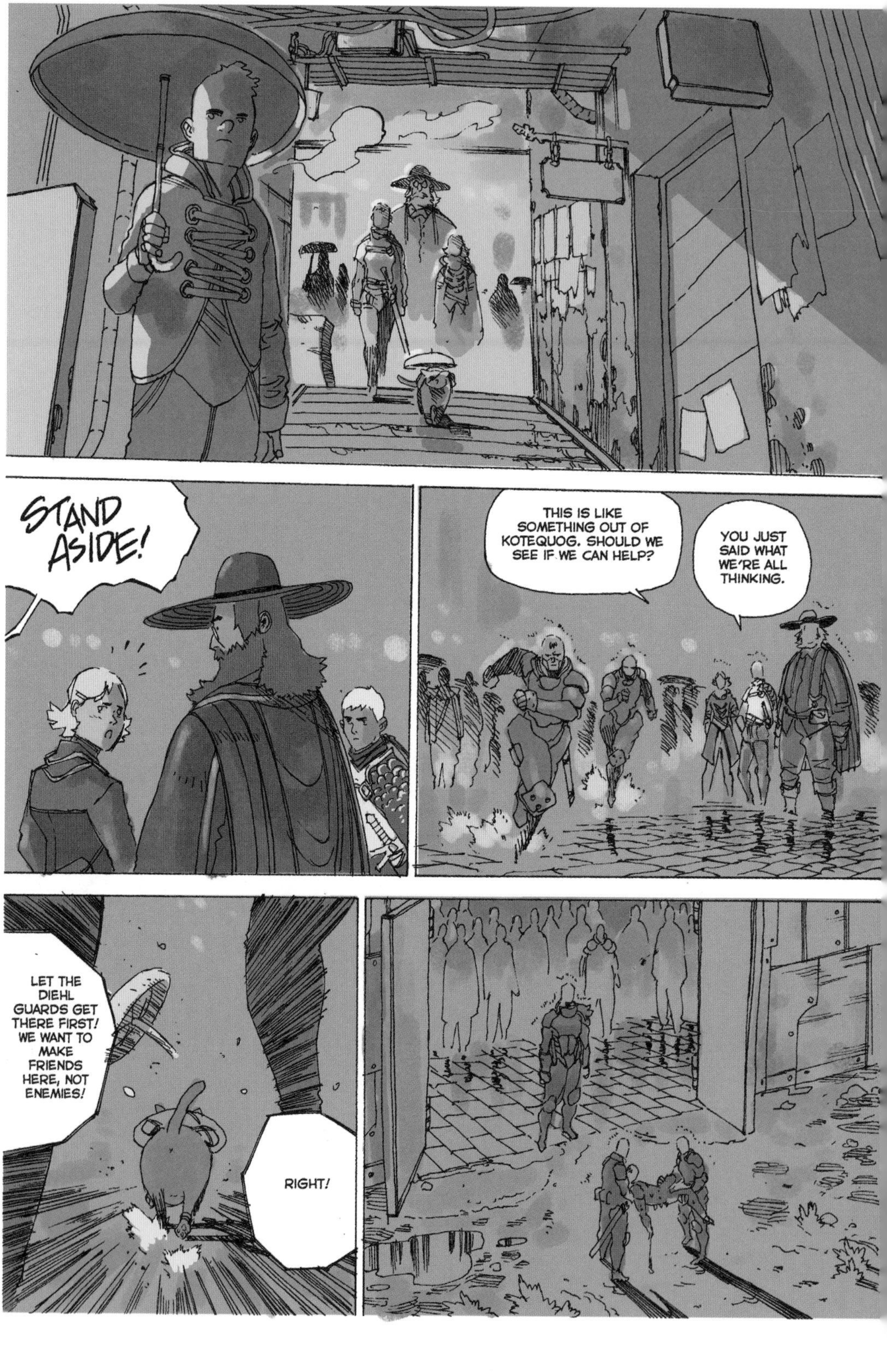
STAND ASIDE!
THIS IS LIKE SOMETHING OUT OF KOTEQUOG. SHOULD WE SEE IF WE CAN HELP?
YOU JUST SAID WHAT WE'RE ALL THINKING.
LET THE DIEHL GUARDS GET THERE FIRST! WE WANT TO MAKE FRIENDS HERE, NOT ENEMIES!
RIGHT!

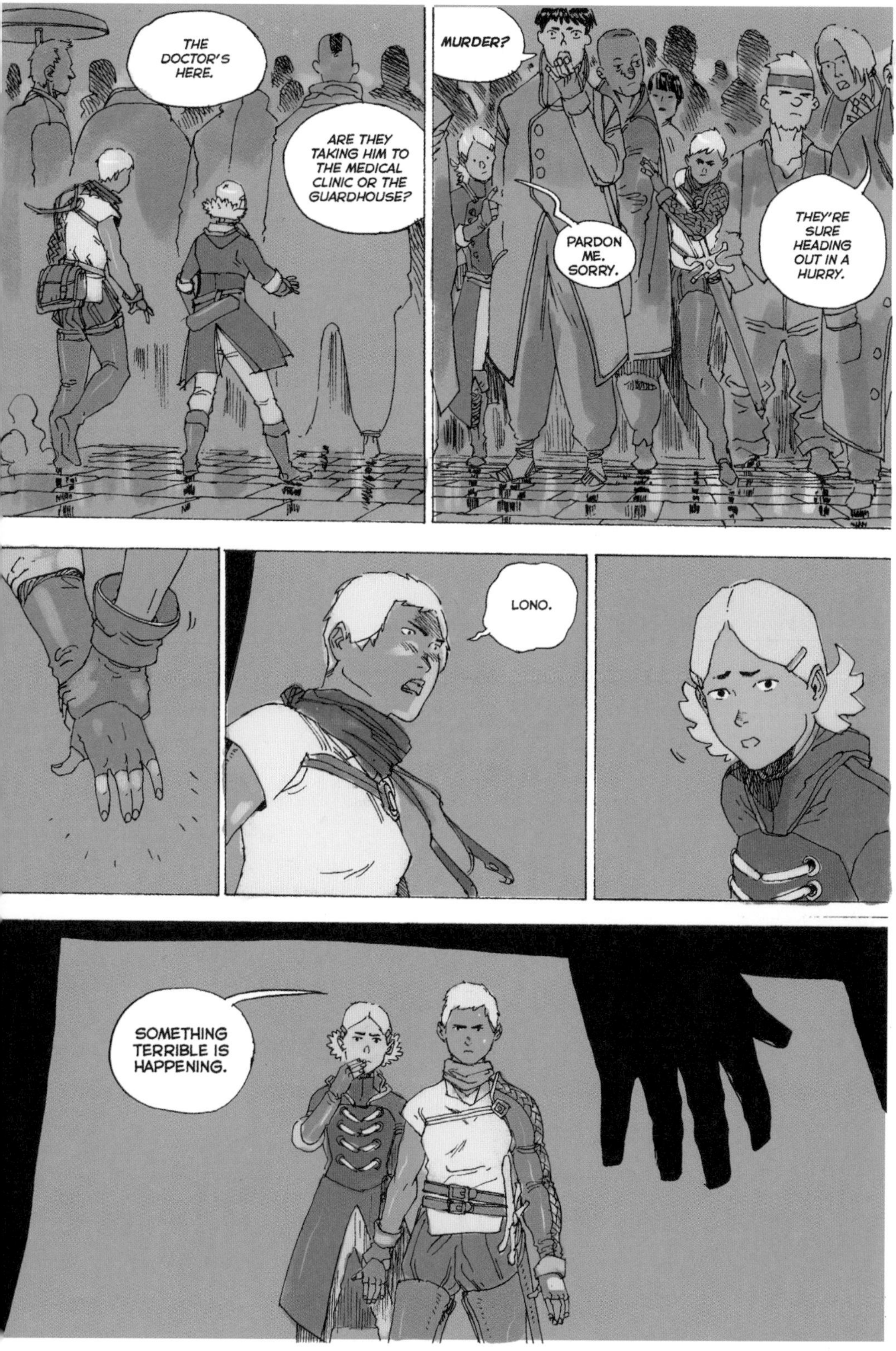
THE DOCTOR'S HERE.
ARE THEY TAKING HIM TO THE MEDICAL CLINIC OR THE GUARDHOUSE?
MURDER?
PARDON ME. SORRY.
THEY'RE SURE HEADING OUT IN A HURRY.
LONO.
SOMETHING TERRIBLE IS HAPPENING.

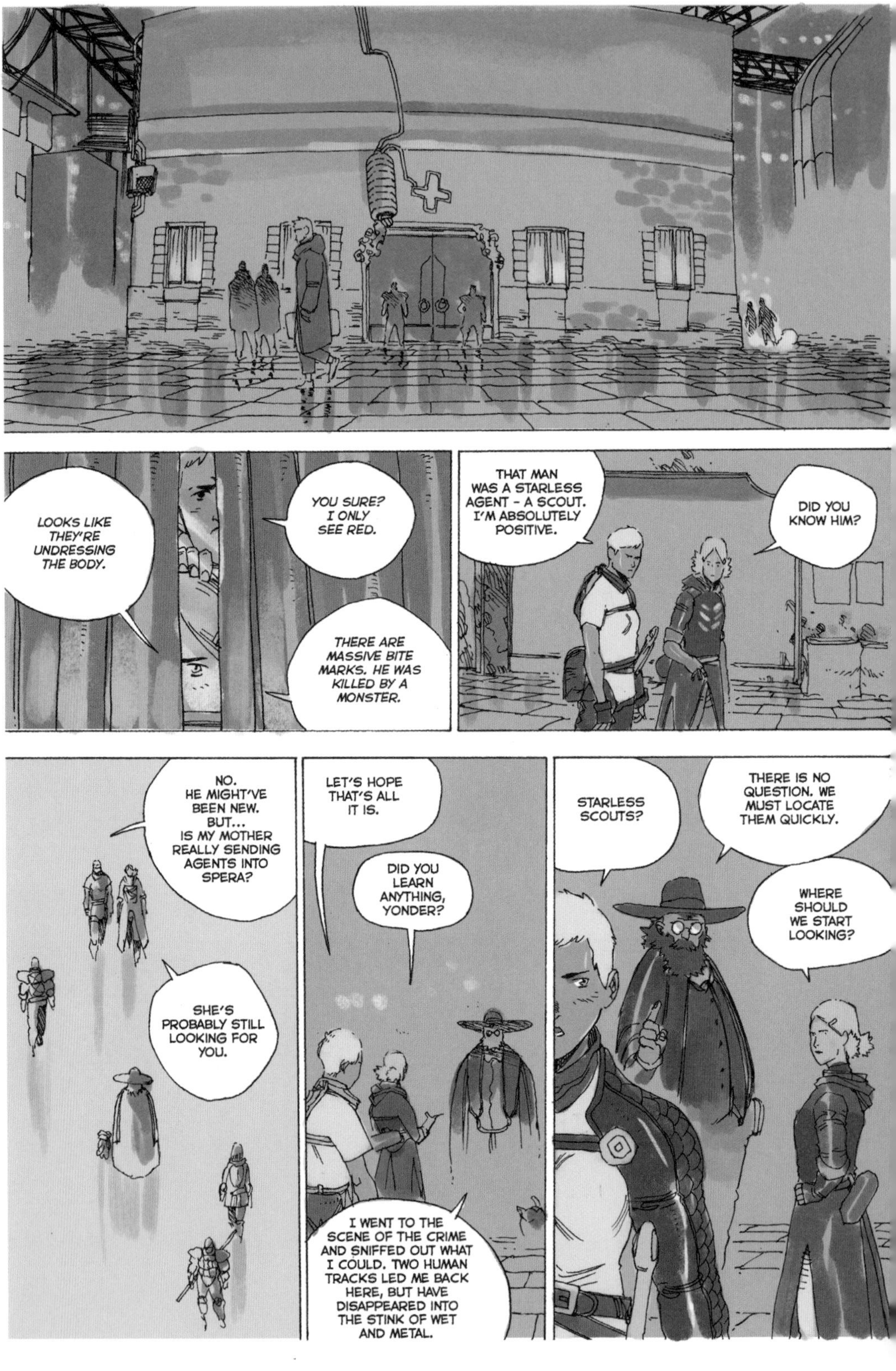
LOOKS LIKE THEY'RE UNDRESSING THE BODY.
YOU SURE? I ONLY SEE RED.
THERE ARE MASSIVE BITE MARKS. HE WAS KILLED BY A MONSTER.
THAT MAN WAS A STARLESS AGENT - A SCOUT. I'M ABSOLUTELY POSITIVE.
DID YOU KNOW HIM?
NO. HE MIGHT'VE BEEN NEW. BUT... IS MY MOTHER REALLY SENDING AGENTS INTO SPERA?
SHE'S PROBABLY STILL LOOKING FOR YOU.
LET'S HOPE THAT'S ALL IT IS.
DID YOU LEARN ANYTHING, YONDER?
I WENT TO THE SCENE OF THE CRIME AND SNIFFED OUT WHAT I COULD. TWO HUMAN TRACKS LED ME BACK HERE, BUT HAVE DISAPPEARED INTO THE STINK OF WET AND METAL.
STARLESS SCOUTS?
THERE IS NO QUESTION. WE MUST LOCATE THEM QUICKLY.
WHERE SHOULD WE START LOOKING?

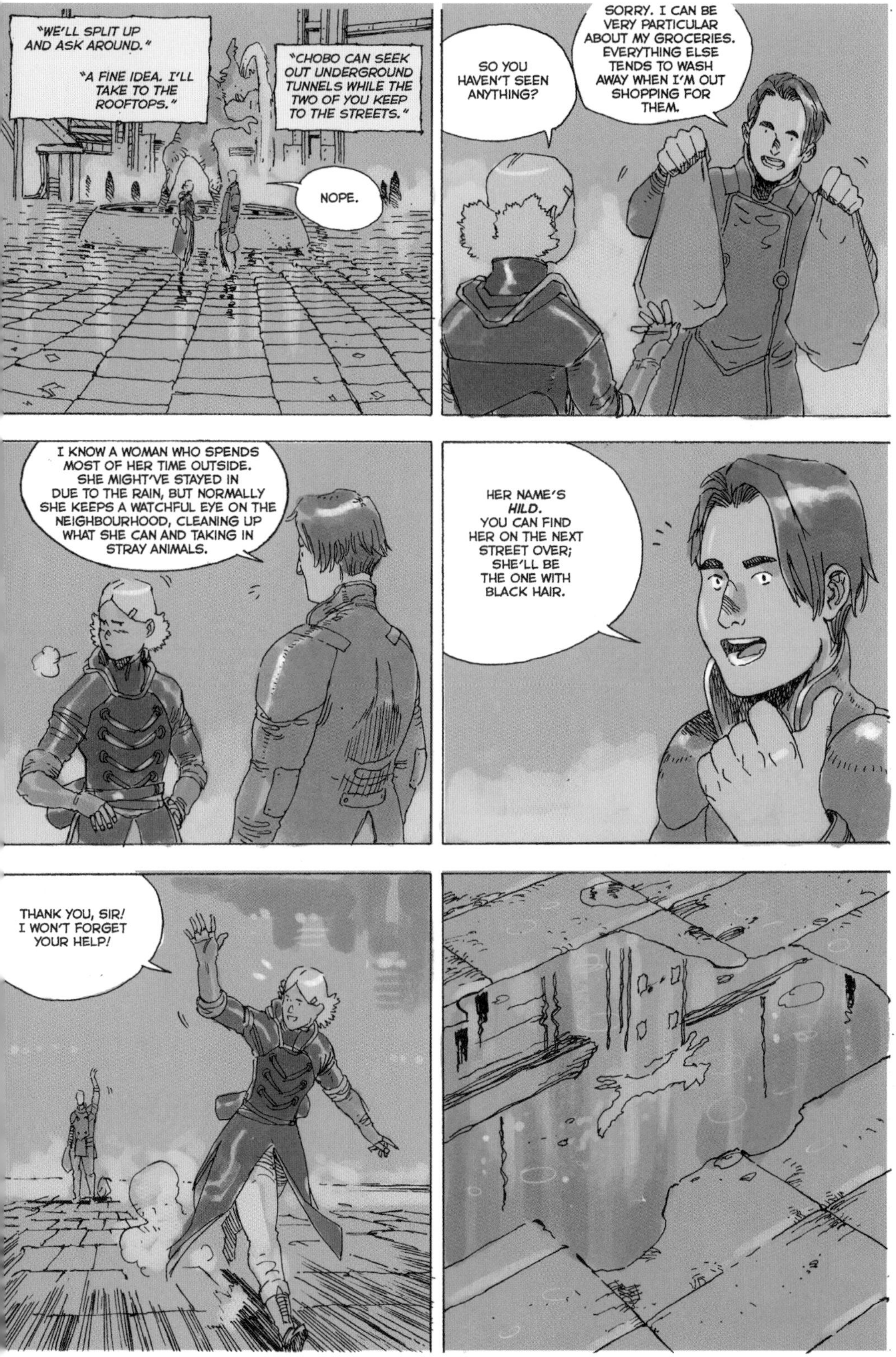
"WE'LL SPLIT UP AND ASK AROUND."
"A FINE IDEA. I'LL TAKE TO THE ROOFTOPS."
"CHOBO CAN SEEK OUT UNDERGROUND TUNNELS WHILE THE TWO OF YOU KEEP TO THE STREETS."
NOPE.
SO YOU HAVEN'T SEEN ANYTHING?
SORRY. I CAN BE VERY PARTICULAR ABOUT MY GROCERIES. EVERYTHING ELSE TENDS TO WASH AWAY WHEN I'M OUT SHOPPING FOR THEM.
I KNOW A WOMAN WHO SPENDS MOST OF HER TIME OUTSIDE. SHE MIGHT'VE STAYED IN DUE TO THE RAIN, BUT NORMALLY SHE KEEPS A WATCHFUL EYE ON THE NEIGHBOURHOOD, CLEANING UP WHAT SHE CAN AND TAKING IN STRAY ANIMALS.
HER NAME'S *HILD*. YOU CAN FIND HER ON THE NEXT STREET OVER; SHE'LL BE THE ONE WITH BLACK HAIR.
THANK YOU, SIR! I WON'T FORGET YOUR HELP!

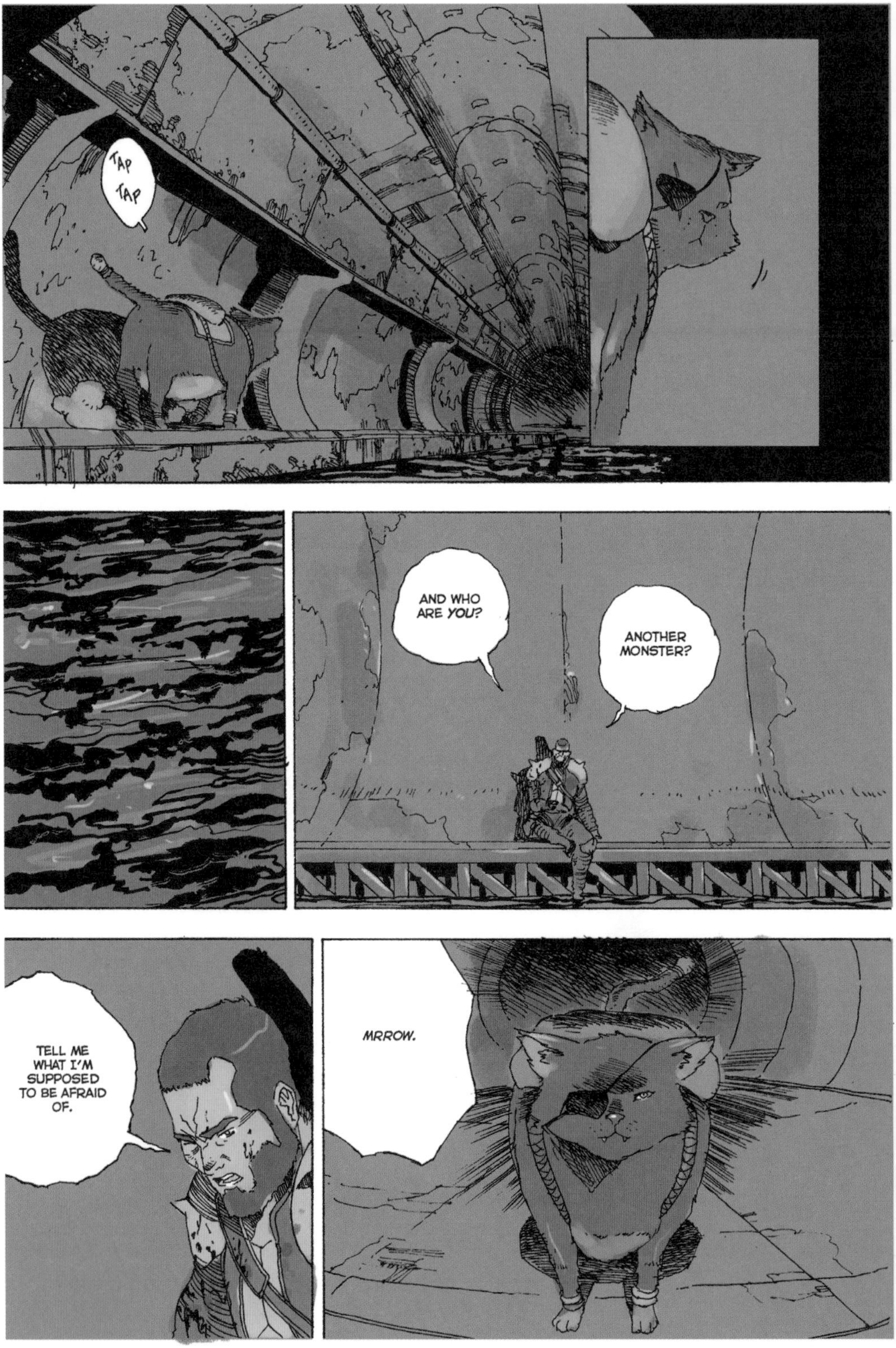
TAP TAP
AND WHO ARE YOU?
ANOTHER MONSTER?
TELL ME WHAT I'M SUPPOSED TO BE AFRAID OF.
MRROW.

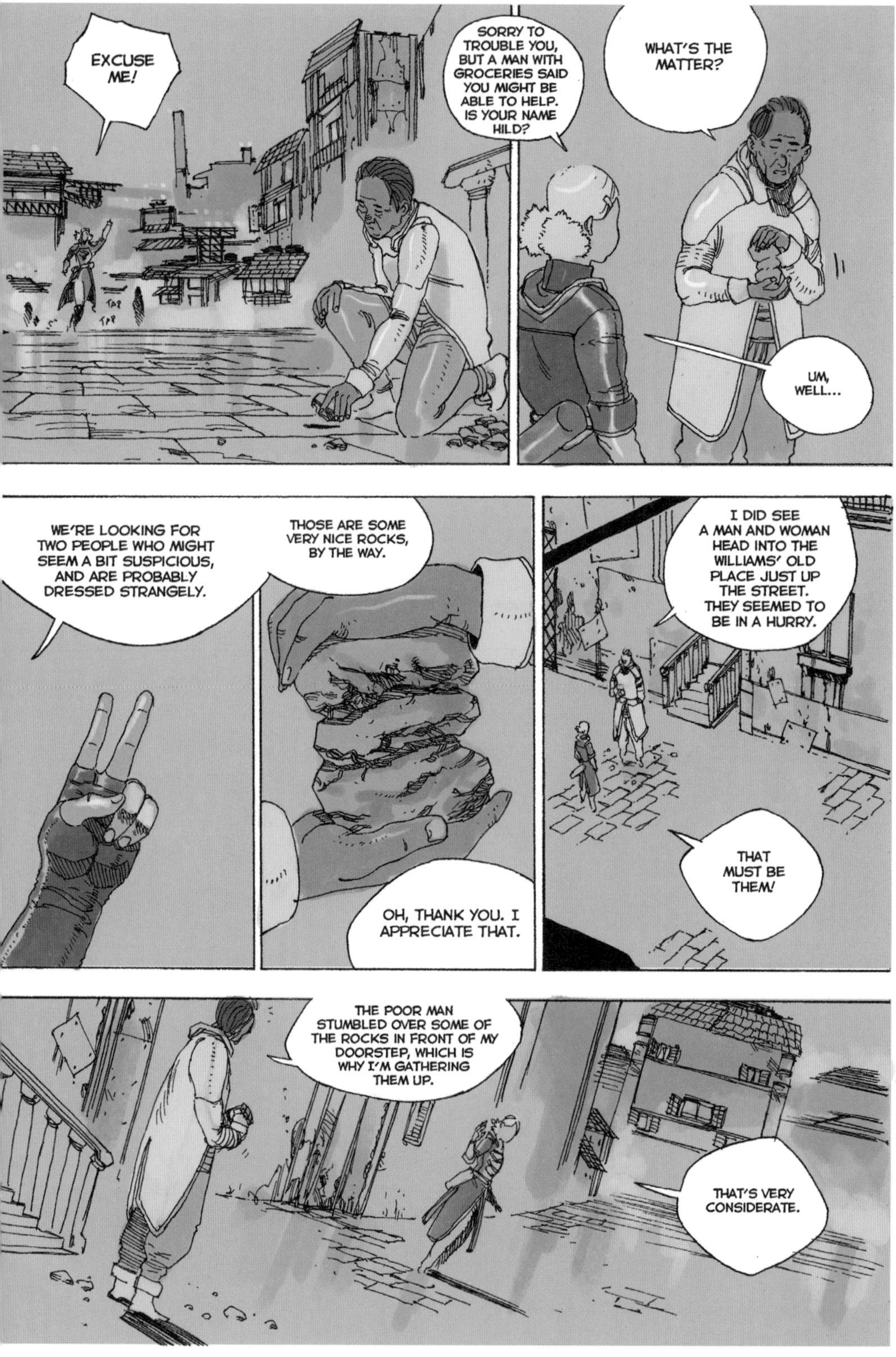
EXCUSE ME!
SORRY TO TROUBLE YOU, BUT A MAN WITH GROCERIES SAID YOU MIGHT BE ABLE TO HELP. IS YOUR NAME HILD?
WHAT'S THE MATTER?
UM, WELL...
WE'RE LOOKING FOR TWO PEOPLE WHO MIGHT SEEM A BIT SUSPICIOUS, AND ARE PROBABLY DRESSED STRANGELY.
THOSE ARE SOME VERY NICE ROCKS, BY THE WAY.
OH, THANK YOU. I APPRECIATE THAT.
I DID SEE A MAN AND WOMAN HEAD INTO THE WILLIAMS' OLD PLACE JUST UP THE STREET. THEY SEEMED TO BE IN A HURRY.
THAT MUST BE THEM!
THE POOR MAN STUMBLED OVER SOME OF THE ROCKS IN FRONT OF MY DOORSTEP, WHICH IS WHY I'M GATHERING THEM UP.
THAT'S VERY CONSIDERATE.

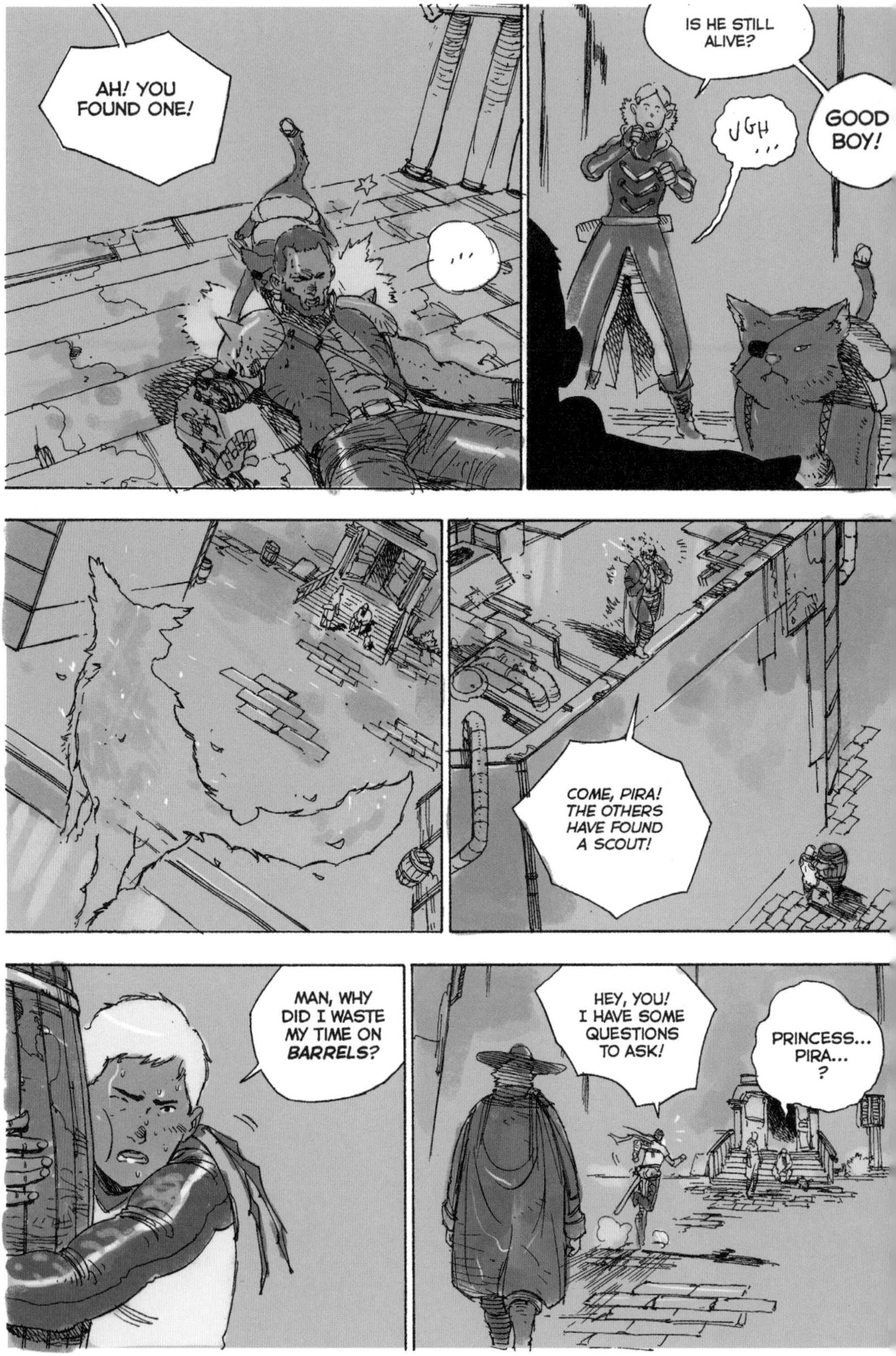
AH! YOU FOUND ONE!
...
IS HE STILL ALIVE?
UGH ...
GOOD BOY!
COME, PIRA! THE OTHERS HAVE FOUND A SCOUT!
MAN, WHY DID I WASTE MY TIME ON *BARRELS*?
HEY, YOU! I HAVE SOME QUESTIONS TO ASK!
PRINCESS... PIRA... ?

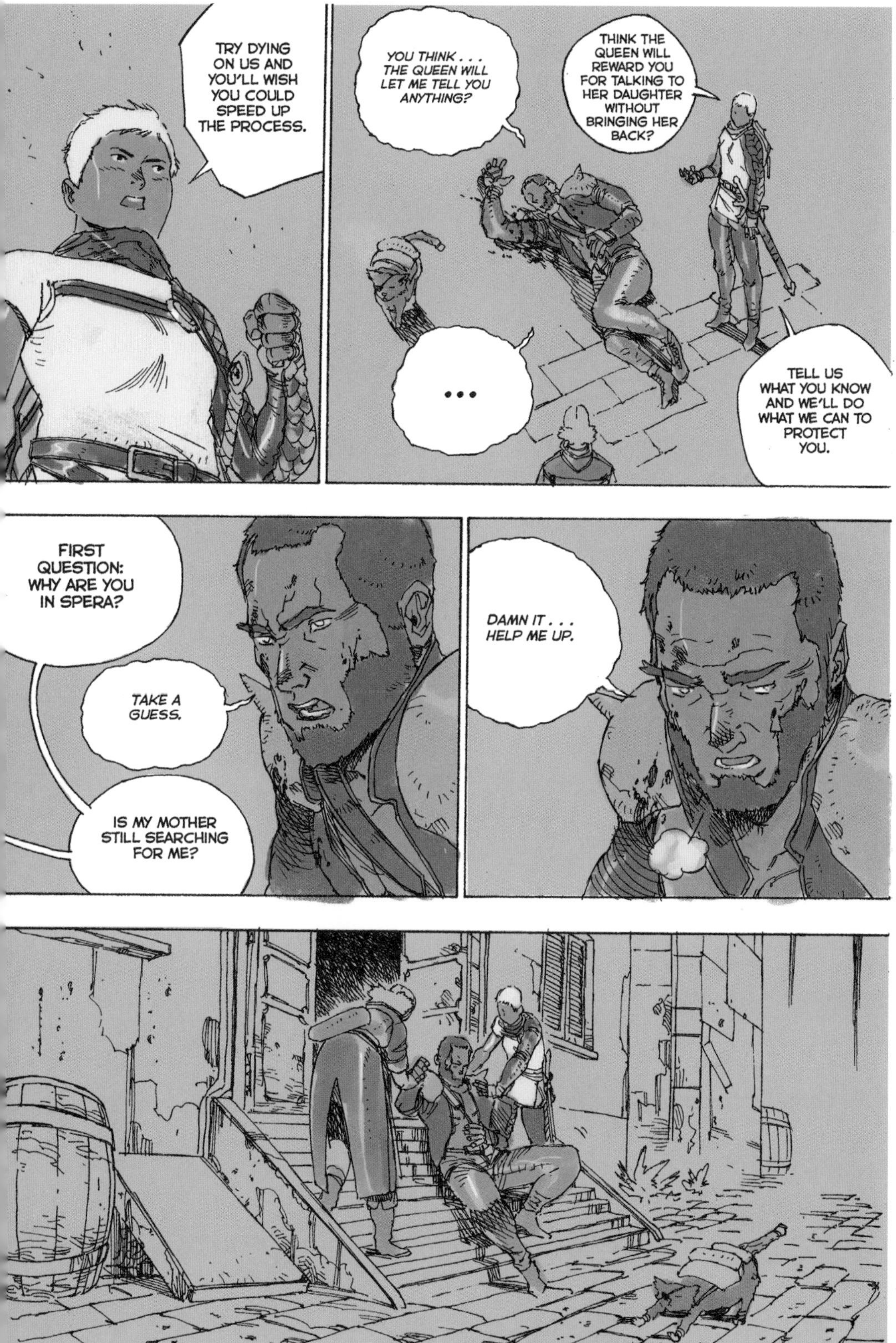
TRY DYING ON US AND YOU'LL WISH YOU COULD SPEED UP THE PROCESS.
YOU THINK . . . THE QUEEN WILL LET ME TELL YOU ANYTHING?
THINK THE QUEEN WILL REWARD YOU FOR TALKING TO HER DAUGHTER WITHOUT BRINGING HER BACK?
...
TELL US WHAT YOU KNOW AND WE'LL DO WHAT WE CAN TO PROTECT YOU.
FIRST QUESTION: WHY ARE YOU IN SPERA?
TAKE A GUESS.
IS MY MOTHER STILL SEARCHING FOR ME?
DAMN IT . . . HELP ME UP.

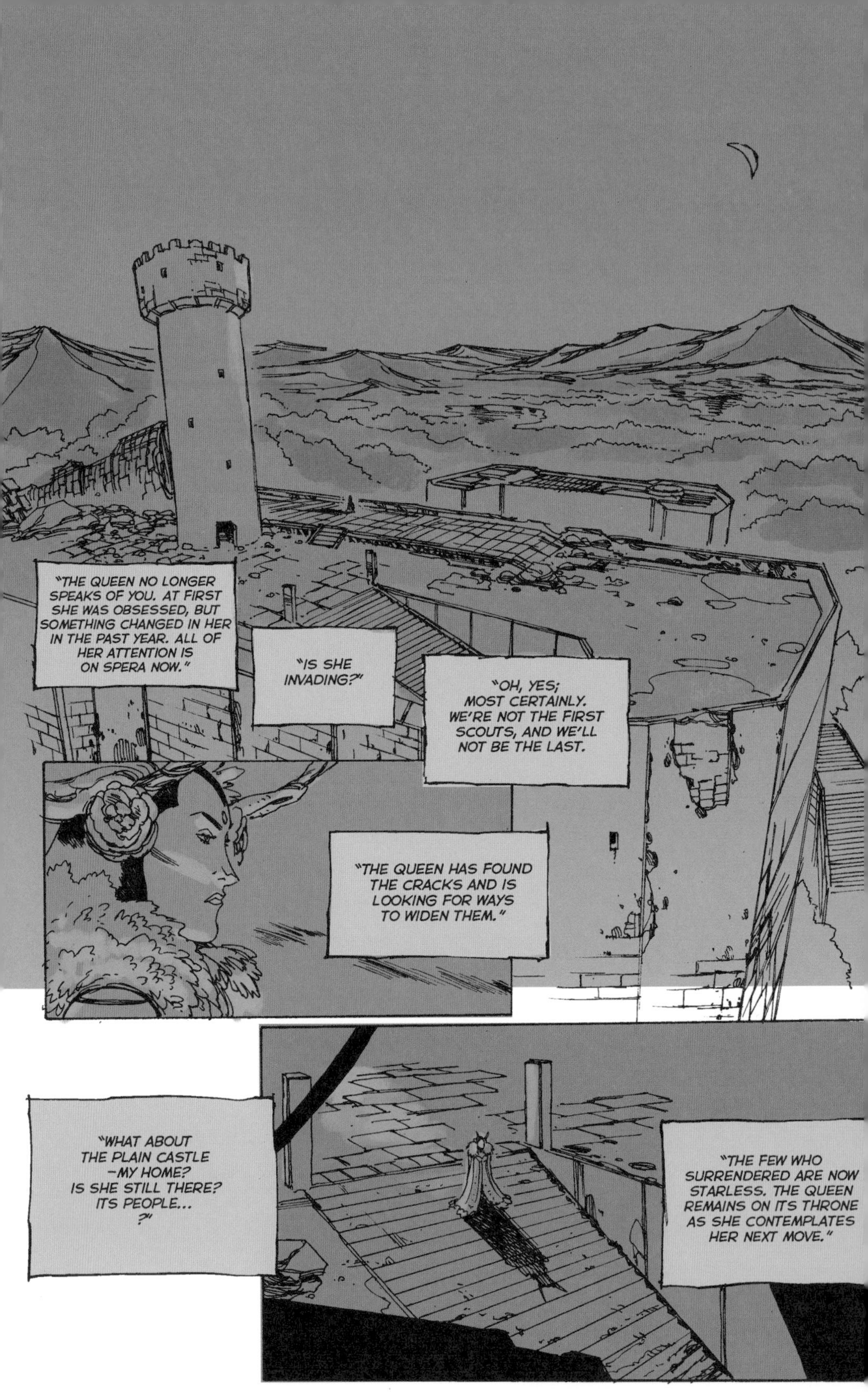
"THE QUEEN NO LONGER SPEAKS OF YOU. AT FIRST SHE WAS OBSESSED, BUT SOMETHING CHANGED IN HER IN THE PAST YEAR. ALL OF HER ATTENTION IS ON SPERA NOW."
"IS SHE INVADING?"
"OH, YES; MOST CERTAINLY. WE'RE NOT THE FIRST SCOUTS, AND WE'LL NOT BE THE LAST.
"THE QUEEN HAS FOUND THE CRACKS AND IS LOOKING FOR WAYS TO WIDEN THEM."
"WHAT ABOUT THE PLAIN CASTLE —MY HOME? IS SHE STILL THERE? ITS PEOPLE... ?"
"THE FEW WHO SURRENDERED ARE NOW STARLESS. THE QUEEN REMAINS ON ITS THRONE AS SHE CONTEMPLATES HER NEXT MOVE."

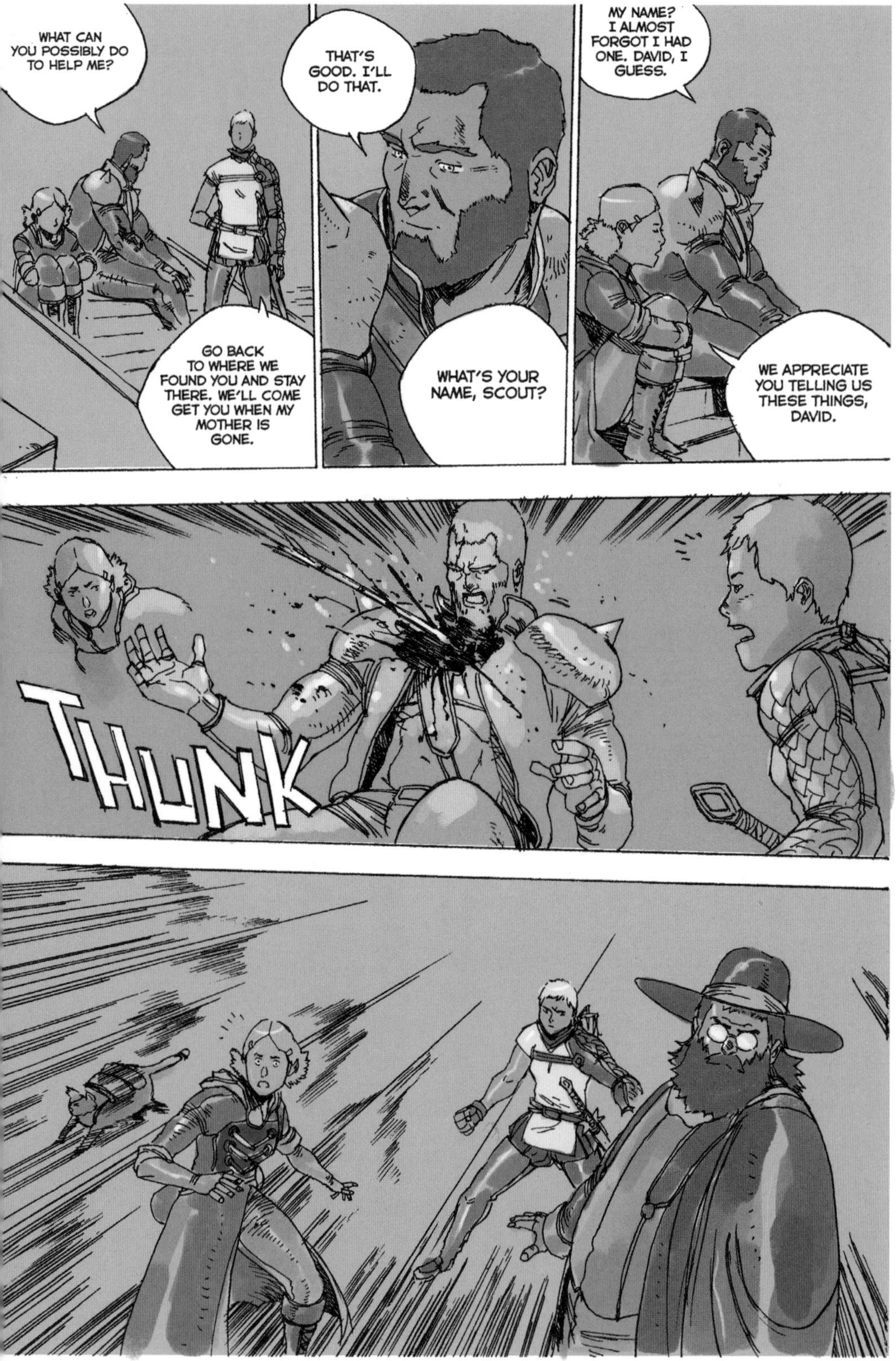
WHAT CAN YOU POSSIBLY DO TO HELP ME?
GO BACK TO WHERE WE FOUND YOU AND STAY THERE. WE'LL COME GET YOU WHEN MY MOTHER IS GONE.
THAT'S GOOD. I'LL DO THAT.
WHAT'S YOUR NAME, SCOUT?
MY NAME? I ALMOST FORGOT I HAD ONE. DAVID, I GUESS.
WE APPRECIATE YOU TELLING US THESE THINGS, DAVID.
THUNK

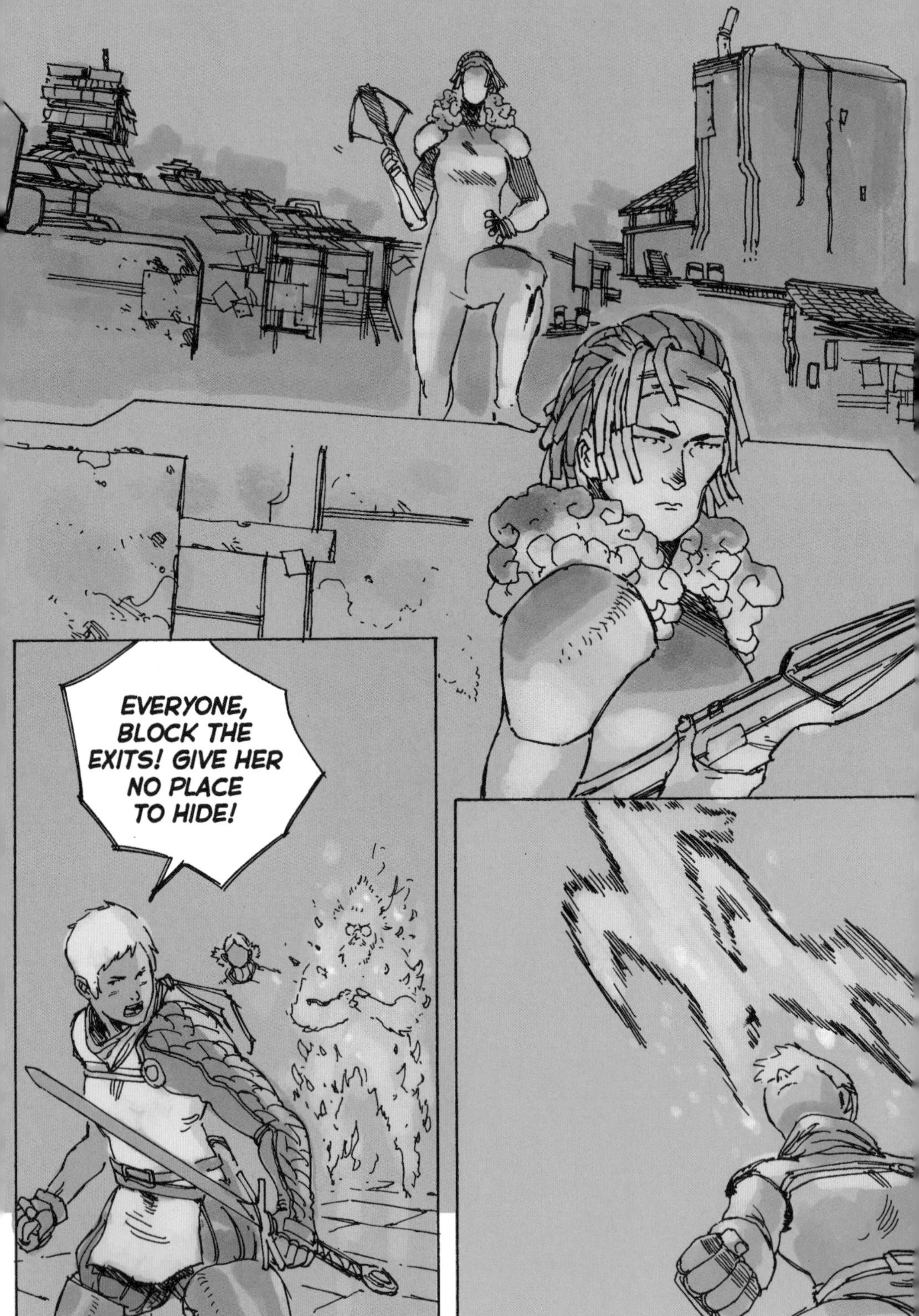
EVERYONE, BLOCK THE EXITS! GIVE HER NO PLACE TO HIDE!

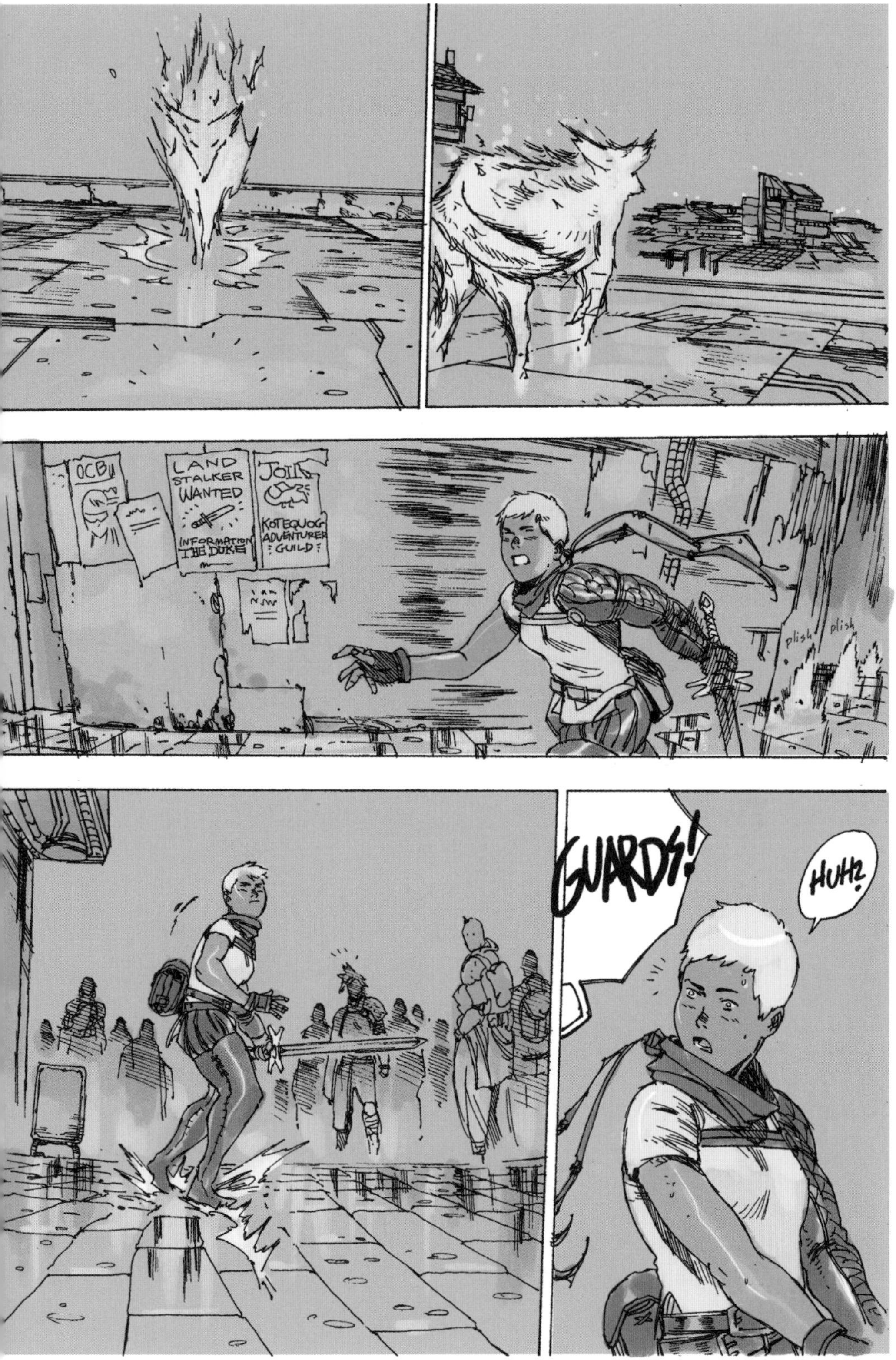
OCB
LAND STALKER WANTED
INFORMATION THE DUKE
KOTEQUOG ADVENTURER GUILD
plish plish
GUARDS!
HUH?

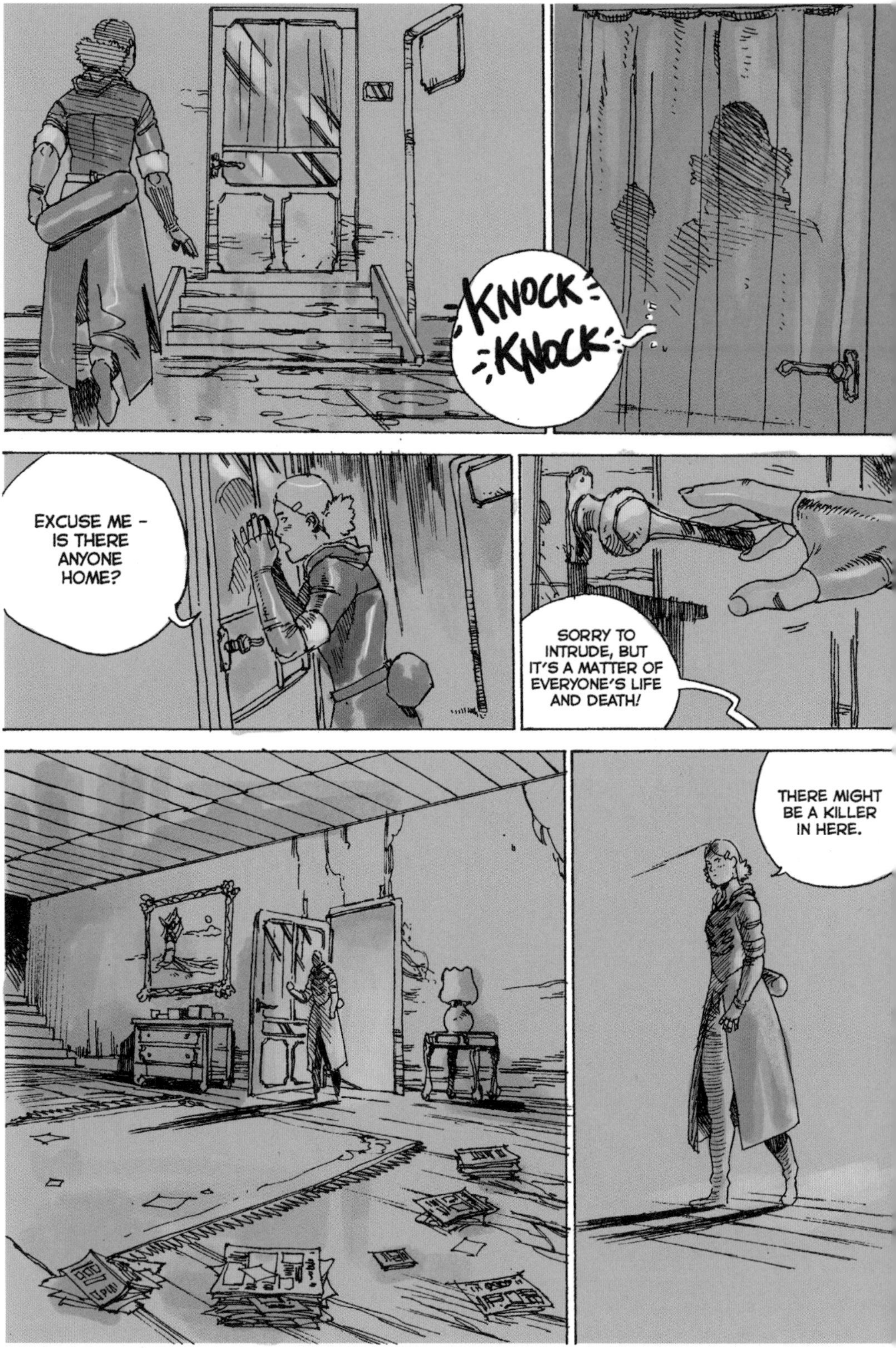
KNOCK KNOCK
EXCUSE ME - IS THERE ANYONE HOME?
SORRY TO INTRUDE, BUT IT'S A MATTER OF EVERYONE'S LIFE AND DEATH!
THERE MIGHT BE A KILLER IN HERE.

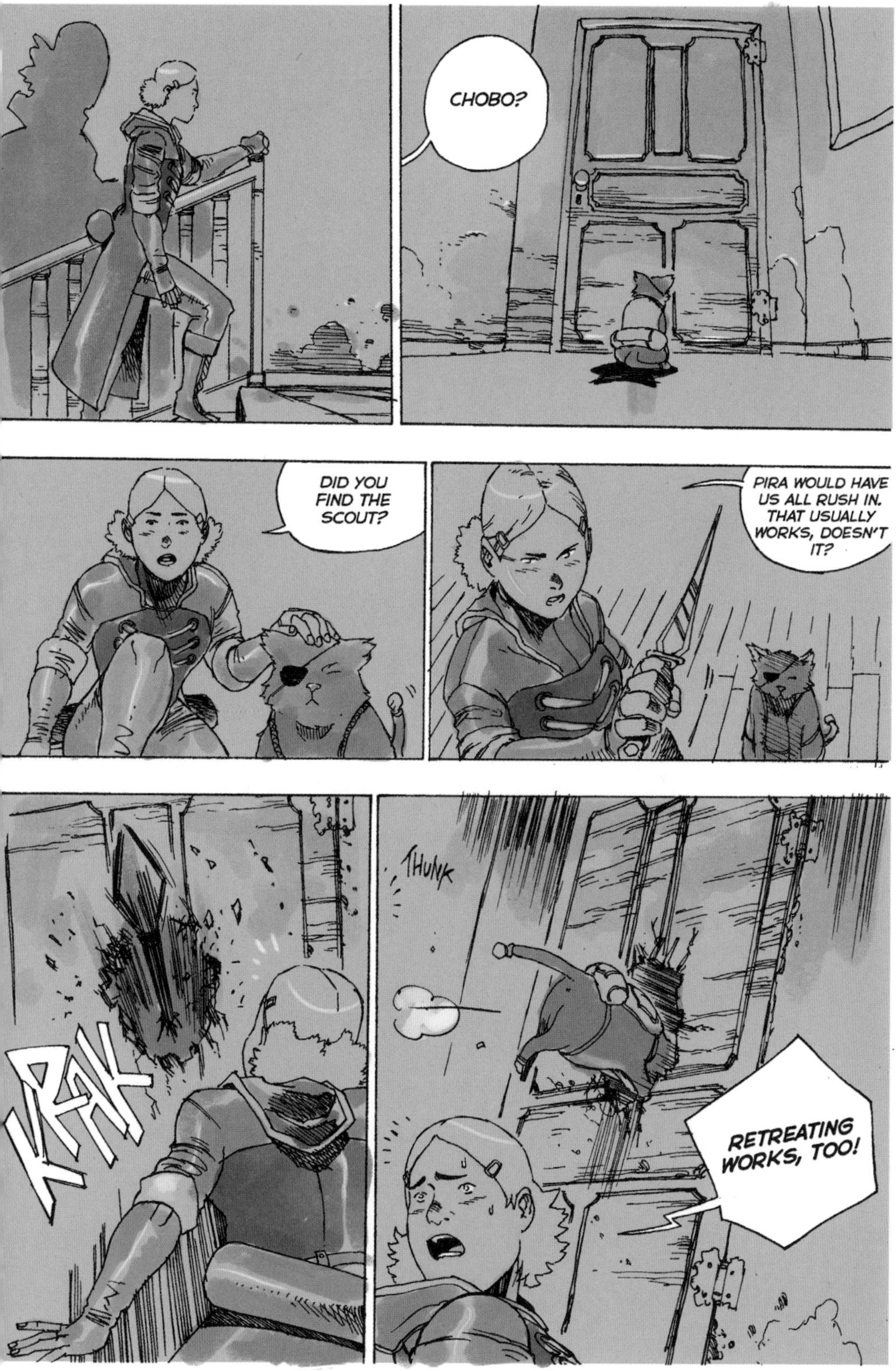
CHOBO?
DID YOU FIND THE SCOUT?
PIRA WOULD HAVE US ALL RUSH IN. THAT USUALLY WORKS, DOESN'T IT?
KRAK
THUNK
RETREATING WORKS, TOO!

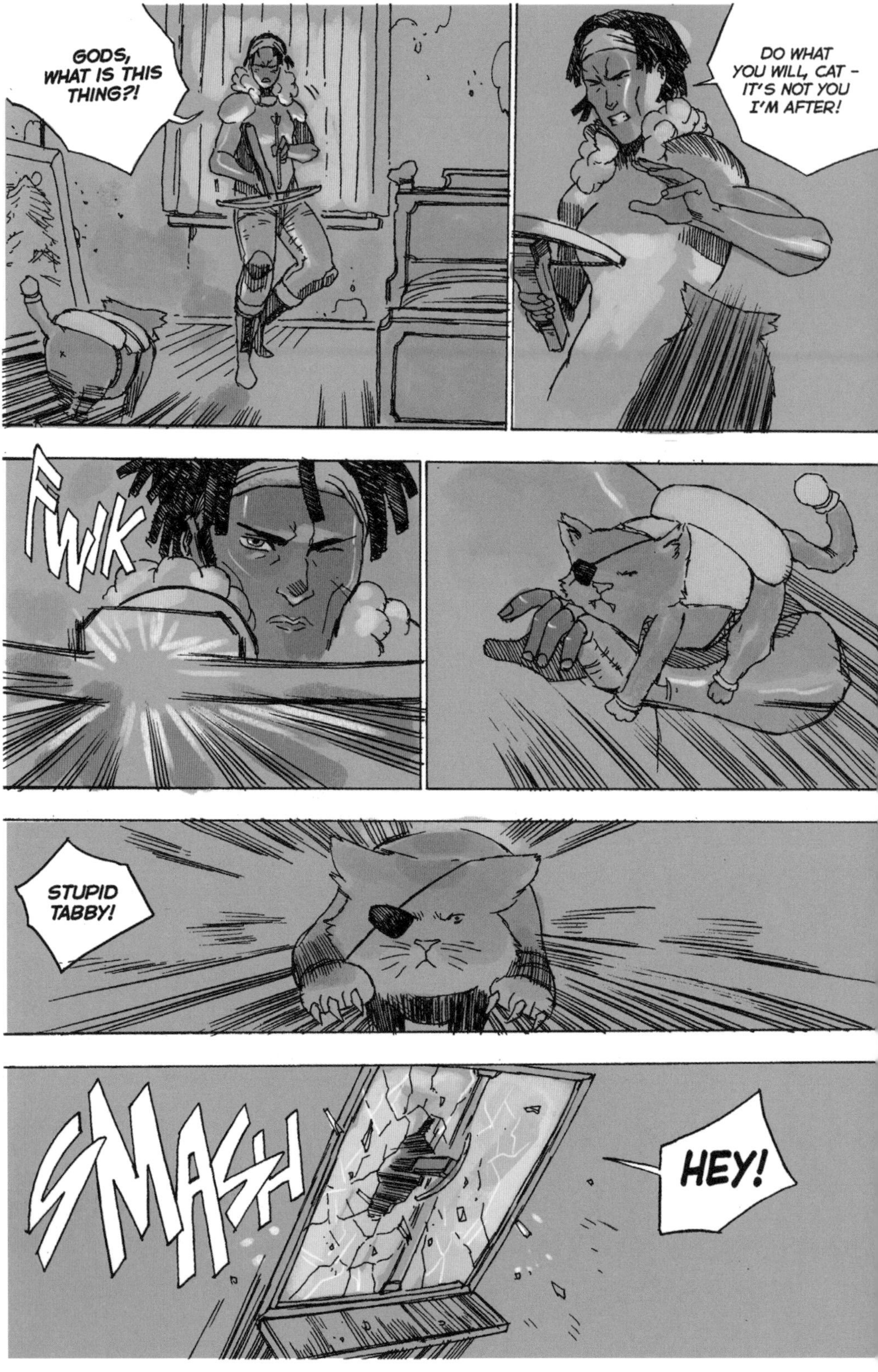
GODS, WHAT IS THIS THING?!
DO WHAT YOU WILL, CAT - IT'S NOT YOU I'M AFTER!
FWIK
STUPID TABBY!
SMASH
HEY!

IF YOU WANT TO QUESTION ME, QUESTION ME ON THE WAY! *AN EVIL AGENT IS IN THAT BUILDING!*
AND HOW DO WE KNOW *YOU'RE* NOT THIS "EVIL AGENT"?
FIRST A DEAD BODY, NOW A STRANGE GIRL WITH A SWORD. I THINK WE HAVE A SUSPECT, MEN.
DOES THIS LOOK LIKE A CROSSBOW TO YOU? HOW ON EARTH DOES THIS PUT A BOLT IN SOMEONE'S CHEST?
... PARDON?
ANOTHER BODY?
THE SCOUT ON THE NEXT STREET OVER - THERE'S NOT A SINGLE SWORD WOUND ON HIM!
WHAT THE HELL IS GOING ON?
SMASH

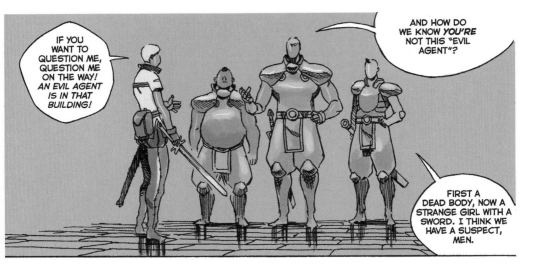

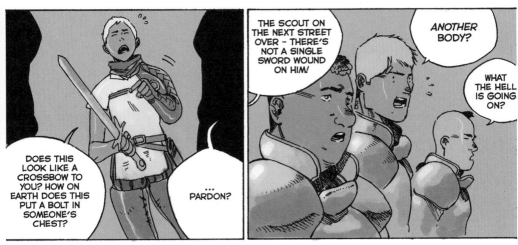

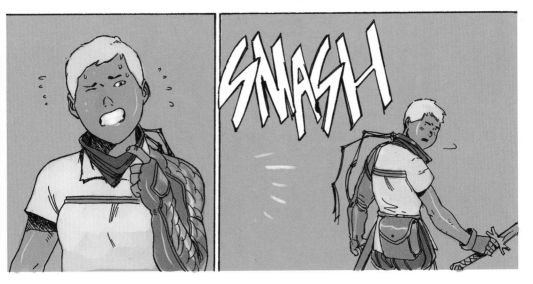

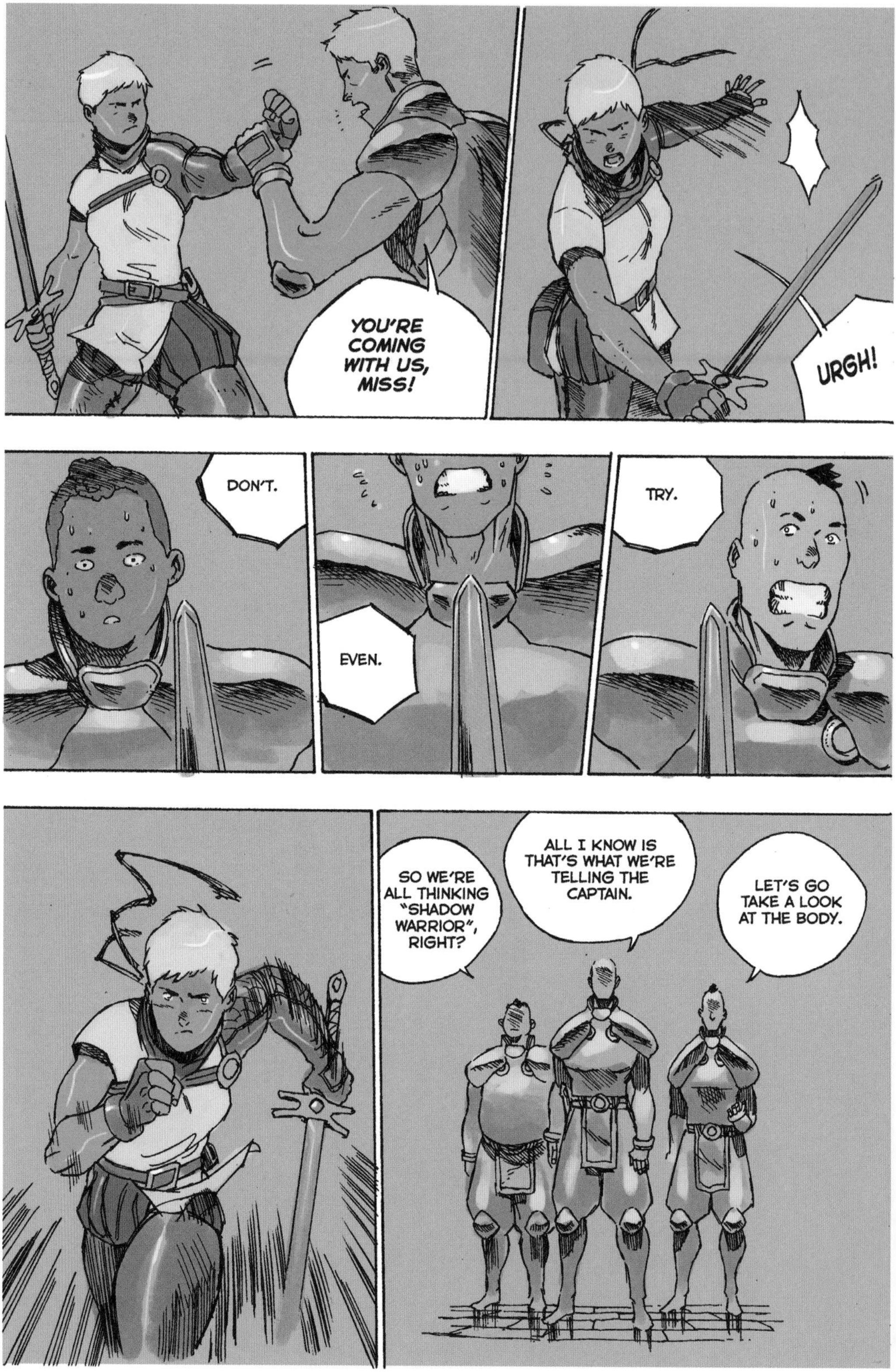
YOU'RE COMING WITH US, MISS!
URGH!
DON'T.
EVEN.
TRY.
SO WE'RE ALL THINKING "SHADOW WARRIOR", RIGHT?
ALL I KNOW IS THAT'S WHAT WE'RE TELLING THE CAPTAIN.
LET'S GO TAKE A LOOK AT THE BODY.

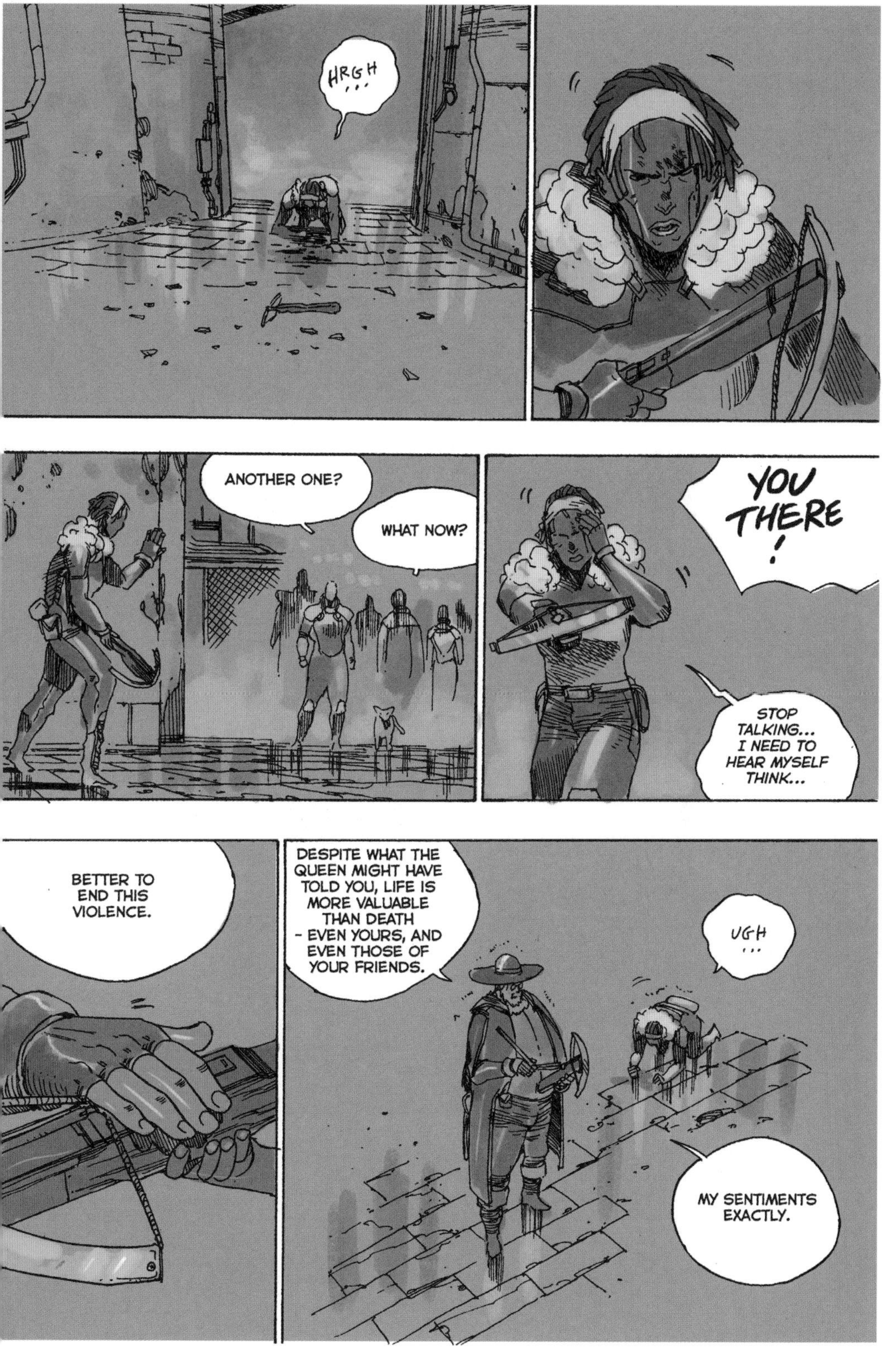
HRGH ...
ANOTHER ONE?
WHAT NOW?
YOU THERE!
STOP TALKING... I NEED TO HEAR MYSELF THINK...
BETTER TO END THIS VIOLENCE.
DESPITE WHAT THE QUEEN MIGHT HAVE TOLD YOU, LIFE IS MORE VALUABLE THAN DEATH - EVEN YOURS, AND EVEN THOSE OF YOUR FRIENDS.
UGH ...
MY SENTIMENTS EXACTLY.

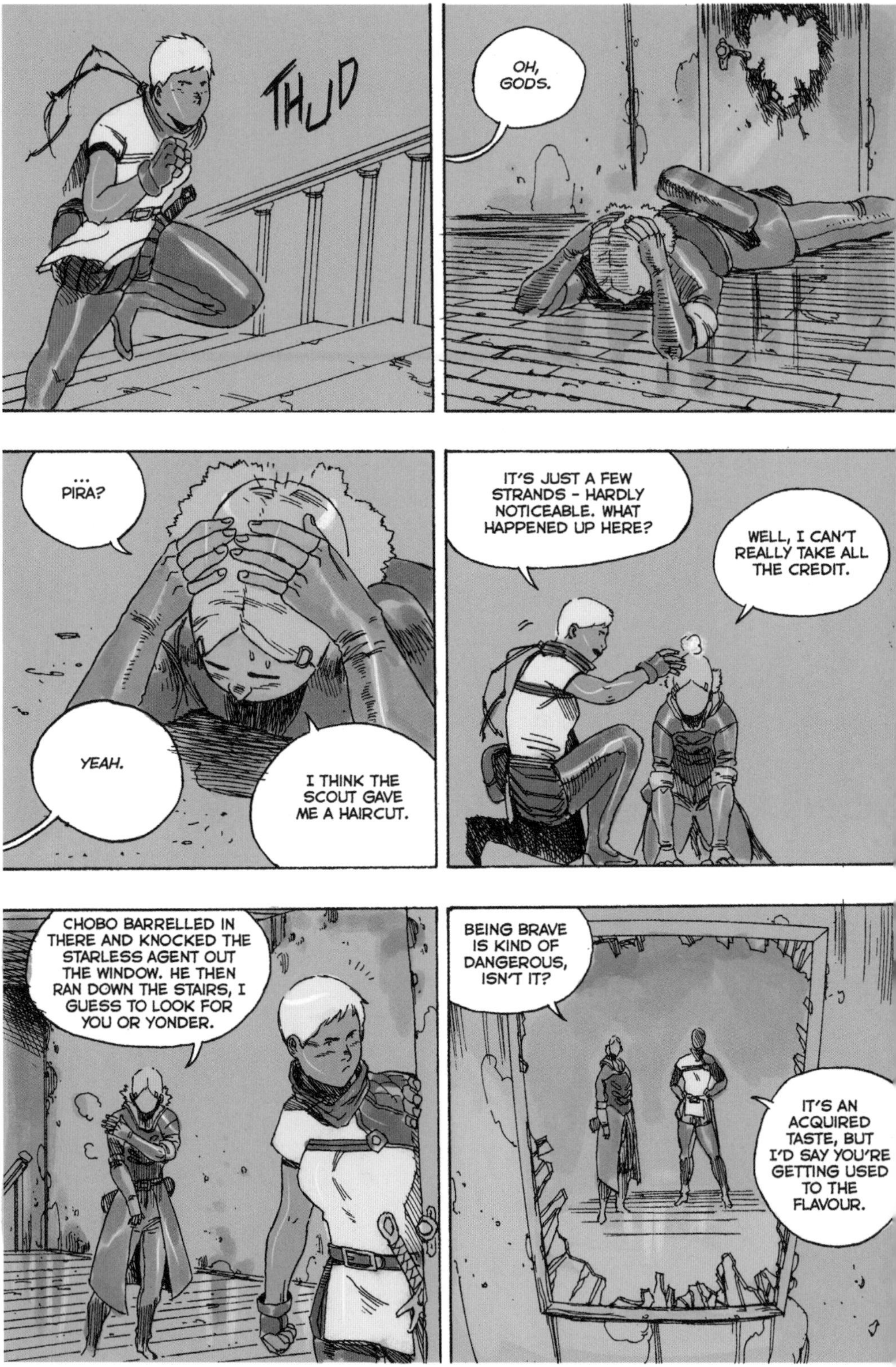
THUD
OH, GODS.
... PIRA?
YEAH.
I THINK THE SCOUT GAVE ME A HAIRCUT.
IT'S JUST A FEW STRANDS - HARDLY NOTICEABLE. WHAT HAPPENED UP HERE?
WELL, I CAN'T REALLY TAKE ALL THE CREDIT.
CHOBO BARRELLED IN THERE AND KNOCKED THE STARLESS AGENT OUT THE WINDOW. HE THEN RAN DOWN THE STAIRS, I GUESS TO LOOK FOR YOU OR YONDER.
BEING BRAVE IS KIND OF DANGEROUS, ISN'T IT?
IT'S AN ACQUIRED TASTE, BUT I'D SAY YOU'RE GETTING USED TO THE FLAVOUR.

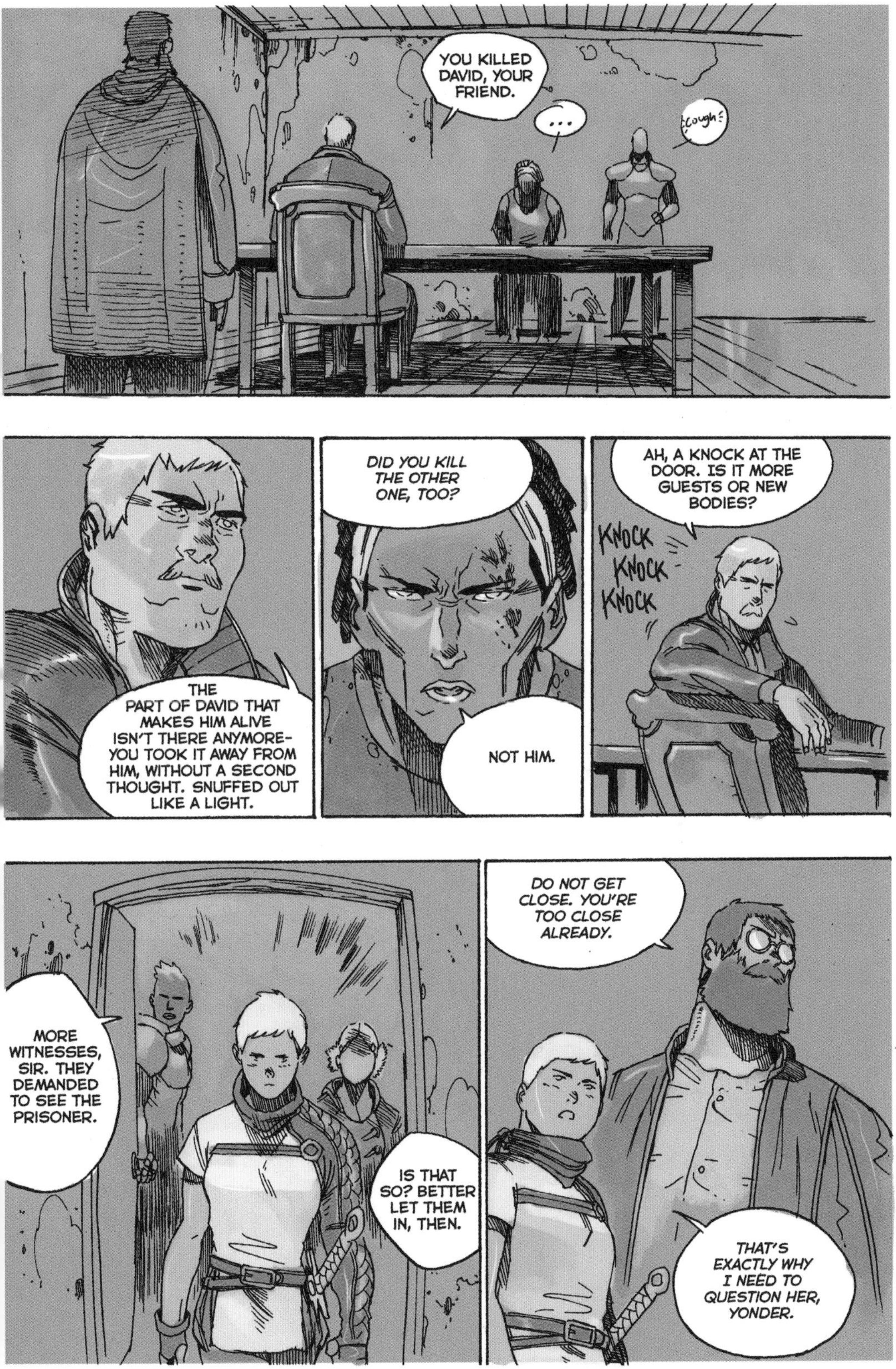
YOU KILLED DAVID, YOUR FRIEND.
...
¡COUGH!
THE PART OF DAVID THAT MAKES HIM ALIVE ISN'T THERE ANYMORE- YOU TOOK IT AWAY FROM HIM, WITHOUT A SECOND THOUGHT. SNUFFED OUT LIKE A LIGHT.
DID YOU KILL THE OTHER ONE, TOO?
NOT HIM.
KNOCK KNOCK KNOCK
AH, A KNOCK AT THE DOOR. IS IT MORE GUESTS OR NEW BODIES?
MORE WITNESSES, SIR. THEY DEMANDED TO SEE THE PRISONER.
IS THAT SO? BETTER LET THEM IN, THEN.
DO NOT GET CLOSE. YOU'RE TOO CLOSE ALREADY.
THAT'S EXACTLY WHY I NEED TO QUESTION HER, YONDER.

WHAT'S YOUR NAME, STARLESS?
SHOULD I BE ANSWERING YOUR QUESTIONS? YOU HAVE NO AUTHORITY OVER ME, PRINCESS.
SHUT UP, INDRID. YOU'RE AN INCONSEQUENTIAL RAT MY MOTHER IS ONLY TOO HAPPY TO BE RID OF. OR DID YOU THINK THE QUEEN WAS PROMOTING YOU BY SUITING UP THE STABLE GIRL?
TELL ME WHAT HER STRATEGY IS.
...
YOU'RE ALREADY DEAD TO HER. YOU KNOW YOU CAN'T GO BACK NOW.
REMEMBER WHEN I LET YOU PLAY WITH THE HORSES, PRINCESS?
HOW CAN I BE AFRAID OF DEATH WHEN I'VE ALWAYS BEEN SURROUNDED BY IT?
TELL ME WHAT YOU KNOW, INDRID.
I WILL, BUT ON ONE CONDITION.
... LET'S HEAR IT.
KEEP MY KINDNESSES SAFE IN YOUR MEMORY.

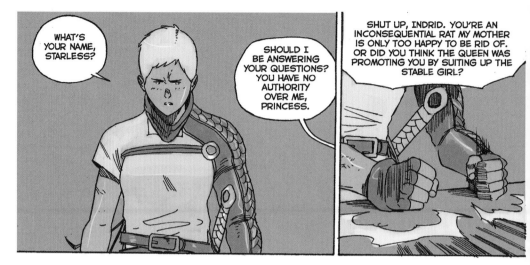

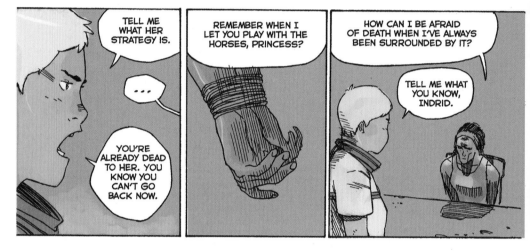

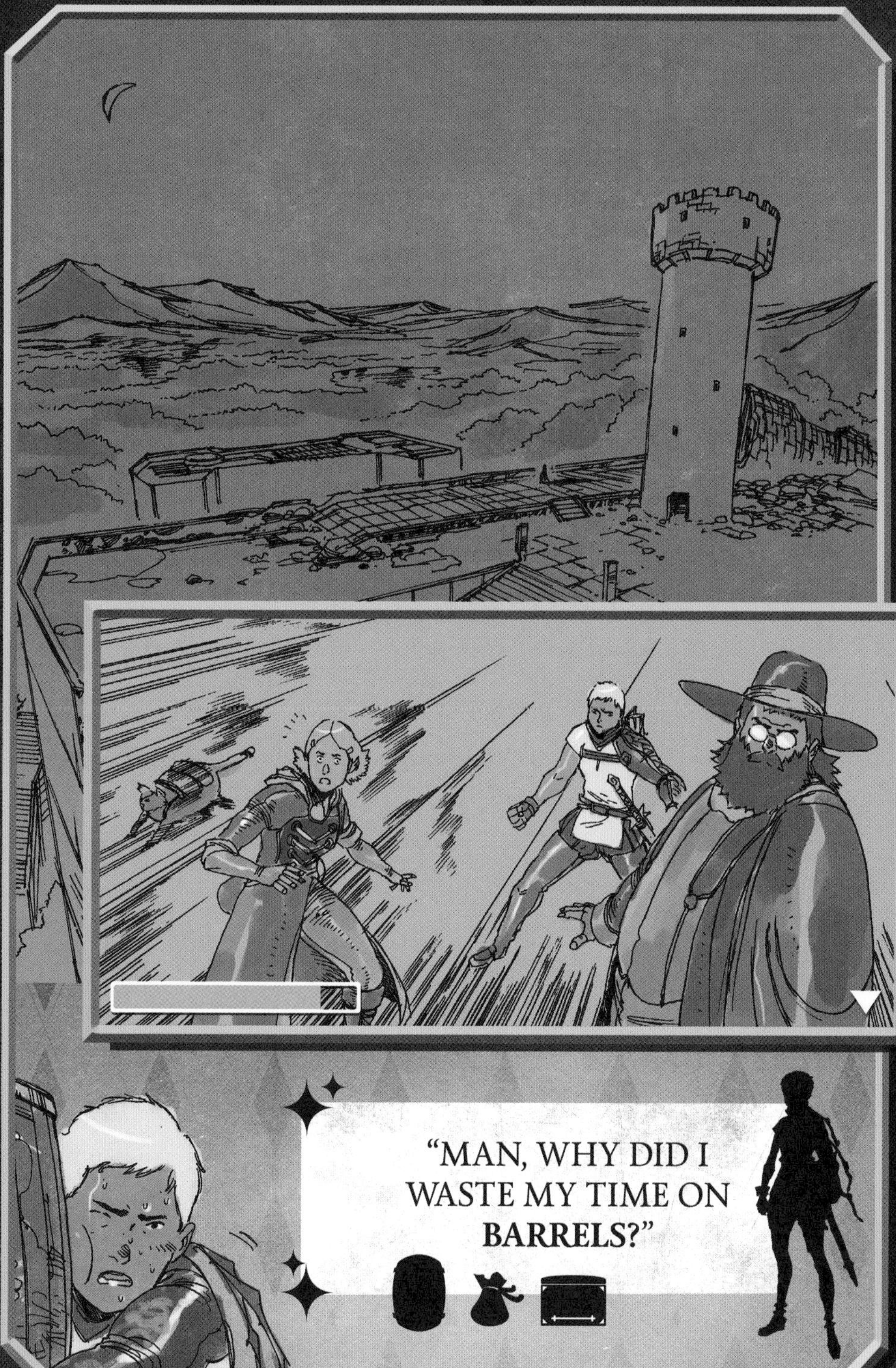
"MAN, WHY DID I
WASTE MY TIME ON
BARRELS?"

CHAPTER TWO

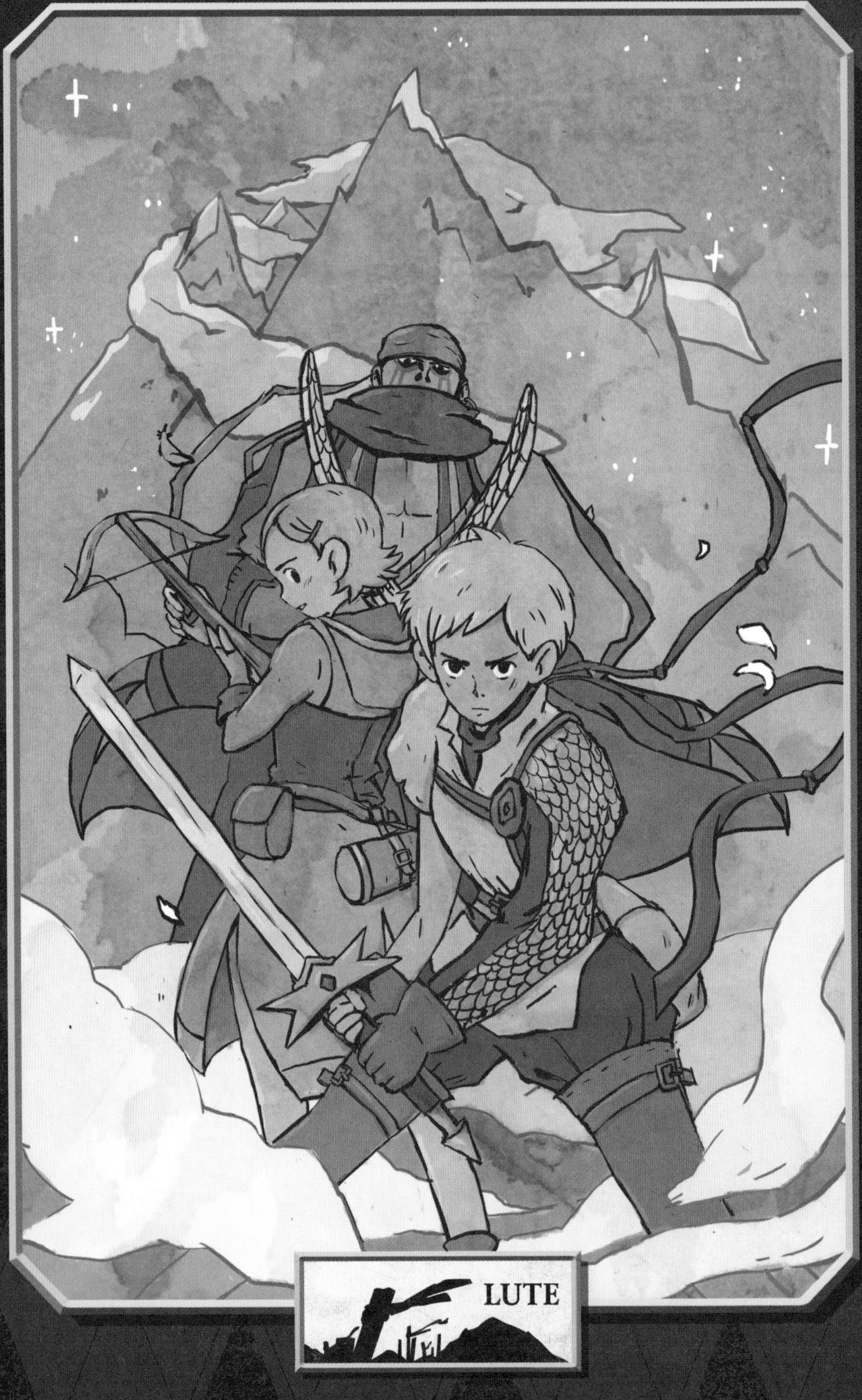
LUTE

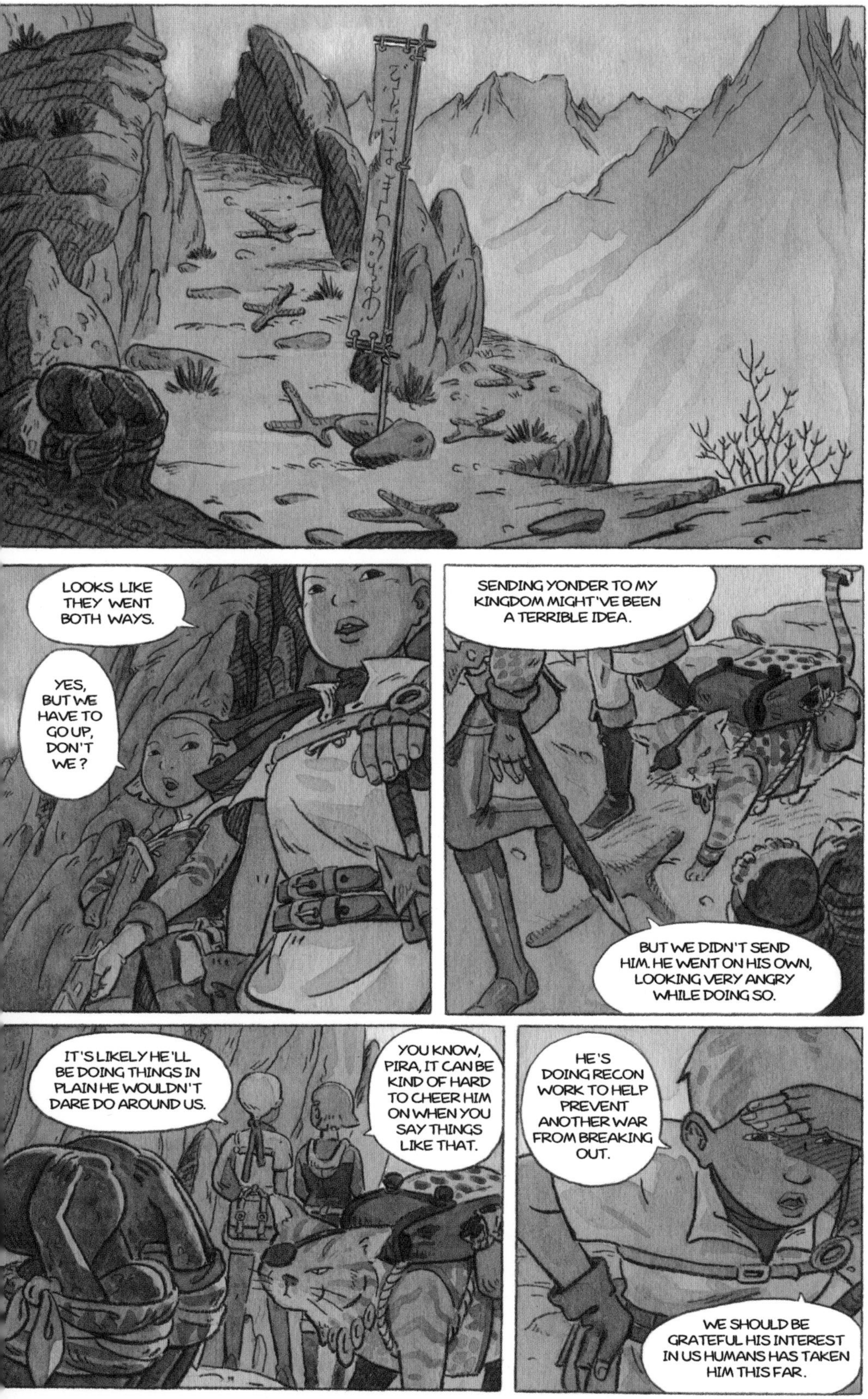

LOOKS LIKE THEY WENT BOTH WAYS.
YES, BUT WE HAVE TO GO UP, DON'T WE?
SENDING YONDER TO MY KINGDOM MIGHT'VE BEEN A TERRIBLE IDEA.
BUT WE DIDN'T SEND HIM. HE WENT ON HIS OWN, LOOKING VERY ANGRY WHILE DOING SO.
IT'S LIKELY HE'LL BE DOING THINGS IN PLAIN HE WOULDN'T DARE DO AROUND US.
YOU KNOW, PIRA, IT CAN BE KIND OF HARD TO CHEER HIM ON WHEN YOU SAY THINGS LIKE THAT.
HE'S DOING RECON WORK TO HELP PREVENT ANOTHER WAR FROM BREAKING OUT.
WE SHOULD BE GRATEFUL HIS INTEREST IN US HUMANS HAS TAKEN HIM THIS FAR.

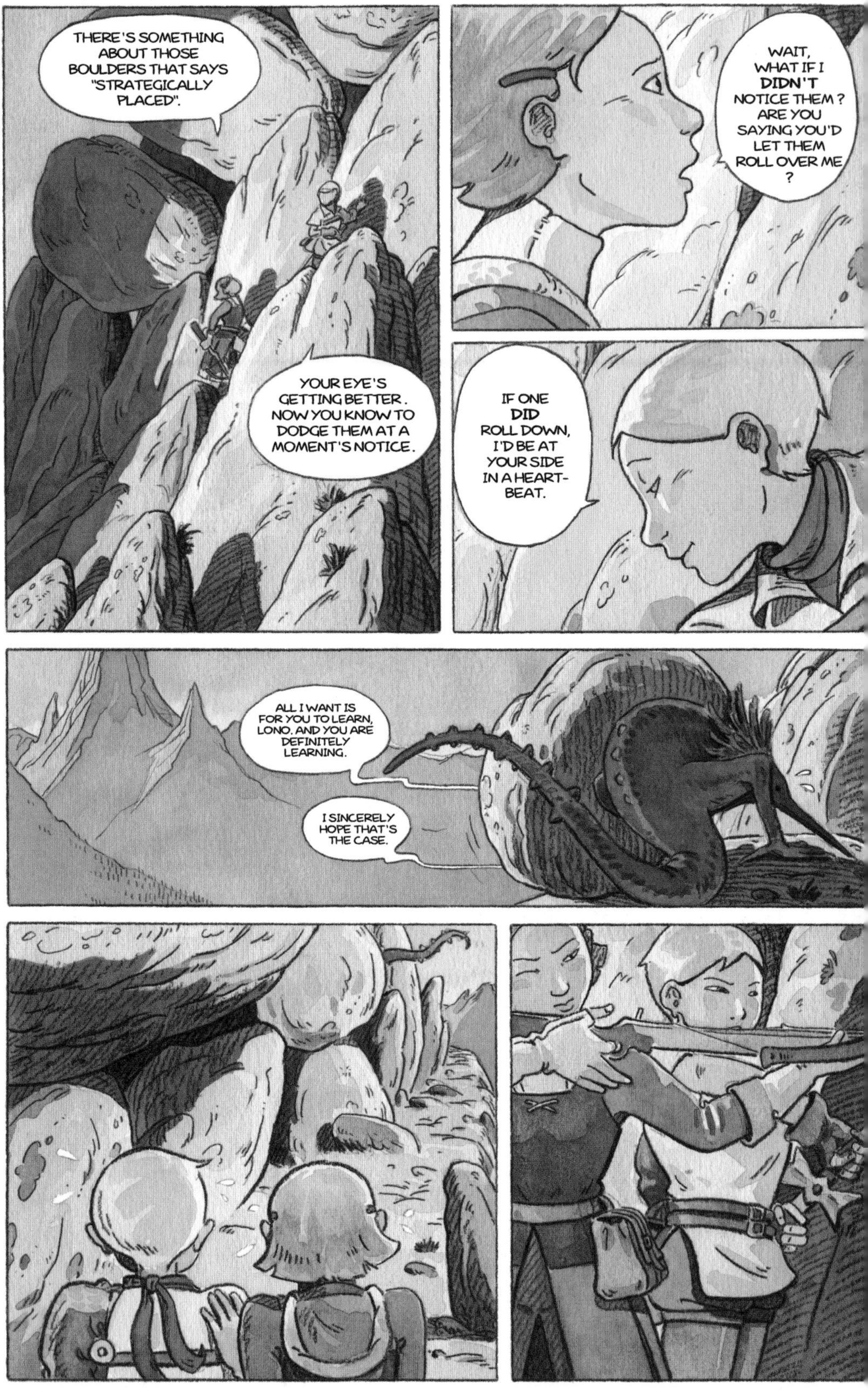
THERE'S SOMETHING ABOUT THOSE BOULDERS THAT SAYS "STRATEGICALLY PLACED".
WAIT, WHAT IF I DIDN'T NOTICE THEM ? ARE YOU SAYING YOU'D LET THEM ROLL OVER ME ?
YOUR EYE'S GETTING BETTER. NOW YOU KNOW TO DODGE THEM AT A MOMENT'S NOTICE.
IF ONE DID ROLL DOWN, I'D BE AT YOUR SIDE IN A HEART-BEAT.
ALL I WANT IS FOR YOU TO LEARN, LONO. AND YOU ARE DEFINITELY LEARNING.
I SINCERELY HOPE THAT'S THE CASE.

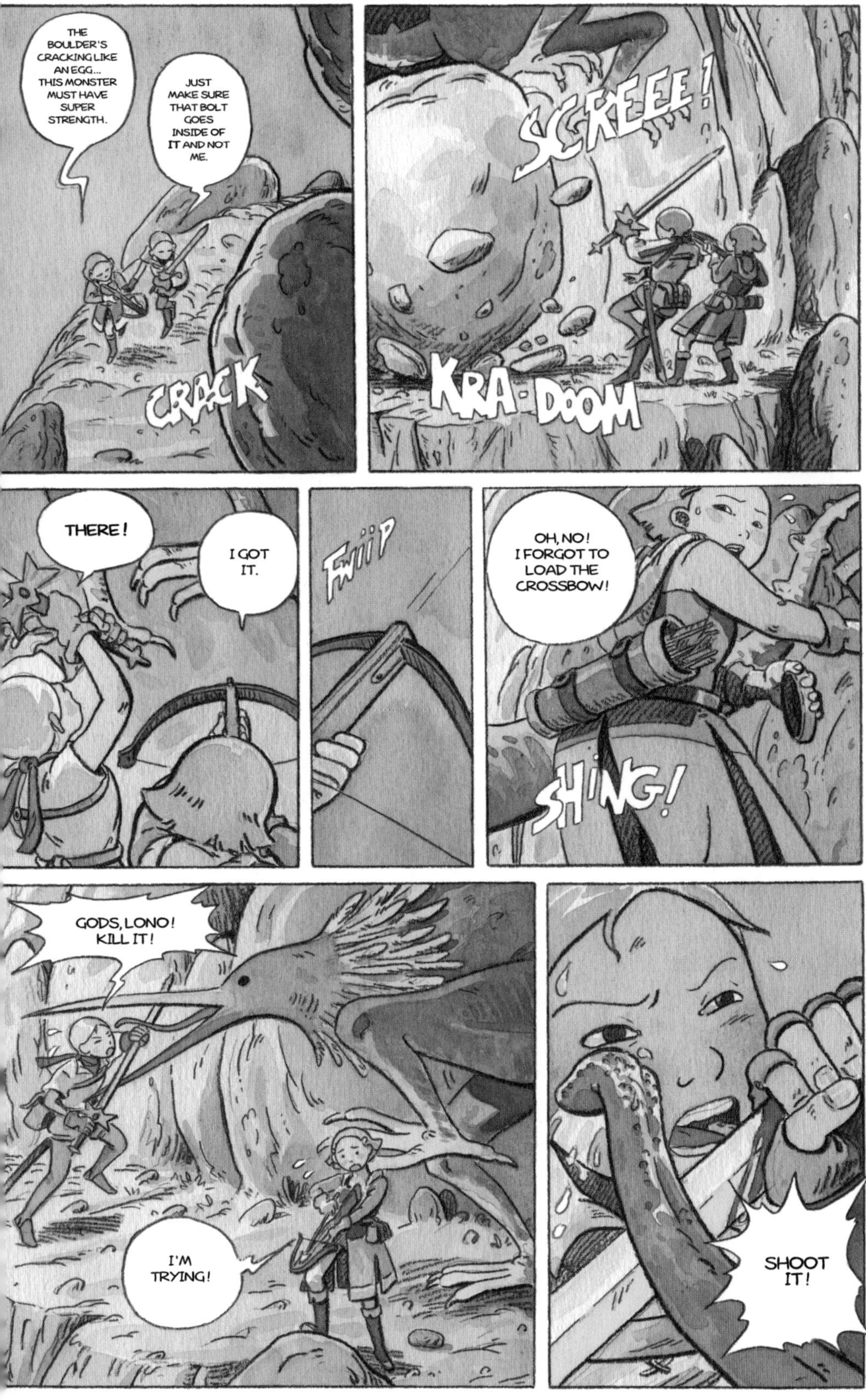
THE BOULDER'S CRACKING LIKE AN EGG... THIS MONSTER MUST HAVE SUPER STRENGTH.
JUST MAKE SURE THAT BOLT GOES INSIDE OF IT AND NOT ME.
CRACK
SCREEE!
KRA-DOOM
THERE!
I GOT IT.
FWIIP
OH, NO! I FORGOT TO LOAD THE CROSSBOW!
SHING!
GODS, LONO! KILL IT!
I'M TRYING!
SHOOT IT!

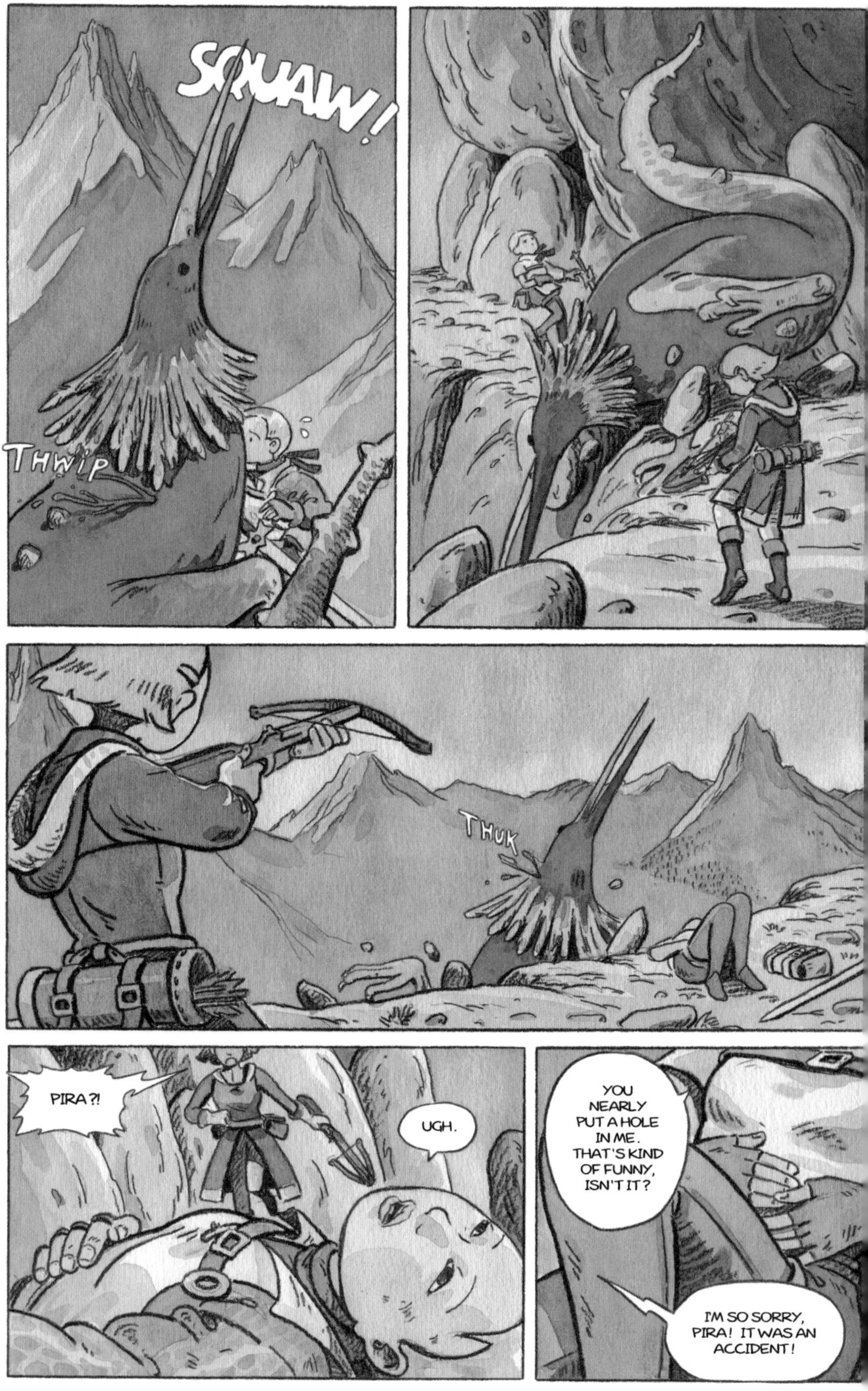
SQUAW!
THWIP
THUK
PIRA?!
UGH.
YOU NEARLY PUT A HOLE IN ME. THAT'S KIND OF FUNNY, ISN'T IT?
I'M SO SORRY, PIRA! IT WAS AN ACCIDENT!

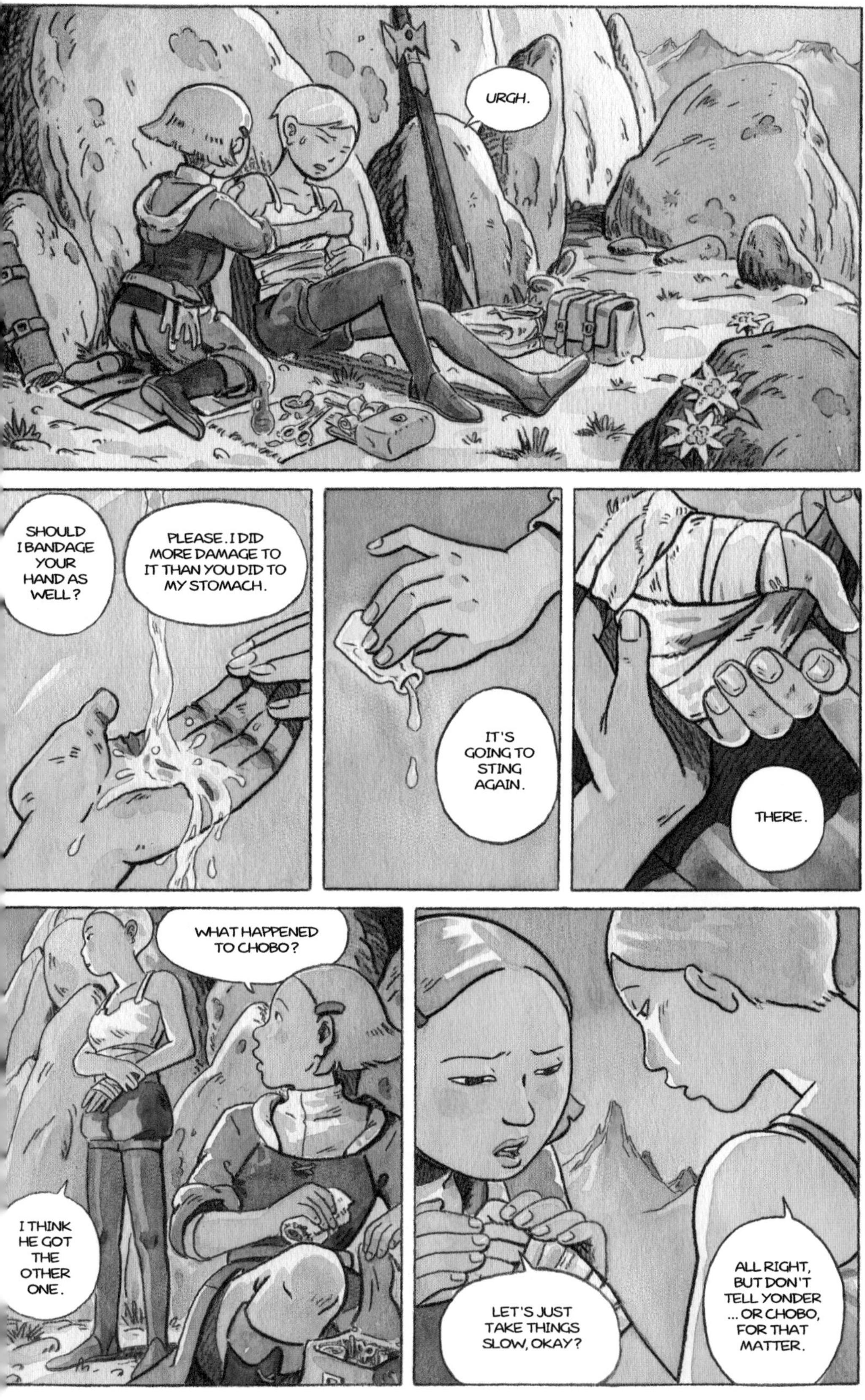
URGH.
SHOULD I BANDAGE YOUR HAND AS WELL?
PLEASE. I DID MORE DAMAGE TO IT THAN YOU DID TO MY STOMACH.
IT'S GOING TO STING AGAIN.
THERE.
WHAT HAPPENED TO CHOBO?
I THINK HE GOT THE OTHER ONE.
ALL RIGHT, BUT DON'T TELL YONDER ...OR CHOBO, FOR THAT MATTER.
LET'S JUST TAKE THINGS SLOW, OKAY?

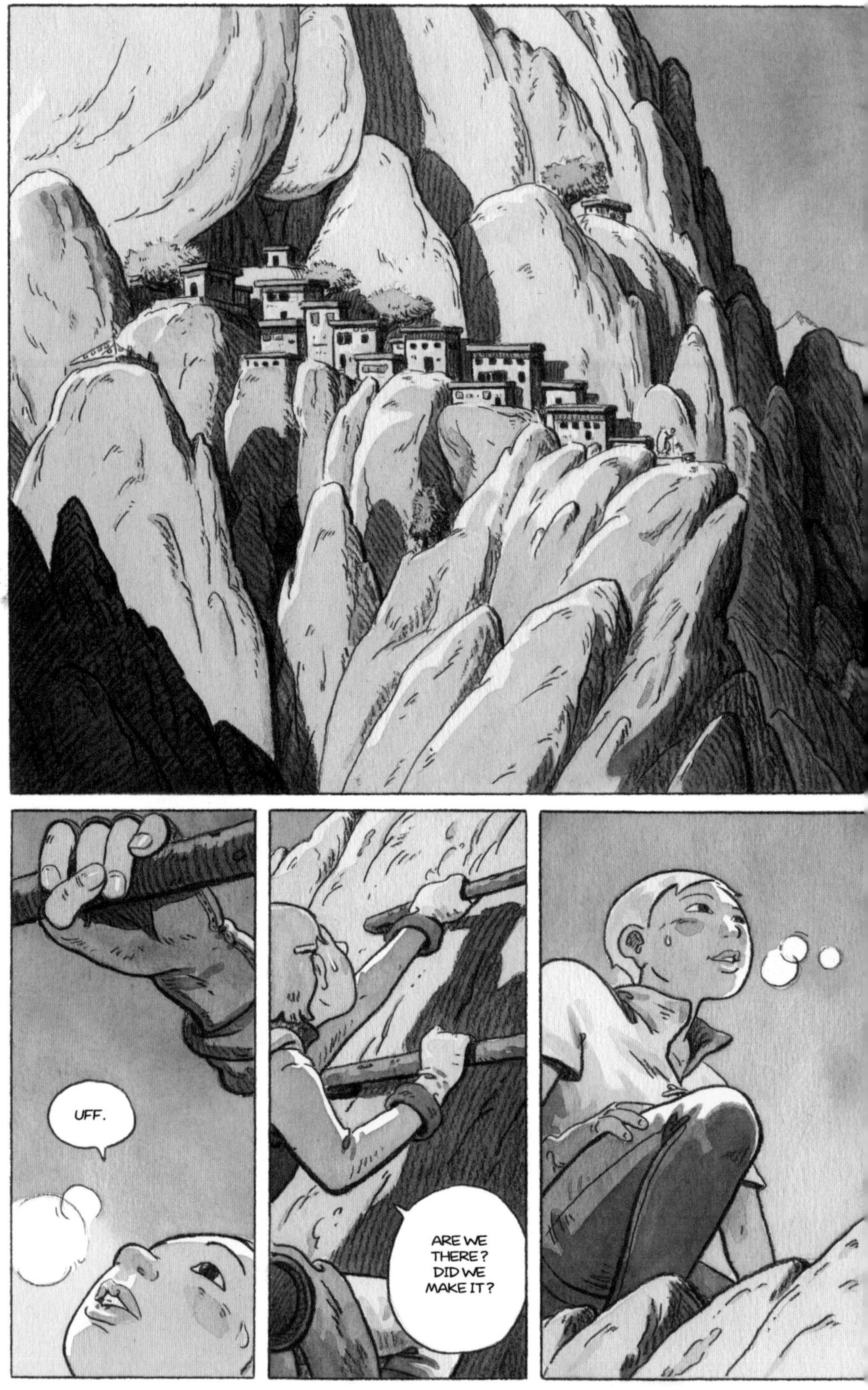
UFF.
ARE WE THERE? DID WE MAKE IT?

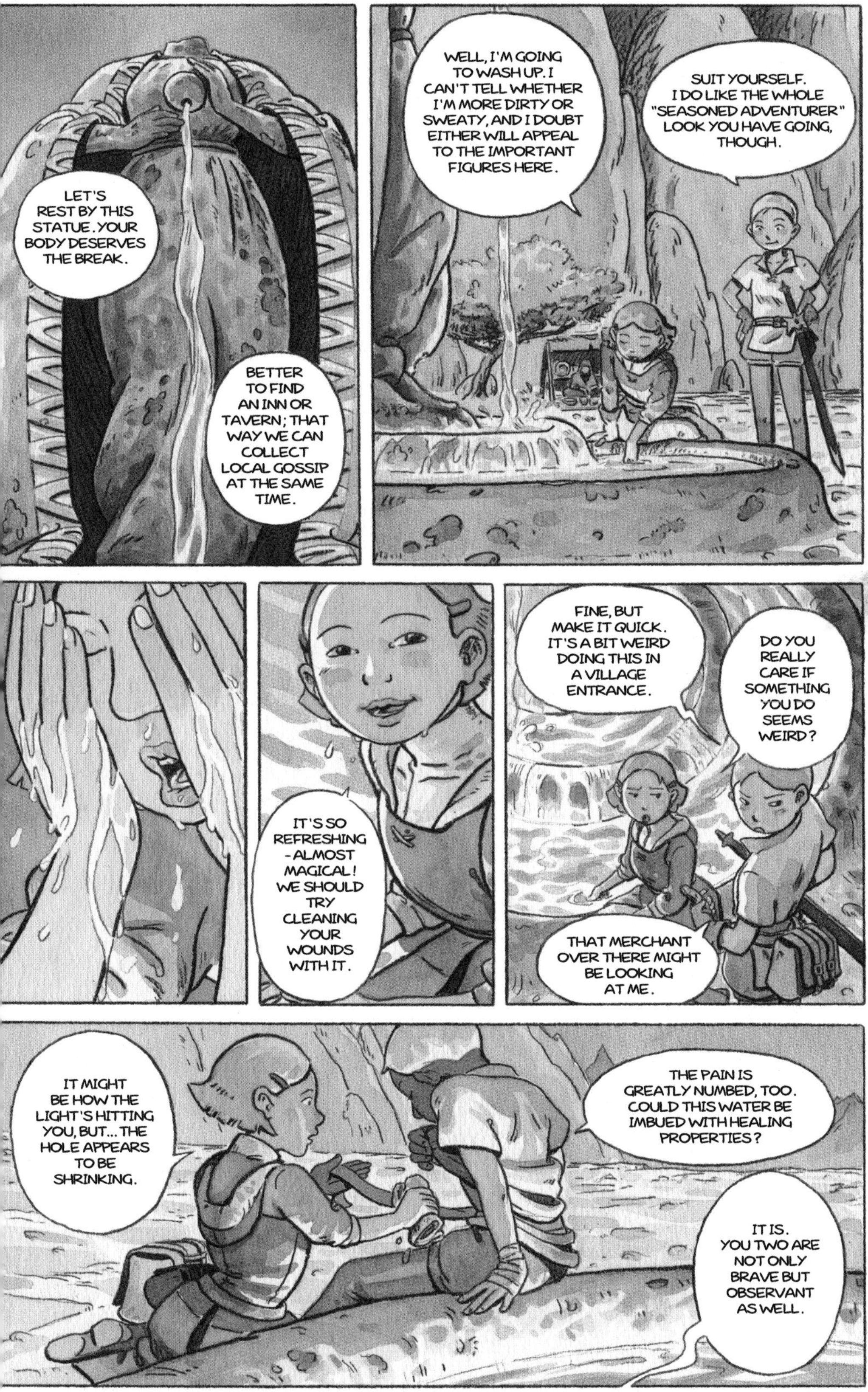
LET'S REST BY THIS STATUE. YOUR BODY DESERVES THE BREAK.
BETTER TO FIND AN INN OR TAVERN; THAT WAY WE CAN COLLECT LOCAL GOSSIP AT THE SAME TIME.
WELL, I'M GOING TO WASH UP. I CAN'T TELL WHETHER I'M MORE DIRTY OR SWEATY, AND I DOUBT EITHER WILL APPEAL TO THE IMPORTANT FIGURES HERE.
SUIT YOURSELF. I DO LIKE THE WHOLE "SEASONED ADVENTURER" LOOK YOU HAVE GOING, THOUGH.
IT'S SO REFRESHING - ALMOST MAGICAL! WE SHOULD TRY CLEANING YOUR WOUNDS WITH IT.
FINE, BUT MAKE IT QUICK. IT'S A BIT WEIRD DOING THIS IN A VILLAGE ENTRANCE.
DO YOU REALLY CARE IF SOMETHING YOU DO SEEMS WEIRD?
THAT MERCHANT OVER THERE MIGHT BE LOOKING AT ME.
IT MIGHT BE HOW THE LIGHT'S HITTING YOU, BUT... THE HOLE APPEARS TO BE SHRINKING.
THE PAIN IS GREATLY NUMBED, TOO. COULD THIS WATER BE IMBUED WITH HEALING PROPERTIES?
IT IS. YOU TWO ARE NOT ONLY BRAVE BUT OBSERVANT AS WELL.

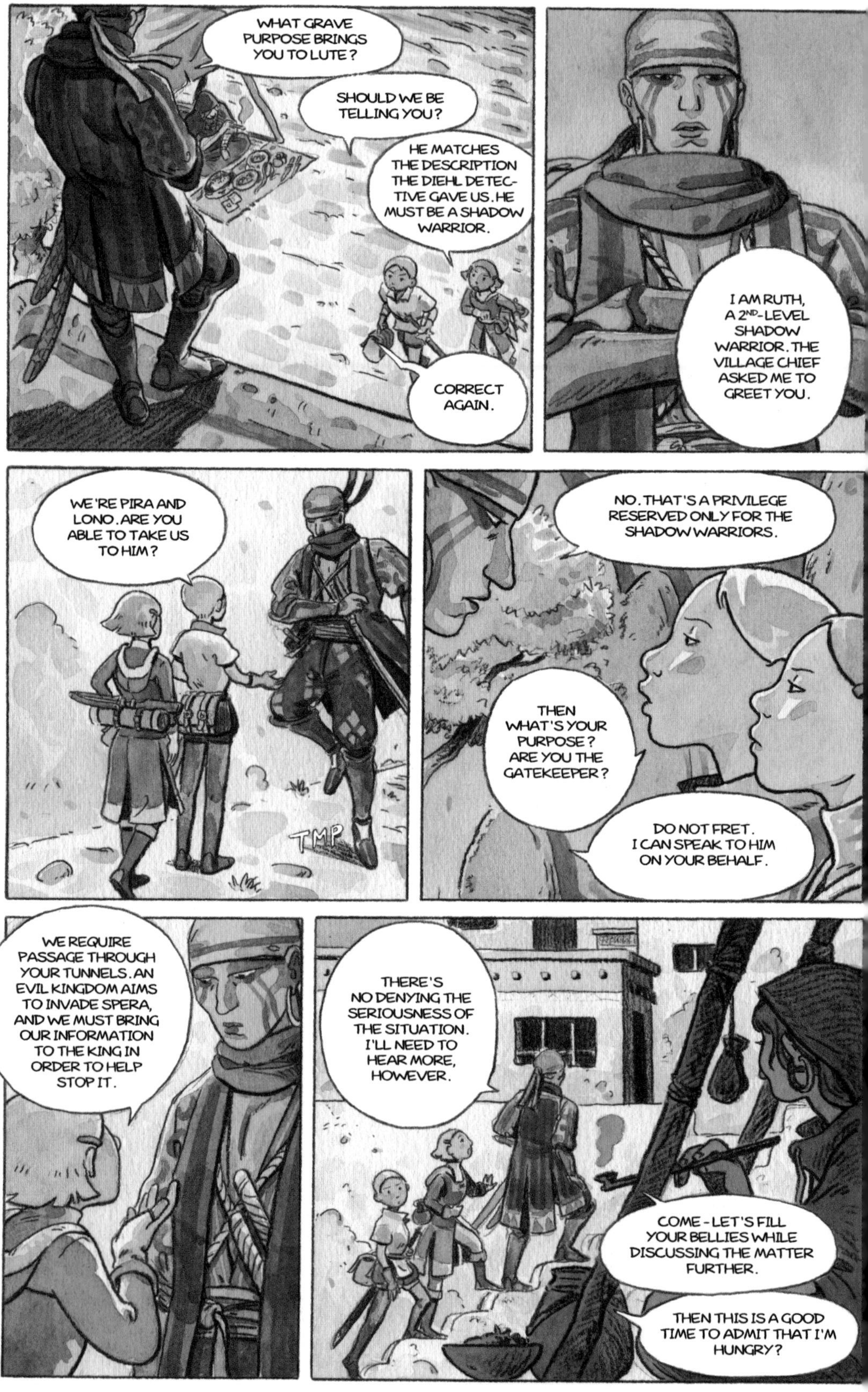
WHAT GRAVE PURPOSE BRINGS YOU TO LUTE?
SHOULD WE BE TELLING YOU?
HE MATCHES THE DESCRIPTION THE DIEHL DETECTIVE GAVE US. HE MUST BE A SHADOW WARRIOR.
CORRECT AGAIN.
I AM RUTH, A 2ND-LEVEL SHADOW WARRIOR. THE VILLAGE CHIEF ASKED ME TO GREET YOU.
WE'RE PIRA AND LONO. ARE YOU ABLE TO TAKE US TO HIM?
TMP
NO. THAT'S A PRIVILEGE RESERVED ONLY FOR THE SHADOW WARRIORS.
THEN WHAT'S YOUR PURPOSE? ARE YOU THE GATEKEEPER?
DO NOT FRET. I CAN SPEAK TO HIM ON YOUR BEHALF.
WE REQUIRE PASSAGE THROUGH YOUR TUNNELS. AN EVIL KINGDOM AIMS TO INVADE SPERA, AND WE MUST BRING OUR INFORMATION TO THE KING IN ORDER TO HELP STOP IT.
THERE'S NO DENYING THE SERIOUSNESS OF THE SITUATION. I'LL NEED TO HEAR MORE, HOWEVER.
COME - LET'S FILL YOUR BELLIES WHILE DISCUSSING THE MATTER FURTHER.
THEN THIS IS A GOOD TIME TO ADMIT THAT I'M HUNGRY?

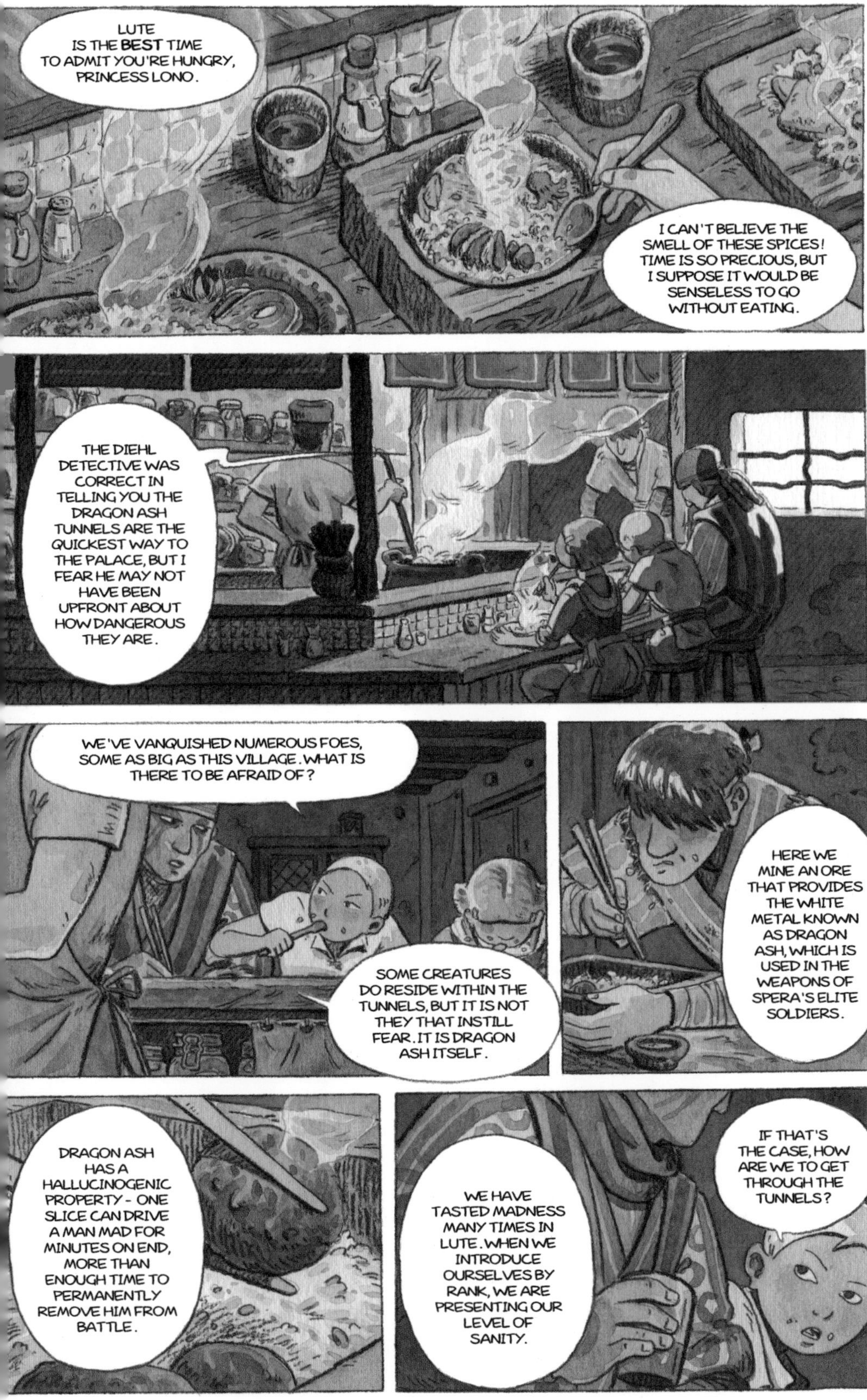

LUTE IS THE BEST TIME TO ADMIT YOU'RE HUNGRY, PRINCESS LONO.
I CAN'T BELIEVE THE SMELL OF THESE SPICES! TIME IS SO PRECIOUS, BUT I SUPPOSE IT WOULD BE SENSELESS TO GO WITHOUT EATING.
THE DIEHL DETECTIVE WAS CORRECT IN TELLING YOU THE DRAGON ASH TUNNELS ARE THE QUICKEST WAY TO THE PALACE, BUT I FEAR HE MAY NOT HAVE BEEN UPFRONT ABOUT HOW DANGEROUS THEY ARE.
WE'VE VANQUISHED NUMEROUS FOES, SOME AS BIG AS THIS VILLAGE. WHAT IS THERE TO BE AFRAID OF?
SOME CREATURES DO RESIDE WITHIN THE TUNNELS, BUT IT IS NOT THEY THAT INSTILL FEAR. IT IS DRAGON ASH ITSELF.
HERE WE MINE AN ORE THAT PROVIDES THE WHITE METAL KNOWN AS DRAGON ASH, WHICH IS USED IN THE WEAPONS OF SPERA'S ELITE SOLDIERS.
DRAGON ASH HAS A HALLUCINOGENIC PROPERTY - ONE SLICE CAN DRIVE A MAN MAD FOR MINUTES ON END, MORE THAN ENOUGH TIME TO PERMANENTLY REMOVE HIM FROM BATTLE.
WE HAVE TASTED MADNESS MANY TIMES IN LUTE. WHEN WE INTRODUCE OURSELVES BY RANK, WE ARE PRESENTING OUR LEVEL OF SANITY.
IF THAT'S THE CASE, HOW ARE WE TO GET THROUGH THE TUNNELS?

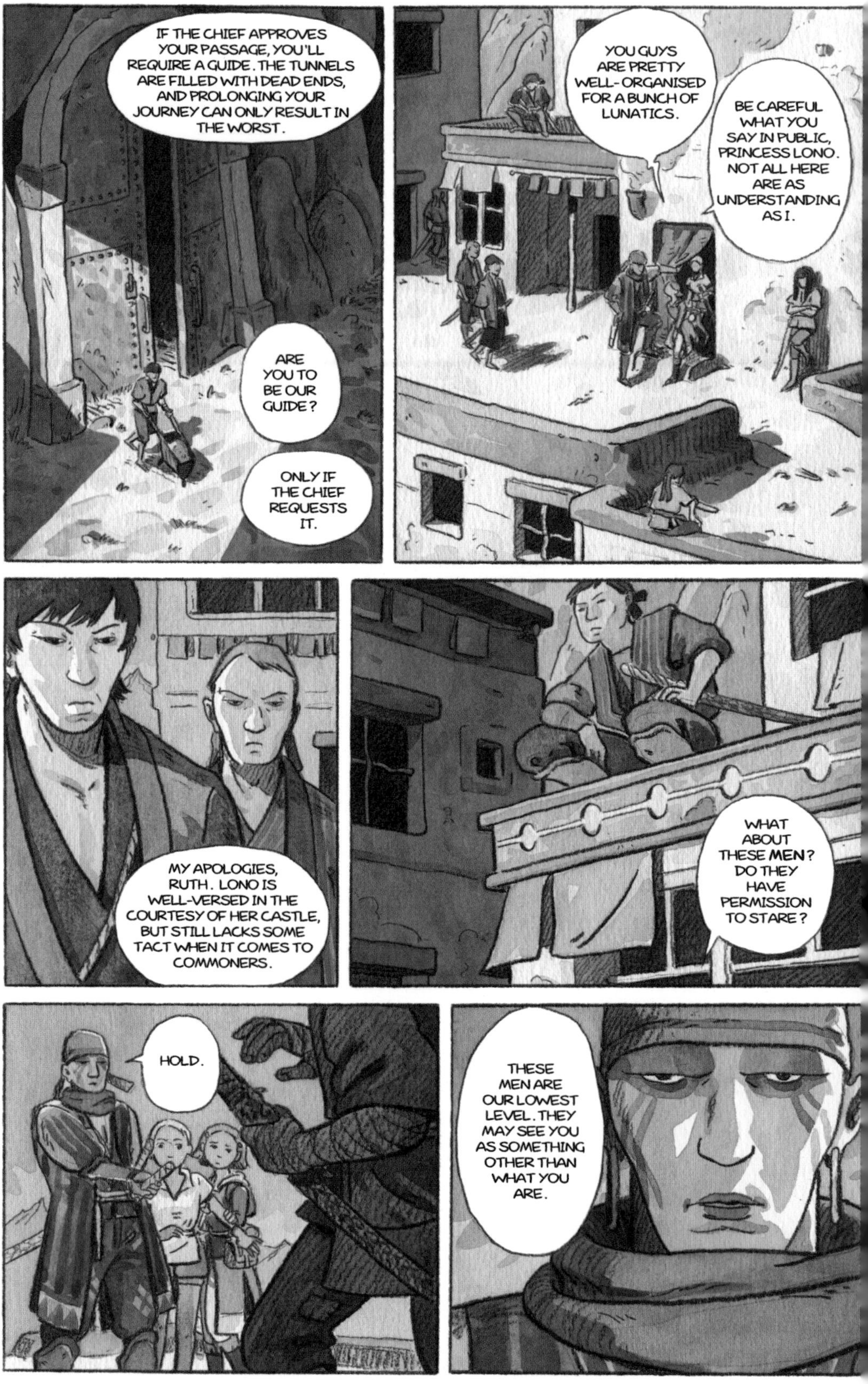
IF THE CHIEF APPROVES YOUR PASSAGE, YOU'LL REQUIRE A GUIDE. THE TUNNELS ARE FILLED WITH DEAD ENDS, AND PROLONGING YOUR JOURNEY CAN ONLY RESULT IN THE WORST.
ARE YOU TO BE OUR GUIDE?
ONLY IF THE CHIEF REQUESTS IT.
YOU GUYS ARE PRETTY WELL-ORGANISED FOR A BUNCH OF LUNATICS.
BE CAREFUL WHAT YOU SAY IN PUBLIC, PRINCESS LONO. NOT ALL HERE ARE AS UNDERSTANDING AS I.
MY APOLOGIES, RUTH. LONO IS WELL-VERSED IN THE COURTESY OF HER CASTLE, BUT STILL LACKS SOME TACT WHEN IT COMES TO COMMONERS.
WHAT ABOUT THESE **MEN**? DO THEY HAVE PERMISSION TO STARE?
HOLD.
THESE MEN ARE OUR LOWEST LEVEL. THEY MAY SEE YOU AS SOMETHING OTHER THAN WHAT YOU ARE.

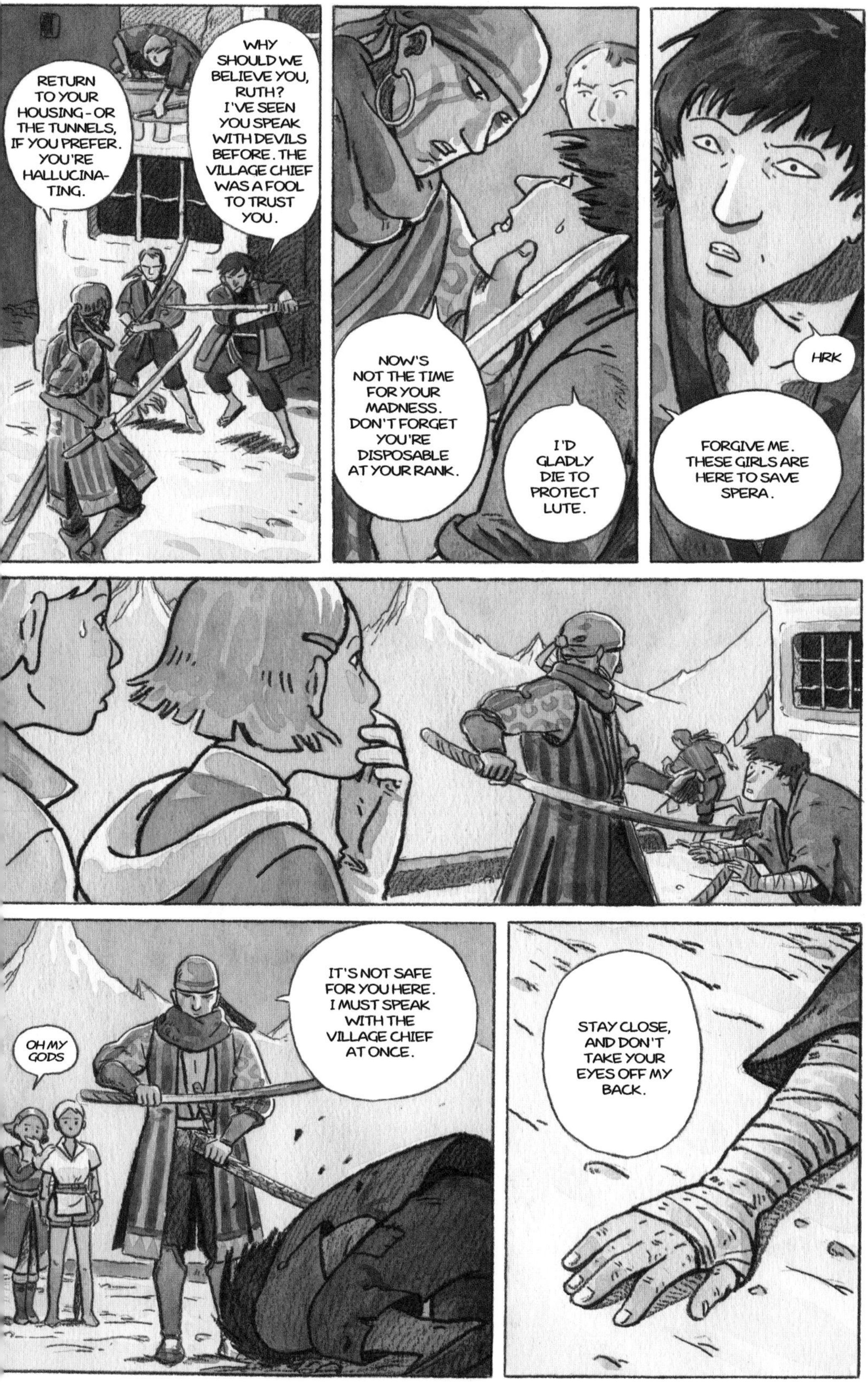
RETURN TO YOUR HOUSING - OR THE TUNNELS, IF YOU PREFER. YOU'RE HALLUCINATING.
WHY SHOULD WE BELIEVE YOU, RUTH? I'VE SEEN YOU SPEAK WITH DEVILS BEFORE. THE VILLAGE CHIEF WAS A FOOL TO TRUST YOU.
NOW'S NOT THE TIME FOR YOUR MADNESS. DON'T FORGET YOU'RE DISPOSABLE AT YOUR RANK.
I'D GLADLY DIE TO PROTECT LUTE.
HRK
FORGIVE ME. THESE GIRLS ARE HERE TO SAVE SPERA.
OH MY GODS
IT'S NOT SAFE FOR YOU HERE. I MUST SPEAK WITH THE VILLAGE CHIEF AT ONCE.
STAY CLOSE, AND DON'T TAKE YOUR EYES OFF MY BACK.

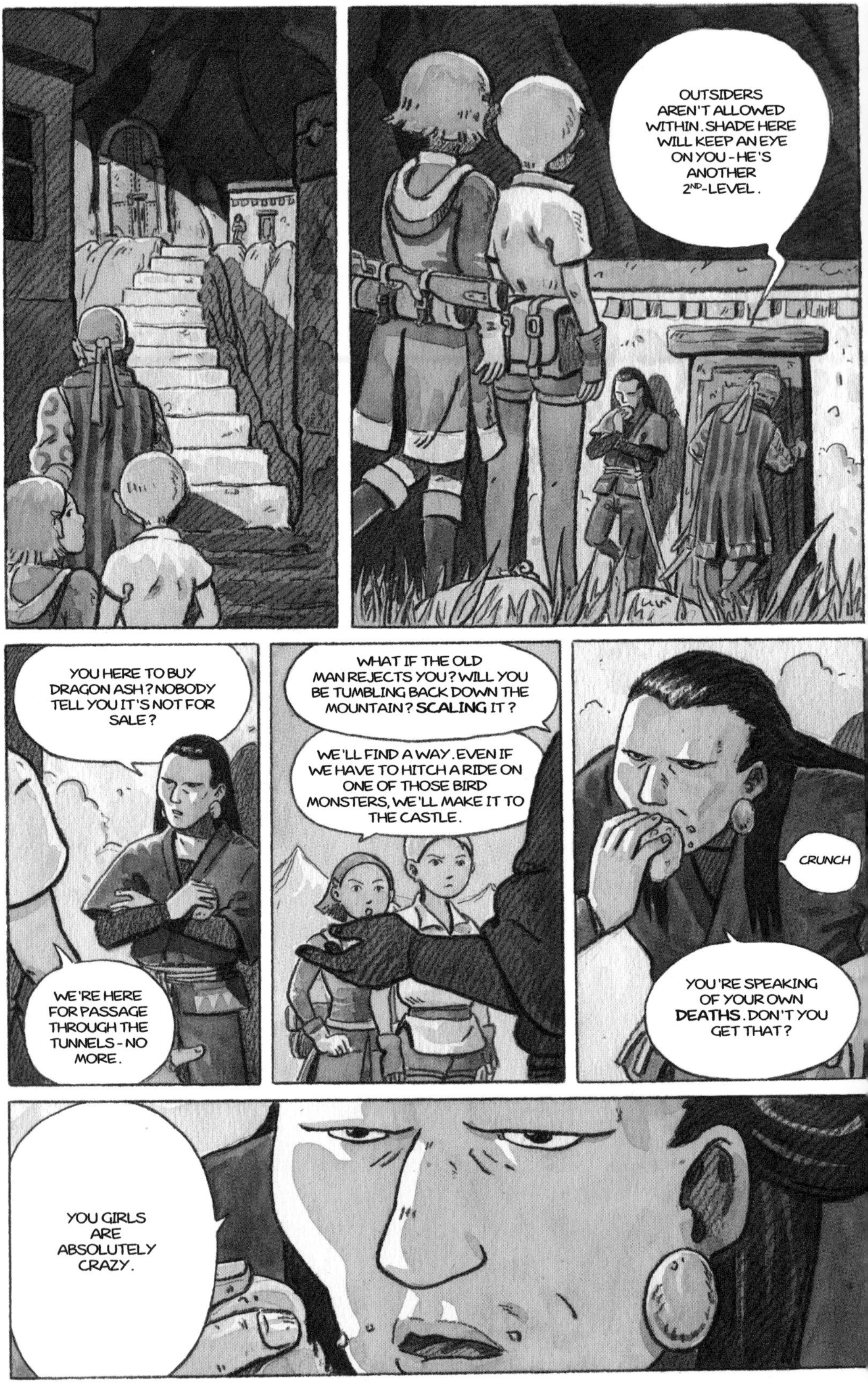
OUTSIDERS AREN'T ALLOWED WITHIN. SHADE HERE WILL KEEP AN EYE ON YOU - HE'S ANOTHER 2ND-LEVEL.
YOU HERE TO BUY DRAGON ASH? NOBODY TELL YOU IT'S NOT FOR SALE?
WE'RE HERE FOR PASSAGE THROUGH THE TUNNELS - NO MORE.
WHAT IF THE OLD MAN REJECTS YOU? WILL YOU BE TUMBLING BACK DOWN THE MOUNTAIN? **SCALING** IT?
WE'LL FIND A WAY. EVEN IF WE HAVE TO HITCH A RIDE ON ONE OF THOSE BIRD MONSTERS, WE'LL MAKE IT TO THE CASTLE.
CRUNCH
YOU'RE SPEAKING OF YOUR OWN **DEATHS**. DON'T YOU GET THAT?
YOU GIRLS ARE ABSOLUTELY CRAZY.

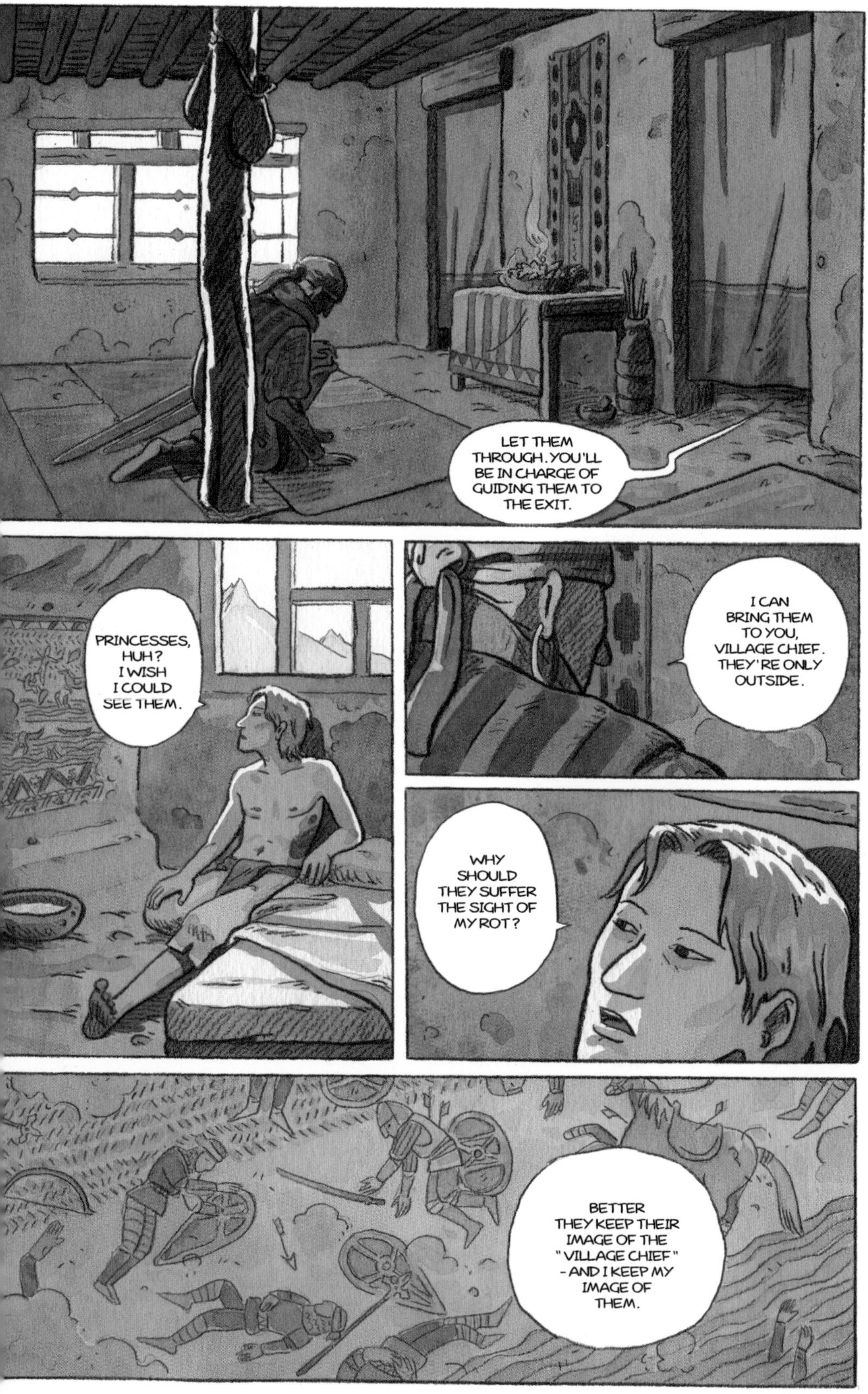
LET THEM THROUGH. YOU'LL BE IN CHARGE OF GUIDING THEM TO THE EXIT.
PRINCESSES, HUH? I WISH I COULD SEE THEM.
I CAN BRING THEM TO YOU, VILLAGE CHIEF. THEY'RE ONLY OUTSIDE.
WHY SHOULD THEY SUFFER THE SIGHT OF MY ROT?
BETTER THEY KEEP THEIR IMAGE OF THE "VILLAGE CHIEF" - AND I KEEP MY IMAGE OF THEM.

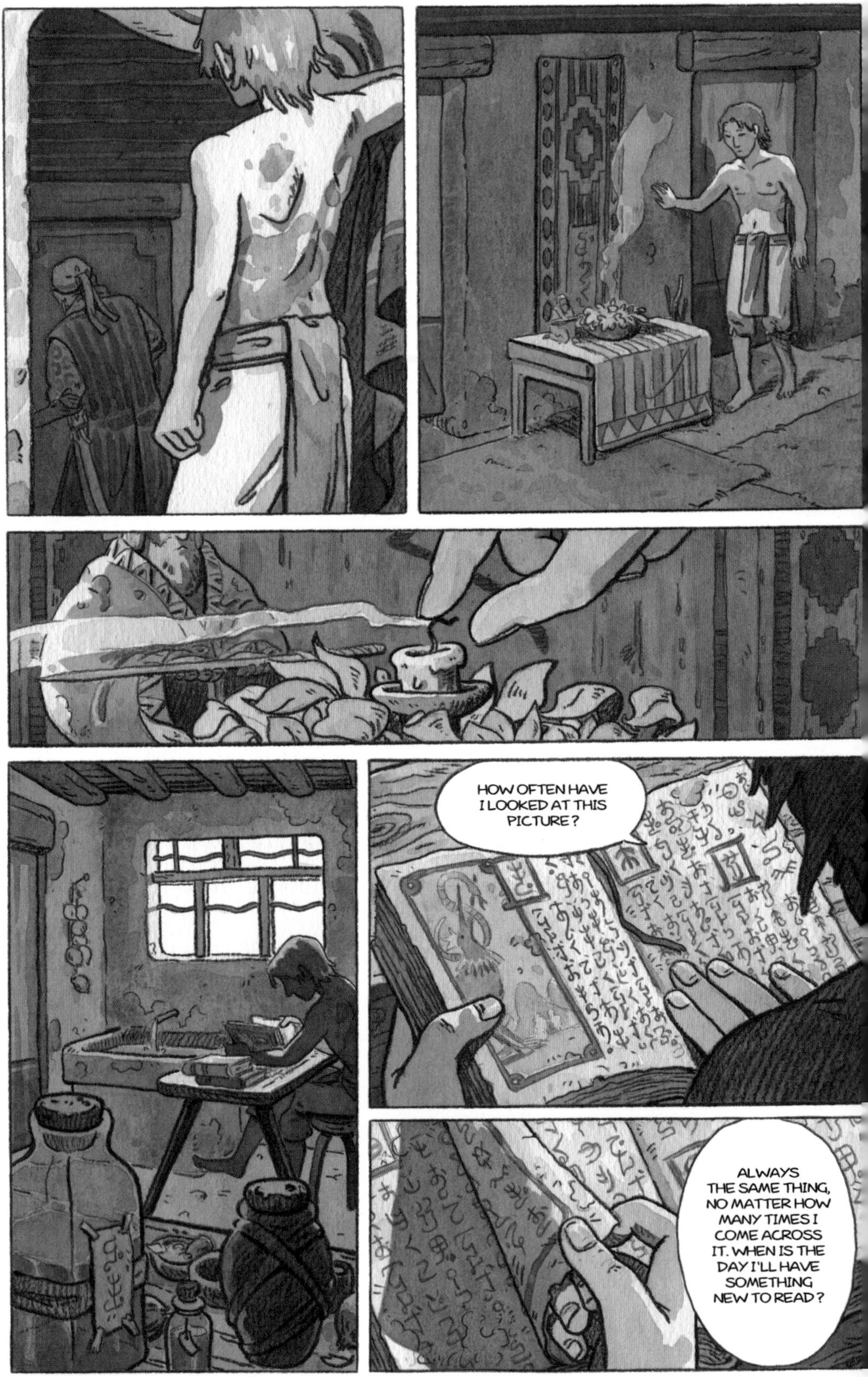
HOW OFTEN HAVE I LOOKED AT THIS PICTURE?
ALWAYS THE SAME THING, NO MATTER HOW MANY TIMES I COME ACROSS IT. WHEN IS THE DAY I'LL HAVE SOMETHING NEW TO READ?

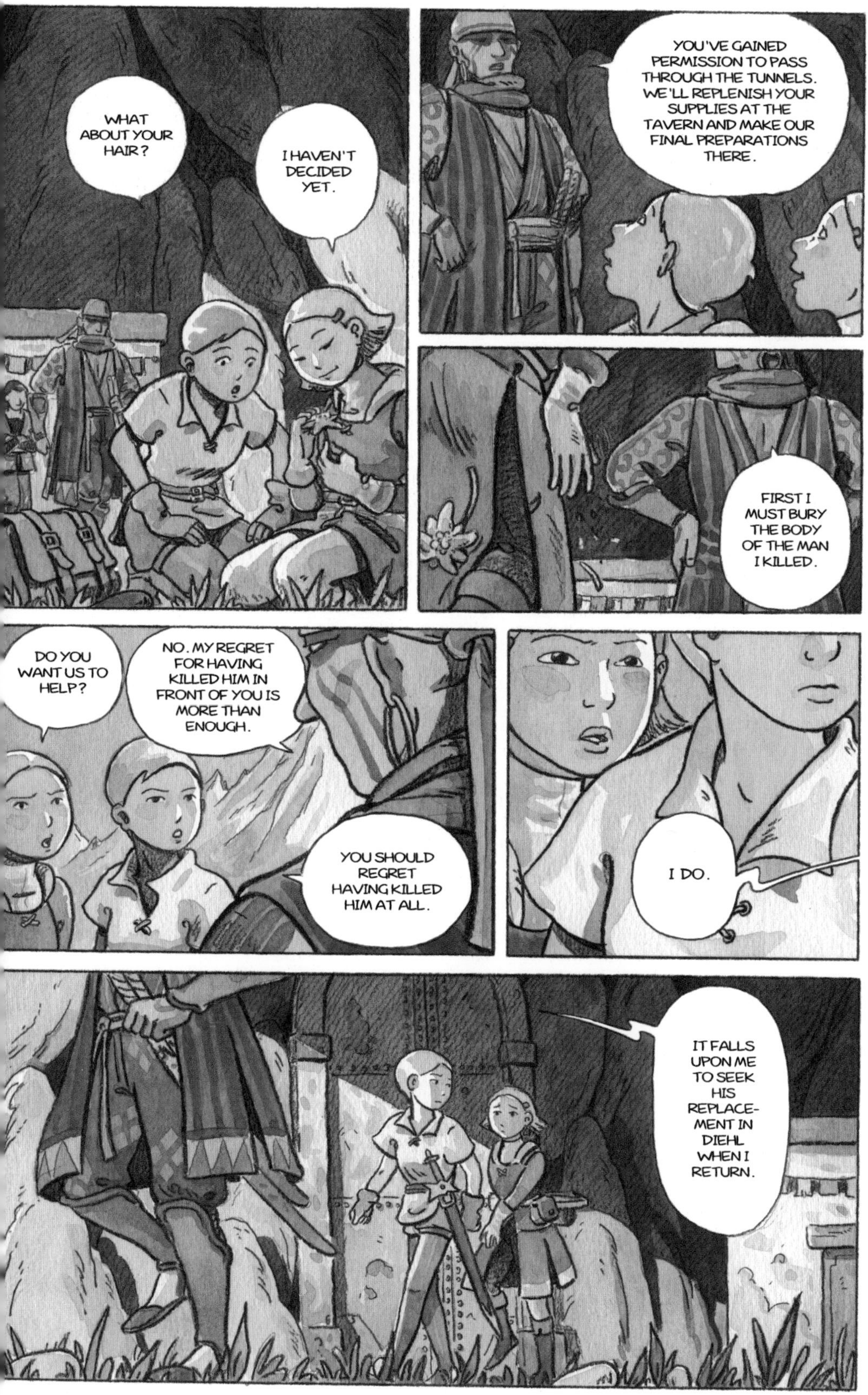
WHAT ABOUT YOUR HAIR?
I HAVEN'T DECIDED YET.
YOU'VE GAINED PERMISSION TO PASS THROUGH THE TUNNELS. WE'LL REPLENISH YOUR SUPPLIES AT THE TAVERN AND MAKE OUR FINAL PREPARATIONS THERE.
FIRST I MUST BURY THE BODY OF THE MAN I KILLED.
DO YOU WANT US TO HELP?
NO. MY REGRET FOR HAVING KILLED HIM IN FRONT OF YOU IS MORE THAN ENOUGH.
YOU SHOULD REGRET HAVING KILLED HIM AT ALL.
I DO.
IT FALLS UPON ME TO SEEK HIS REPLACE-MENT IN DIEHL WHEN I RETURN.

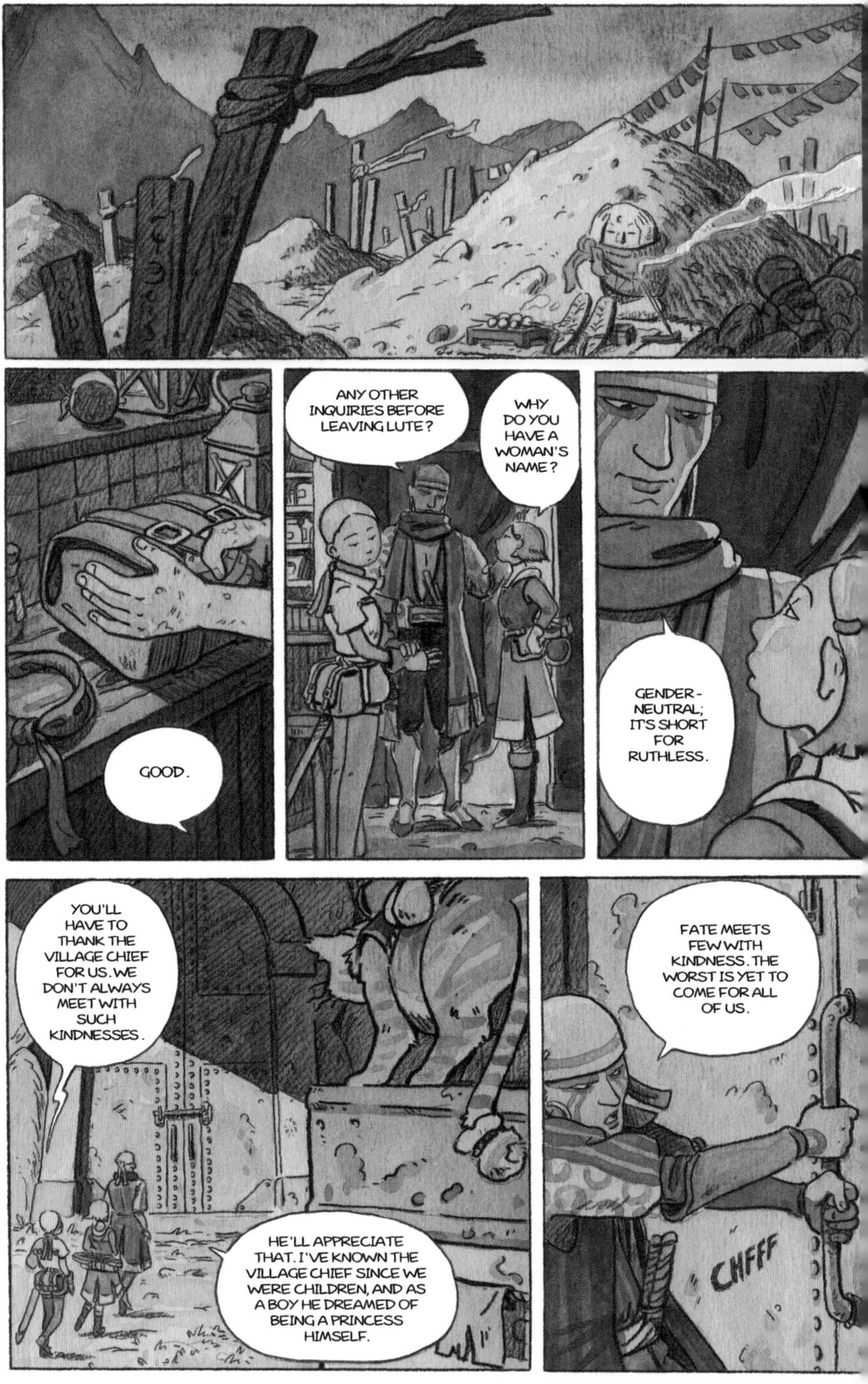
GOOD.
ANY OTHER INQUIRIES BEFORE LEAVING LUTE?
WHY DO YOU HAVE A WOMAN'S NAME?
GENDER-NEUTRAL; IT'S SHORT FOR RUTHLESS.
YOU'LL HAVE TO THANK THE VILLAGE CHIEF FOR US. WE DON'T ALWAYS MEET WITH SUCH KINDNESSES.
HE'LL APPRECIATE THAT. I'VE KNOWN THE VILLAGE CHIEF SINCE WE WERE CHILDREN, AND AS A BOY HE DREAMED OF BEING A PRINCESS HIMSELF.
FATE MEETS FEW WITH KINDNESS. THE WORST IS YET TO COME FOR ALL OF US.
CHFFF

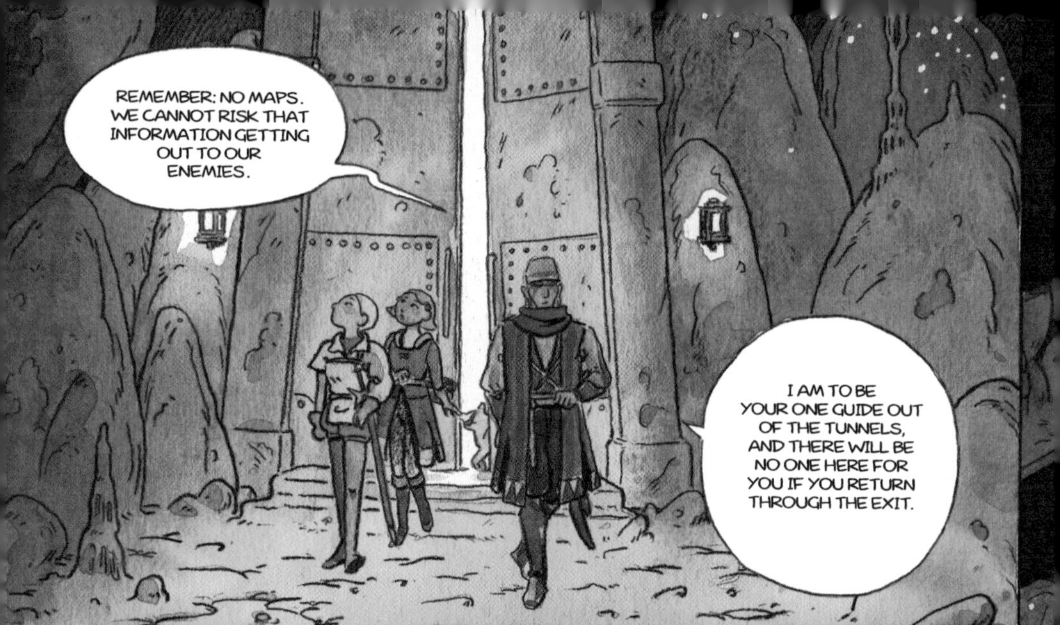
REMEMBER: NO MAPS. WE CANNOT RISK THAT INFORMATION GETTING OUT TO OUR ENEMIES.
I AM TO BE YOUR ONE GUIDE OUT OF THE TUNNELS, AND THERE WILL BE NO ONE HERE FOR YOU IF YOU RETURN THROUGH THE EXIT.

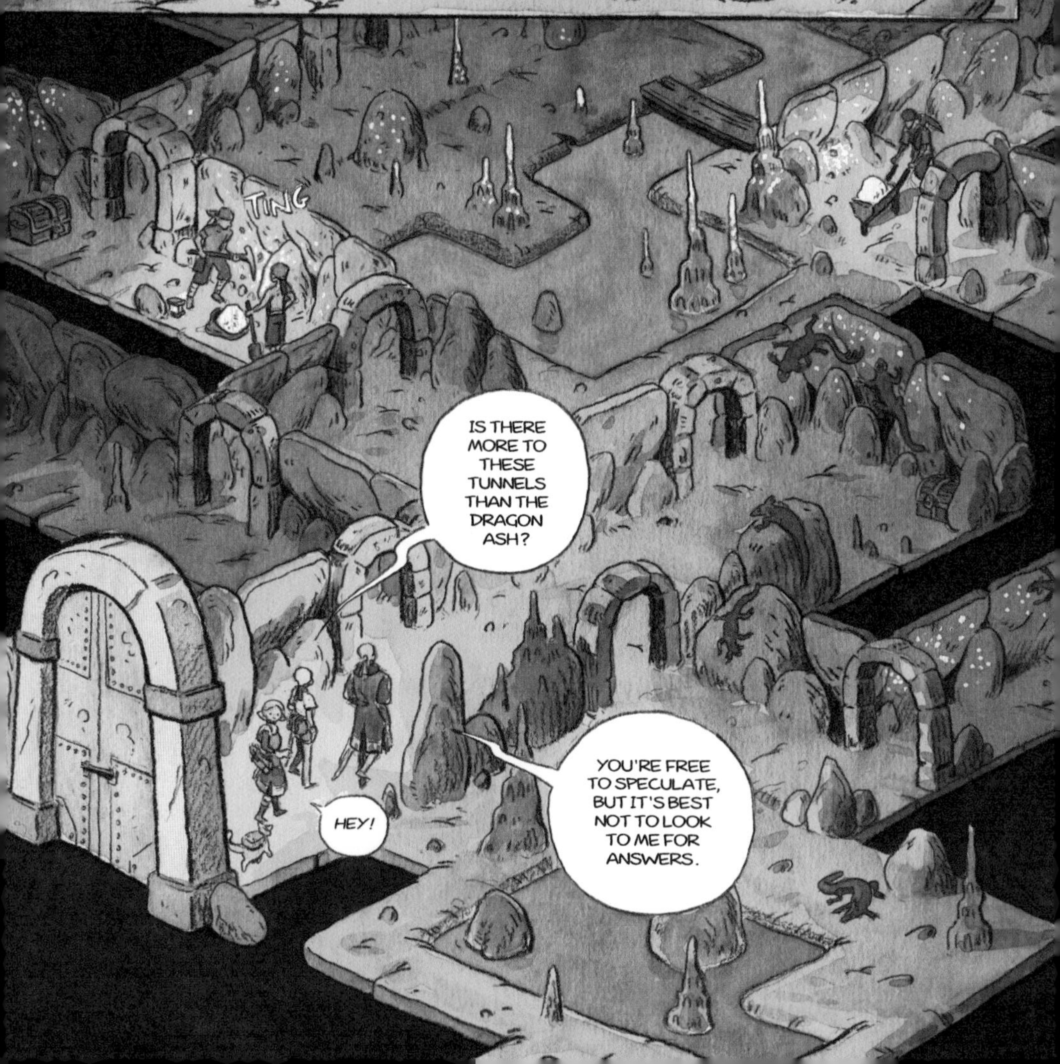
TING
IS THERE MORE TO THESE TUNNELS THAN THE DRAGON ASH?
HEY!
YOU'RE FREE TO SPECULATE, BUT IT'S BEST NOT TO LOOK TO ME FOR ANSWERS.

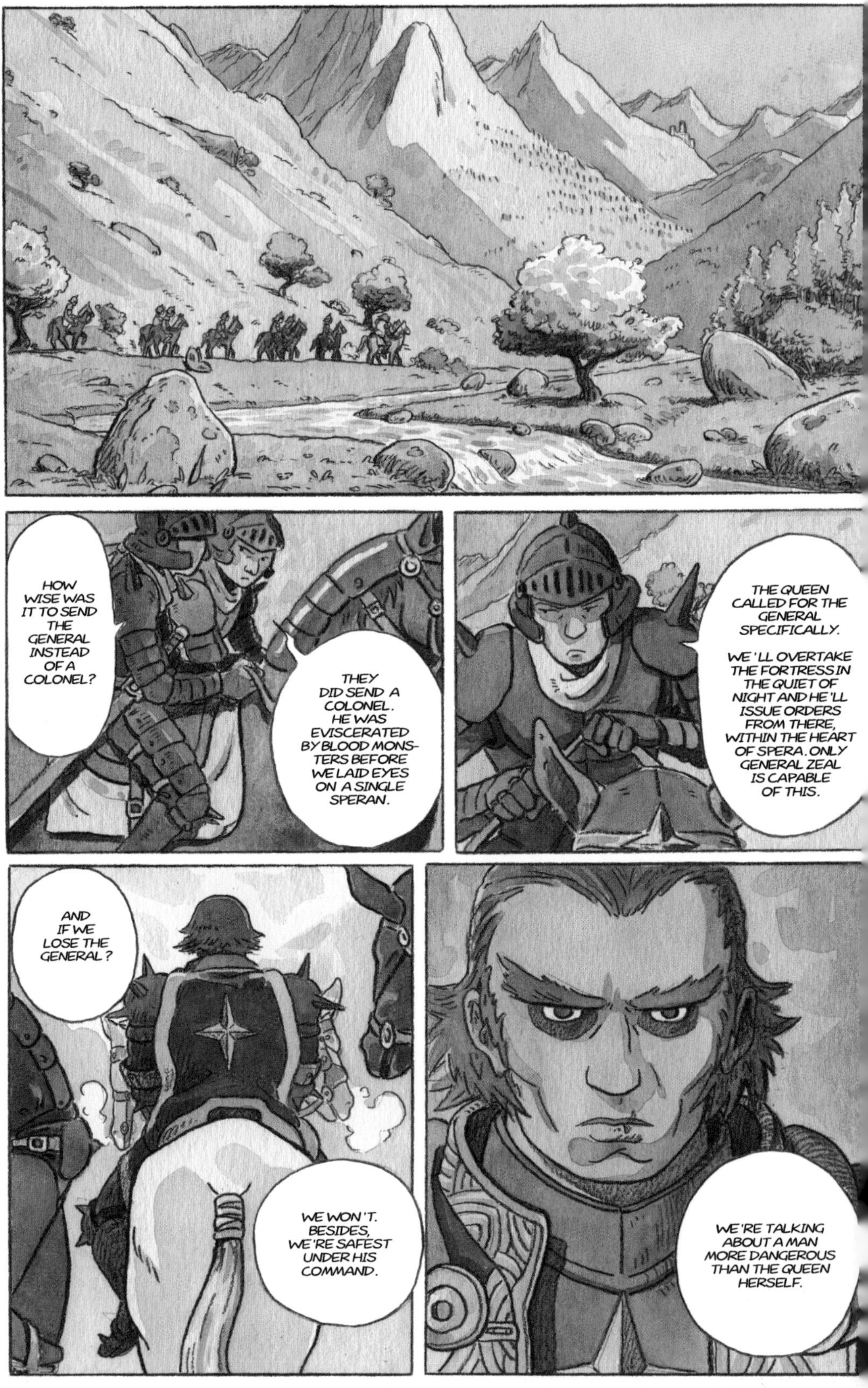
HOW WISE WAS IT TO SEND THE GENERAL INSTEAD OF A COLONEL?
THEY DID SEND A COLONEL. HE WAS EVISCERATED BY BLOOD MONSTERS BEFORE WE LAID EYES ON A SINGLE SPERAN.
THE QUEEN CALLED FOR THE GENERAL SPECIFICALLY.
WE'LL OVERTAKE THE FORTRESS IN THE QUIET OF NIGHT AND HE'LL ISSUE ORDERS FROM THERE, WITHIN THE HEART OF SPERA. ONLY GENERAL ZEAL IS CAPABLE OF THIS.
AND IF WE LOSE THE GENERAL?
WE WON'T. BESIDES, WE'RE SAFEST UNDER HIS COMMAND.
WE'RE TALKING ABOUT A MAN MORE DANGEROUS THAN THE QUEEN HERSELF.

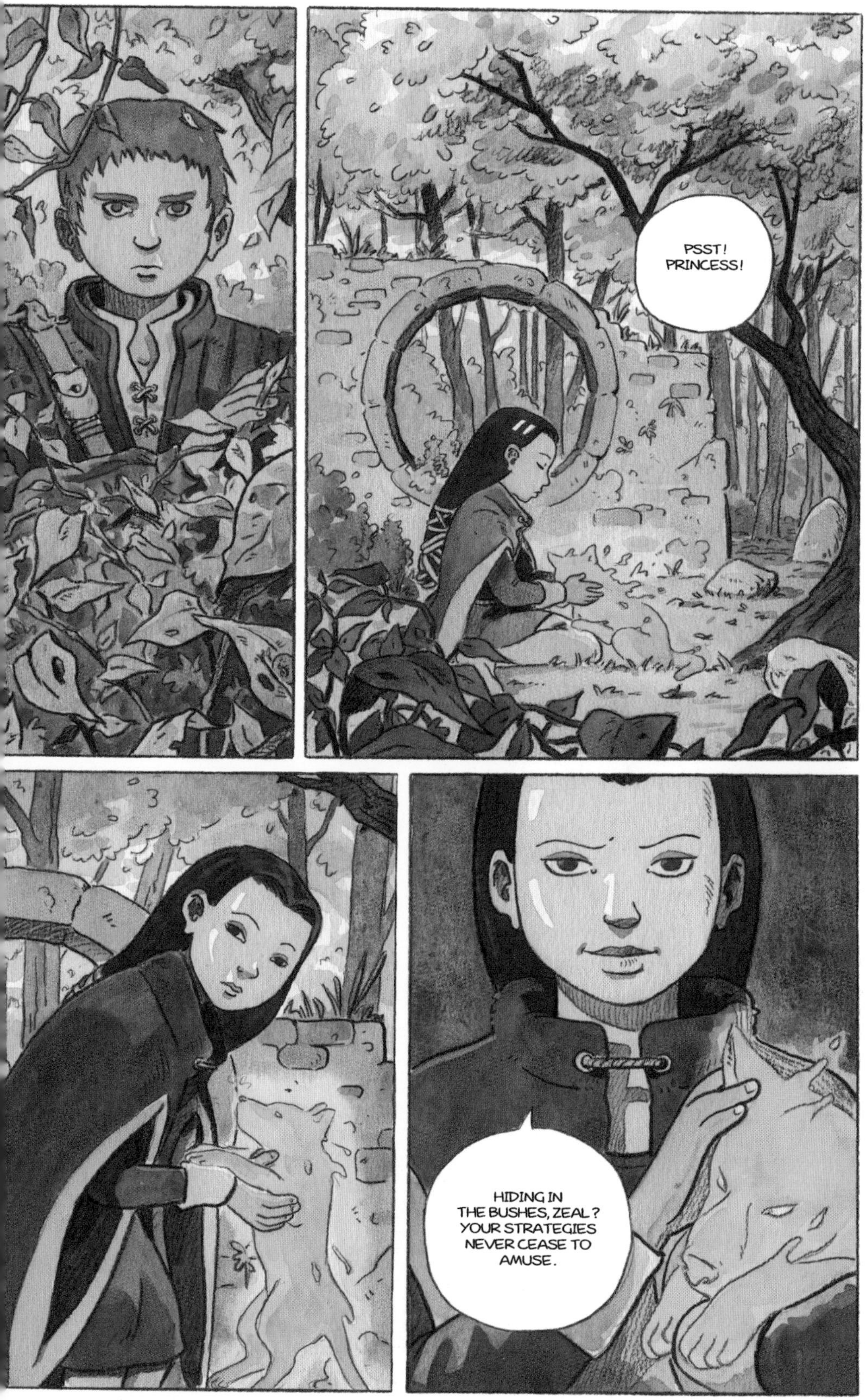
PSST! PRINCESS!
HIDING IN THE BUSHES, ZEAL? YOUR STRATEGIES NEVER CEASE TO AMUSE.

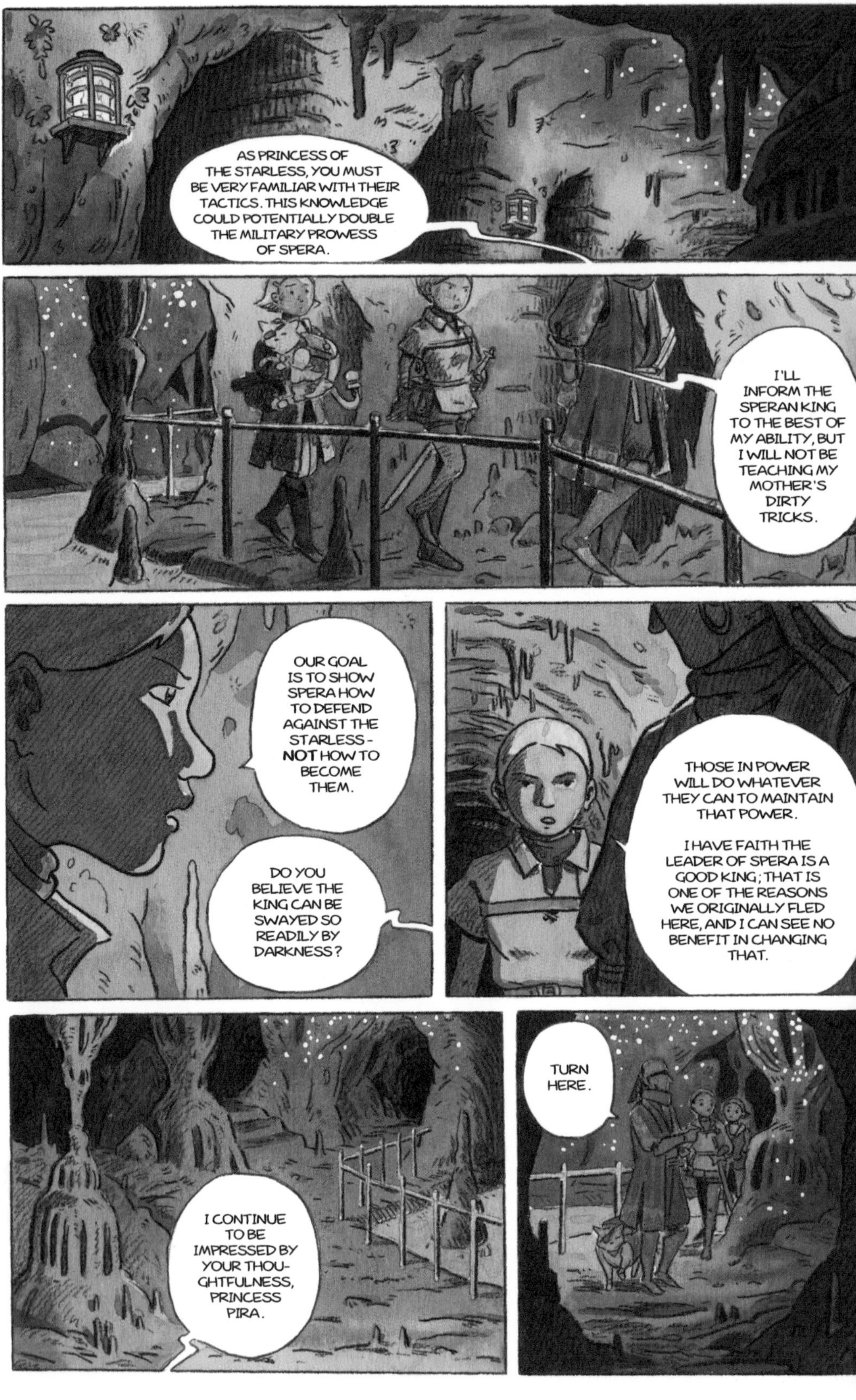
AS PRINCESS OF THE STARLESS, YOU MUST BE VERY FAMILIAR WITH THEIR TACTICS. THIS KNOWLEDGE COULD POTENTIALLY DOUBLE THE MILITARY PROWESS OF SPERA.
I'LL INFORM THE SPERAN KING TO THE BEST OF MY ABILITY, BUT I WILL NOT BE TEACHING MY MOTHER'S DIRTY TRICKS.
OUR GOAL IS TO SHOW SPERA HOW TO DEFEND AGAINST THE STARLESS - **NOT** HOW TO BECOME THEM.
DO YOU BELIEVE THE KING CAN BE SWAYED SO READILY BY DARKNESS?
THOSE IN POWER WILL DO WHATEVER THEY CAN TO MAINTAIN THAT POWER.
I HAVE FAITH THE LEADER OF SPERA IS A GOOD KING; THAT IS ONE OF THE REASONS WE ORIGINALLY FLED HERE, AND I CAN SEE NO BENEFIT IN CHANGING THAT.
I CONTINUE TO BE IMPRESSED BY YOUR THOUGHTFULNESS, PRINCESS PIRA.
TURN HERE.

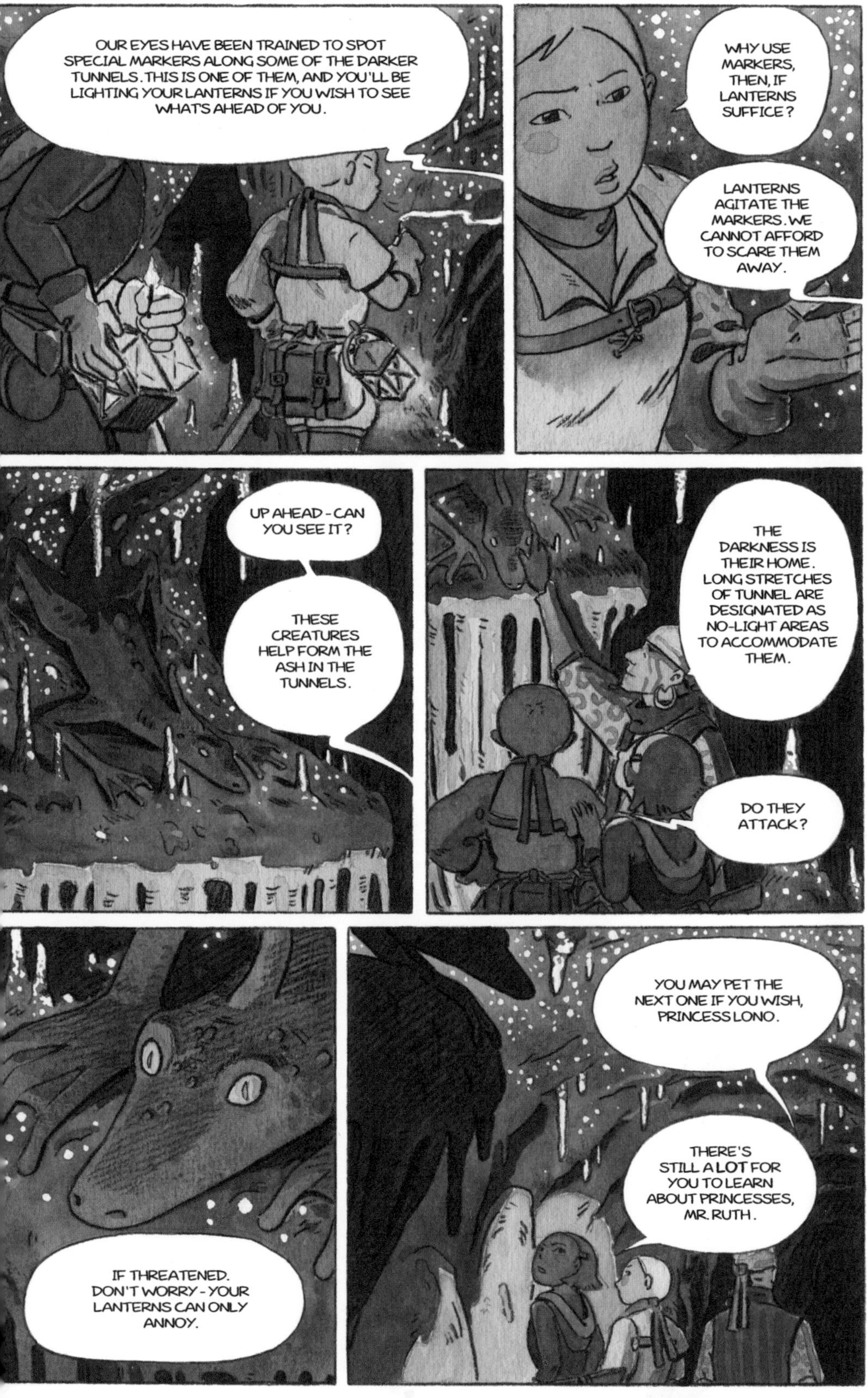
OUR EYES HAVE BEEN TRAINED TO SPOT SPECIAL MARKERS ALONG SOME OF THE DARKER TUNNELS. THIS IS ONE OF THEM, AND YOU'LL BE LIGHTING YOUR LANTERNS IF YOU WISH TO SEE WHAT'S AHEAD OF YOU.
WHY USE MARKERS, THEN, IF LANTERNS SUFFICE?
LANTERNS AGITATE THE MARKERS. WE CANNOT AFFORD TO SCARE THEM AWAY.
UP AHEAD - CAN YOU SEE IT?
THESE CREATURES HELP FORM THE ASH IN THE TUNNELS.
THE DARKNESS IS THEIR HOME. LONG STRETCHES OF TUNNEL ARE DESIGNATED AS NO-LIGHT AREAS TO ACCOMMODATE THEM.
DO THEY ATTACK?
IF THREATENED. DON'T WORRY - YOUR LANTERNS CAN ONLY ANNOY.
YOU MAY PET THE NEXT ONE IF YOU WISH, PRINCESS LONO.
THERE'S STILL A **LOT** FOR YOU TO LEARN ABOUT PRINCESSES, MR. RUTH.

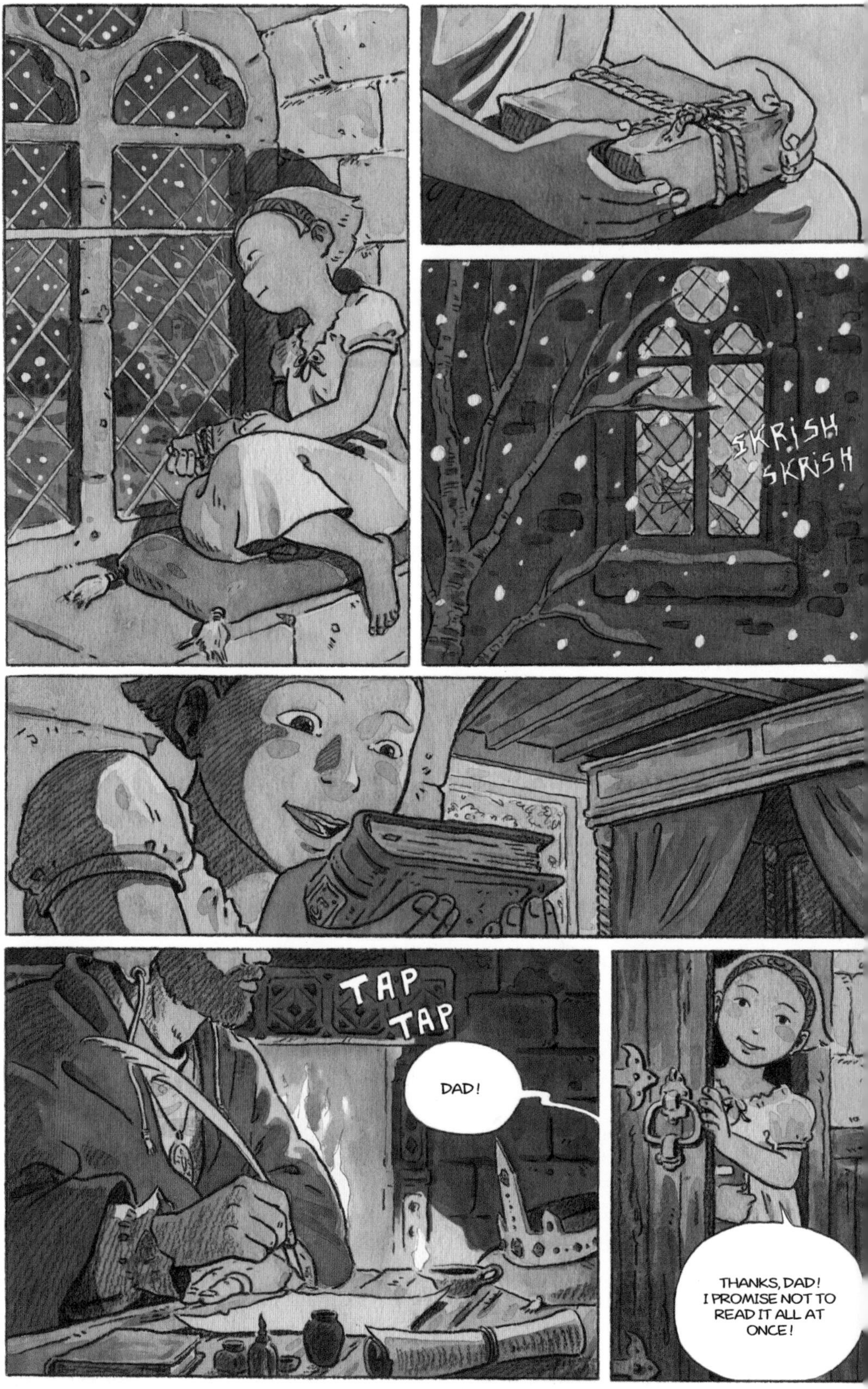
SKRISH
SKRISH
TAP
TAP
DAD!
THANKS, DAD! I PROMISE NOT TO READ IT ALL AT ONCE!

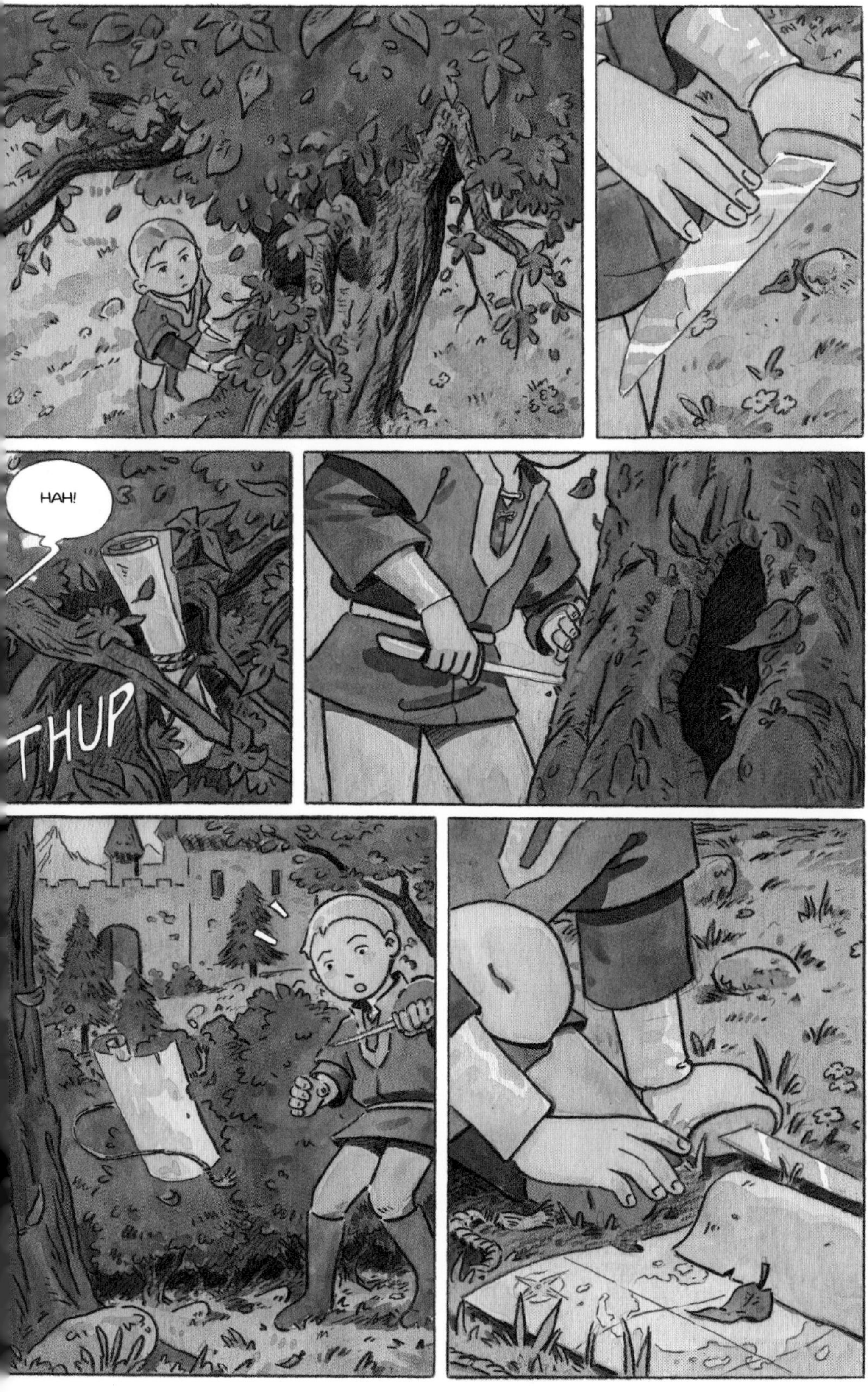
HAH!
THUP

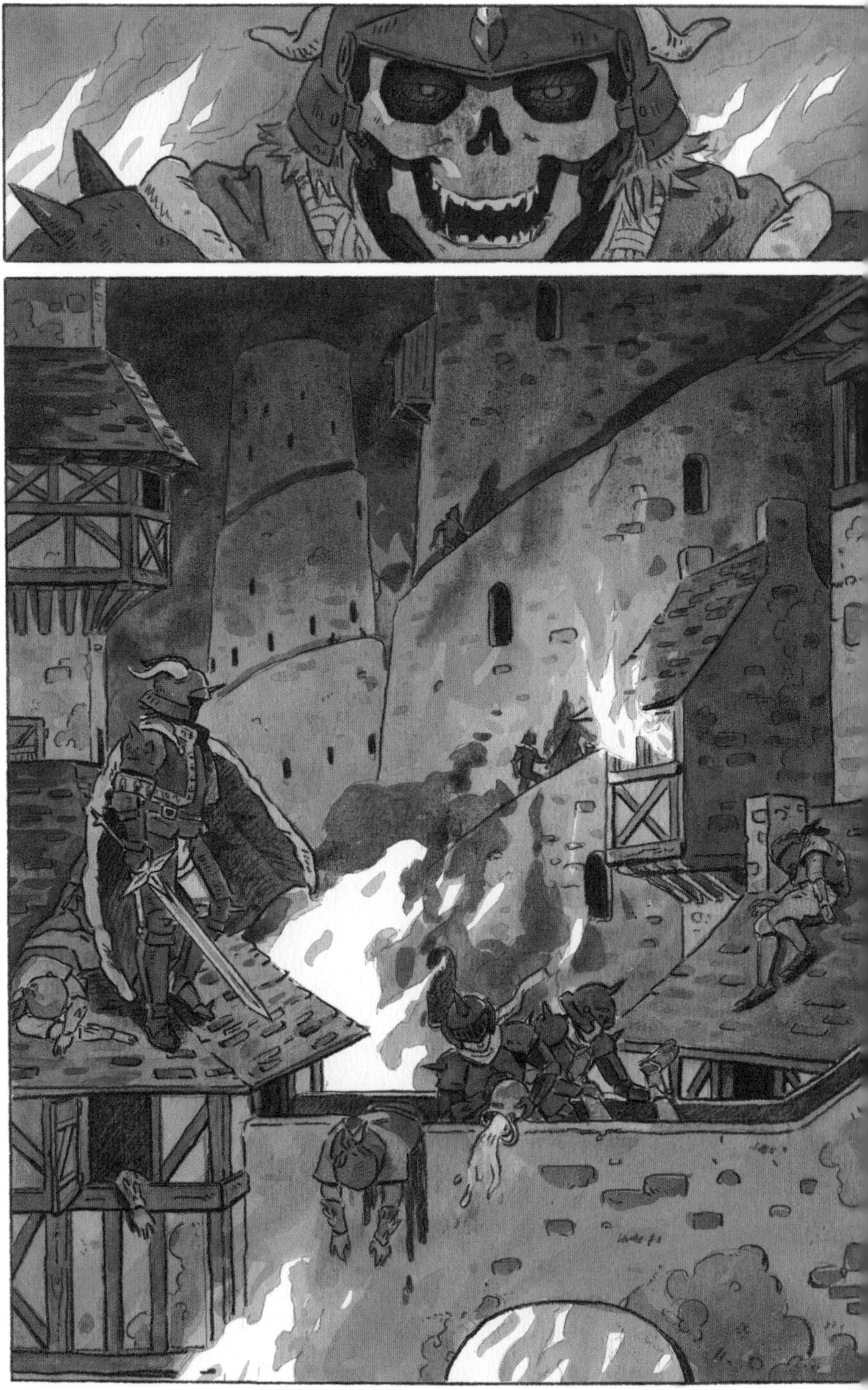

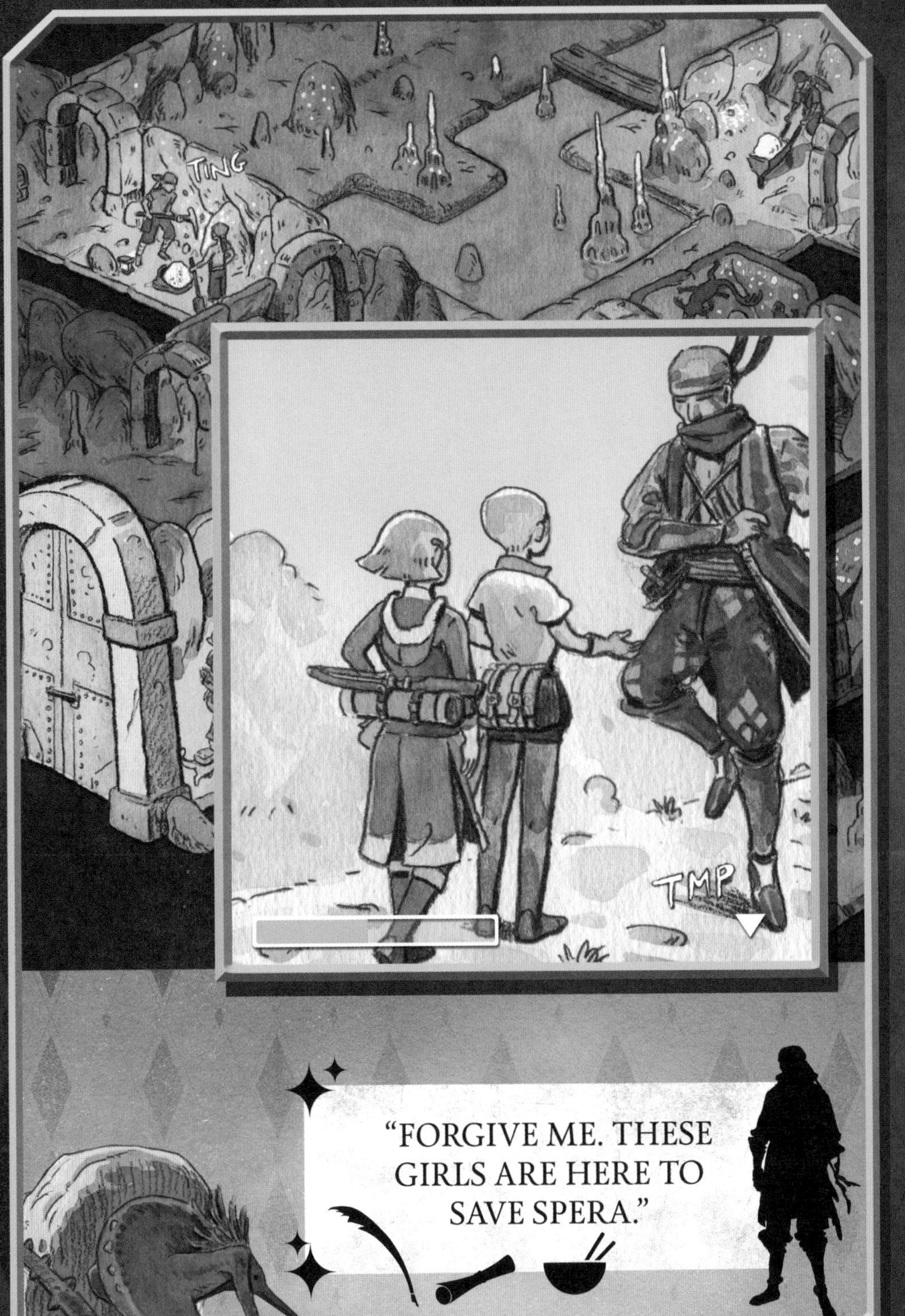
TING
TMP
"FORGIVE ME. THESE GIRLS ARE HERE TO SAVE SPERA."

CHAPTER THREE

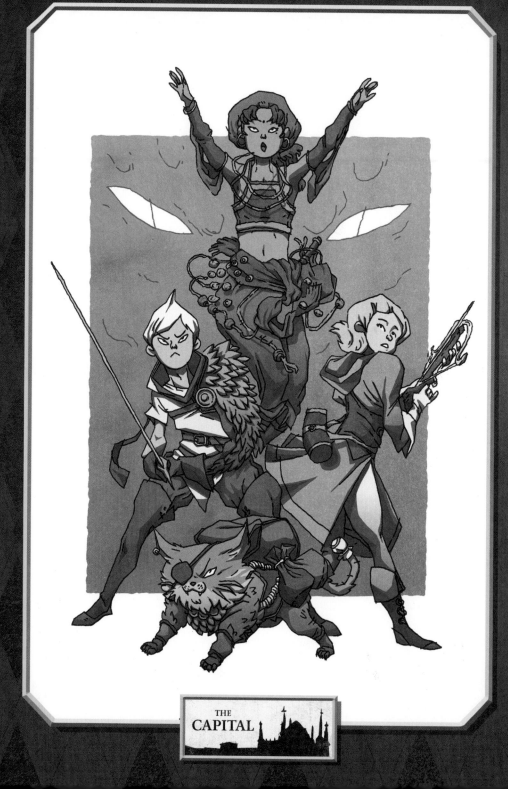

THE
CAPITAL

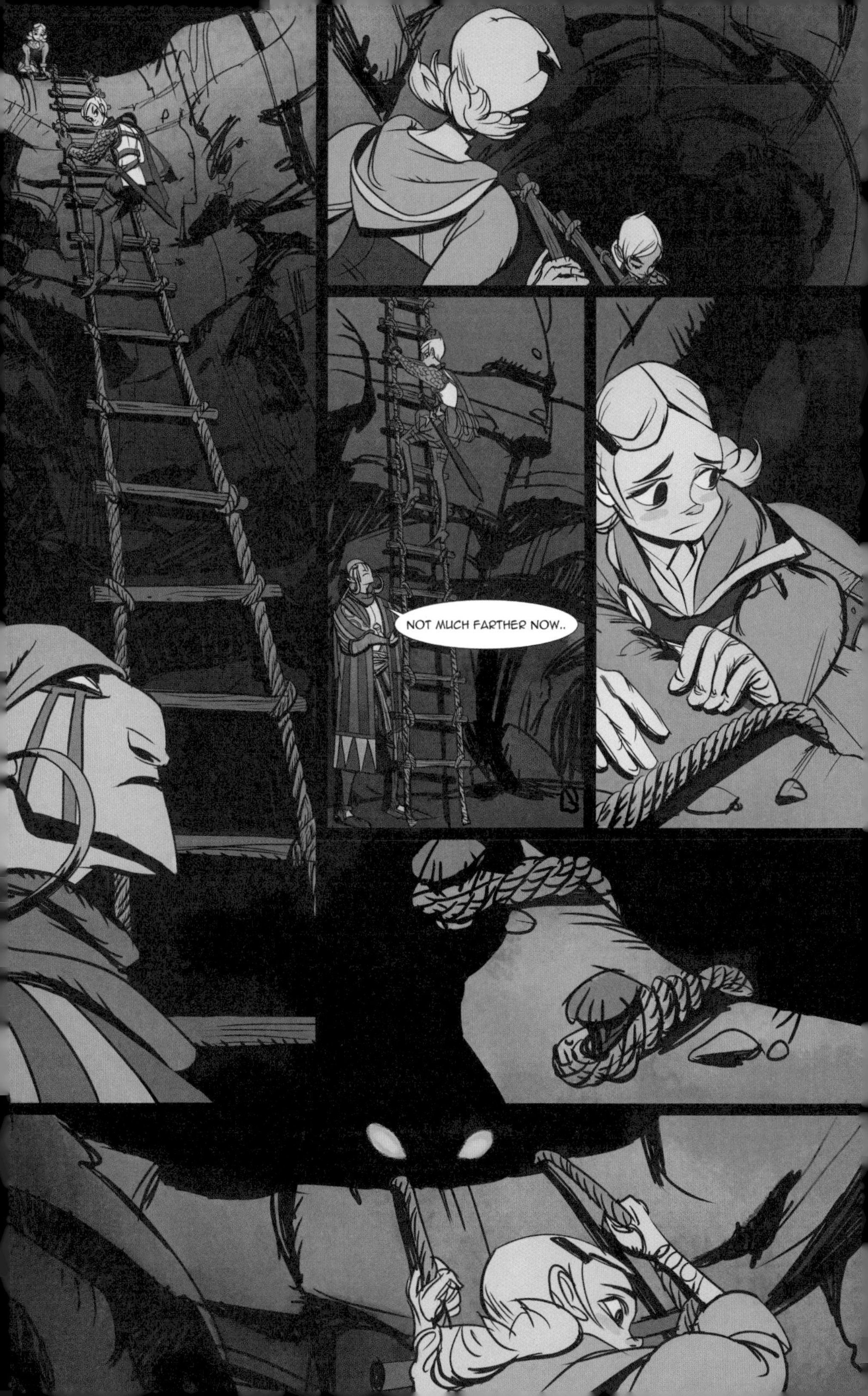
NOT MUCH FARTHER NOW..

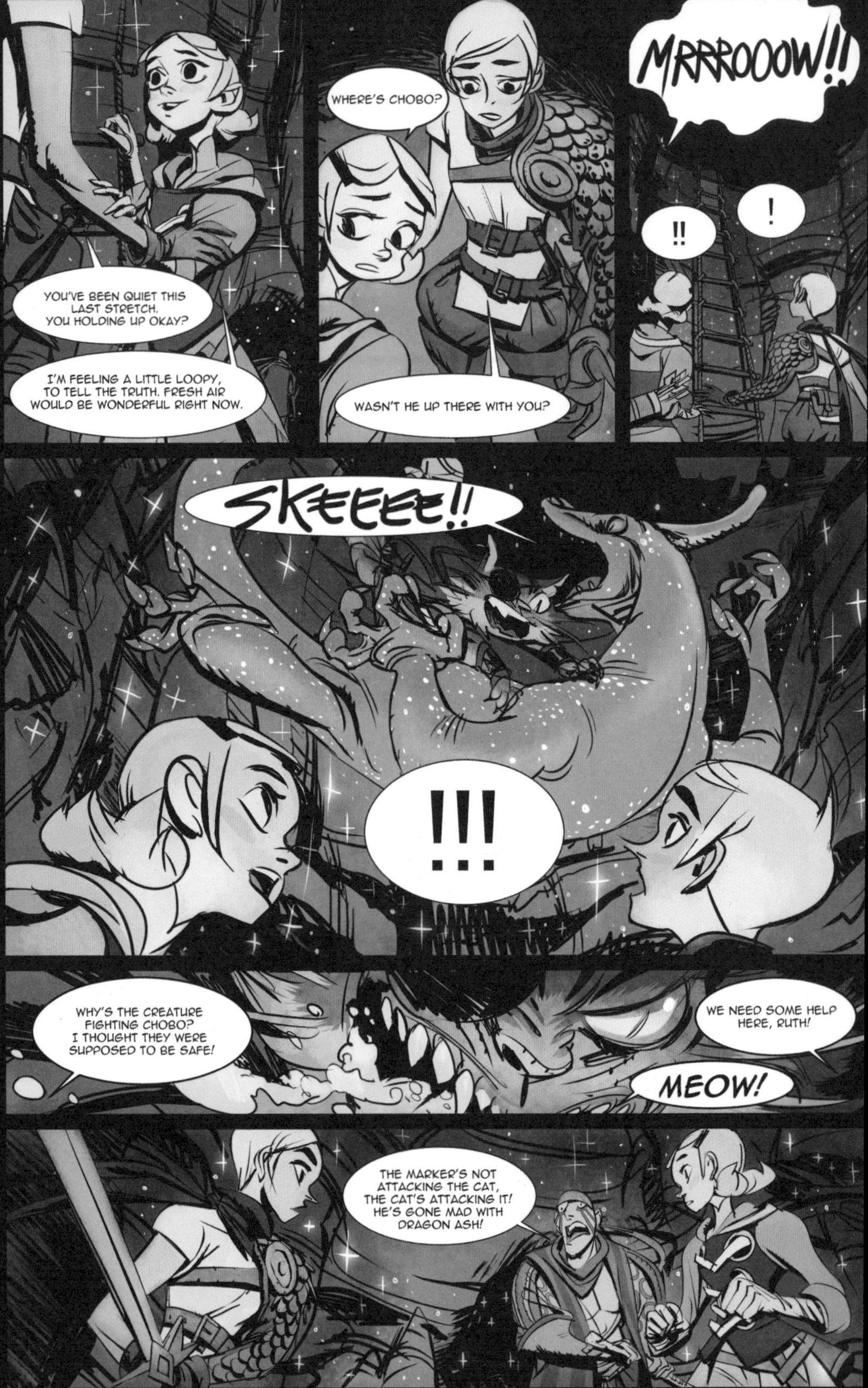
YOU'VE BEEN QUIET THIS LAST STRETCH. YOU HOLDING UP OKAY?
I'M FEELING A LITTLE LOOPY, TO TELL THE TRUTH. FRESH AIR WOULD BE WONDERFUL RIGHT NOW.
WHERE'S CHOBO?
WASN'T HE UP THERE WITH YOU?
MRRROOOW!!
!!
!
SKEEEEE!!
!!!
WHY'S THE CREATURE FIGHTING CHOBO? I THOUGHT THEY WERE SUPPOSED TO BE SAFE!
WE NEED SOME HELP HERE, RUTH!
MEOW!
THE MARKER'S NOT ATTACKING THE CAT, THE CAT'S ATTACKING IT! HE'S GONE MAD WITH DRAGON ASH!

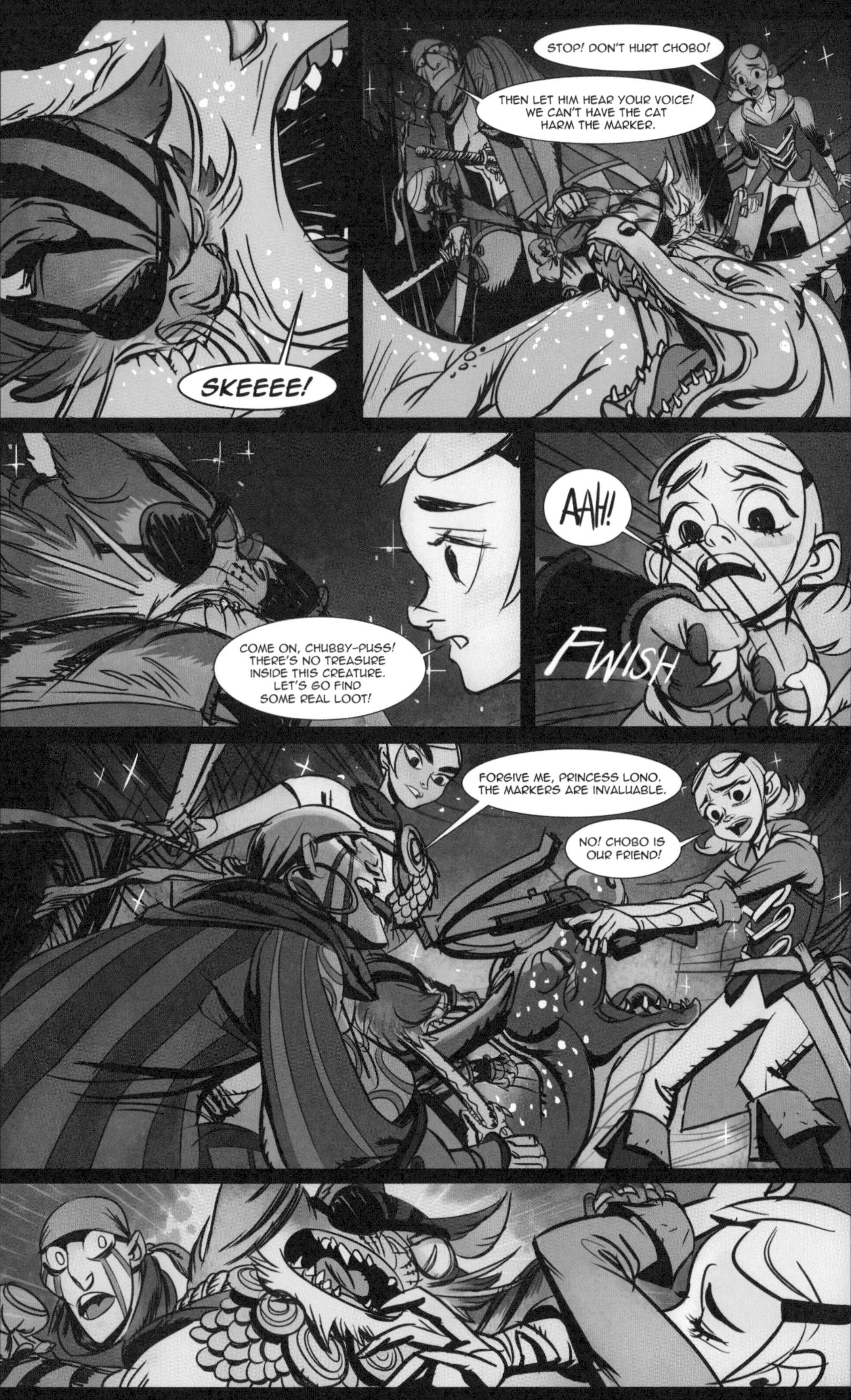
SKEEEE!
STOP! DON'T HURT CHOBO!
THEN LET HIM HEAR YOUR VOICE! WE CAN'T HAVE THE CAT HARM THE MARKER.
COME ON, CHUBBY-PUSS! THERE'S NO TREASURE INSIDE THIS CREATURE. LET'S GO FIND SOME REAL LOOT!
AAH!
FWISH
FORGIVE ME, PRINCESS LONO. THE MARKERS ARE INVALUABLE.
NO! CHOBO IS OUR FRIEND!

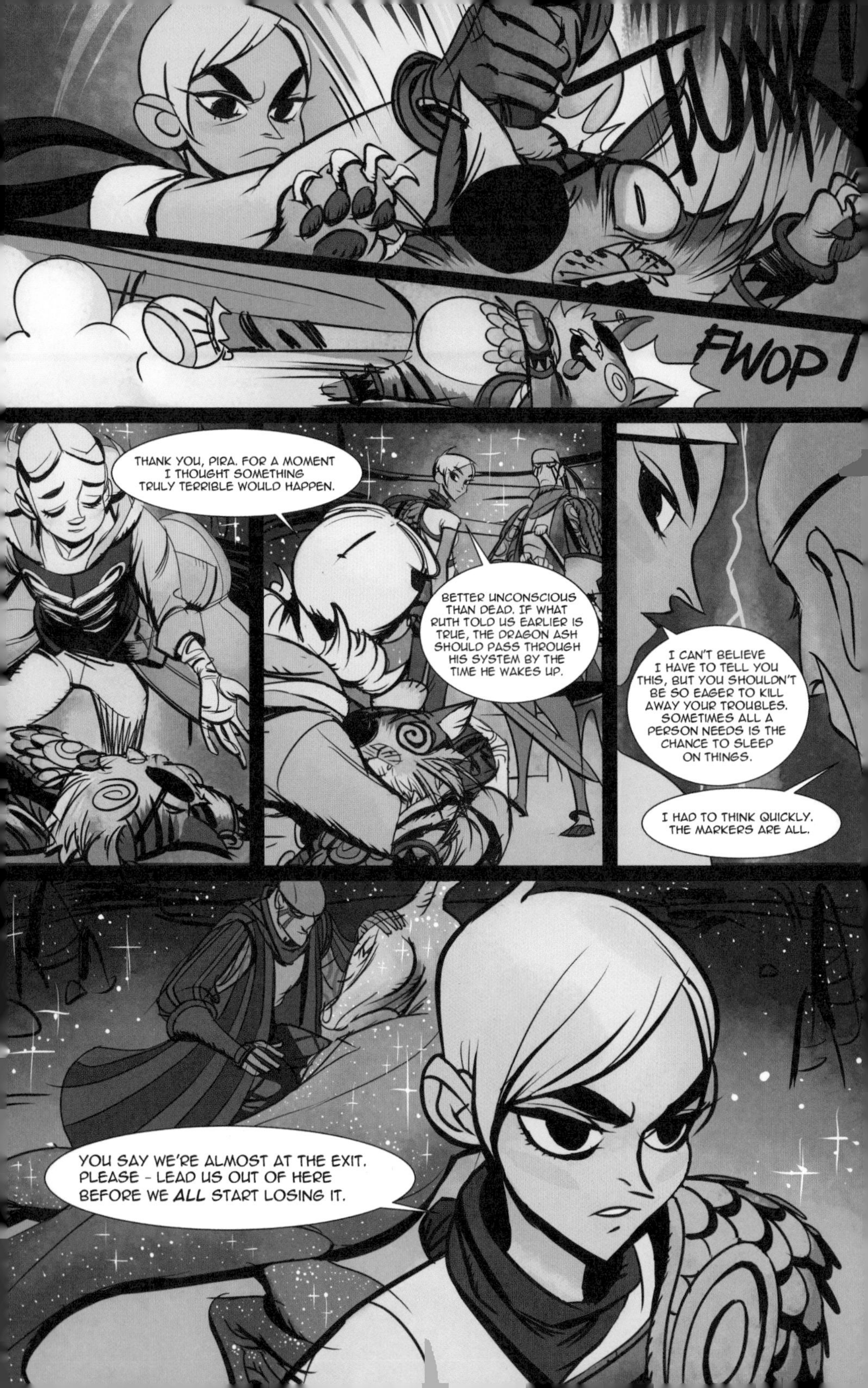
TUNK!!
FWOP!
THANK YOU, PIRA. FOR A MOMENT I THOUGHT SOMETHING TRULY TERRIBLE WOULD HAPPEN.
BETTER UNCONSCIOUS THAN DEAD. IF WHAT RUTH TOLD US EARLIER IS TRUE, THE DRAGON ASH SHOULD PASS THROUGH HIS SYSTEM BY THE TIME HE WAKES UP.
I CAN'T BELIEVE I HAVE TO TELL YOU THIS, BUT YOU SHOULDN'T BE SO EAGER TO KILL AWAY YOUR TROUBLES. SOMETIMES ALL A PERSON NEEDS IS THE CHANCE TO SLEEP ON THINGS.
I HAD TO THINK QUICKLY. THE MARKERS ARE ALL.
YOU SAY WE'RE ALMOST AT THE EXIT. PLEASE - LEAD US OUT OF HERE BEFORE WE *ALL* START LOSING IT.

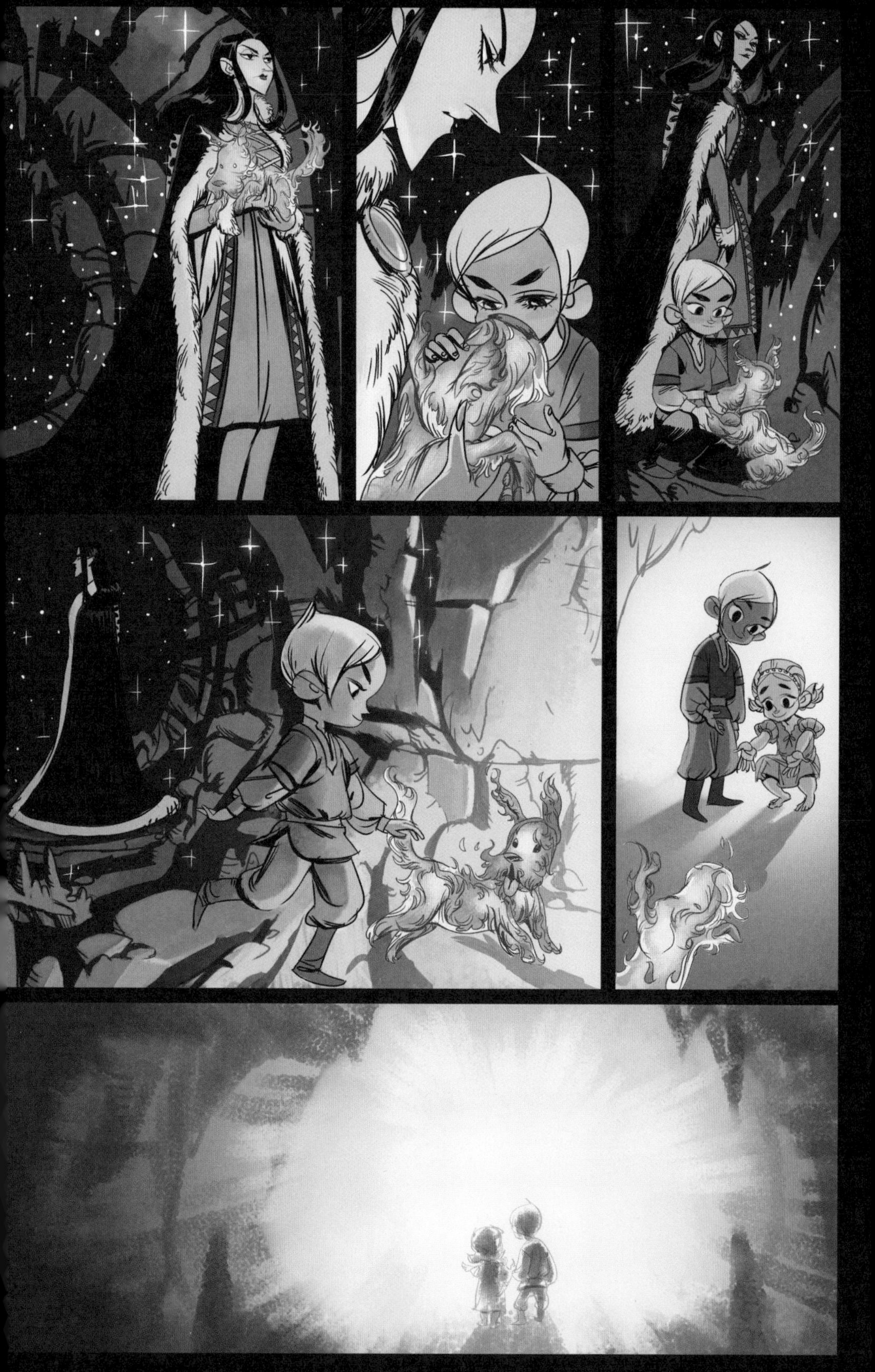

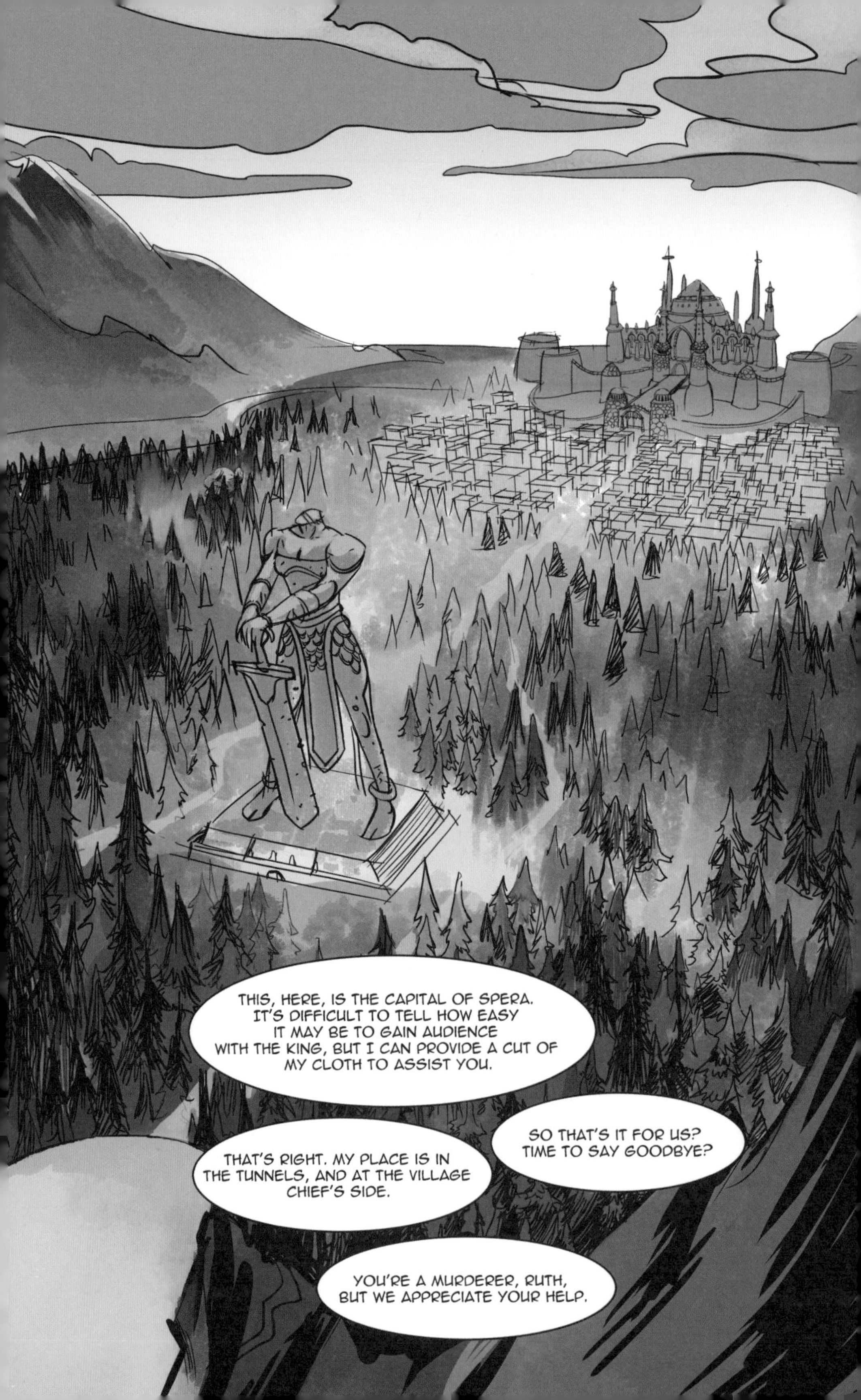
THIS, HERE, IS THE CAPITAL OF SPERA. IT'S DIFFICULT TO TELL HOW EASY IT MAY BE TO GAIN AUDIENCE WITH THE KING, BUT I CAN PROVIDE A CUT OF MY CLOTH TO ASSIST YOU.
SO THAT'S IT FOR US? TIME TO SAY GOODBYE?
THAT'S RIGHT. MY PLACE IS IN THE TUNNELS, AND AT THE VILLAGE CHIEF'S SIDE.
YOU'RE A MURDERER, RUTH, BUT WE APPRECIATE YOUR HELP.

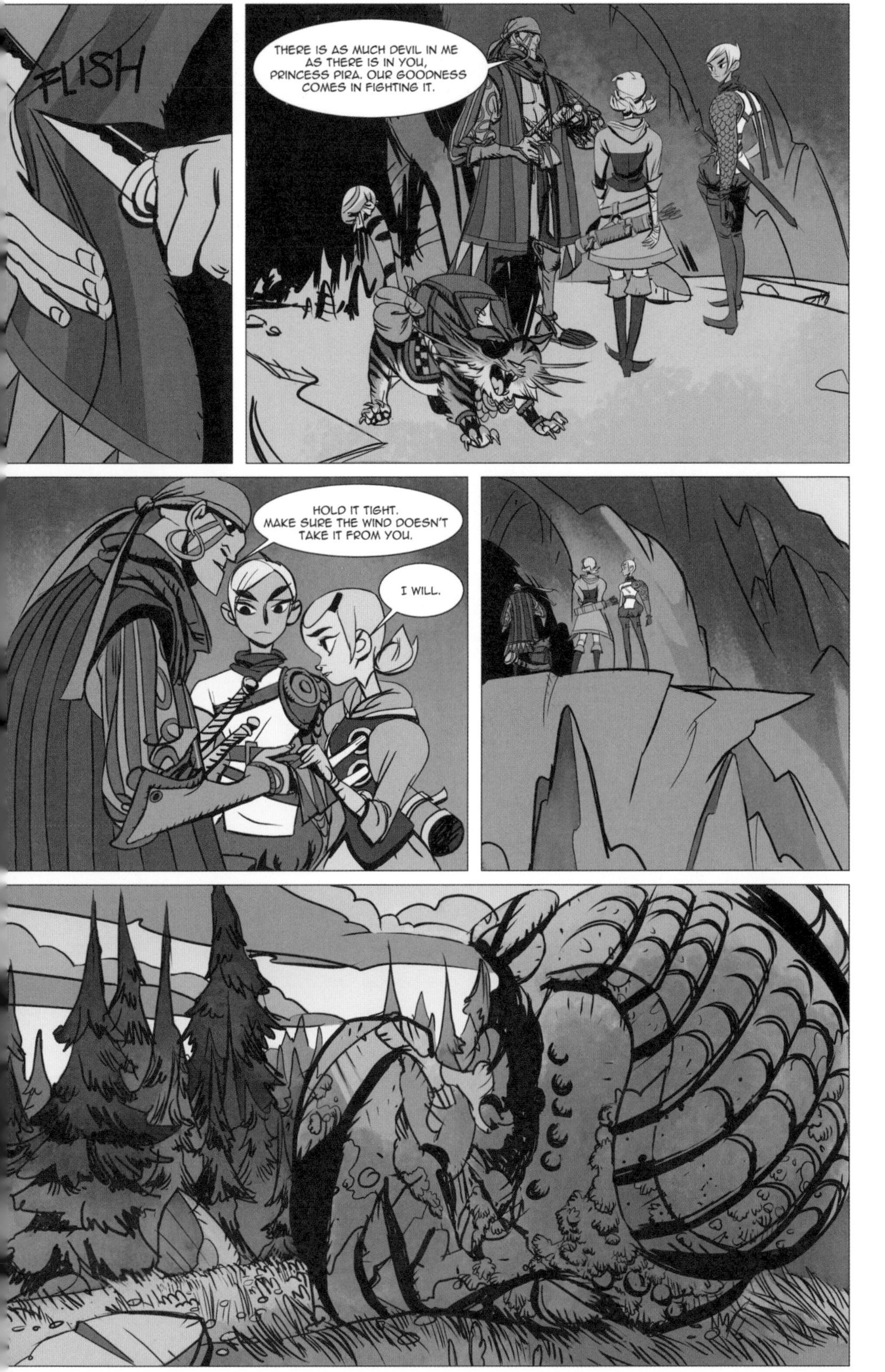
FLISH
THERE IS AS MUCH DEVIL IN ME AS THERE IS IN YOU, PRINCESS PIRA. OUR GOODNESS COMES IN FIGHTING IT.
HOLD IT TIGHT. MAKE SURE THE WIND DOESN'T TAKE IT FROM YOU.
I WILL.

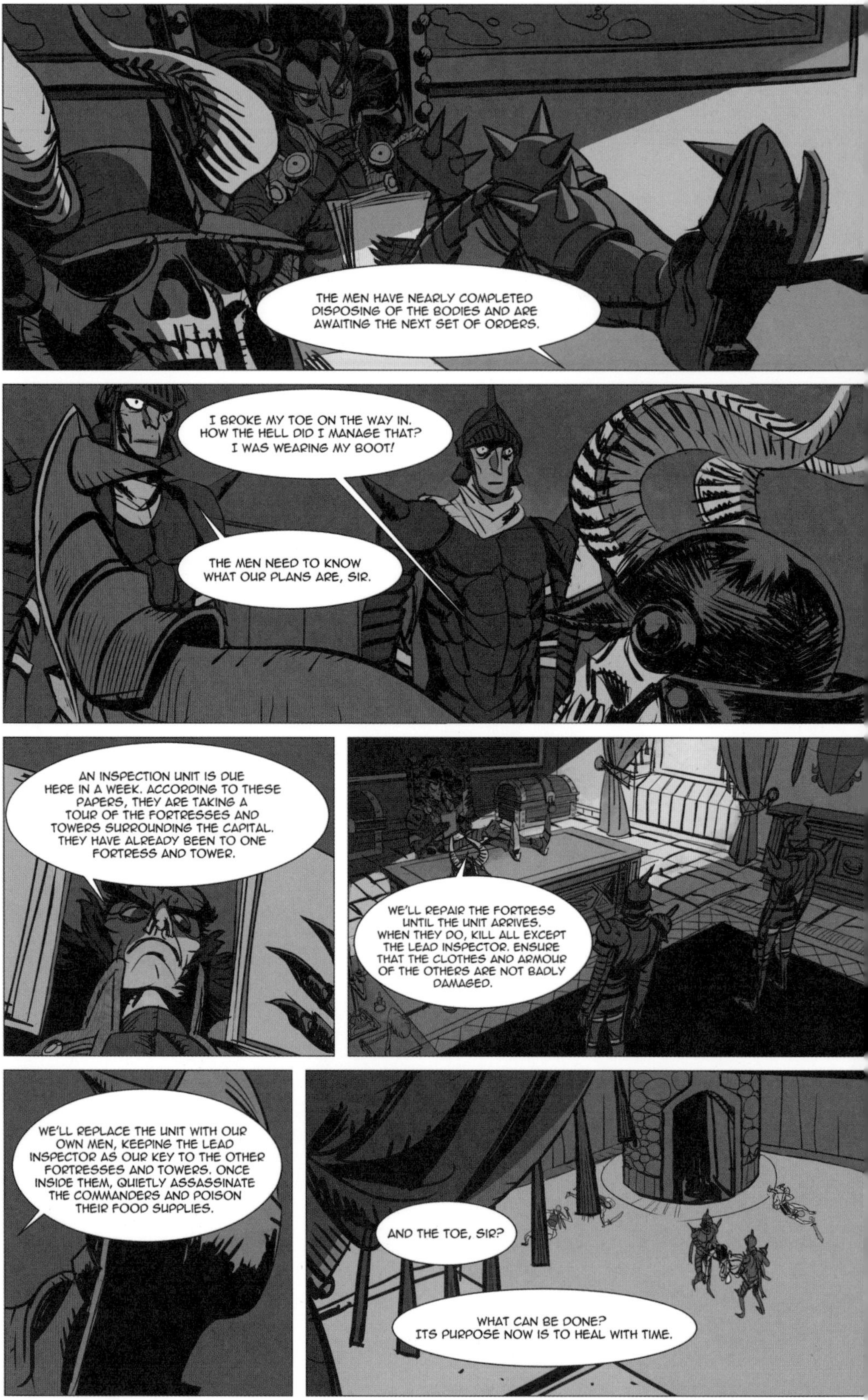
THE MEN HAVE NEARLY COMPLETED DISPOSING OF THE BODIES AND ARE AWAITING THE NEXT SET OF ORDERS.
I BROKE MY TOE ON THE WAY IN. HOW THE HELL DID I MANAGE THAT? I WAS WEARING MY BOOT!
THE MEN NEED TO KNOW WHAT OUR PLANS ARE, SIR.
AN INSPECTION UNIT IS DUE HERE IN A WEEK. ACCORDING TO THESE PAPERS, THEY ARE TAKING A TOUR OF THE FORTRESSES AND TOWERS SURROUNDING THE CAPITAL. THEY HAVE ALREADY BEEN TO ONE FORTRESS AND TOWER.
WE'LL REPAIR THE FORTRESS UNTIL THE UNIT ARRIVES. WHEN THEY DO, KILL ALL EXCEPT THE LEAD INSPECTOR. ENSURE THAT THE CLOTHES AND ARMOUR OF THE OTHERS ARE NOT BADLY DAMAGED.
WE'LL REPLACE THE UNIT WITH OUR OWN MEN, KEEPING THE LEAD INSPECTOR AS OUR KEY TO THE OTHER FORTRESSES AND TOWERS. ONCE INSIDE THEM, QUIETLY ASSASSINATE THE COMMANDERS AND POISON THEIR FOOD SUPPLIES.
AND THE TOE, SIR?
WHAT CAN BE DONE? ITS PURPOSE NOW IS TO HEAL WITH TIME.

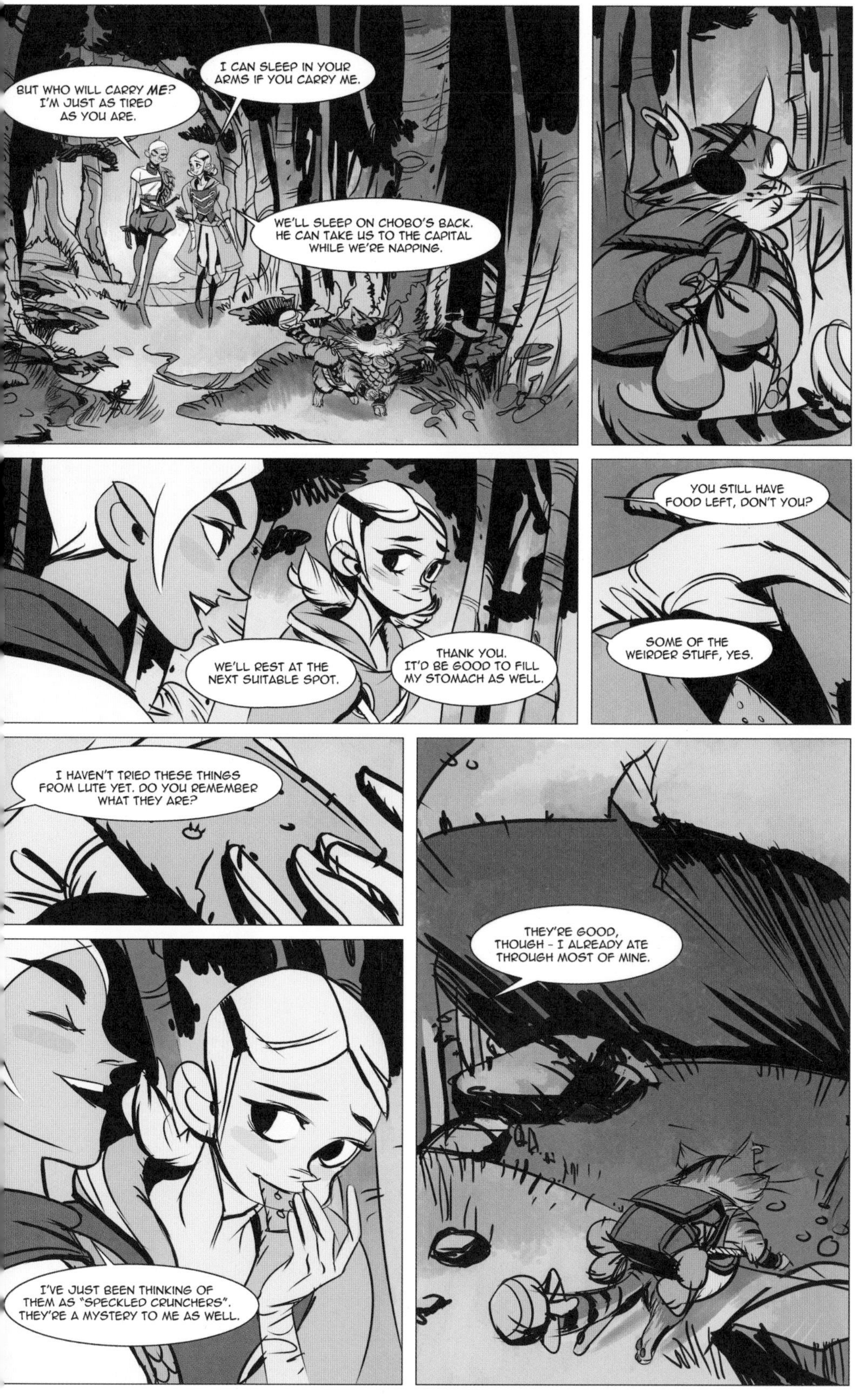
BUT WHO WILL CARRY *ME*? I'M JUST AS TIRED AS YOU ARE.
I CAN SLEEP IN YOUR ARMS IF YOU CARRY ME.
WE'LL SLEEP ON CHOBO'S BACK. HE CAN TAKE US TO THE CAPITAL WHILE WE'RE NAPPING.
WE'LL REST AT THE NEXT SUITABLE SPOT.
THANK YOU. IT'D BE GOOD TO FILL MY STOMACH AS WELL.
YOU STILL HAVE FOOD LEFT, DON'T YOU?
SOME OF THE WEIRDER STUFF, YES.
I HAVEN'T TRIED THESE THINGS FROM LUTE YET. DO YOU REMEMBER WHAT THEY ARE?
I'VE JUST BEEN THINKING OF THEM AS "SPECKLED CRUNCHERS". THEY'RE A MYSTERY TO ME AS WELL.
THEY'RE GOOD, THOUGH - I ALREADY ATE THROUGH MOST OF MINE.

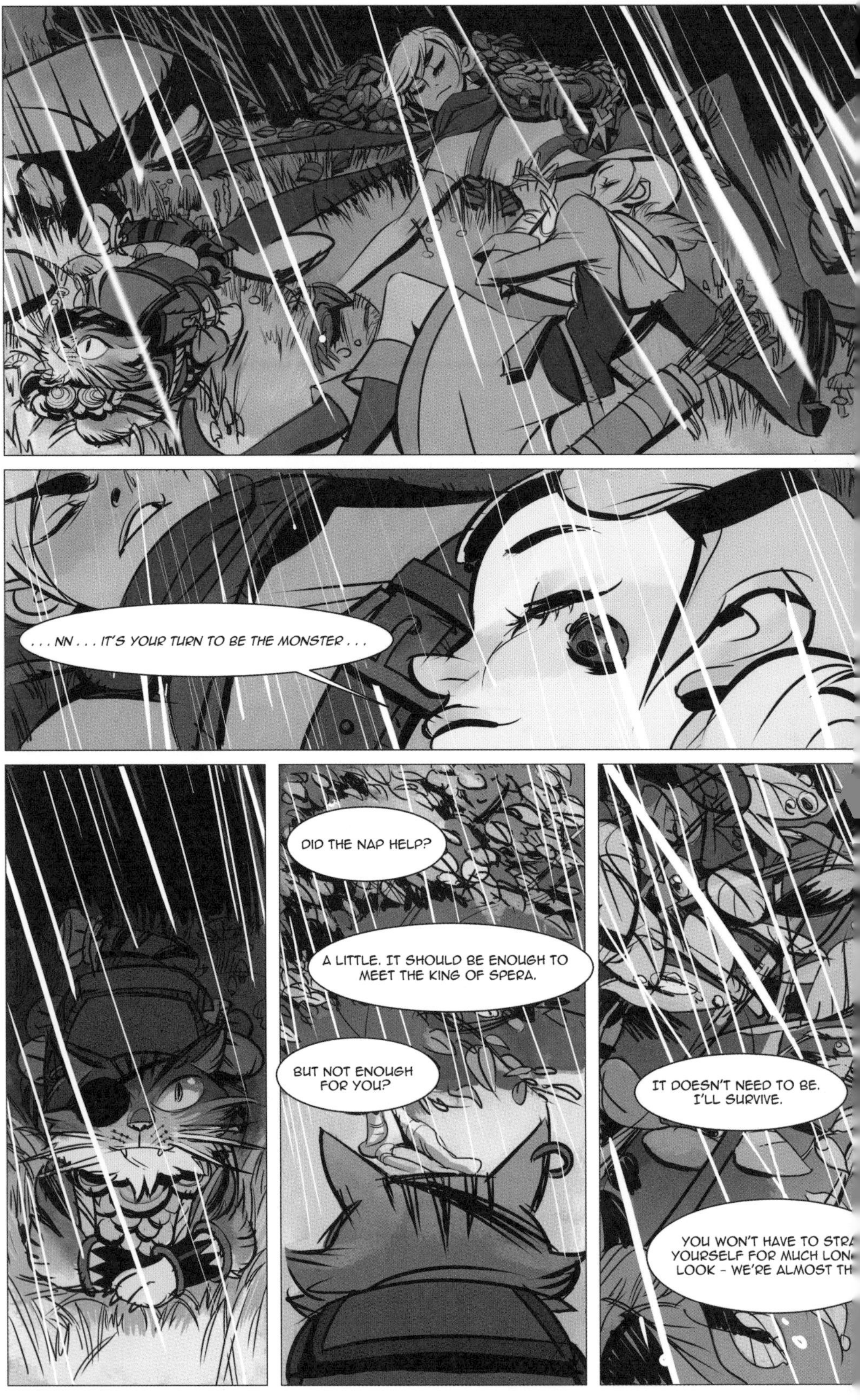
. . . NN . . . IT'S YOUR TURN TO BE THE MONSTER . . .
DID THE NAP HELP?
A LITTLE. IT SHOULD BE ENOUGH TO MEET THE KING OF SPERA.
BUT NOT ENOUGH FOR YOU?
IT DOESN'T NEED TO BE. I'LL SURVIVE.
YOU WON'T HAVE TO STR
YOURSELF FOR MUCH LON
LOOK - WE'RE ALMOST TH

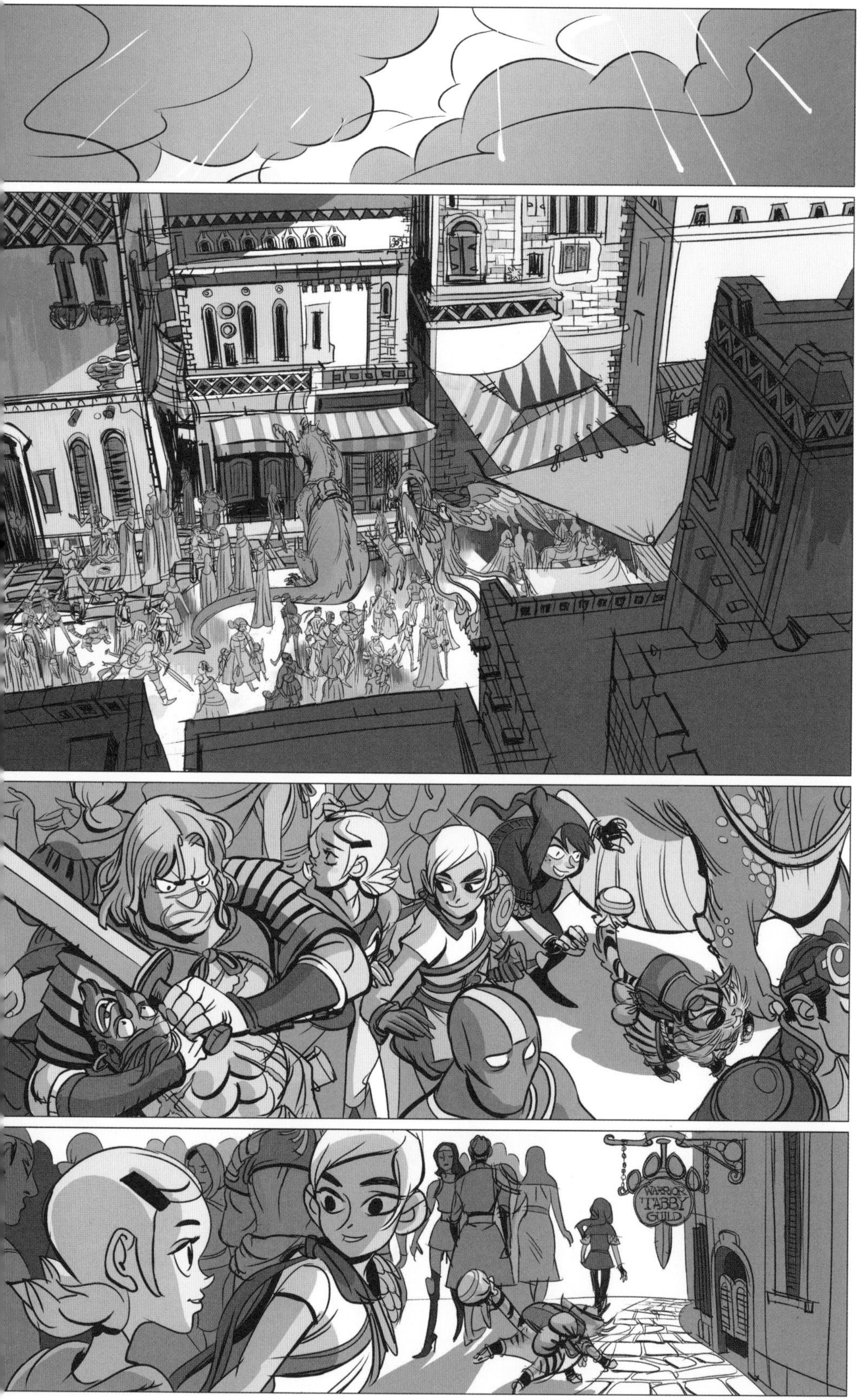
WARRIOR TABBY GUILD

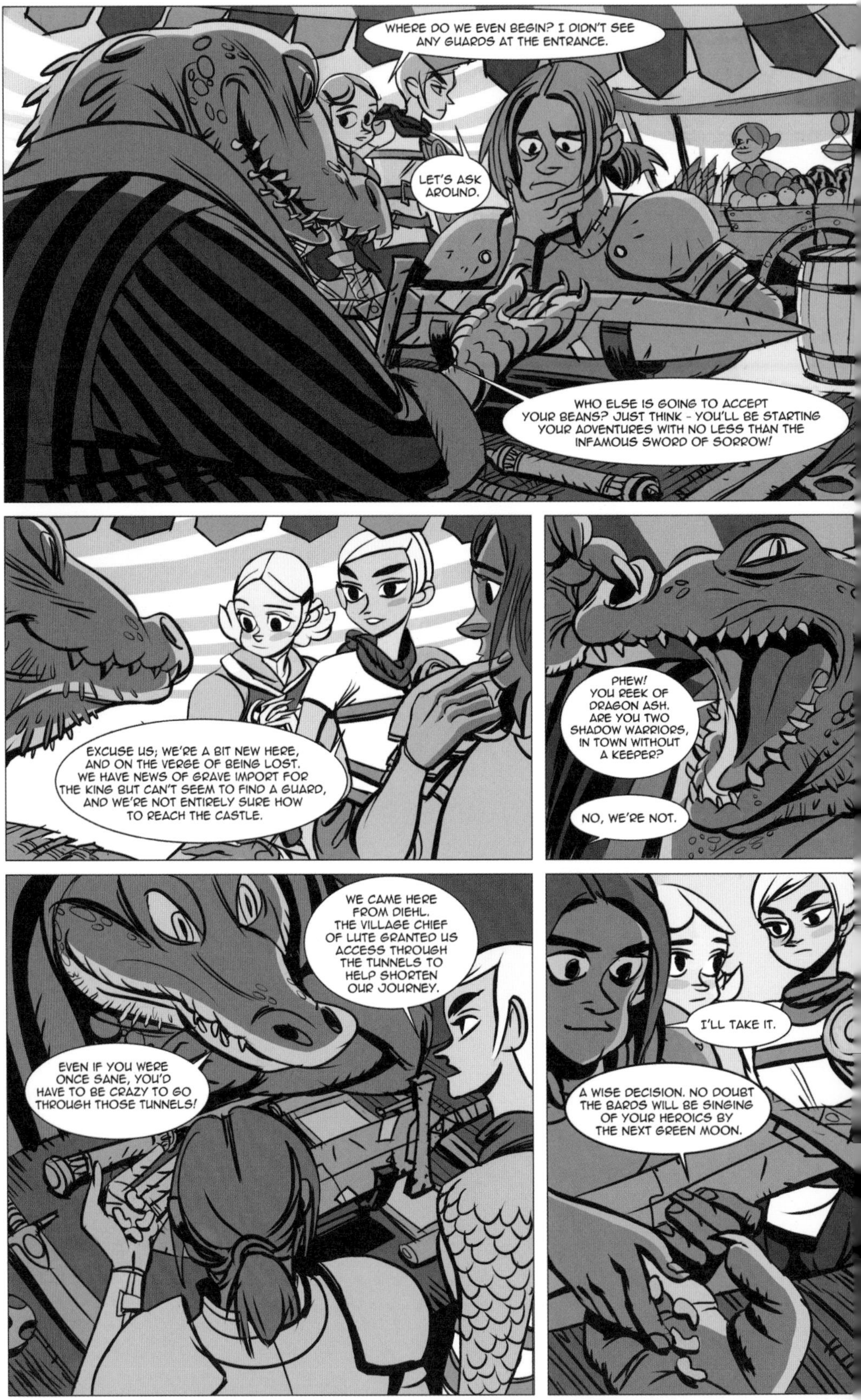
WHERE DO WE EVEN BEGIN? I DIDN'T SEE ANY GUARDS AT THE ENTRANCE.
LET'S ASK AROUND.
WHO ELSE IS GOING TO ACCEPT YOUR BEANS? JUST THINK - YOU'LL BE STARTING YOUR ADVENTURES WITH NO LESS THAN THE INFAMOUS SWORD OF SORROW!
EXCUSE US; WE'RE A BIT NEW HERE, AND ON THE VERGE OF BEING LOST. WE HAVE NEWS OF GRAVE IMPORT FOR THE KING BUT CAN'T SEEM TO FIND A GUARD, AND WE'RE NOT ENTIRELY SURE HOW TO REACH THE CASTLE.
PHEW! YOU REEK OF DRAGON ASH. ARE YOU TWO SHADOW WARRIORS, IN TOWN WITHOUT A KEEPER?
NO, WE'RE NOT.
WE CAME HERE FROM DIEHL. THE VILLAGE CHIEF OF LUTE GRANTED US ACCESS THROUGH THE TUNNELS TO HELP SHORTEN OUR JOURNEY.
EVEN IF YOU WERE ONCE SANE, YOU'D HAVE TO BE CRAZY TO GO THROUGH THOSE TUNNELS!
I'LL TAKE IT.
A WISE DECISION. NO DOUBT THE BARDS WILL BE SINGING OF YOUR HEROICS BY THE NEXT GREEN MOON.

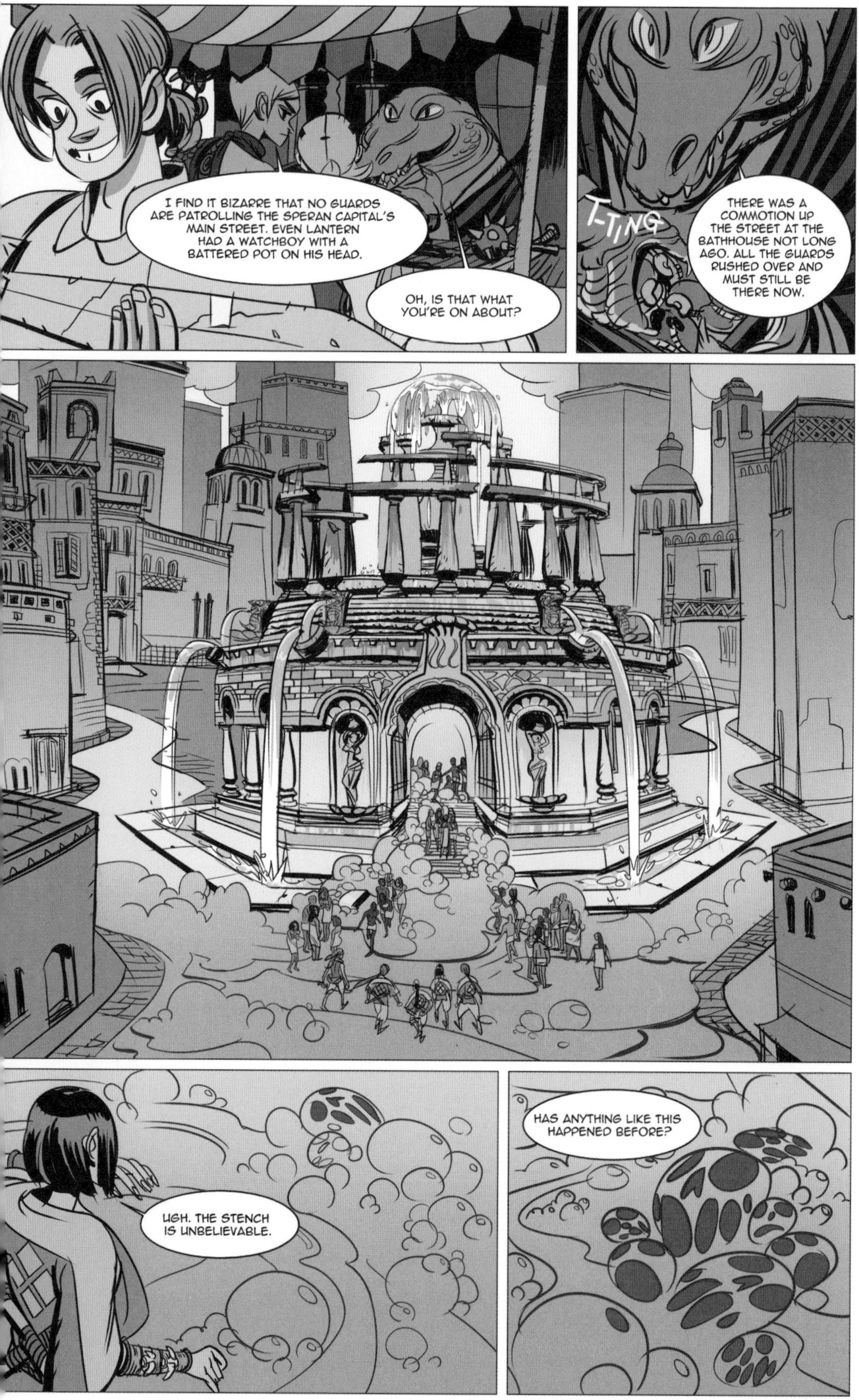
I FIND IT BIZARRE THAT NO GUARDS ARE PATROLLING THE SPERAN CAPITAL'S MAIN STREET. EVEN LANTERN HAD A WATCHBOY WITH A BATTERED POT ON HIS HEAD.
OH, IS THAT WHAT YOU'RE ON ABOUT?
T-TING
THERE WAS A COMMOTION UP THE STREET AT THE BATHHOUSE NOT LONG AGO. ALL THE GUARDS RUSHED OVER AND MUST STILL BE THERE NOW.
UGH. THE STENCH IS UNBELIEVABLE.
HAS ANYTHING LIKE THIS HAPPENED BEFORE?

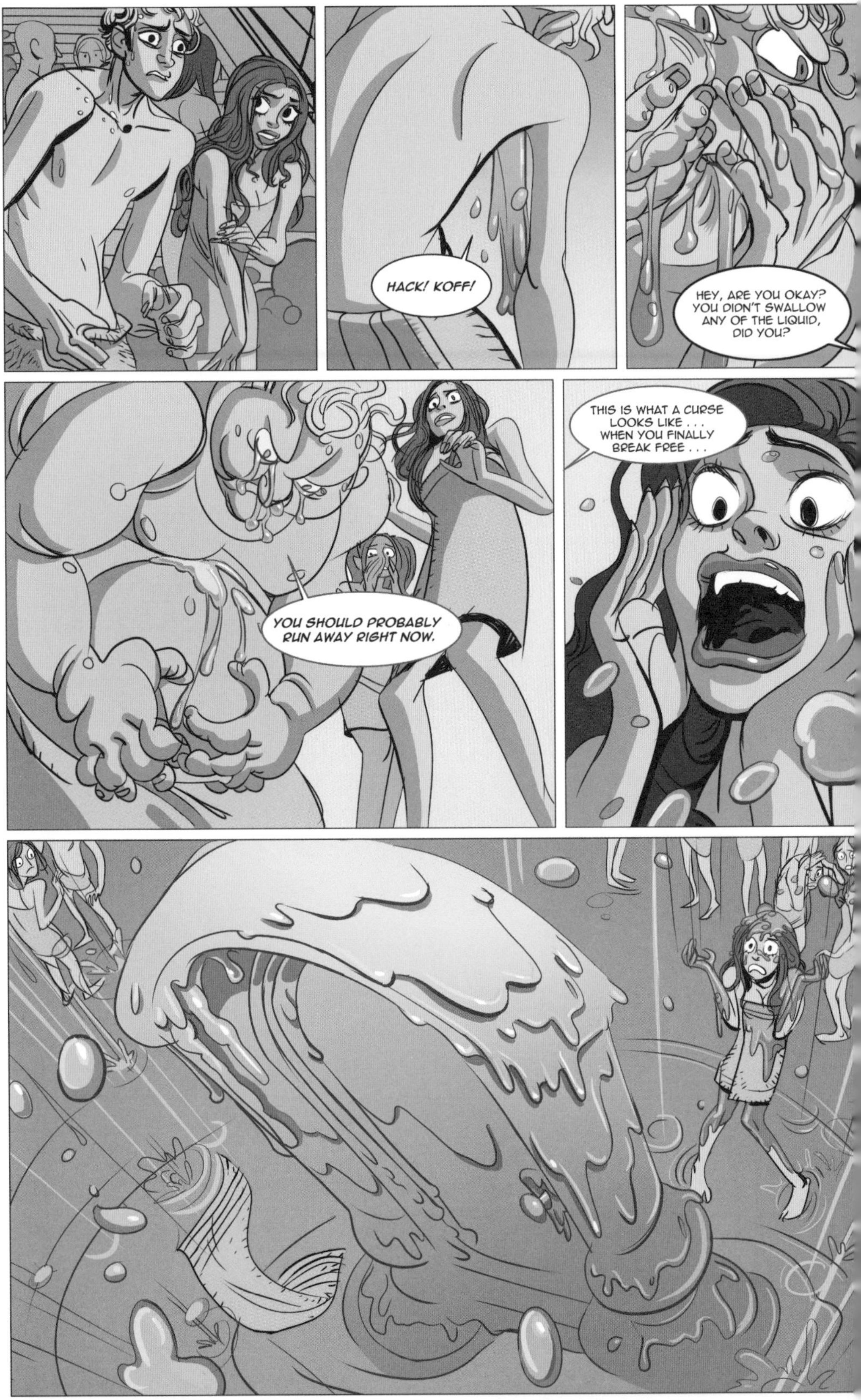
HACK! KOFF!
HEY, ARE YOU OKAY? YOU DIDN'T SWALLOW ANY OF THE LIQUID, DID YOU?
YOU SHOULD PROBABLY RUN AWAY RIGHT NOW.
THIS IS WHAT A CURSE LOOKS LIKE . . . WHEN YOU FINALLY BREAK FREE . . .

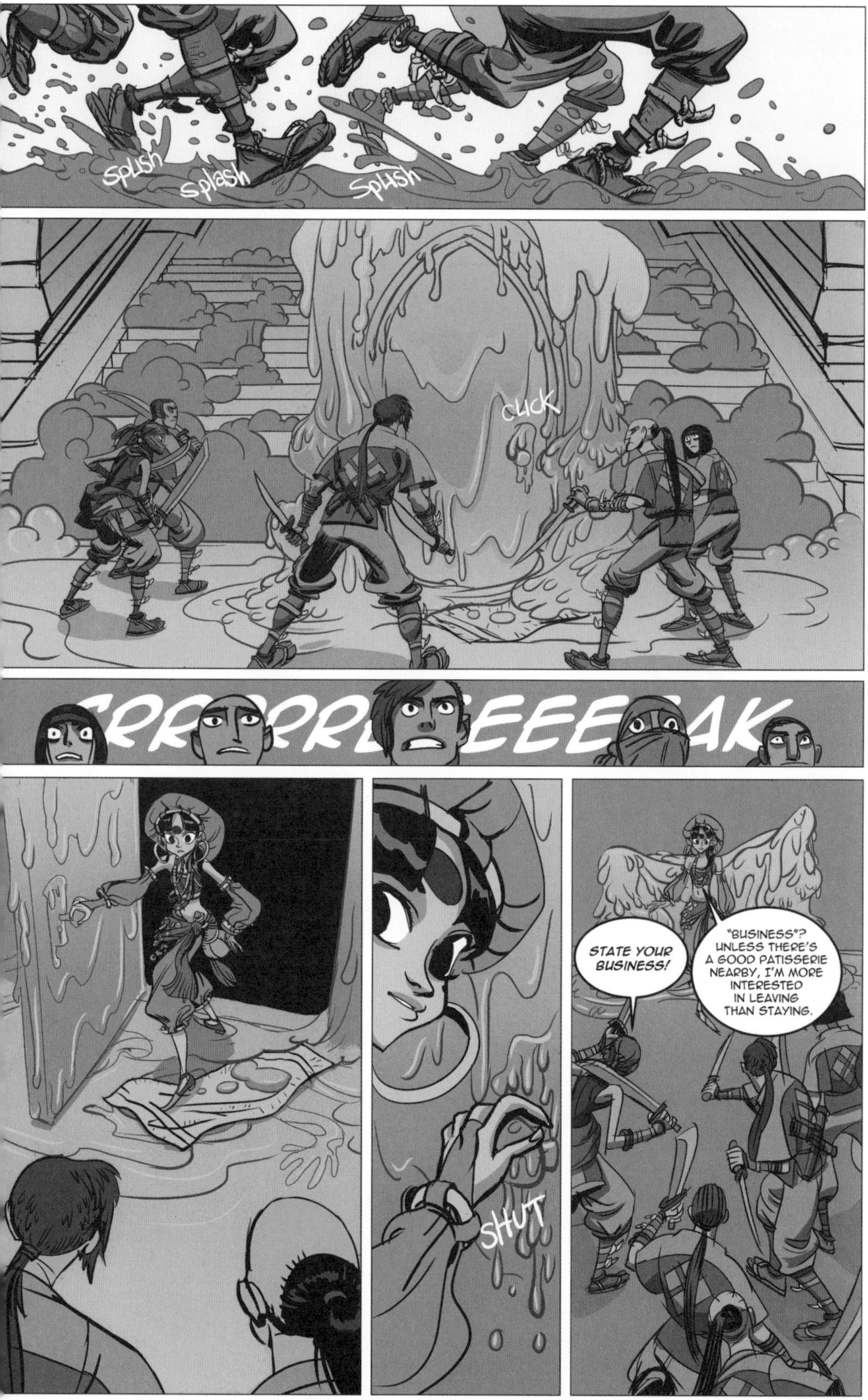
SPLISH
SPLASH
SPLISH
CLICK
CRRRRREEEEEAK
SHUT
STATE YOUR BUSINESS!
"BUSINESS"? UNLESS THERE'S A GOOD PATISSERIE NEARBY, I'M MORE INTERESTED IN LEAVING THAN STAYING.

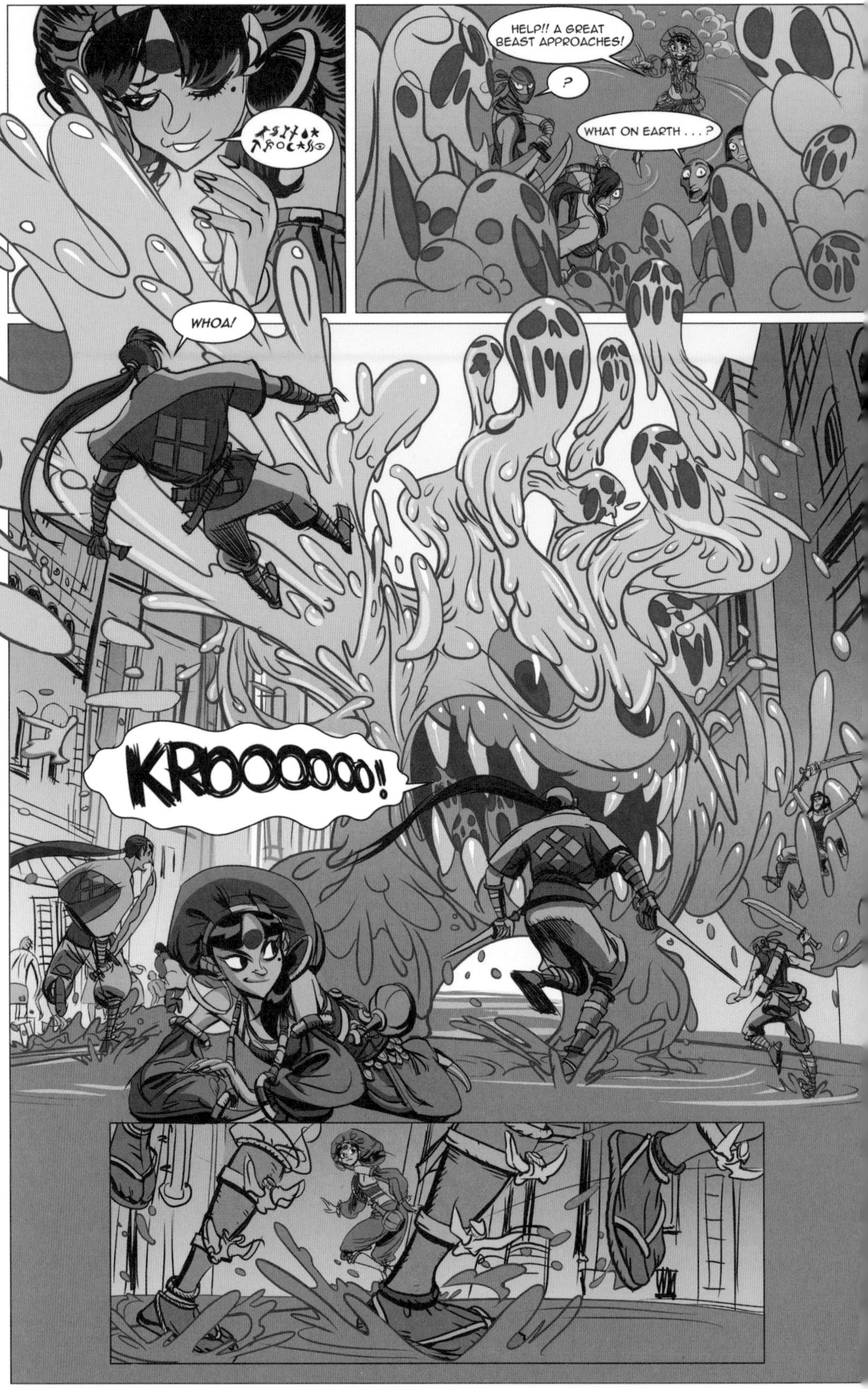
HELP!! A GREAT BEAST APPROACHES!
?
WHAT ON EARTH . . . ?
WHOA!
KROOOOOOO!!

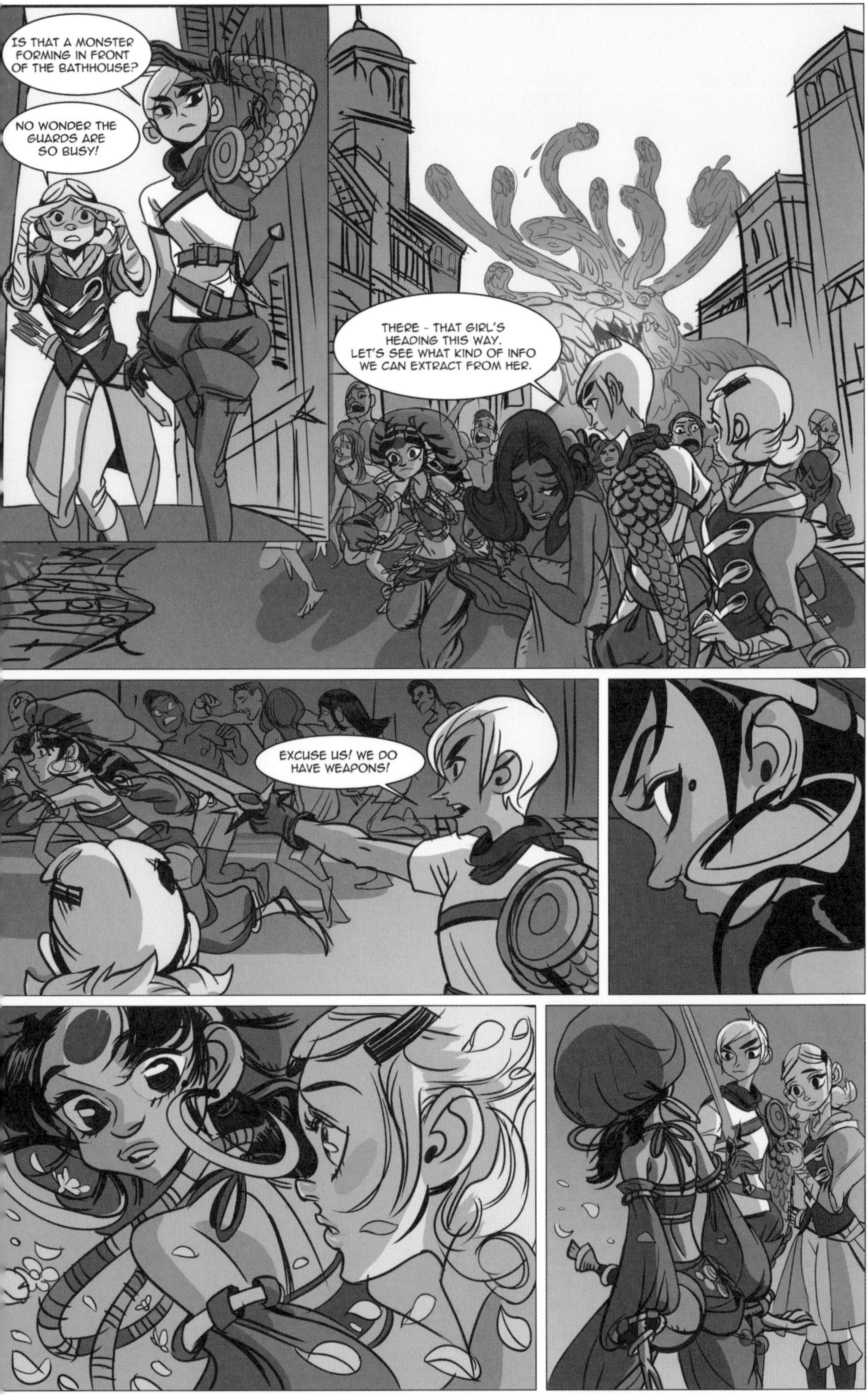
IS THAT A MONSTER FORMING IN FRONT OF THE BATHHOUSE?
NO WONDER THE GUARDS ARE SO BUSY!
THERE - THAT GIRL'S HEADING THIS WAY. LET'S SEE WHAT KIND OF INFO WE CAN EXTRACT FROM HER.
EXCUSE US! WE DO HAVE WEAPONS!

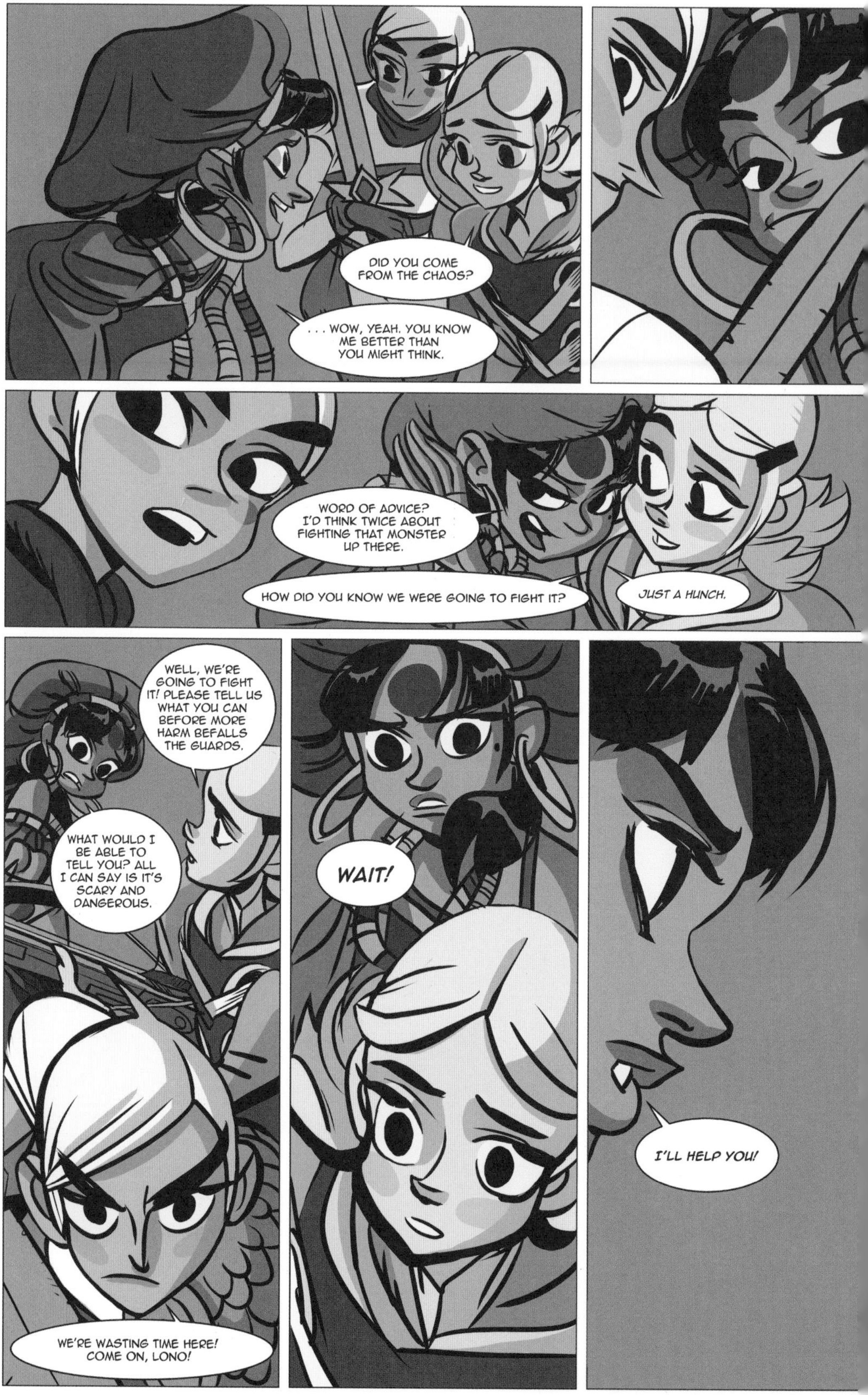
DID YOU COME FROM THE CHAOS?
. . . WOW, YEAH. YOU KNOW ME BETTER THAN YOU MIGHT THINK.
WORD OF ADVICE? I'D THINK TWICE ABOUT FIGHTING THAT MONSTER UP THERE.
HOW DID YOU KNOW WE WERE GOING TO FIGHT IT?
JUST A HUNCH.
WELL, WE'RE GOING TO FIGHT IT! PLEASE TELL US WHAT YOU CAN BEFORE MORE HARM BEFALLS THE GUARDS.
WHAT WOULD I BE ABLE TO TELL YOU? ALL I CAN SAY IS IT'S SCARY AND DANGEROUS.
WE'RE WASTING TIME HERE! COME ON, LONO!
WAIT!
I'LL HELP YOU!

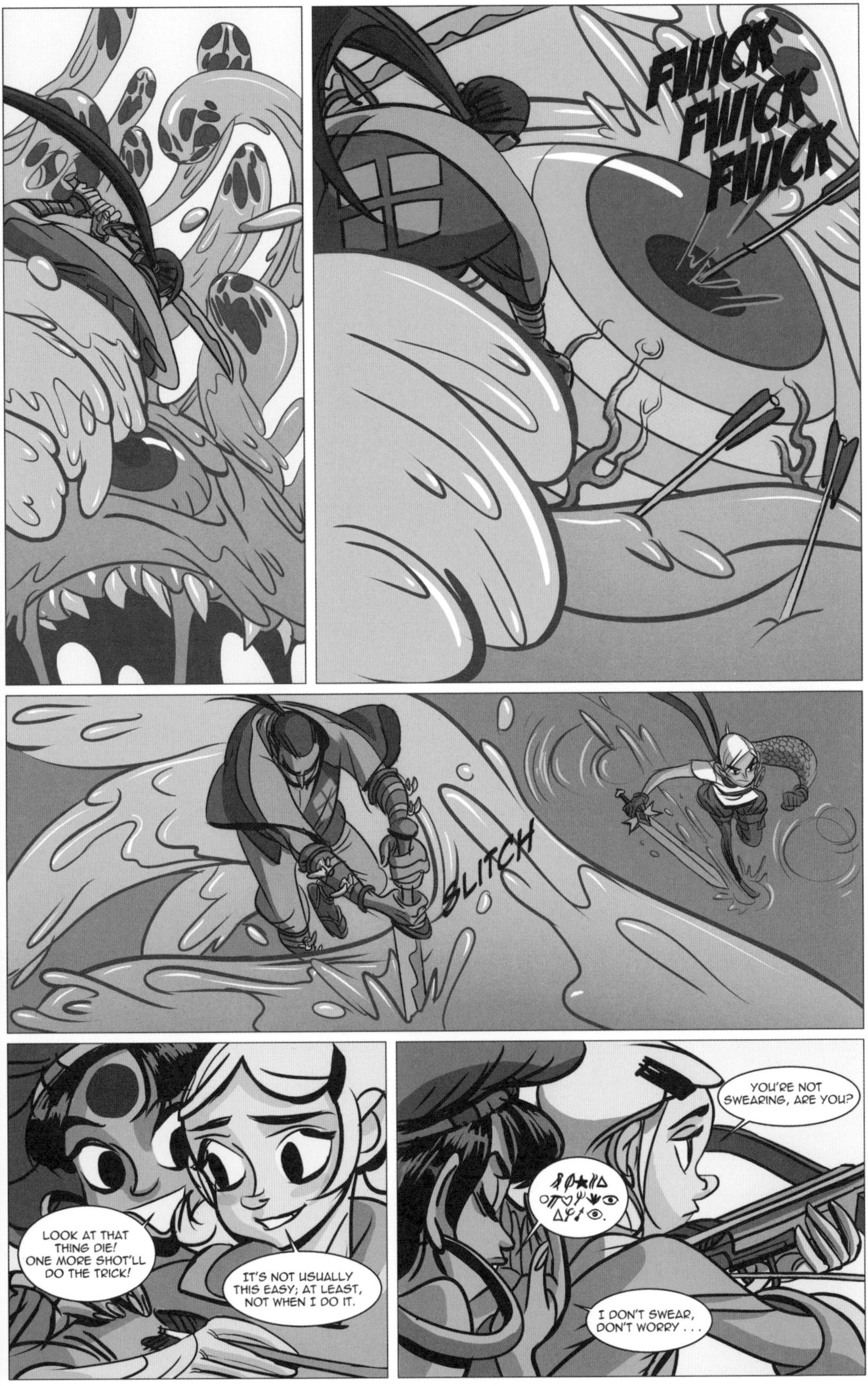
FWICK
FWICK
FWICK
SLITCH
LOOK AT THAT THING DIE! ONE MORE SHOT'LL DO THE TRICK!
IT'S NOT USUALLY THIS EASY; AT LEAST, NOT WHEN I DO IT.
YOU'RE NOT SWEARING, ARE YOU?
I DON'T SWEAR, DON'T WORRY . . .

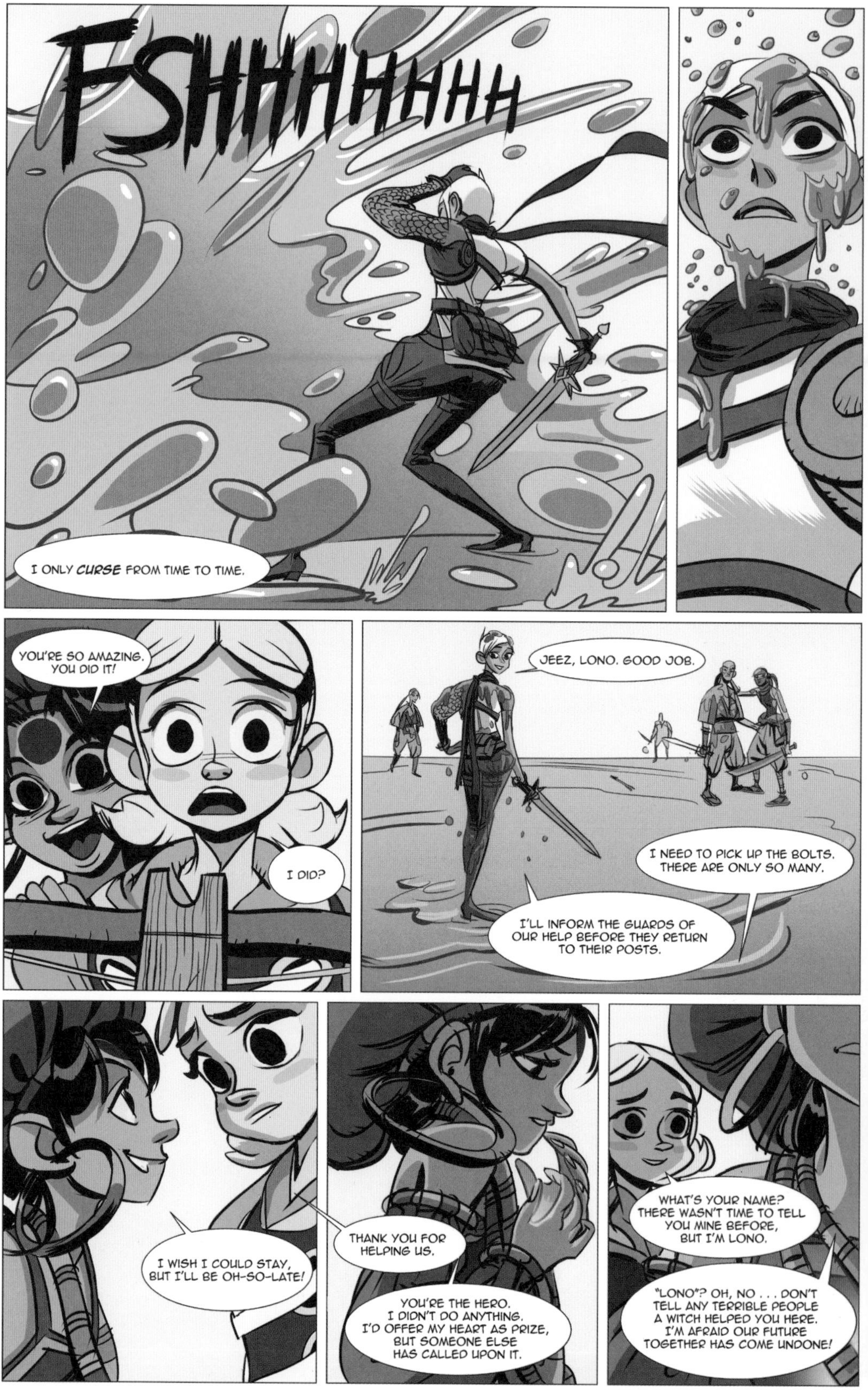

FSHHHHHHH
I ONLY CURSE FROM TIME TO TIME.
YOU'RE SO AMAZING. YOU DID IT!
I DID?
JEEZ, LONO. GOOD JOB.
I NEED TO PICK UP THE BOLTS. THERE ARE ONLY SO MANY.
I'LL INFORM THE GUARDS OF OUR HELP BEFORE THEY RETURN TO THEIR POSTS.
I WISH I COULD STAY, BUT I'LL BE OH-SO-LATE!
THANK YOU FOR HELPING US.
YOU'RE THE HERO. I DIDN'T DO ANYTHING. I'D OFFER MY HEART AS PRIZE, BUT SOMEONE ELSE HAS CALLED UPON IT.
WHAT'S YOUR NAME? THERE WASN'T TIME TO TELL YOU MINE BEFORE, BUT I'M LONO.
"LONO"? OH, NO . . . DON'T TELL ANY TERRIBLE PEOPLE A WITCH HELPED YOU HERE. I'M AFRAID OUR FUTURE TOGETHER HAS COME UNDONE!

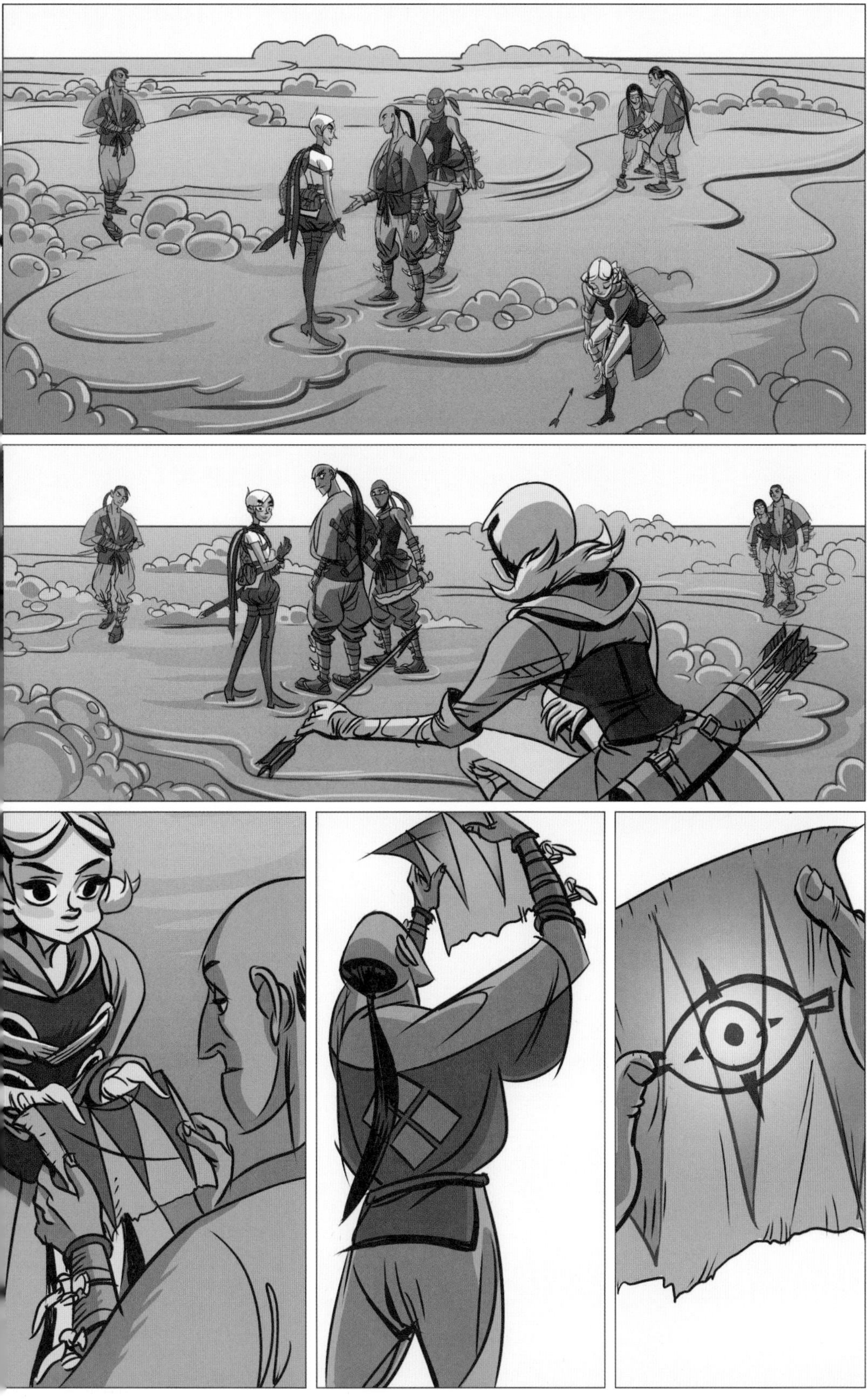

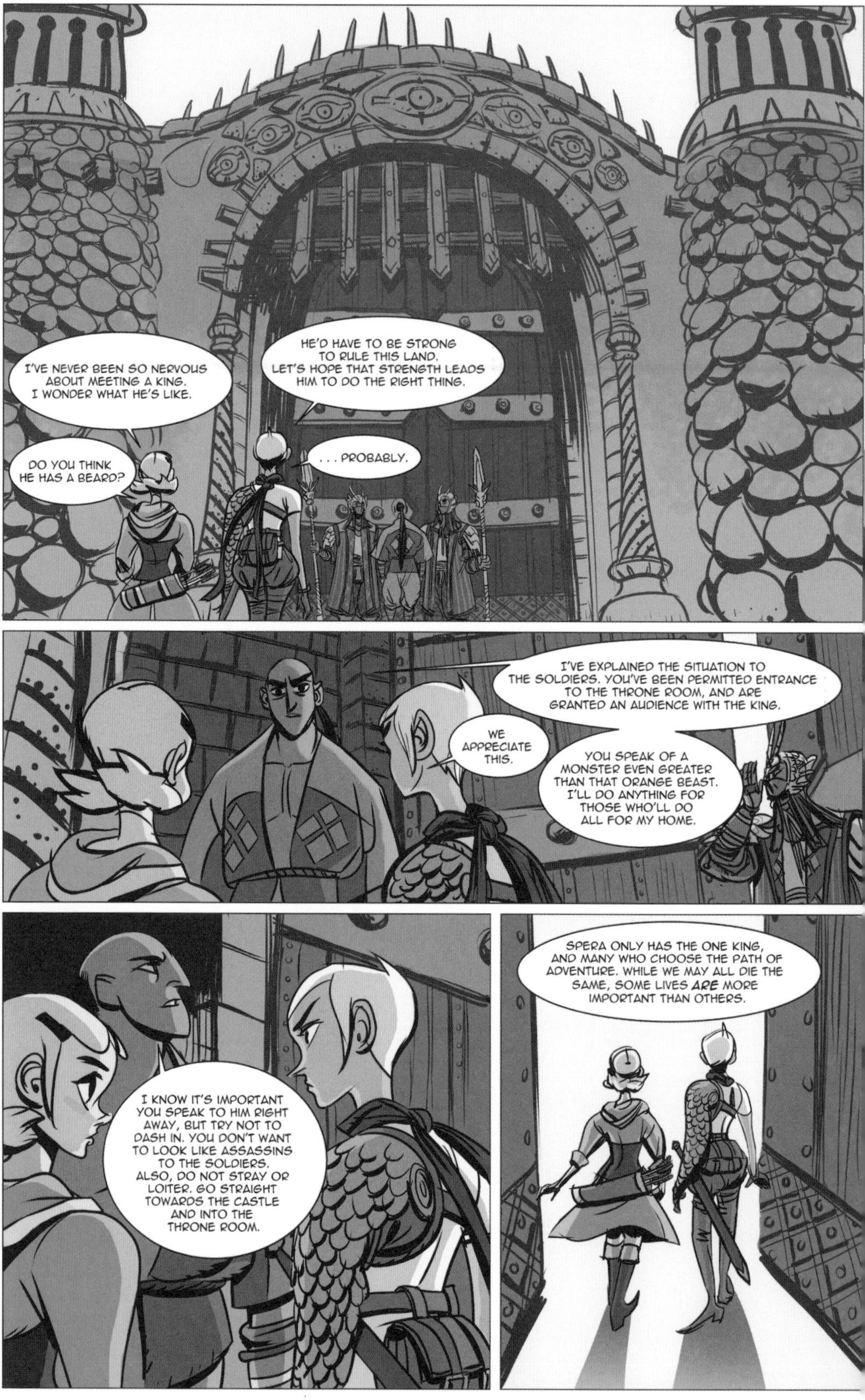
I'VE NEVER BEEN SO NERVOUS ABOUT MEETING A KING. I WONDER WHAT HE'S LIKE.
HE'D HAVE TO BE STRONG TO RULE THIS LAND. LET'S HOPE THAT STRENGTH LEADS HIM TO DO THE RIGHT THING.
DO YOU THINK HE HAS A BEARD?
. . . PROBABLY.
I'VE EXPLAINED THE SITUATION TO THE SOLDIERS. YOU'VE BEEN PERMITTED ENTRANCE TO THE THRONE ROOM, AND ARE GRANTED AN AUDIENCE WITH THE KING.
WE APPRECIATE THIS.
YOU SPEAK OF A MONSTER EVEN GREATER THAN THAT ORANGE BEAST. I'LL DO ANYTHING FOR THOSE WHO'LL DO ALL FOR MY HOME.
I KNOW IT'S IMPORTANT YOU SPEAK TO HIM RIGHT AWAY, BUT TRY NOT TO DASH IN. YOU DON'T WANT TO LOOK LIKE ASSASSINS TO THE SOLDIERS. ALSO, DO NOT STRAY OR LOITER. GO STRAIGHT TOWARDS THE CASTLE AND INTO THE THRONE ROOM.
SPERA ONLY HAS THE ONE KING, AND MANY WHO CHOOSE THE PATH OF ADVENTURE. WHILE WE MAY ALL DIE THE SAME, SOME LIVES ARE MORE IMPORTANT THAN OTHERS.

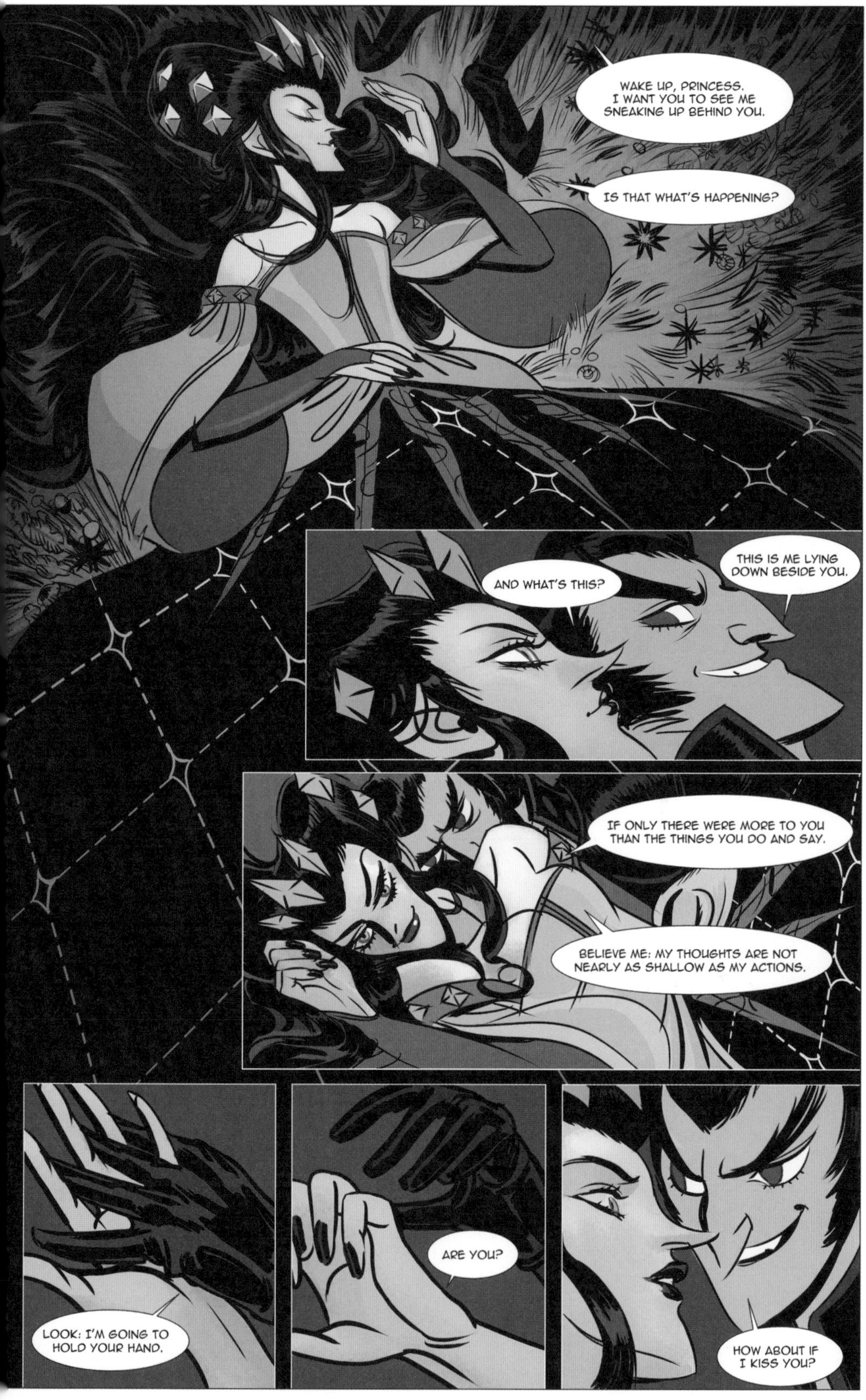
WAKE UP, PRINCESS. I WANT YOU TO SEE ME SNEAKING UP BEHIND YOU.
IS THAT WHAT'S HAPPENING?
AND WHAT'S THIS?
THIS IS ME LYING DOWN BESIDE YOU.
IF ONLY THERE WERE MORE TO YOU THAN THE THINGS YOU DO AND SAY.
BELIEVE ME: MY THOUGHTS ARE NOT NEARLY AS SHALLOW AS MY ACTIONS.
LOOK: I'M GOING TO HOLD YOUR HAND.
ARE YOU?
HOW ABOUT IF I KISS YOU?

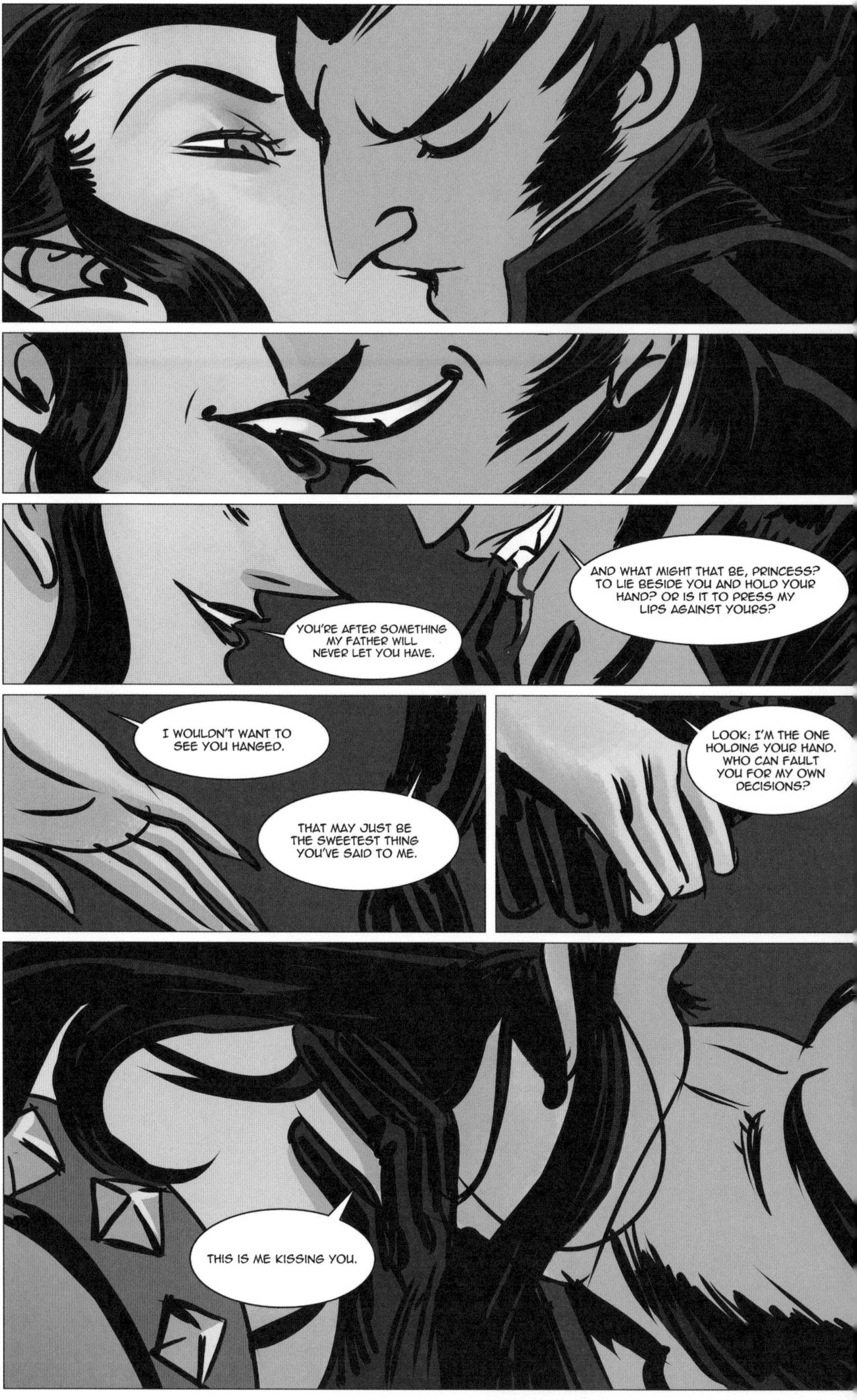
YOU'RE AFTER SOMETHING MY FATHER WILL NEVER LET YOU HAVE.
AND WHAT MIGHT THAT BE, PRINCESS? TO LIE BESIDE YOU AND HOLD YOUR HAND? OR IS IT TO PRESS MY LIPS AGAINST YOURS?
I WOULDN'T WANT TO SEE YOU HANGED.
THAT MAY JUST BE THE SWEETEST THING YOU'VE SAID TO ME.
LOOK: I'M THE ONE HOLDING YOUR HAND. WHO CAN FAULT YOU FOR MY OWN DECISIONS?
THIS IS ME KISSING YOU.

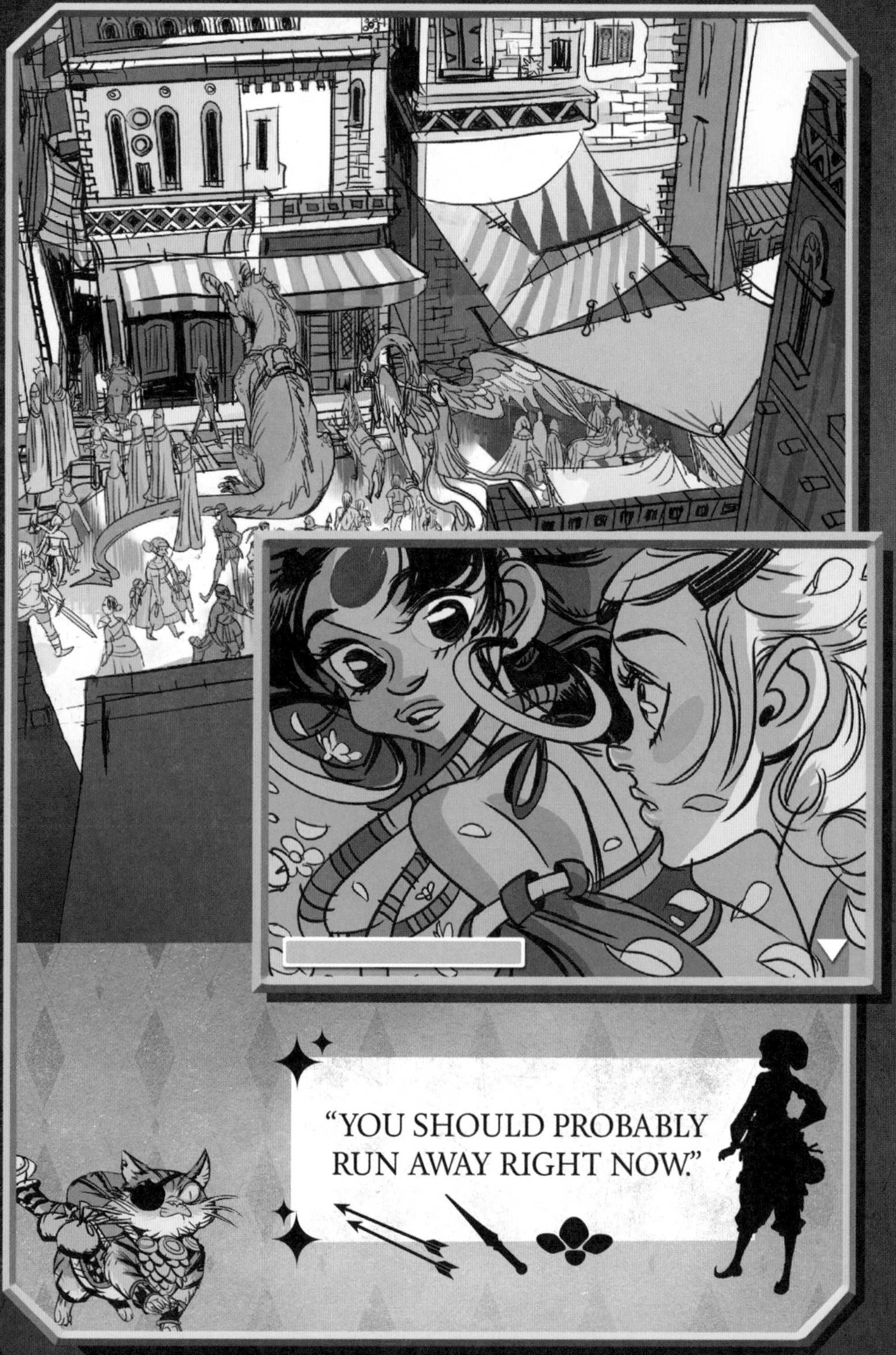
"YOU SHOULD PROBABLY RUN AWAY RIGHT NOW."

CHAPTER FOUR

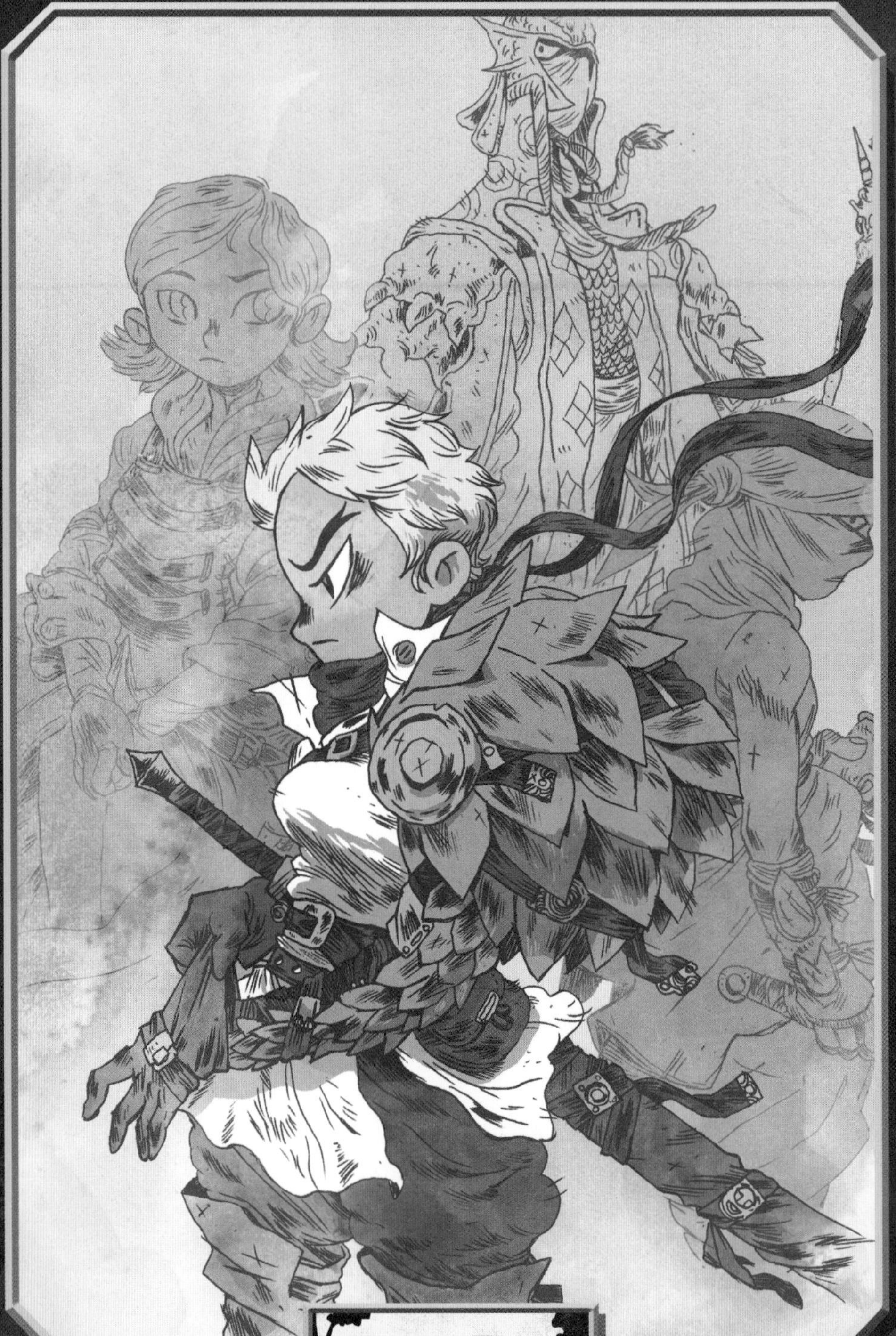

THE CASTLE

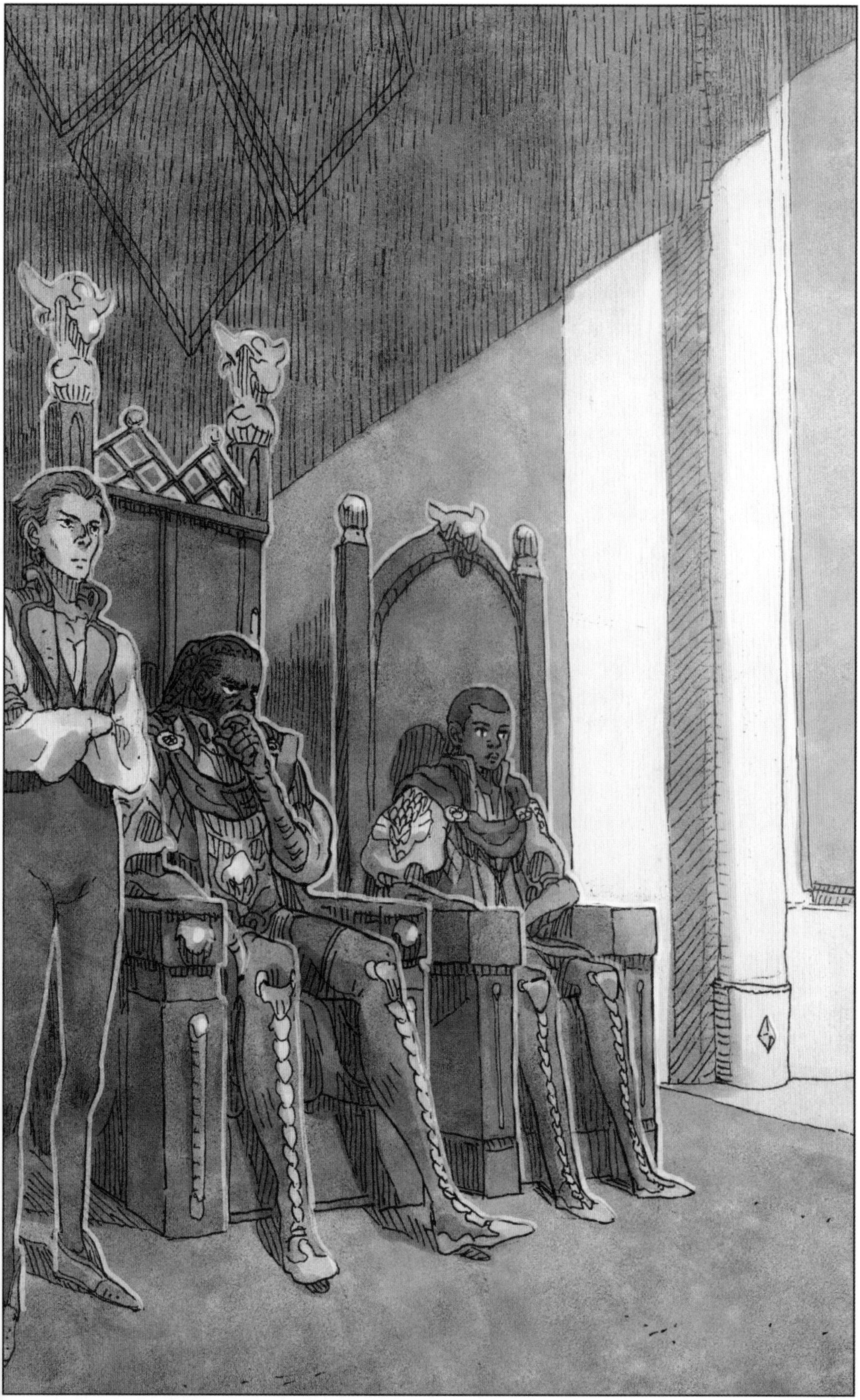

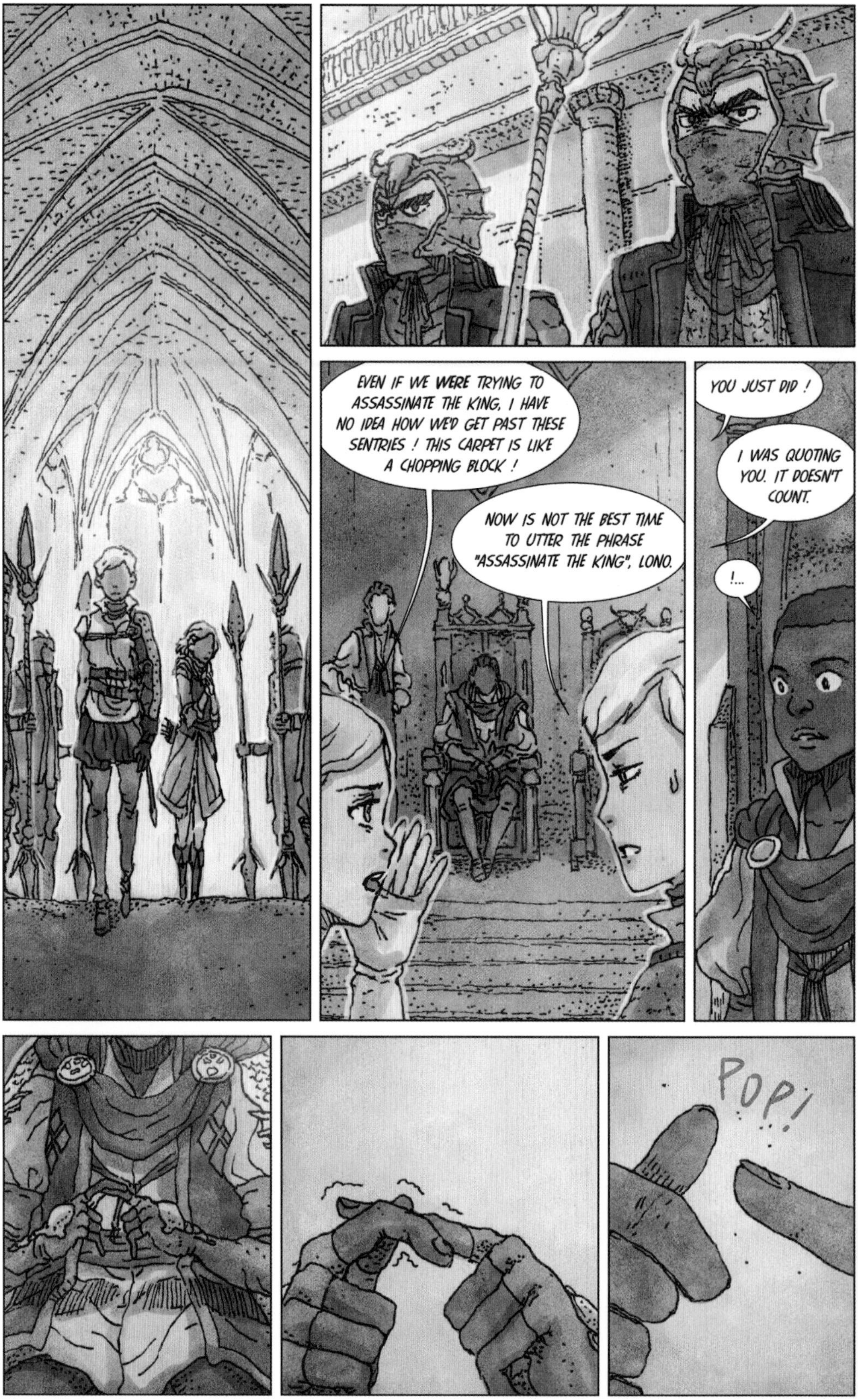
EVEN IF WE WERE TRYING TO ASSASSINATE THE KING, I HAVE NO IDEA HOW WE'D GET PAST THESE SENTRIES ! THIS CARPET IS LIKE A CHOPPING BLOCK !
NOW IS NOT THE BEST TIME TO UTTER THE PHRASE "ASSASSINATE THE KING", LONO.
YOU JUST DID !
I WAS QUOTING YOU. IT DOESN'T COUNT.
!...
POP!

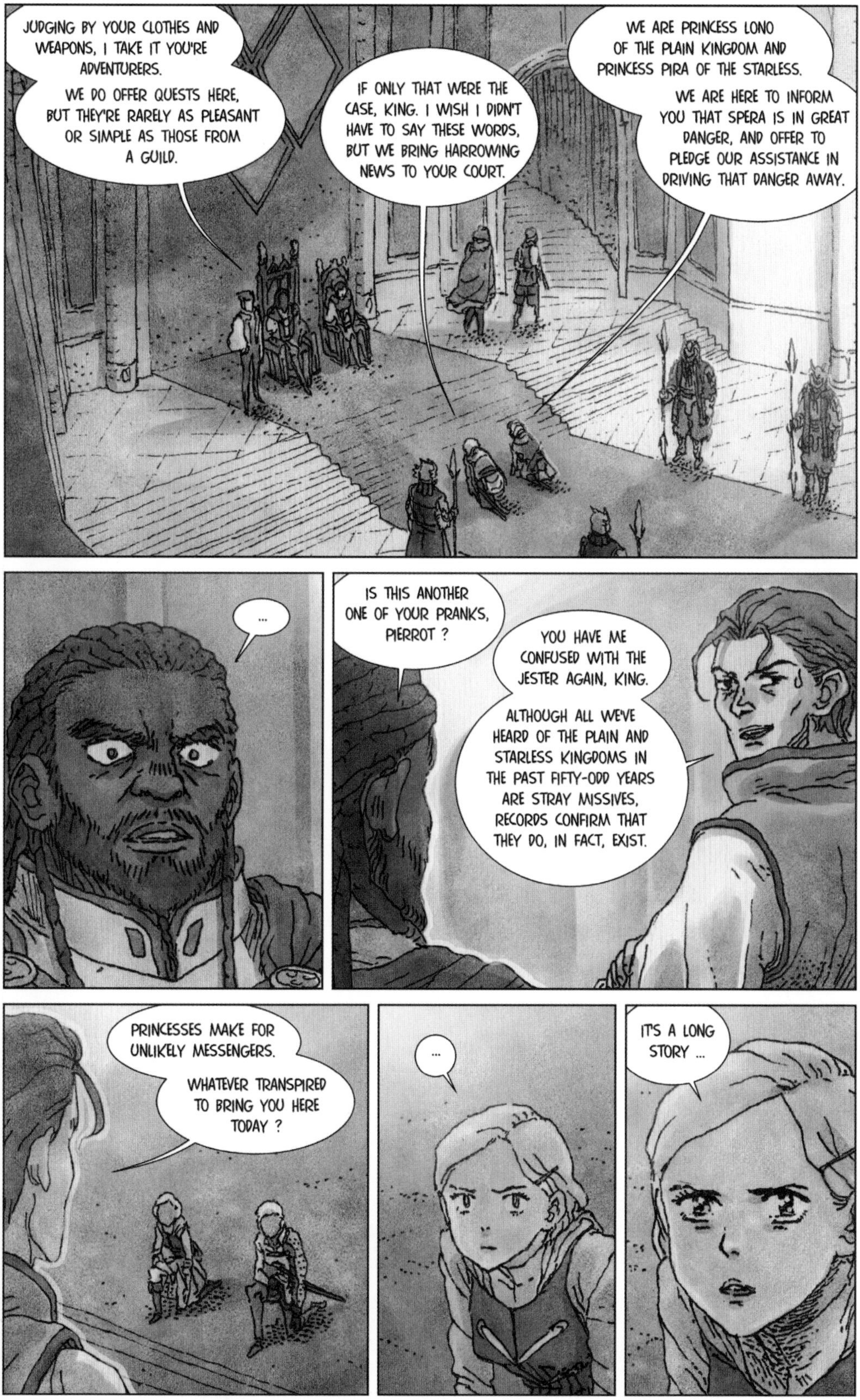
JUDGING BY YOUR CLOTHES AND WEAPONS, I TAKE IT YOU'RE ADVENTURERS.
WE DO OFFER QUESTS HERE, BUT THEY'RE RARELY AS PLEASANT OR SIMPLE AS THOSE FROM A GUILD.
IF ONLY THAT WERE THE CASE, KING. I WISH I DIDN'T HAVE TO SAY THESE WORDS, BUT WE BRING HARROWING NEWS TO YOUR COURT.
WE ARE PRINCESS LONO OF THE PLAIN KINGDOM AND PRINCESS PIRA OF THE STARLESS.
WE ARE HERE TO INFORM YOU THAT SPERA IS IN GREAT DANGER, AND OFFER TO PLEDGE OUR ASSISTANCE IN DRIVING THAT DANGER AWAY.
...
IS THIS ANOTHER ONE OF YOUR PRANKS, PIERROT ?
YOU HAVE ME CONFUSED WITH THE JESTER AGAIN, KING.
ALTHOUGH ALL WE'VE HEARD OF THE PLAIN AND STARLESS KINGDOMS IN THE PAST FIFTY-ODD YEARS ARE STRAY MISSIVES, RECORDS CONFIRM THAT THEY DO, IN FACT, EXIST.
PRINCESSES MAKE FOR UNLIKELY MESSENGERS.
WHATEVER TRANSPIRED TO BRING YOU HERE TODAY ?
...
IT'S A LONG STORY ...

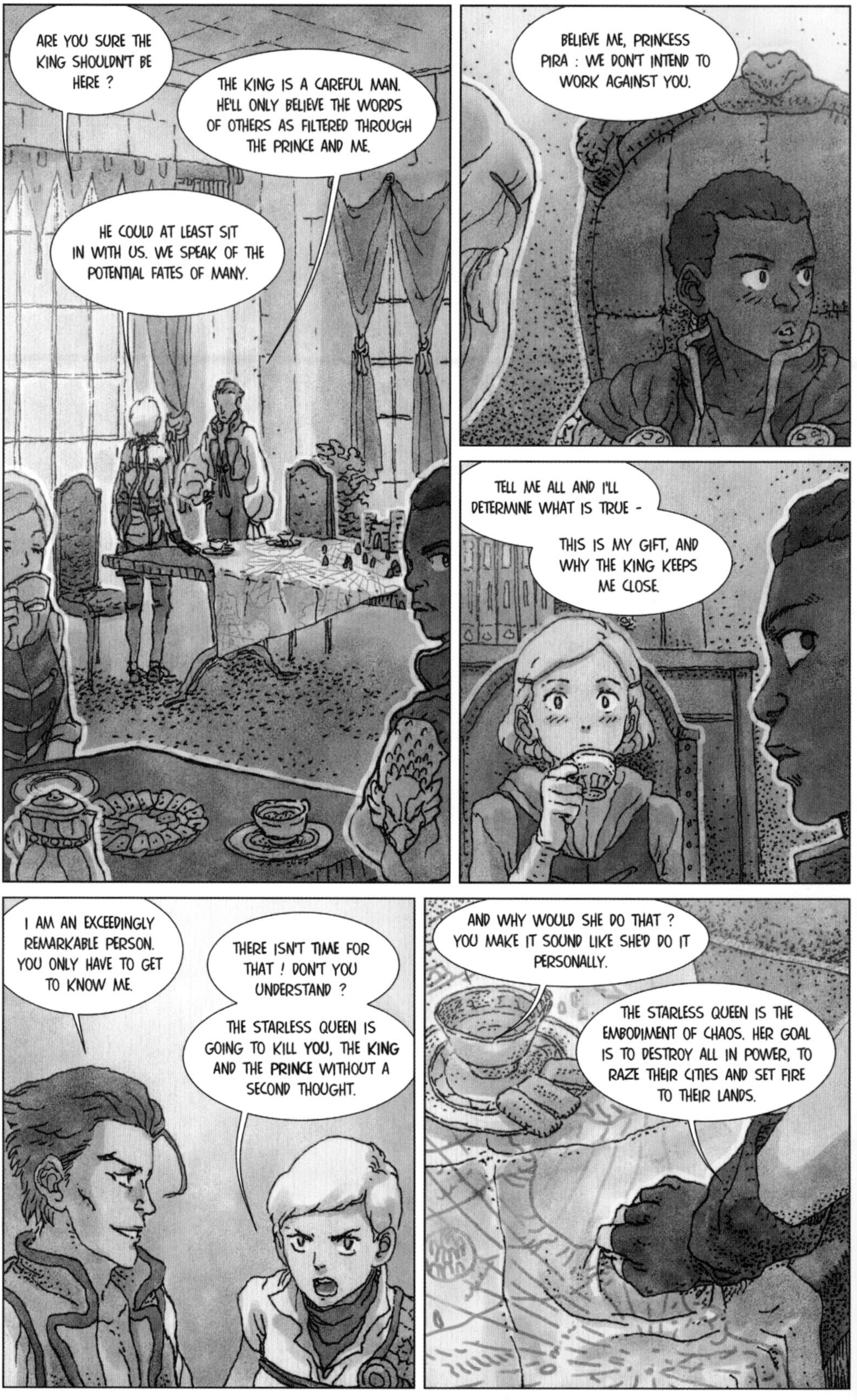
ARE YOU SURE THE KING SHOULDN'T BE HERE ?
THE KING IS A CAREFUL MAN. HE'LL ONLY BELIEVE THE WORDS OF OTHERS AS FILTERED THROUGH THE PRINCE AND ME.
HE COULD AT LEAST SIT IN WITH US. WE SPEAK OF THE POTENTIAL FATES OF MANY.
BELIEVE ME, PRINCESS PIRA : WE DON'T INTEND TO WORK AGAINST YOU.
TELL ME ALL AND I'LL DETERMINE WHAT IS TRUE -
THIS IS MY GIFT, AND WHY THE KING KEEPS ME CLOSE.
I AM AN EXCEEDINGLY REMARKABLE PERSON. YOU ONLY HAVE TO GET TO KNOW ME.
THERE ISN'T TIME FOR THAT ! DON'T YOU UNDERSTAND ?
THE STARLESS QUEEN IS GOING TO KILL YOU, THE KING AND THE PRINCE WITHOUT A SECOND THOUGHT.
AND WHY WOULD SHE DO THAT ? YOU MAKE IT SOUND LIKE SHE'D DO IT PERSONALLY.
THE STARLESS QUEEN IS THE EMBODIMENT OF CHAOS. HER GOAL IS TO DESTROY ALL IN POWER, TO RAZE THEIR CITIES AND SET FIRE TO THEIR LANDS.

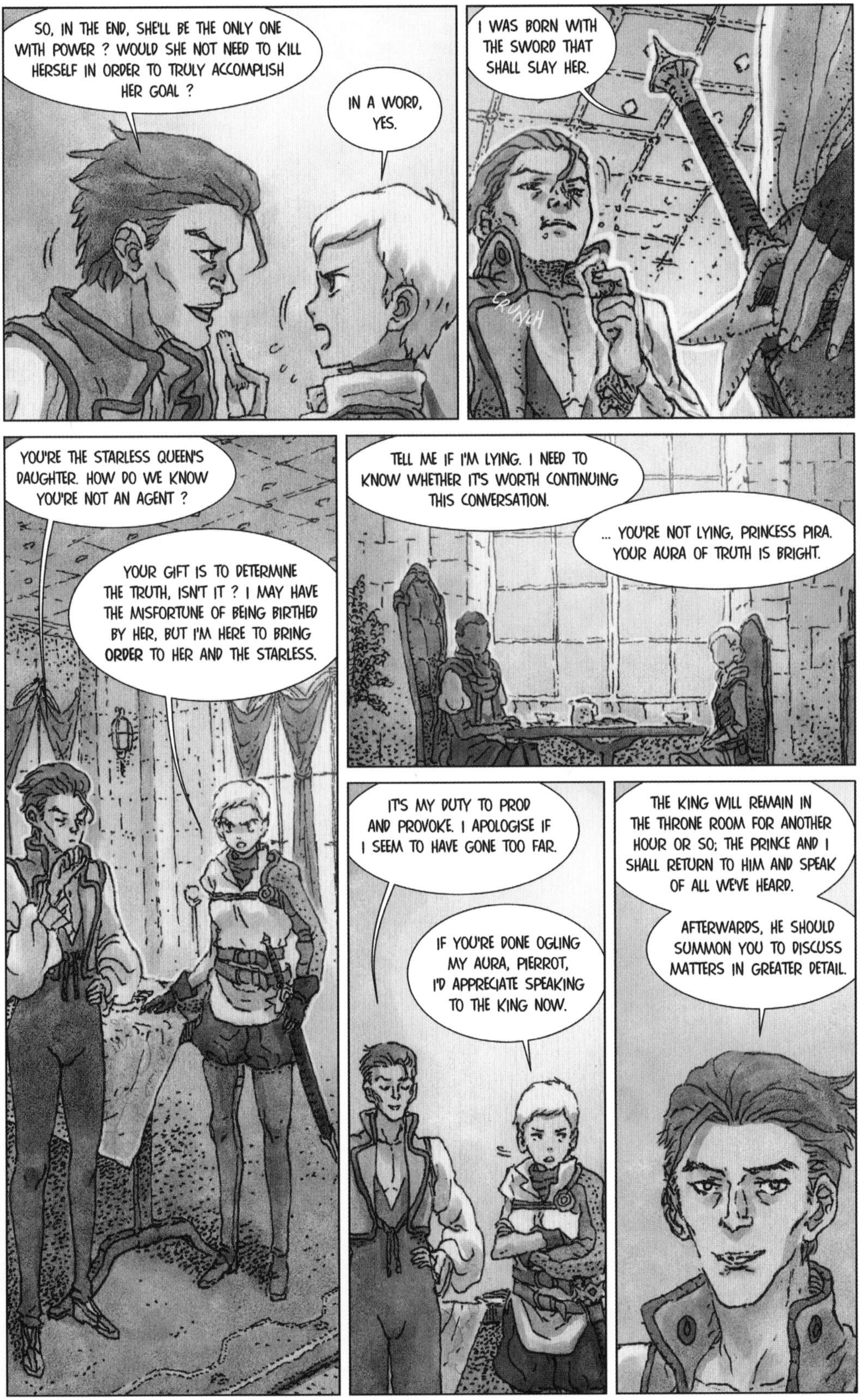
SO, IN THE END, SHE'LL BE THE ONLY ONE WITH POWER ? WOULD SHE NOT NEED TO KILL HERSELF IN ORDER TO TRULY ACCOMPLISH HER GOAL ?
IN A WORD, YES.
I WAS BORN WITH THE SWORD THAT SHALL SLAY HER.
CRUNCH
YOU'RE THE STARLESS QUEEN'S DAUGHTER. HOW DO WE KNOW YOU'RE NOT AN AGENT ?
YOUR GIFT IS TO DETERMINE THE TRUTH, ISN'T IT ? I MAY HAVE THE MISFORTUNE OF BEING BIRTHED BY HER, BUT I'M HERE TO BRING ORDER TO HER AND THE STARLESS.
TELL ME IF I'M LYING. I NEED TO KNOW WHETHER IT'S WORTH CONTINUING THIS CONVERSATION.
... YOU'RE NOT LYING, PRINCESS PIRA. YOUR AURA OF TRUTH IS BRIGHT.
IT'S MY DUTY TO PROD AND PROVOKE. I APOLOGISE IF I SEEM TO HAVE GONE TOO FAR.
IF YOU'RE DONE OGLING MY AURA, PIERROT, I'D APPRECIATE SPEAKING TO THE KING NOW.
THE KING WILL REMAIN IN THE THRONE ROOM FOR ANOTHER HOUR OR SO; THE PRINCE AND I SHALL RETURN TO HIM AND SPEAK OF ALL WE'VE HEARD.
AFTERWARDS, HE SHOULD SUMMON YOU TO DISCUSS MATTERS IN GREATER DETAIL.

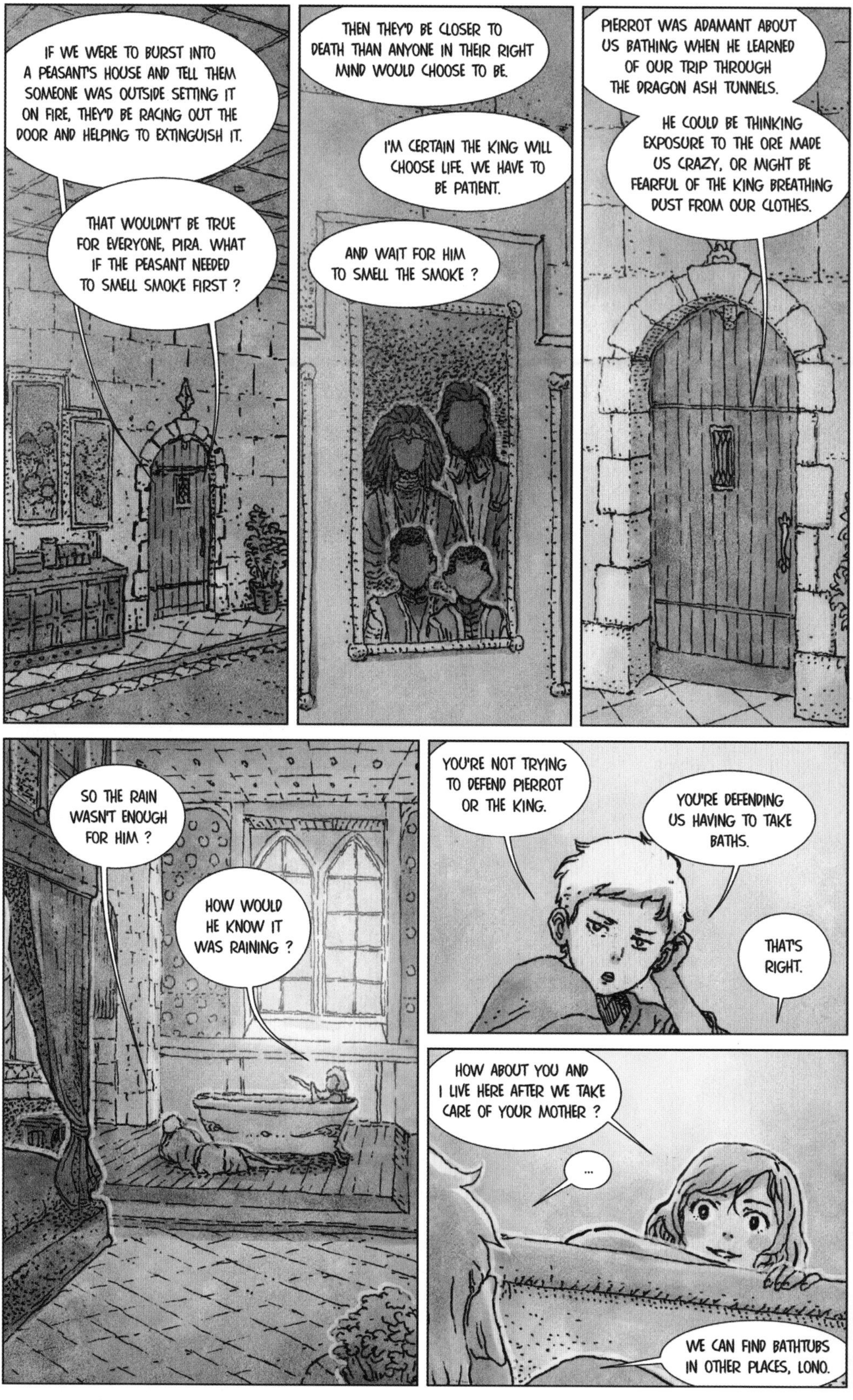
IF WE WERE TO BURST INTO A PEASANT'S HOUSE AND TELL THEM SOMEONE WAS OUTSIDE SETTING IT ON FIRE, THEY'D BE RACING OUT THE DOOR AND HELPING TO EXTINGUISH IT.
THAT WOULDN'T BE TRUE FOR EVERYONE, PIRA. WHAT IF THE PEASANT NEEDED TO SMELL SMOKE FIRST ?
THEN THEY'D BE CLOSER TO DEATH THAN ANYONE IN THEIR RIGHT MIND WOULD CHOOSE TO BE.
I'M CERTAIN THE KING WILL CHOOSE LIFE. WE HAVE TO BE PATIENT.
AND WAIT FOR HIM TO SMELL THE SMOKE ?
PIERROT WAS ADAMANT ABOUT US BATHING WHEN HE LEARNED OF OUR TRIP THROUGH THE DRAGON ASH TUNNELS.
HE COULD BE THINKING EXPOSURE TO THE ORE MADE US CRAZY, OR MIGHT BE FEARFUL OF THE KING BREATHING DUST FROM OUR CLOTHES.
SO THE RAIN WASN'T ENOUGH FOR HIM ?
HOW WOULD HE KNOW IT WAS RAINING ?
YOU'RE NOT TRYING TO DEFEND PIERROT OR THE KING.
YOU'RE DEFENDING US HAVING TO TAKE BATHS.
THAT'S RIGHT.
HOW ABOUT YOU AND I LIVE HERE AFTER WE TAKE CARE OF YOUR MOTHER ?
...
WE CAN FIND BATHTUBS IN OTHER PLACES, LONO.

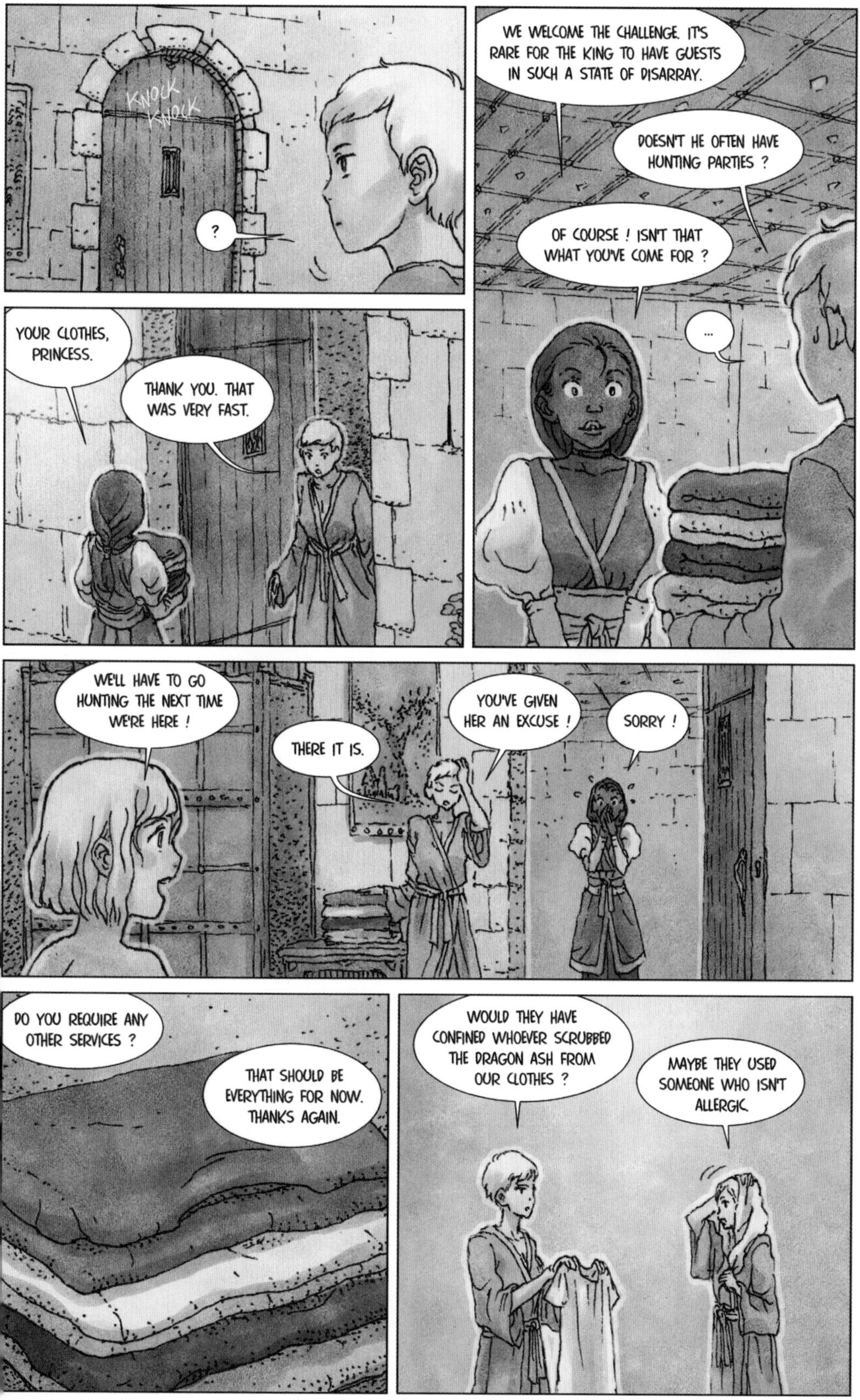
KNOCK KNOCK
?
WE WELCOME THE CHALLENGE. IT'S RARE FOR THE KING TO HAVE GUESTS IN SUCH A STATE OF DISARRAY.
DOESN'T HE OFTEN HAVE HUNTING PARTIES ?
OF COURSE ! ISN'T THAT WHAT YOU'VE COME FOR ?
...
YOUR CLOTHES, PRINCESS.
THANK YOU. THAT WAS VERY FAST.
WE'LL HAVE TO GO HUNTING THE NEXT TIME WE'RE HERE !
THERE IT IS.
YOU'VE GIVEN HER AN EXCUSE !
SORRY !
DO YOU REQUIRE ANY OTHER SERVICES ?
THAT SHOULD BE EVERYTHING FOR NOW. THANKS AGAIN.
WOULD THEY HAVE CONFINED WHOEVER SCRUBBED THE DRAGON ASH FROM OUR CLOTHES ?
MAYBE THEY USED SOMEONE WHO ISN'T ALLERGIC.

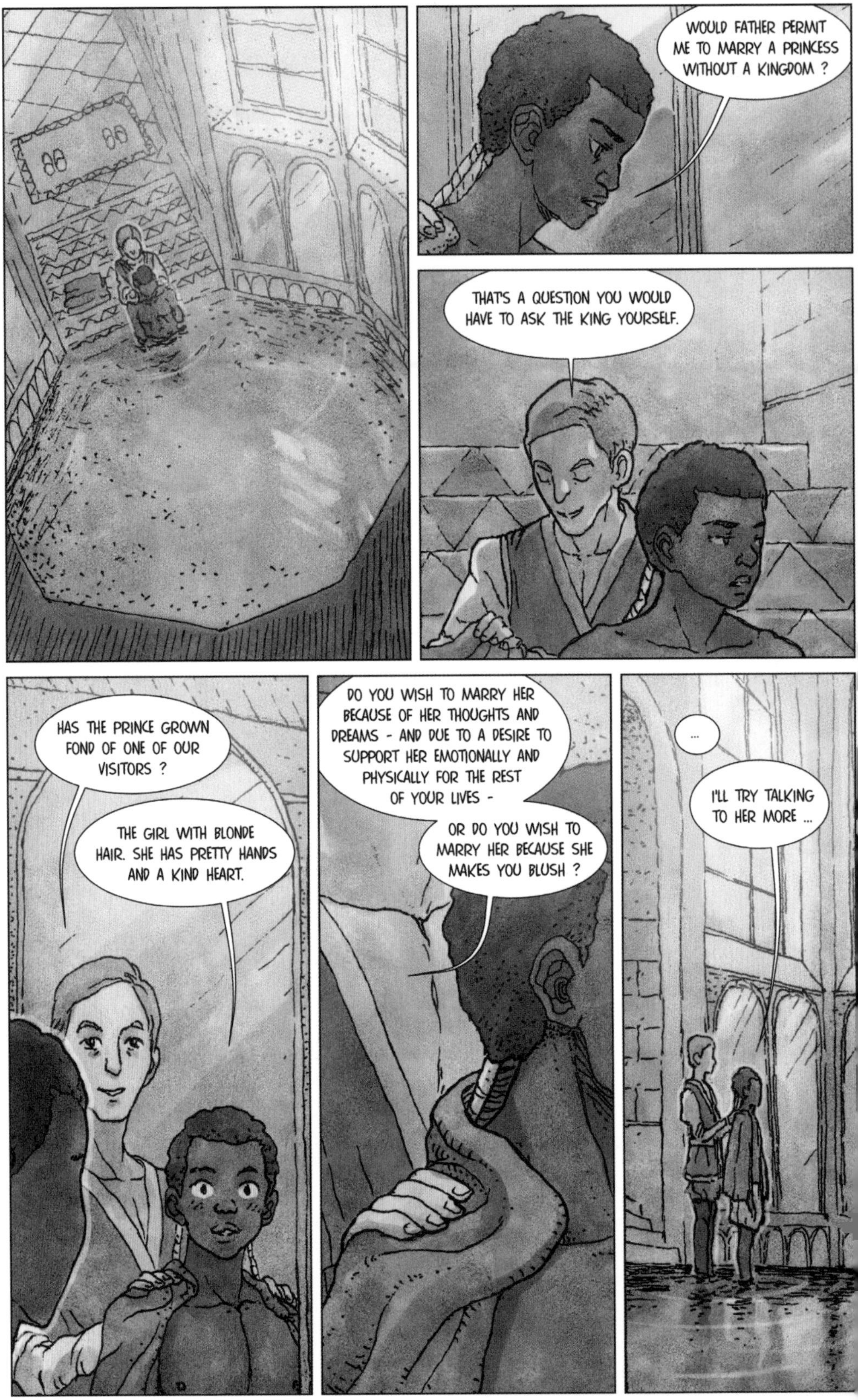
WOULD FATHER PERMIT ME TO MARRY A PRINCESS WITHOUT A KINGDOM ?
THAT'S A QUESTION YOU WOULD HAVE TO ASK THE KING YOURSELF.
HAS THE PRINCE GROWN FOND OF ONE OF OUR VISITORS ?
THE GIRL WITH BLONDE HAIR. SHE HAS PRETTY HANDS AND A KIND HEART.
DO YOU WISH TO MARRY HER BECAUSE OF HER THOUGHTS AND DREAMS - AND DUE TO A DESIRE TO SUPPORT HER EMOTIONALLY AND PHYSICALLY FOR THE REST OF YOUR LIVES -
OR DO YOU WISH TO MARRY HER BECAUSE SHE MAKES YOU BLUSH ?
...
I'LL TRY TALKING TO HER MORE ...

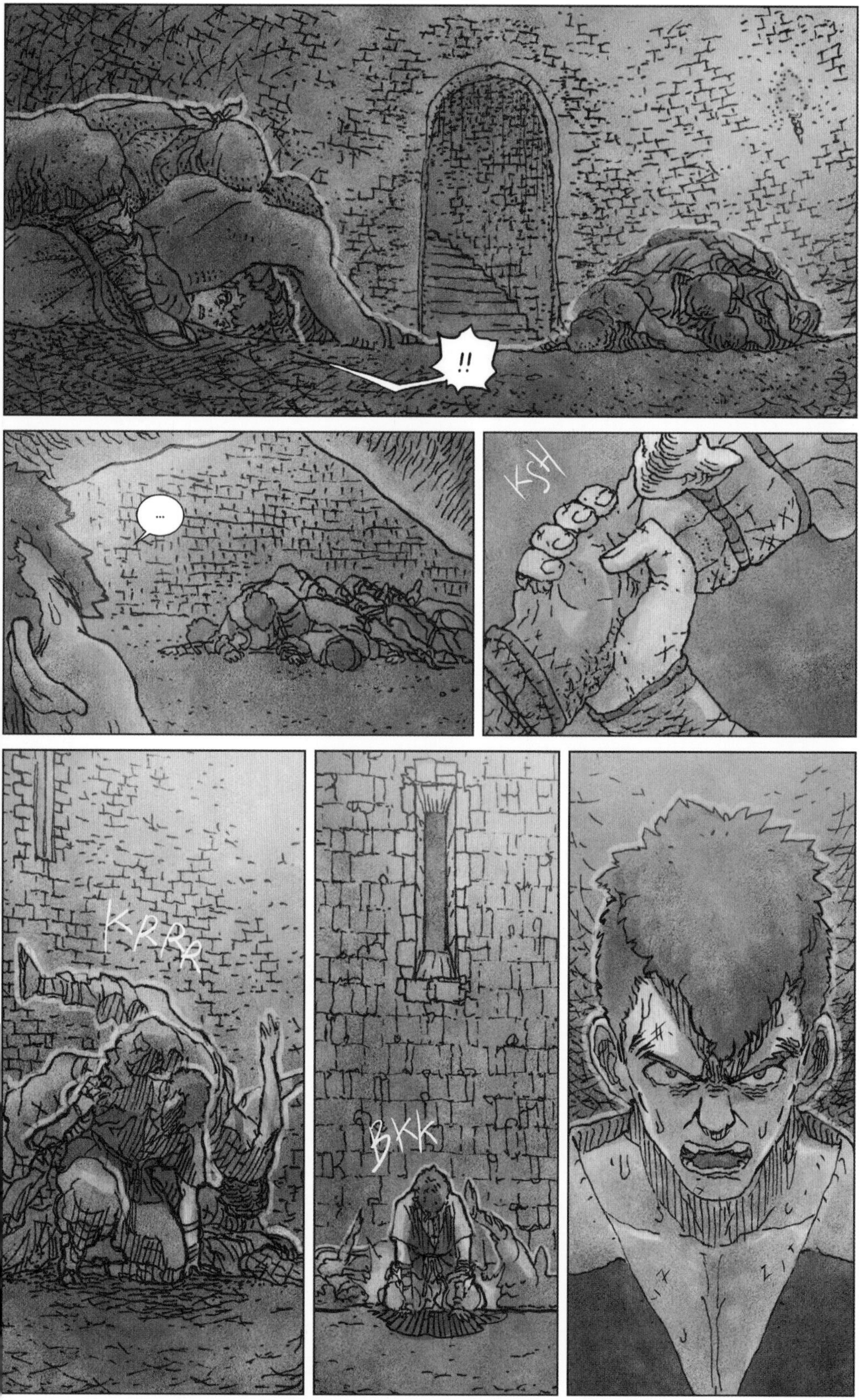
!!
...
KSH
KRRR
BKK

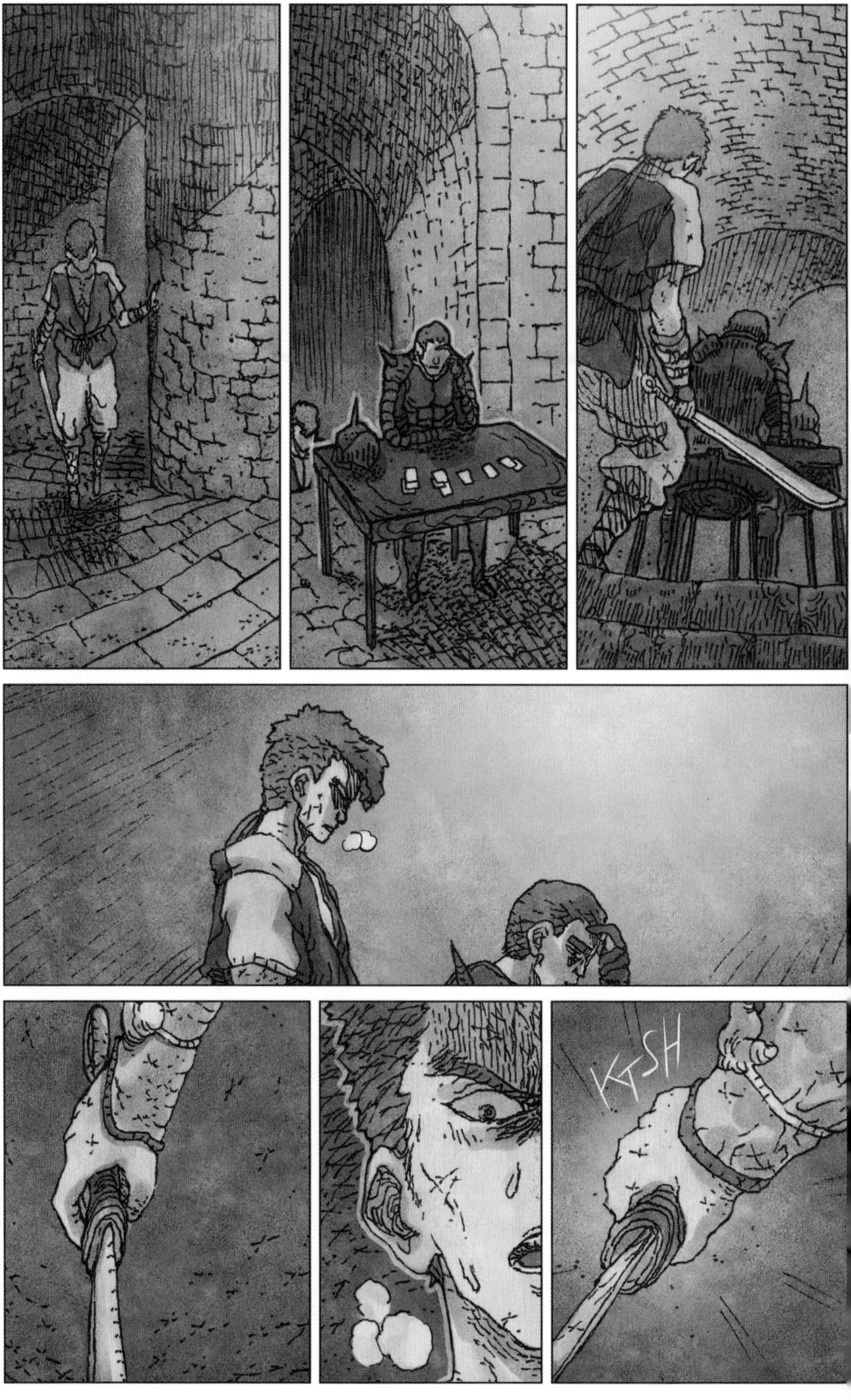
KTSH

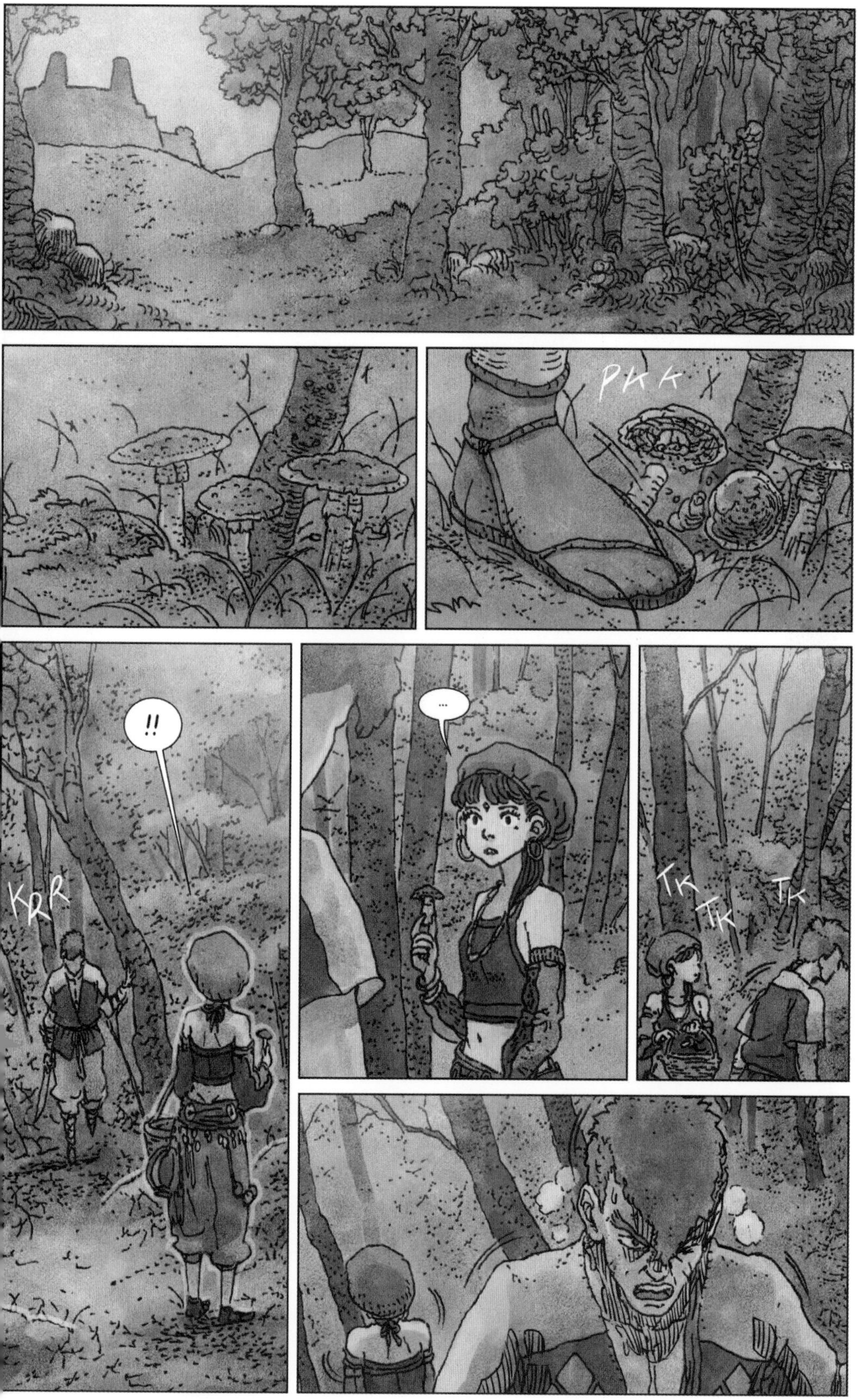
PKK
!!
KRR
...
TK
TK
TK

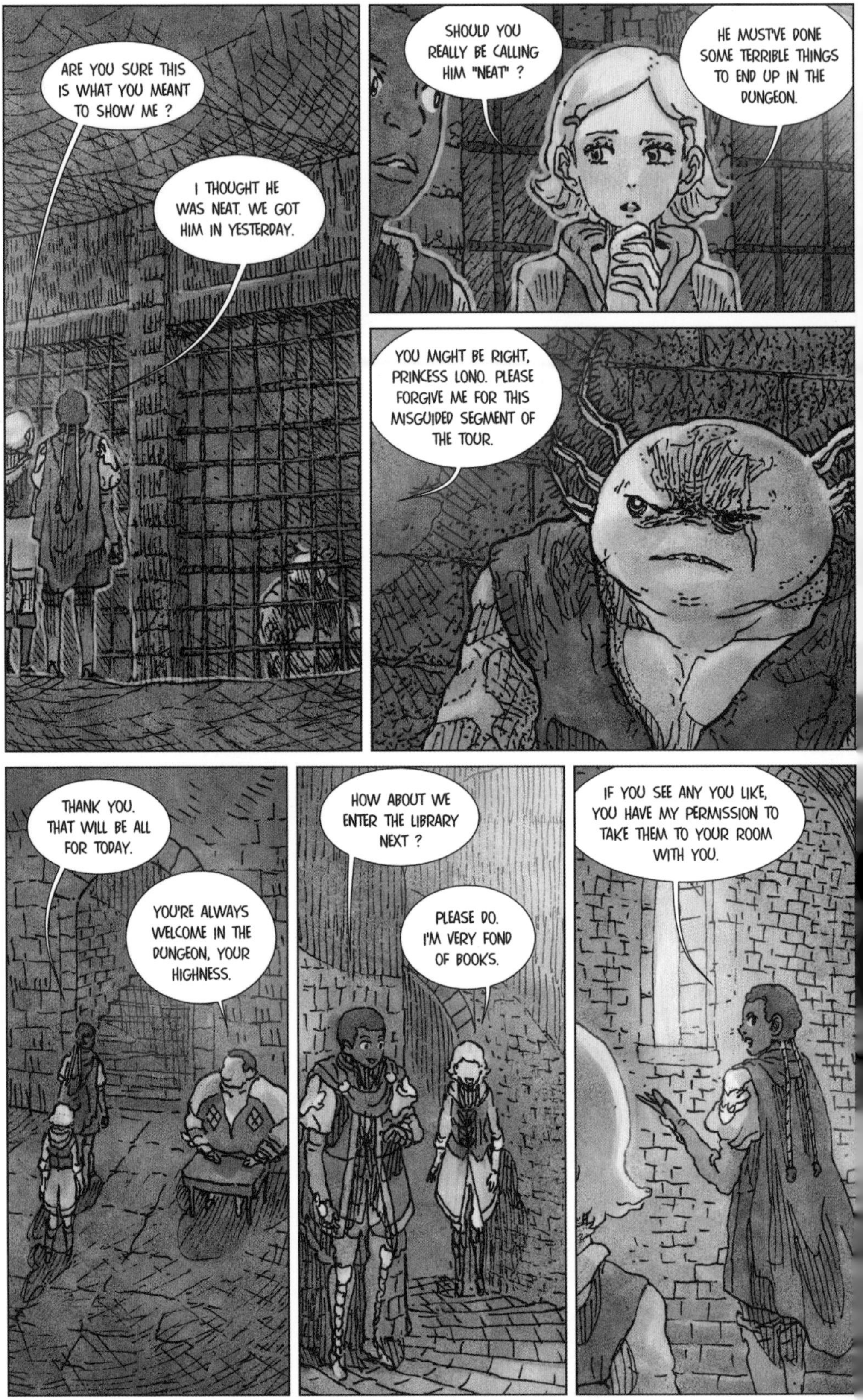

ARE YOU SURE THIS IS WHAT YOU MEANT TO SHOW ME ?
I THOUGHT HE WAS NEAT. WE GOT HIM IN YESTERDAY.
SHOULD YOU REALLY BE CALLING HIM "NEAT" ?
HE MUST'VE DONE SOME TERRIBLE THINGS TO END UP IN THE DUNGEON.
YOU MIGHT BE RIGHT, PRINCESS LONO. PLEASE FORGIVE ME FOR THIS MISGUIDED SEGMENT OF THE TOUR.
THANK YOU. THAT WILL BE ALL FOR TODAY.
YOU'RE ALWAYS WELCOME IN THE DUNGEON, YOUR HIGHNESS.
HOW ABOUT WE ENTER THE LIBRARY NEXT ?
PLEASE DO. I'M VERY FOND OF BOOKS.
IF YOU SEE ANY YOU LIKE, YOU HAVE MY PERMISSION TO TAKE THEM TO YOUR ROOM WITH YOU.

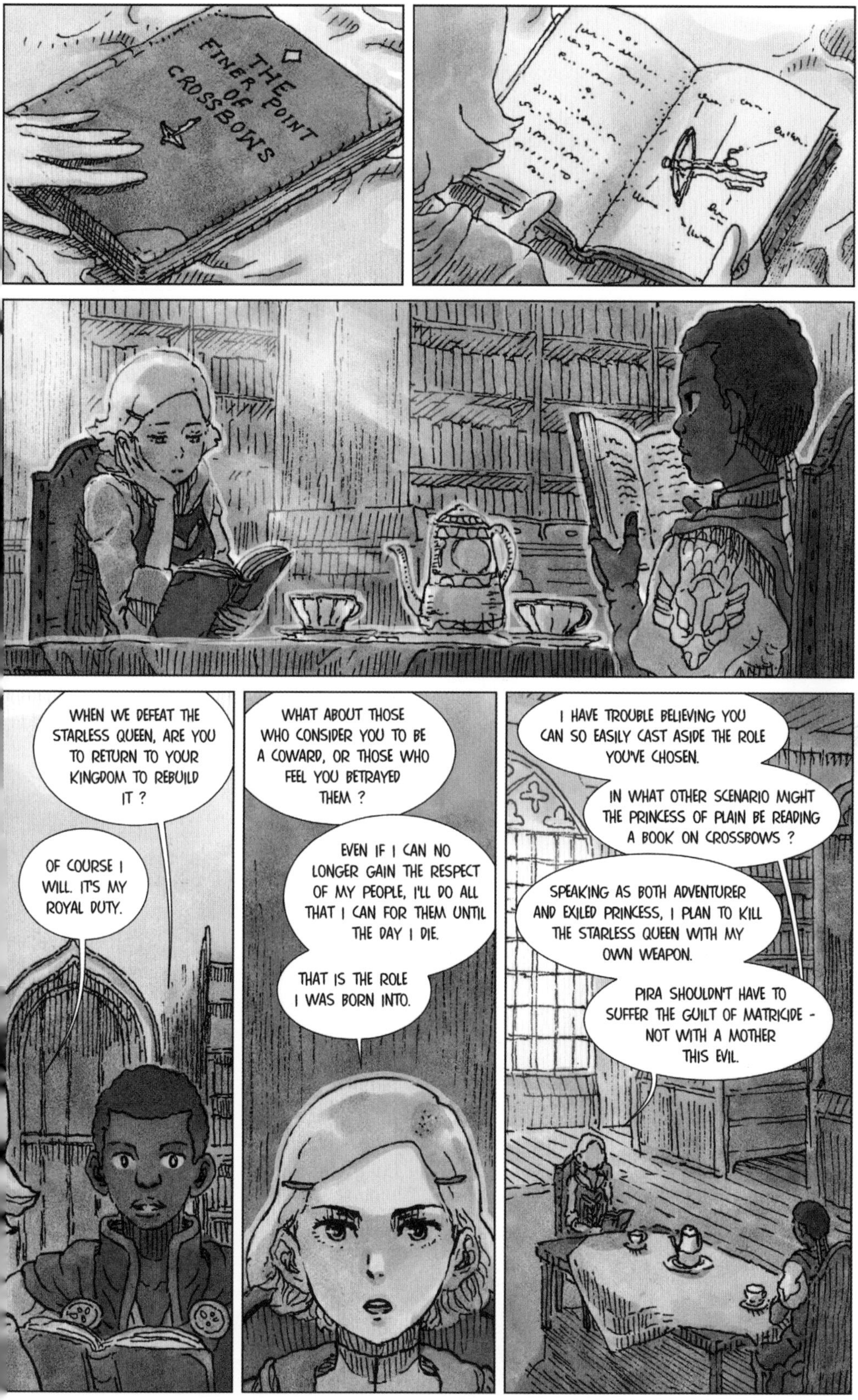
THE FINER POINT OF CROSSBOWS
WHEN WE DEFEAT THE STARLESS QUEEN, ARE YOU TO RETURN TO YOUR KINGDOM TO REBUILD IT ?
OF COURSE I WILL. IT'S MY ROYAL DUTY.
WHAT ABOUT THOSE WHO CONSIDER YOU TO BE A COWARD, OR THOSE WHO FEEL YOU BETRAYED THEM ?
EVEN IF I CAN NO LONGER GAIN THE RESPECT OF MY PEOPLE, I'LL DO ALL THAT I CAN FOR THEM UNTIL THE DAY I DIE.
THAT IS THE ROLE I WAS BORN INTO.
I HAVE TROUBLE BELIEVING YOU CAN SO EASILY CAST ASIDE THE ROLE YOU'VE CHOSEN.
IN WHAT OTHER SCENARIO MIGHT THE PRINCESS OF PLAIN BE READING A BOOK ON CROSSBOWS ?
SPEAKING AS BOTH ADVENTURER AND EXILED PRINCESS, I PLAN TO KILL THE STARLESS QUEEN WITH MY OWN WEAPON.
PIRA SHOULDN'T HAVE TO SUFFER THE GUILT OF MATRICIDE - NOT WITH A MOTHER THIS EVIL.

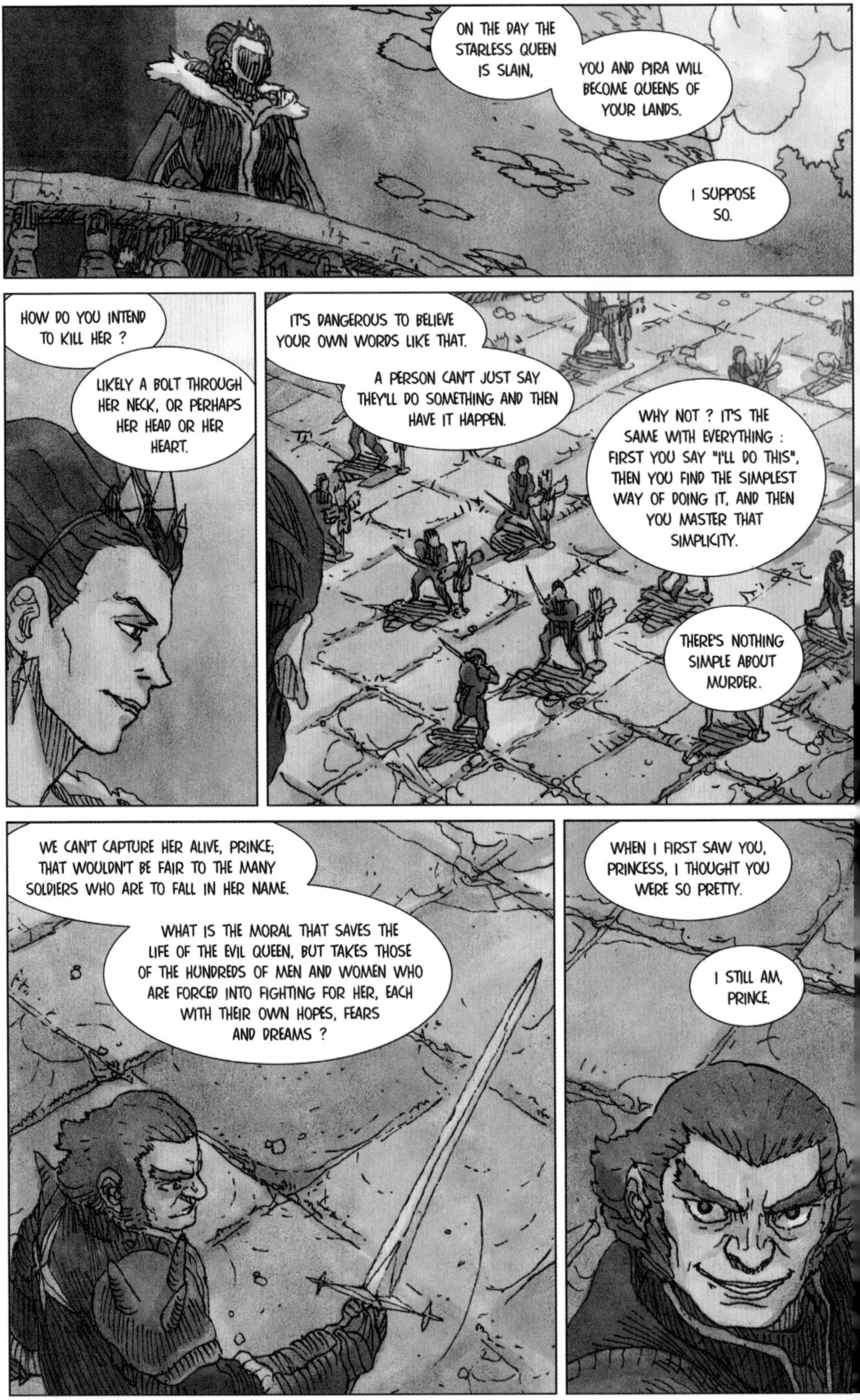
ON THE DAY THE STARLESS QUEEN IS SLAIN,
YOU AND PIRA WILL BECOME QUEENS OF YOUR LANDS.
I SUPPOSE SO.
HOW DO YOU INTEND TO KILL HER ?
LIKELY A BOLT THROUGH HER NECK, OR PERHAPS HER HEAD OR HER HEART.
IT'S DANGEROUS TO BELIEVE YOUR OWN WORDS LIKE THAT.
A PERSON CAN'T JUST SAY THEY'LL DO SOMETHING AND THEN HAVE IT HAPPEN.
WHY NOT ? IT'S THE SAME WITH EVERYTHING : FIRST YOU SAY "I'LL DO THIS", THEN YOU FIND THE SIMPLEST WAY OF DOING IT, AND THEN YOU MASTER THAT SIMPLICITY.
THERE'S NOTHING SIMPLE ABOUT MURDER.
WE CAN'T CAPTURE HER ALIVE, PRINCE; THAT WOULDN'T BE FAIR TO THE MANY SOLDIERS WHO ARE TO FALL IN HER NAME.
WHAT IS THE MORAL THAT SAVES THE LIFE OF THE EVIL QUEEN, BUT TAKES THOSE OF THE HUNDREDS OF MEN AND WOMEN WHO ARE FORCED INTO FIGHTING FOR HER, EACH WITH THEIR OWN HOPES, FEARS AND DREAMS ?
WHEN I FIRST SAW YOU, PRINCESS, I THOUGHT YOU WERE SO PRETTY.
I STILL AM, PRINCE.

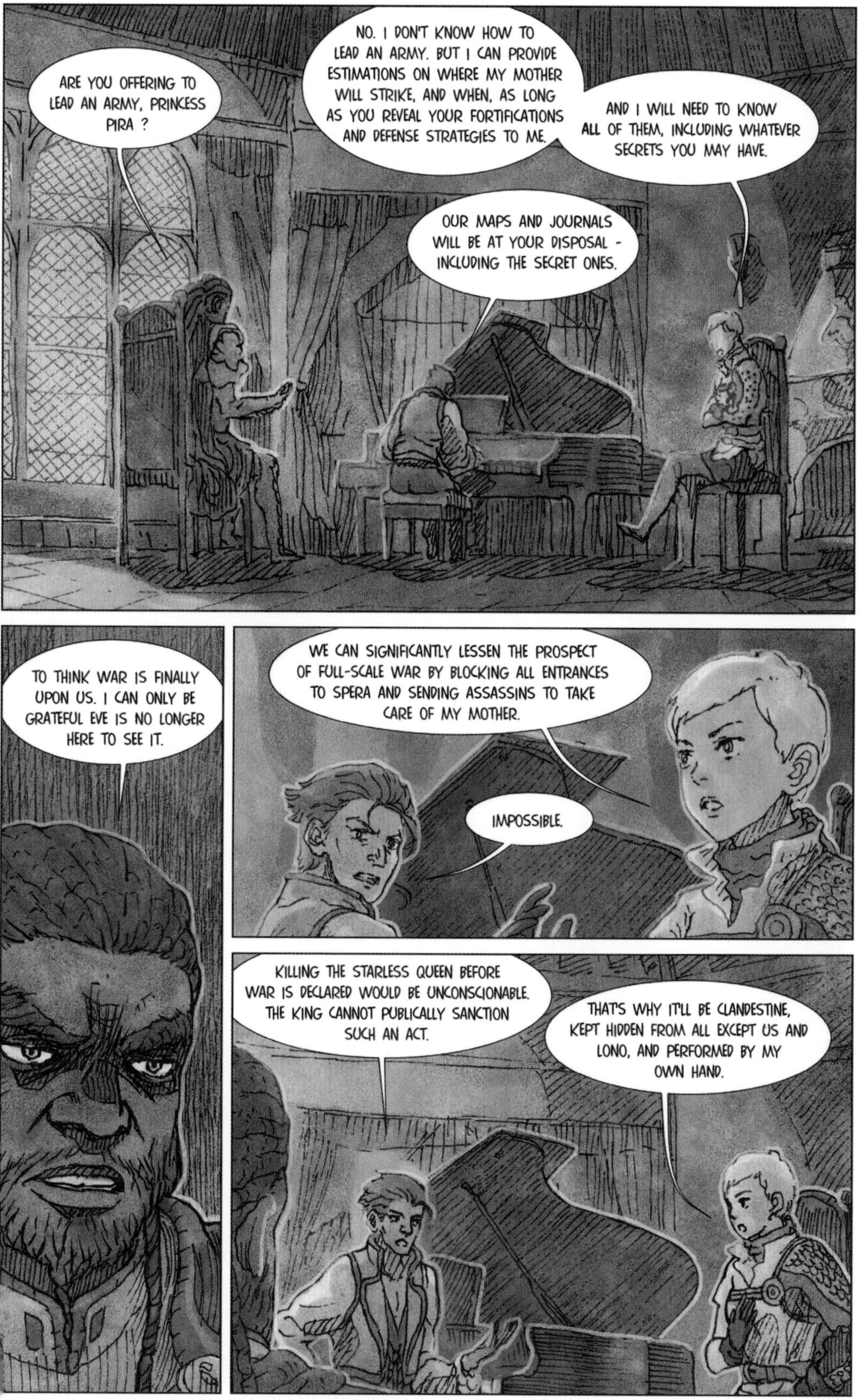
ARE YOU OFFERING TO LEAD AN ARMY, PRINCESS PIRA ?
NO. I DON'T KNOW HOW TO LEAD AN ARMY. BUT I CAN PROVIDE ESTIMATIONS ON WHERE MY MOTHER WILL STRIKE, AND WHEN, AS LONG AS YOU REVEAL YOUR FORTIFICATIONS AND DEFENSE STRATEGIES TO ME.
AND I WILL NEED TO KNOW **ALL** OF THEM, INCLUDING WHATEVER SECRETS YOU MAY HAVE.
OUR MAPS AND JOURNALS WILL BE AT YOUR DISPOSAL - INCLUDING THE SECRET ONES.
TO THINK WAR IS FINALLY UPON US. I CAN ONLY BE GRATEFUL EVE IS NO LONGER HERE TO SEE IT.
WE CAN SIGNIFICANTLY LESSEN THE PROSPECT OF FULL-SCALE WAR BY BLOCKING ALL ENTRANCES TO SPERA AND SENDING ASSASSINS TO TAKE CARE OF MY MOTHER.
IMPOSSIBLE.
KILLING THE STARLESS QUEEN BEFORE WAR IS DECLARED WOULD BE UNCONSCIONABLE. THE KING CANNOT PUBLICALLY SANCTION SUCH AN ACT.
THAT'S WHY IT'LL BE CLANDESTINE, KEPT HIDDEN FROM ALL EXCEPT US AND LONO, AND PERFORMED BY MY OWN HAND.

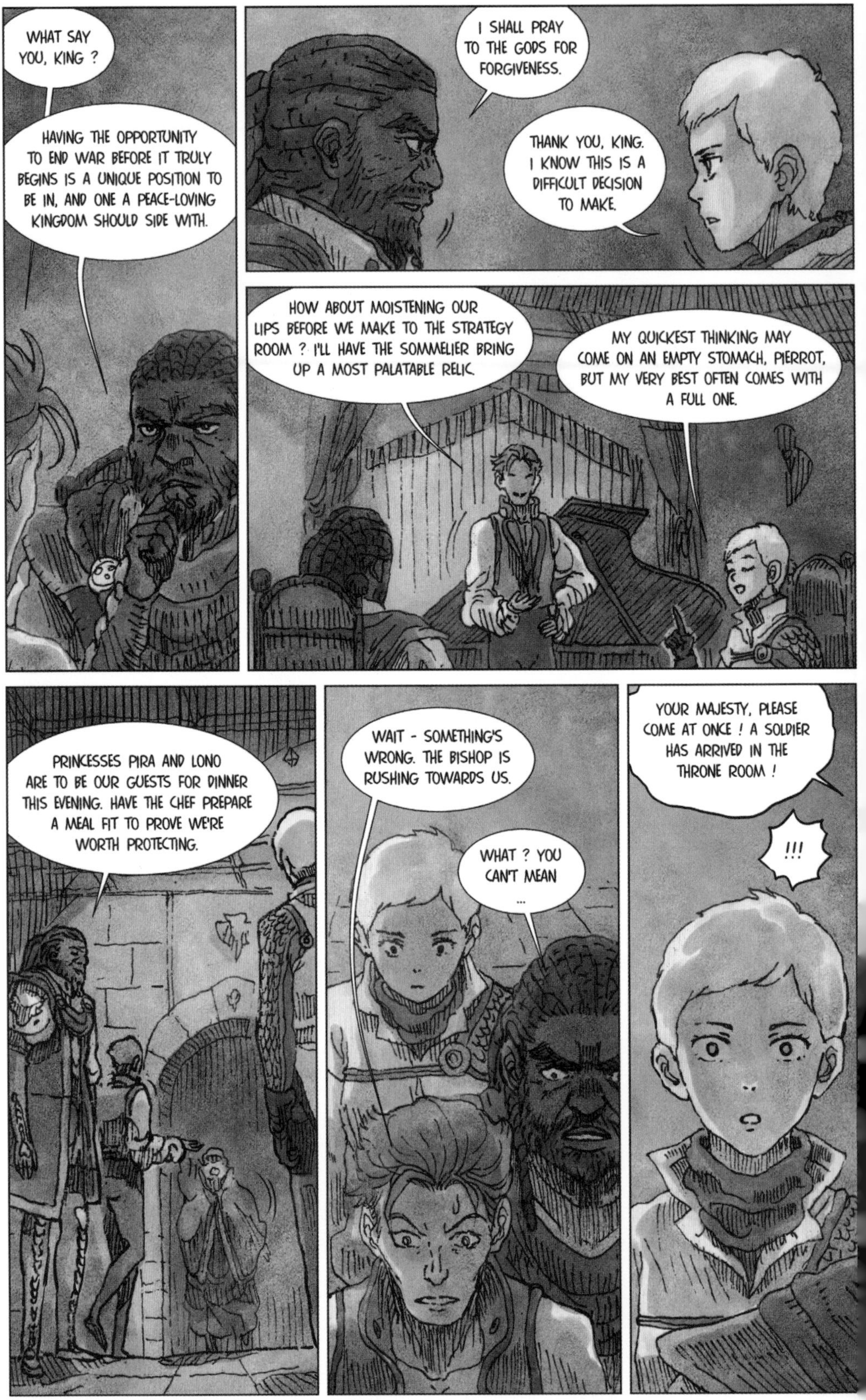
WHAT SAY YOU, KING ?
HAVING THE OPPORTUNITY TO END WAR BEFORE IT TRULY BEGINS IS A UNIQUE POSITION TO BE IN, AND ONE A PEACE-LOVING KINGDOM SHOULD SIDE WITH.
I SHALL PRAY TO THE GODS FOR FORGIVENESS.
THANK YOU, KING. I KNOW THIS IS A DIFFICULT DECISION TO MAKE.
HOW ABOUT MOISTENING OUR LIPS BEFORE WE MAKE TO THE STRATEGY ROOM ? I'LL HAVE THE SOMMELIER BRING UP A MOST PALATABLE RELIC.
MY QUICKEST THINKING MAY COME ON AN EMPTY STOMACH, PIERROT, BUT MY VERY BEST OFTEN COMES WITH A FULL ONE.
PRINCESSES PIRA AND LONO ARE TO BE OUR GUESTS FOR DINNER THIS EVENING. HAVE THE CHEF PREPARE A MEAL FIT TO PROVE WE'RE WORTH PROTECTING.
WAIT - SOMETHING'S WRONG. THE BISHOP IS RUSHING TOWARDS US.
WHAT ? YOU CAN'T MEAN ...
YOUR MAJESTY, PLEASE COME AT ONCE ! A SOLDIER HAS ARRIVED IN THE THRONE ROOM !
!!!

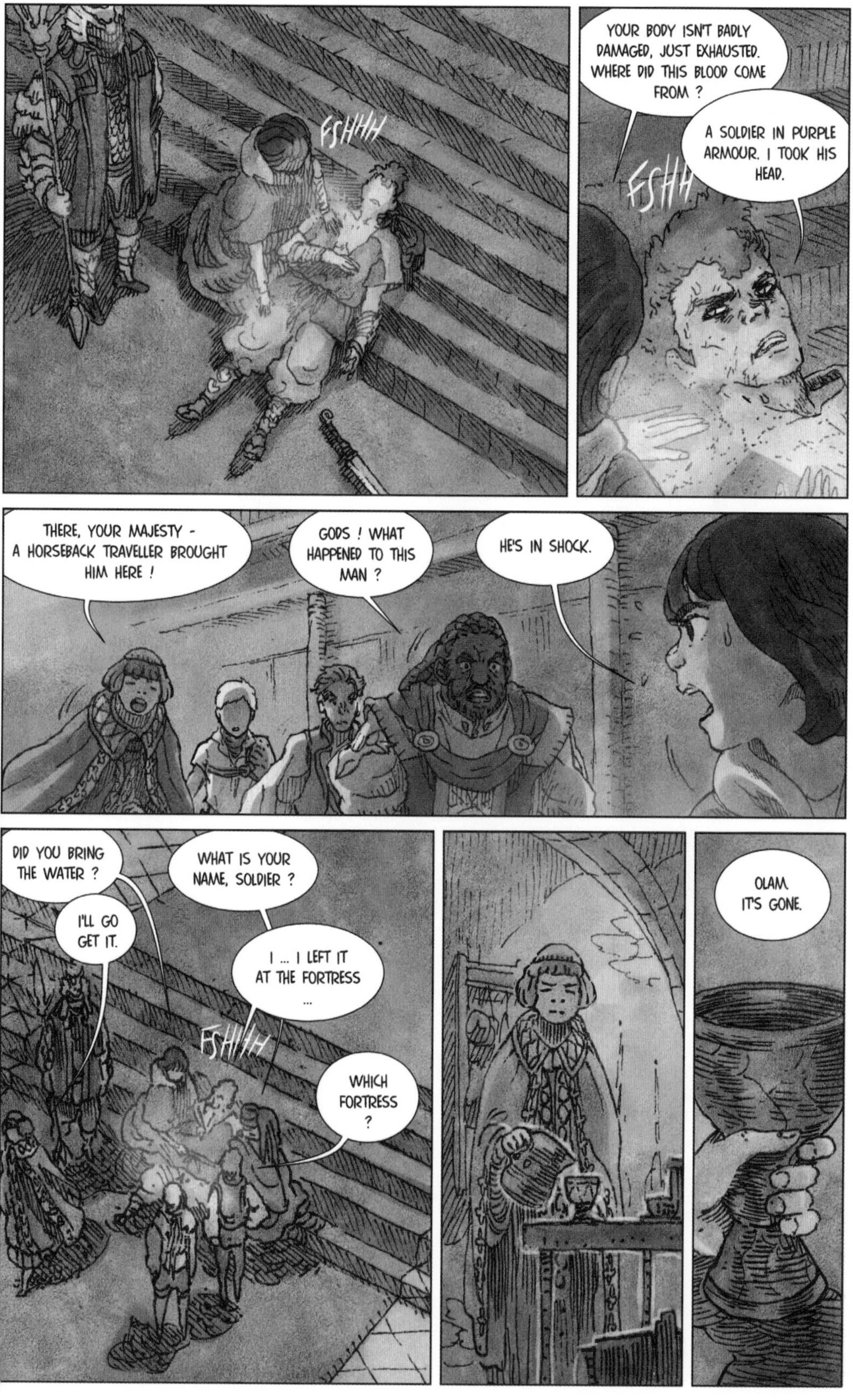
FSHHH
YOUR BODY ISN'T BADLY DAMAGED, JUST EXHAUSTED. WHERE DID THIS BLOOD COME FROM ?
FSHH
A SOLDIER IN PURPLE ARMOUR. I TOOK HIS HEAD.
THERE, YOUR MAJESTY - A HORSEBACK TRAVELLER BROUGHT HIM HERE !
GODS ! WHAT HAPPENED TO THIS MAN ?
HE'S IN SHOCK.
DID YOU BRING THE WATER ?
WHAT IS YOUR NAME, SOLDIER ?
I'LL GO GET IT.
I ... I LEFT IT AT THE FORTRESS ...
FSHHH
WHICH FORTRESS ?
OLAM IT'S GONE.

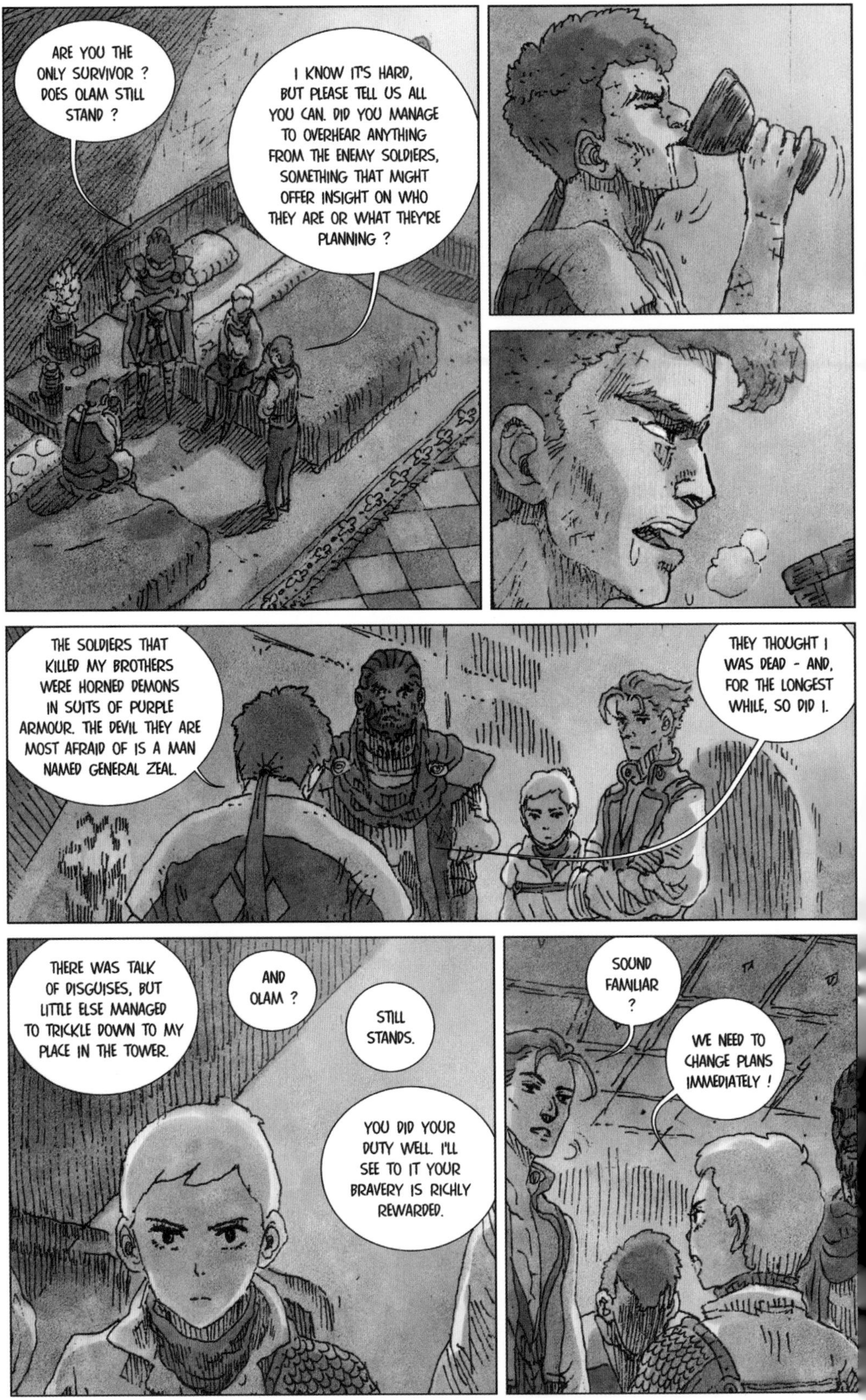
ARE YOU THE ONLY SURVIVOR ? DOES OLAM STILL STAND ?
I KNOW IT'S HARD, BUT PLEASE TELL US ALL YOU CAN. DID YOU MANAGE TO OVERHEAR ANYTHING FROM THE ENEMY SOLDIERS, SOMETHING THAT MIGHT OFFER INSIGHT ON WHO THEY ARE OR WHAT THEY'RE PLANNING ?
THE SOLDIERS THAT KILLED MY BROTHERS WERE HORNED DEMONS IN SUITS OF PURPLE ARMOUR. THE DEVIL THEY ARE MOST AFRAID OF IS A MAN NAMED GENERAL ZEAL.
THEY THOUGHT I WAS DEAD - AND, FOR THE LONGEST WHILE, SO DID I.
THERE WAS TALK OF DISGUISES, BUT LITTLE ELSE MANAGED TO TRICKLE DOWN TO MY PLACE IN THE TOWER.
AND OLAM ?
STILL STANDS.
YOU DID YOUR DUTY WELL. I'LL SEE TO IT YOUR BRAVERY IS RICHLY REWARDED.
SOUND FAMILIAR ?
WE NEED TO CHANGE PLANS IMMEDIATELY !

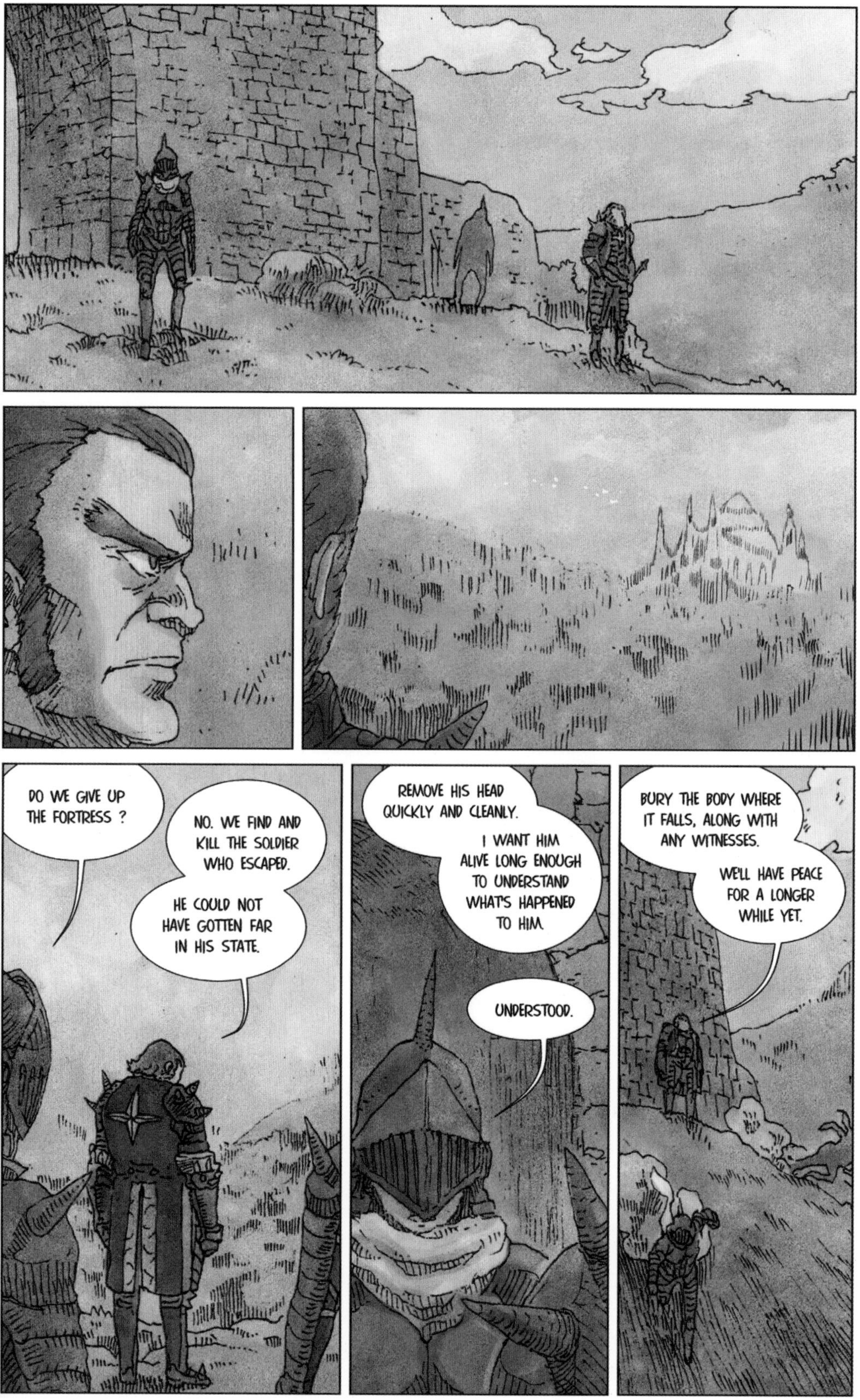
DO WE GIVE UP THE FORTRESS ?
NO. WE FIND AND KILL THE SOLDIER WHO ESCAPED.
HE COULD NOT HAVE GOTTEN FAR IN HIS STATE.
REMOVE HIS HEAD QUICKLY AND CLEANLY.
I WANT HIM ALIVE LONG ENOUGH TO UNDERSTAND WHAT'S HAPPENED TO HIM.
UNDERSTOOD.
BURY THE BODY WHERE IT FALLS, ALONG WITH ANY WITNESSES.
WE'LL HAVE PEACE FOR A LONGER WHILE YET.

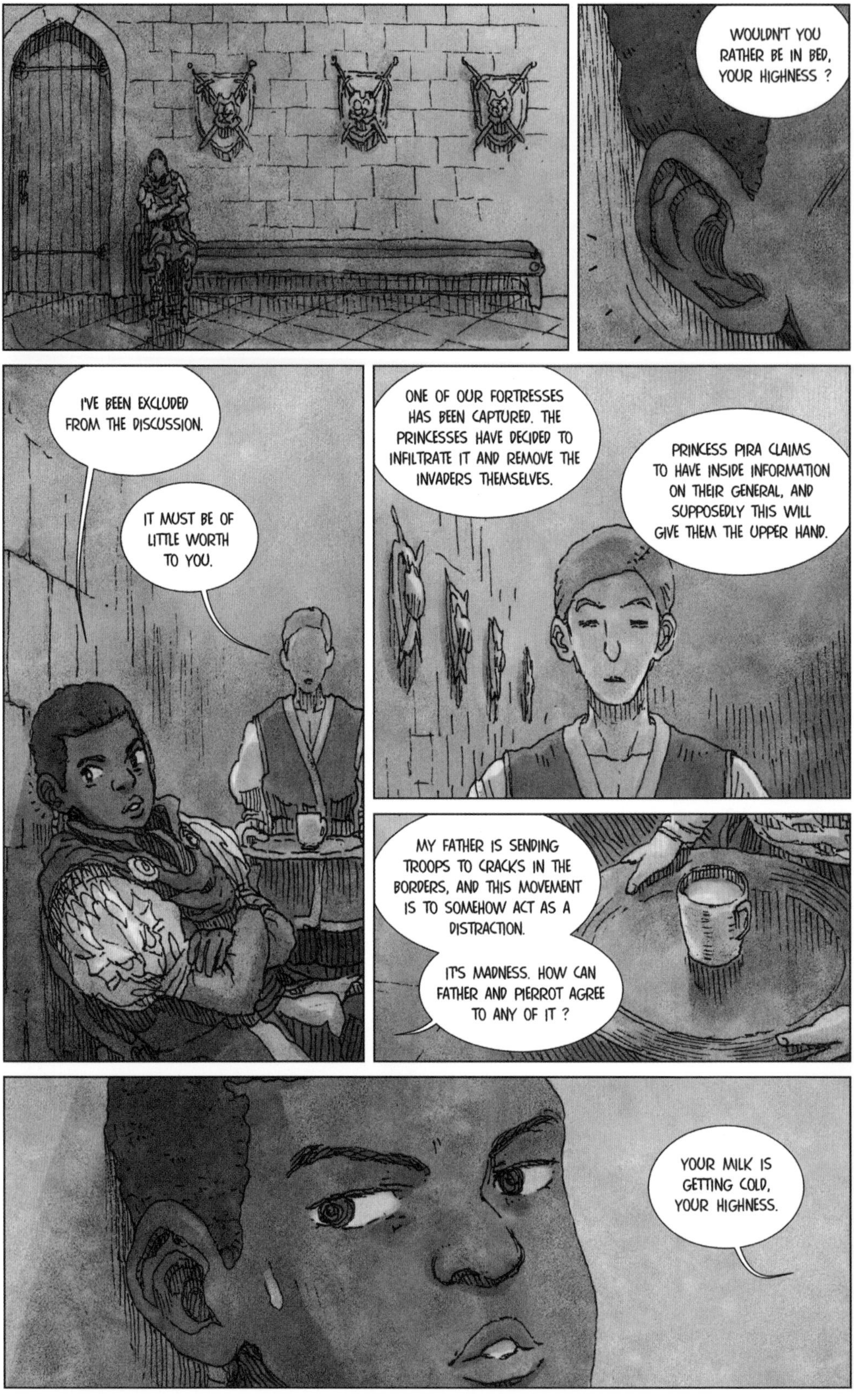
WOULDN'T YOU RATHER BE IN BED, YOUR HIGHNESS ?
I'VE BEEN EXCLUDED FROM THE DISCUSSION.
IT MUST BE OF LITTLE WORTH TO YOU.
ONE OF OUR FORTRESSES HAS BEEN CAPTURED. THE PRINCESSES HAVE DECIDED TO INFILTRATE IT AND REMOVE THE INVADERS THEMSELVES.
PRINCESS PIRA CLAIMS TO HAVE INSIDE INFORMATION ON THEIR GENERAL, AND SUPPOSEDLY THIS WILL GIVE THEM THE UPPER HAND.
MY FATHER IS SENDING TROOPS TO CRACKS IN THE BORDERS, AND THIS MOVEMENT IS TO SOMEHOW ACT AS A DISTRACTION.
IT'S MADNESS. HOW CAN FATHER AND PIERROT AGREE TO ANY OF IT ?
YOUR MILK IS GETTING COLD, YOUR HIGHNESS.

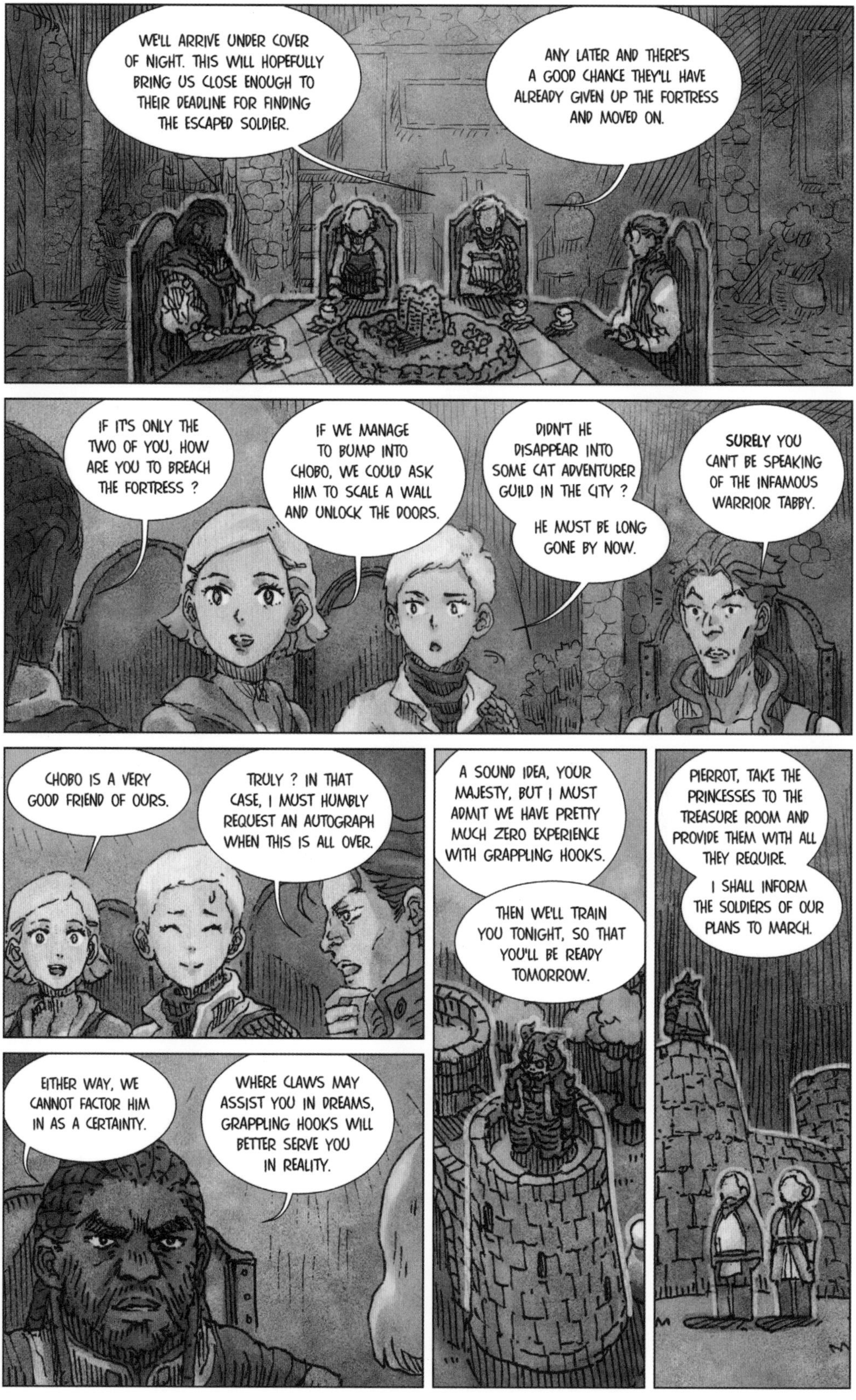
WE'LL ARRIVE UNDER COVER OF NIGHT. THIS WILL HOPEFULLY BRING US CLOSE ENOUGH TO THEIR DEADLINE FOR FINDING THE ESCAPED SOLDIER.
ANY LATER AND THERE'S A GOOD CHANCE THEY'LL HAVE ALREADY GIVEN UP THE FORTRESS AND MOVED ON.
IF IT'S ONLY THE TWO OF YOU, HOW ARE YOU TO BREACH THE FORTRESS ?
IF WE MANAGE TO BUMP INTO CHOBO, WE COULD ASK HIM TO SCALE A WALL AND UNLOCK THE DOORS.
DIDN'T HE DISAPPEAR INTO SOME CAT ADVENTURER GUILD IN THE CITY ?
HE MUST BE LONG GONE BY NOW.
SURELY YOU CAN'T BE SPEAKING OF THE INFAMOUS WARRIOR TABBY.
CHOBO IS A VERY GOOD FRIEND OF OURS.
TRULY ? IN THAT CASE, I MUST HUMBLY REQUEST AN AUTOGRAPH WHEN THIS IS ALL OVER.
EITHER WAY, WE CANNOT FACTOR HIM IN AS A CERTAINTY.
WHERE CLAWS MAY ASSIST YOU IN DREAMS, GRAPPLING HOOKS WILL BETTER SERVE YOU IN REALITY.
A SOUND IDEA, YOUR MAJESTY, BUT I MUST ADMIT WE HAVE PRETTY MUCH ZERO EXPERIENCE WITH GRAPPLING HOOKS.
THEN WE'LL TRAIN YOU TONIGHT, SO THAT YOU'LL BE READY TOMORROW.
PIERROT, TAKE THE PRINCESSES TO THE TREASURE ROOM AND PROVIDE THEM WITH ALL THEY REQUIRE.
I SHALL INFORM THE SOLDIERS OF OUR PLANS TO MARCH.

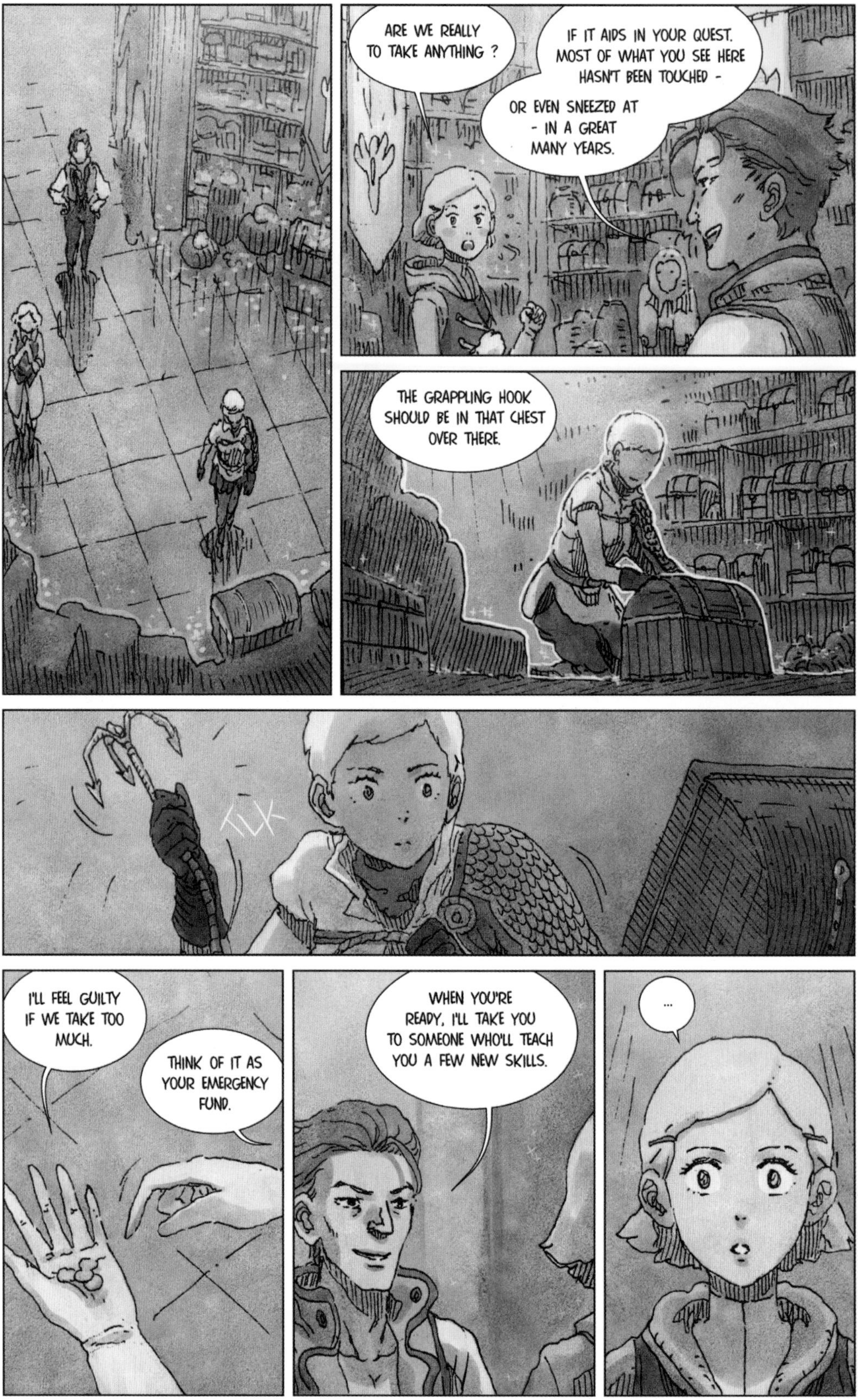
ARE WE REALLY TO TAKE ANYTHING ?
IF IT AIDS IN YOUR QUEST. MOST OF WHAT YOU SEE HERE HASN'T BEEN TOUCHED -
OR EVEN SNEEZED AT - IN A GREAT MANY YEARS.
THE GRAPPLING HOOK SHOULD BE IN THAT CHEST OVER THERE.
TLK
I'LL FEEL GUILTY IF WE TAKE TOO MUCH.
THINK OF IT AS YOUR EMERGENCY FUND.
WHEN YOU'RE READY, I'LL TAKE YOU TO SOMEONE WHO'LL TEACH YOU A FEW NEW SKILLS.
...

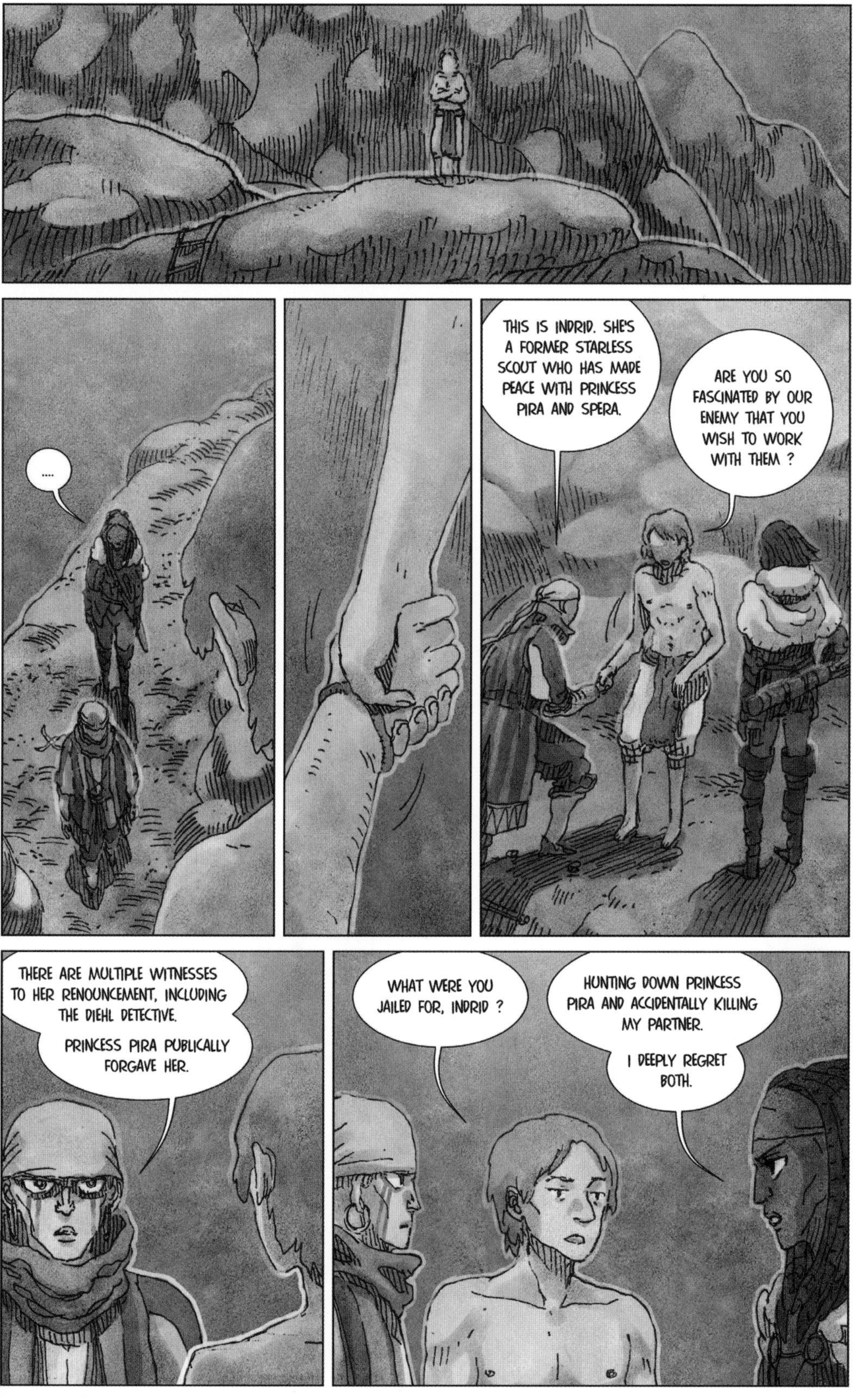
....
THIS IS INDRID. SHE'S A FORMER STARLESS SCOUT WHO HAS MADE PEACE WITH PRINCESS PIRA AND SPERA.
ARE YOU SO FASCINATED BY OUR ENEMY THAT YOU WISH TO WORK WITH THEM ?
THERE ARE MULTIPLE WITNESSES TO HER RENOUNCEMENT, INCLUDING THE DIEHL DETECTIVE.
PRINCESS PIRA PUBLICALLY FORGAVE HER.
WHAT WERE YOU JAILED FOR, INDRID ?
HUNTING DOWN PRINCESS PIRA AND ACCIDENTALLY KILLING MY PARTNER.
I DEEPLY REGRET BOTH.

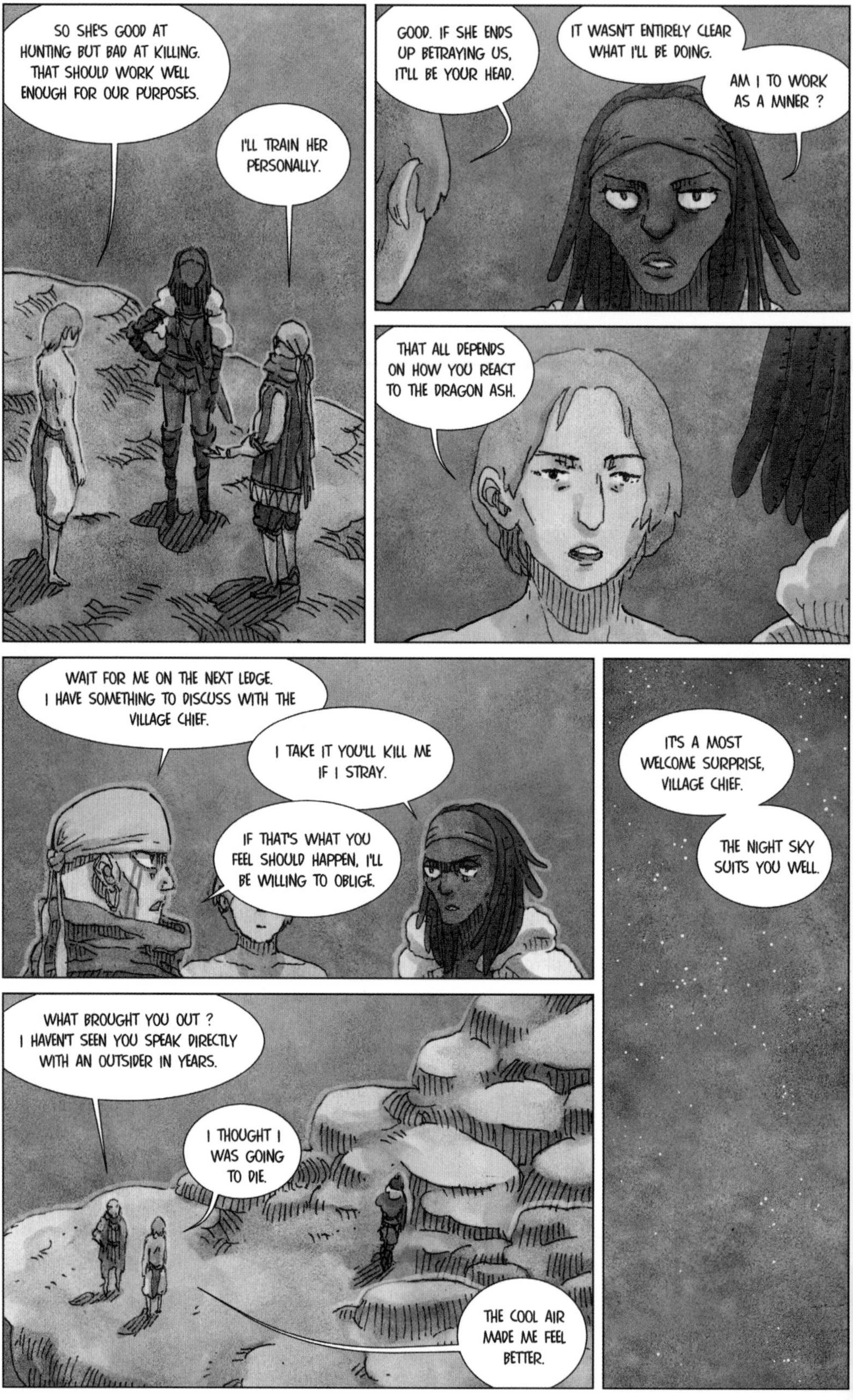
SO SHE'S GOOD AT HUNTING BUT BAD AT KILLING. THAT SHOULD WORK WELL ENOUGH FOR OUR PURPOSES.
I'LL TRAIN HER PERSONALLY.
GOOD. IF SHE ENDS UP BETRAYING US, IT'LL BE YOUR HEAD.
IT WASN'T ENTIRELY CLEAR WHAT I'LL BE DOING.
AM I TO WORK AS A MINER ?
THAT ALL DEPENDS ON HOW YOU REACT TO THE DRAGON ASH.
WAIT FOR ME ON THE NEXT LEDGE. I HAVE SOMETHING TO DISCUSS WITH THE VILLAGE CHIEF.
I TAKE IT YOU'LL KILL ME IF I STRAY.
IF THAT'S WHAT YOU FEEL SHOULD HAPPEN, I'LL BE WILLING TO OBLIGE.
WHAT BROUGHT YOU OUT ? I HAVEN'T SEEN YOU SPEAK DIRECTLY WITH AN OUTSIDER IN YEARS.
I THOUGHT I WAS GOING TO DIE.
THE COOL AIR MADE ME FEEL BETTER.
IT'S A MOST WELCOME SURPRISE, VILLAGE CHIEF.
THE NIGHT SKY SUITS YOU WELL.

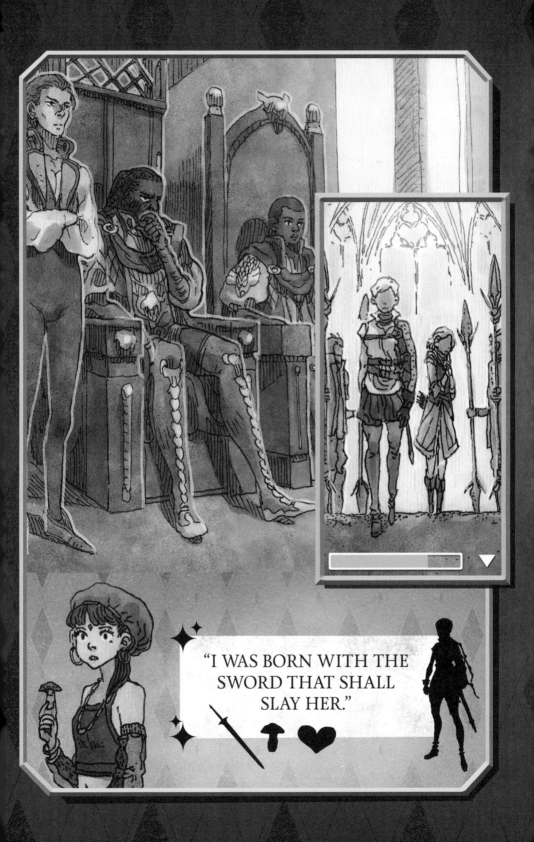

"I WAS BORN WITH THE SWORD THAT SHALL SLAY HER."

CHAPTER FIVE

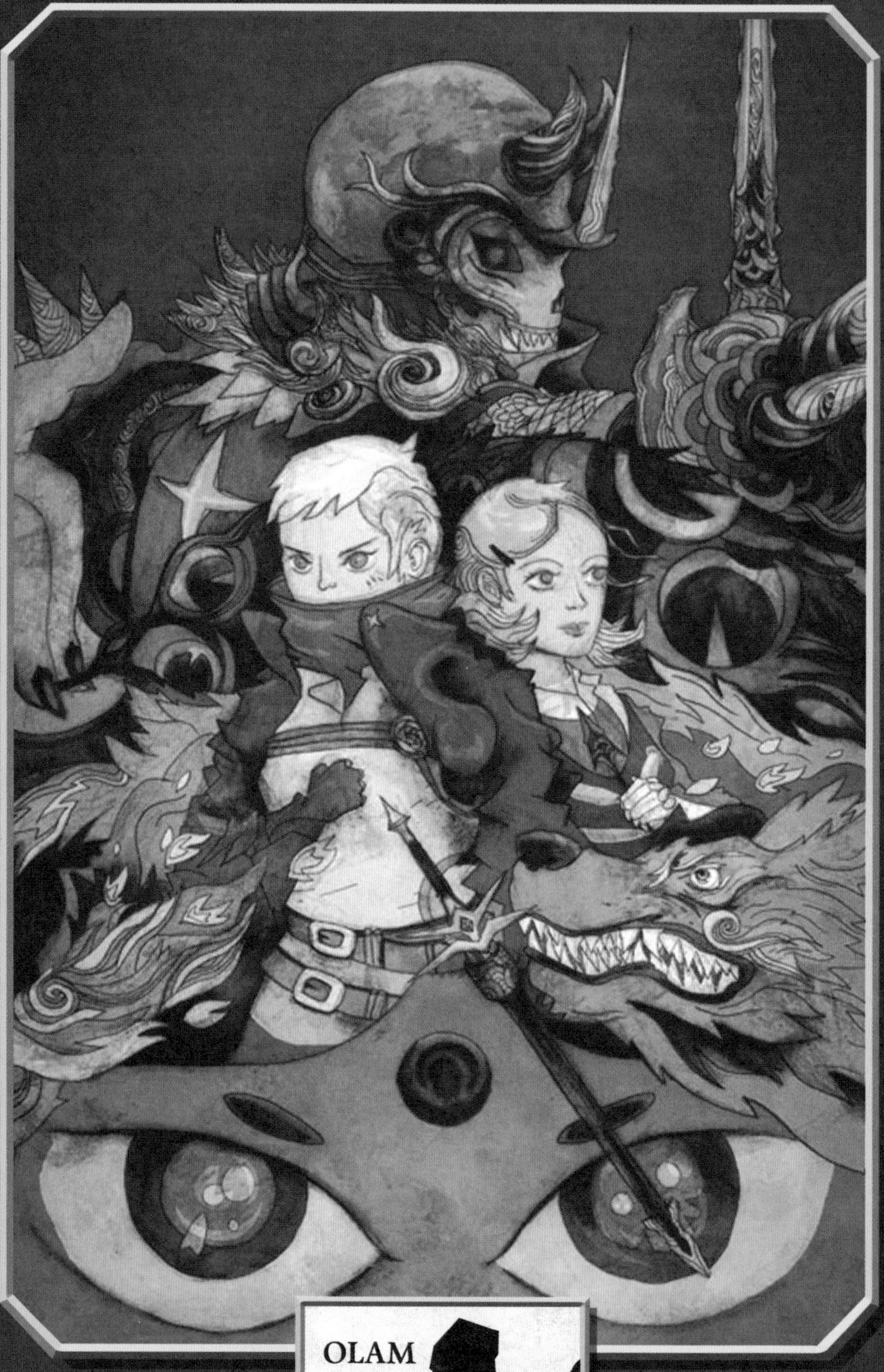

OLAM

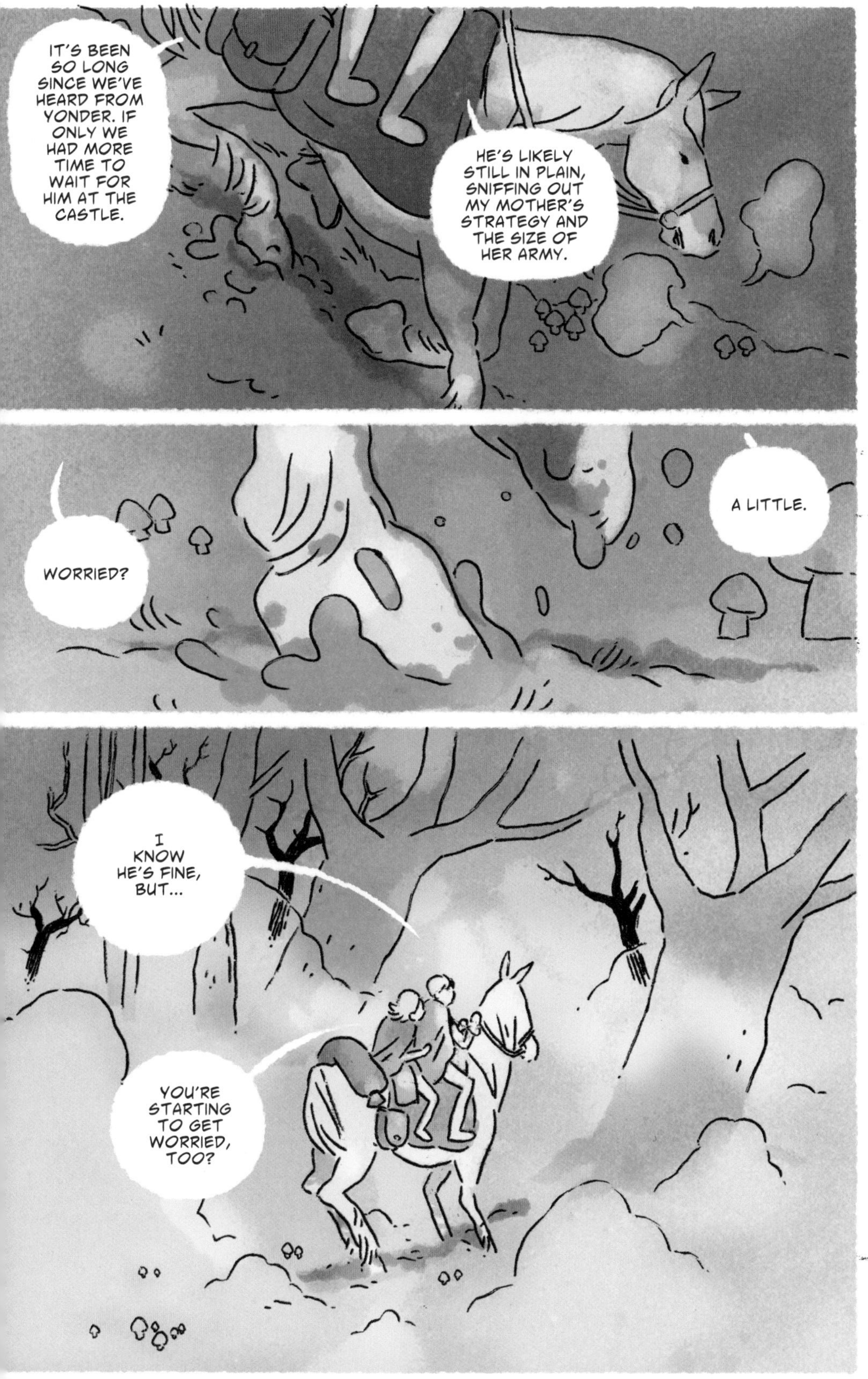
IT'S BEEN SO LONG SINCE WE'VE HEARD FROM YONDER. IF ONLY WE HAD MORE TIME TO WAIT FOR HIM AT THE CASTLE.
HE'S LIKELY STILL IN PLAIN, SNIFFING OUT MY MOTHER'S STRATEGY AND THE SIZE OF HER ARMY.
WORRIED?
A LITTLE.
I KNOW HE'S FINE, BUT...
YOU'RE STARTING TO GET WORRIED, TOO?

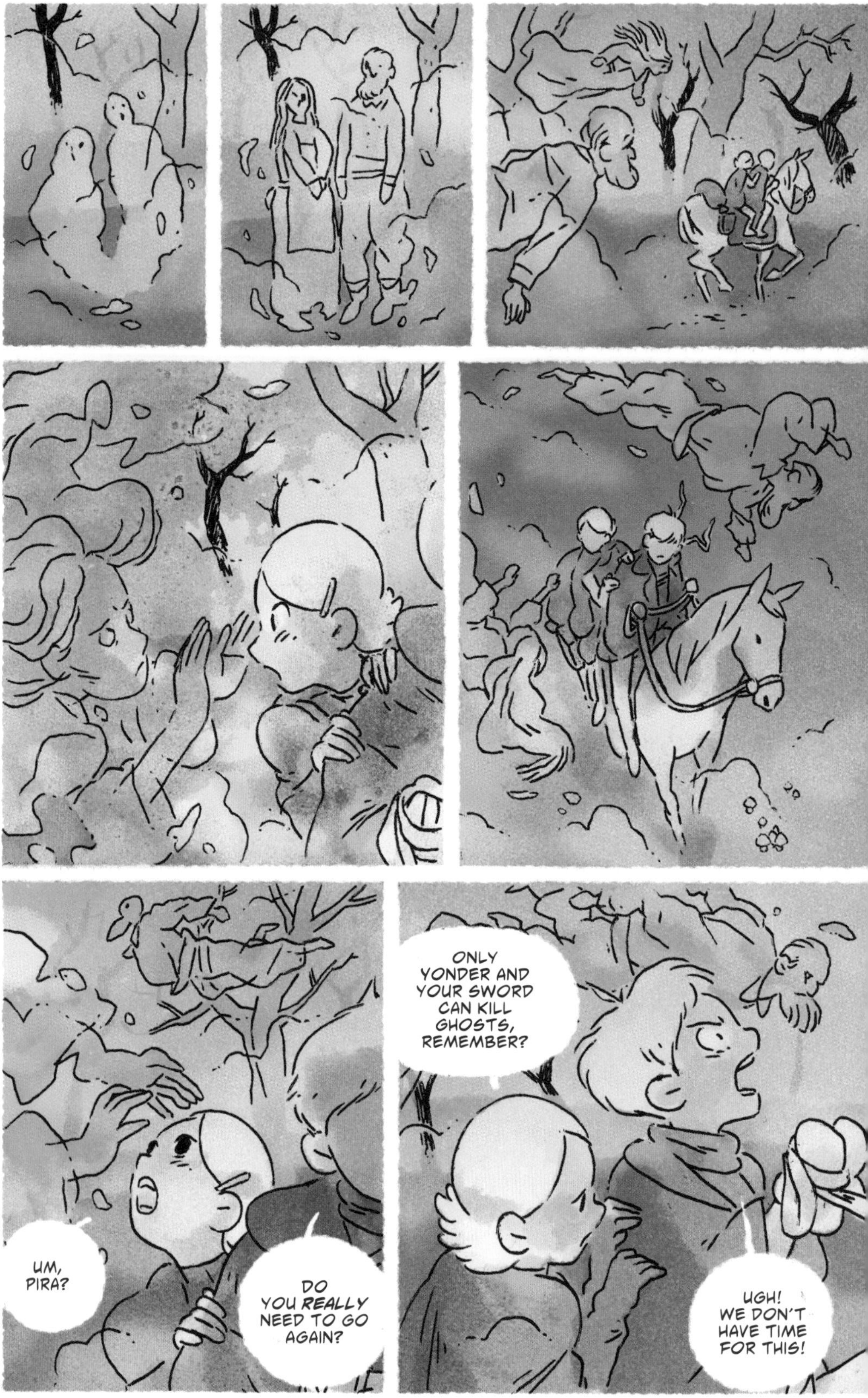
UM, PIRA?
DO YOU REALLY NEED TO GO AGAIN?
ONLY YONDER AND YOUR SWORD CAN KILL GHOSTS, REMEMBER?
UGH! WE DON'T HAVE TIME FOR THIS!

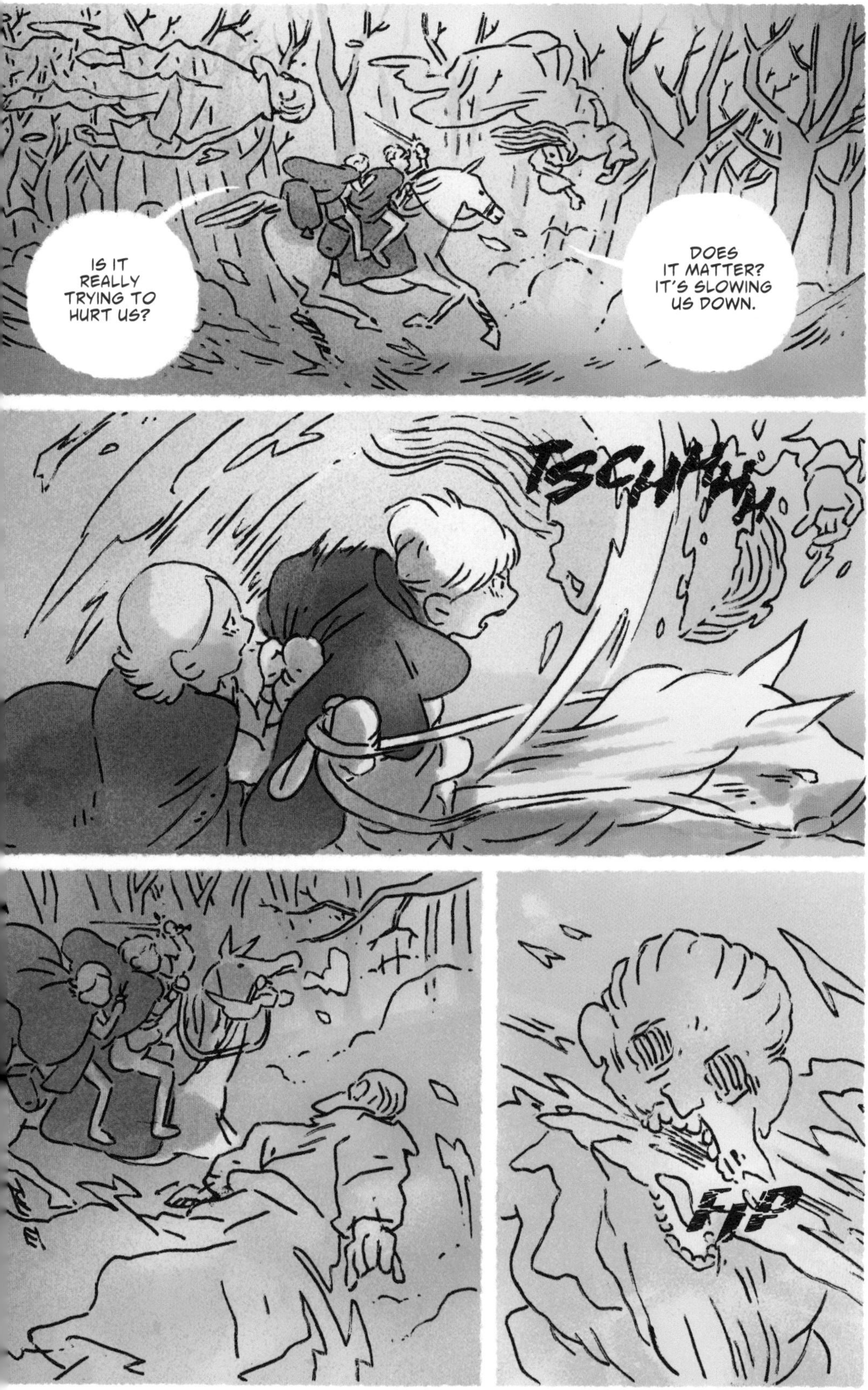
IS IT REALLY TRYING TO HURT US?
DOES IT MATTER? IT'S SLOWING US DOWN.
TSCHHH
HP

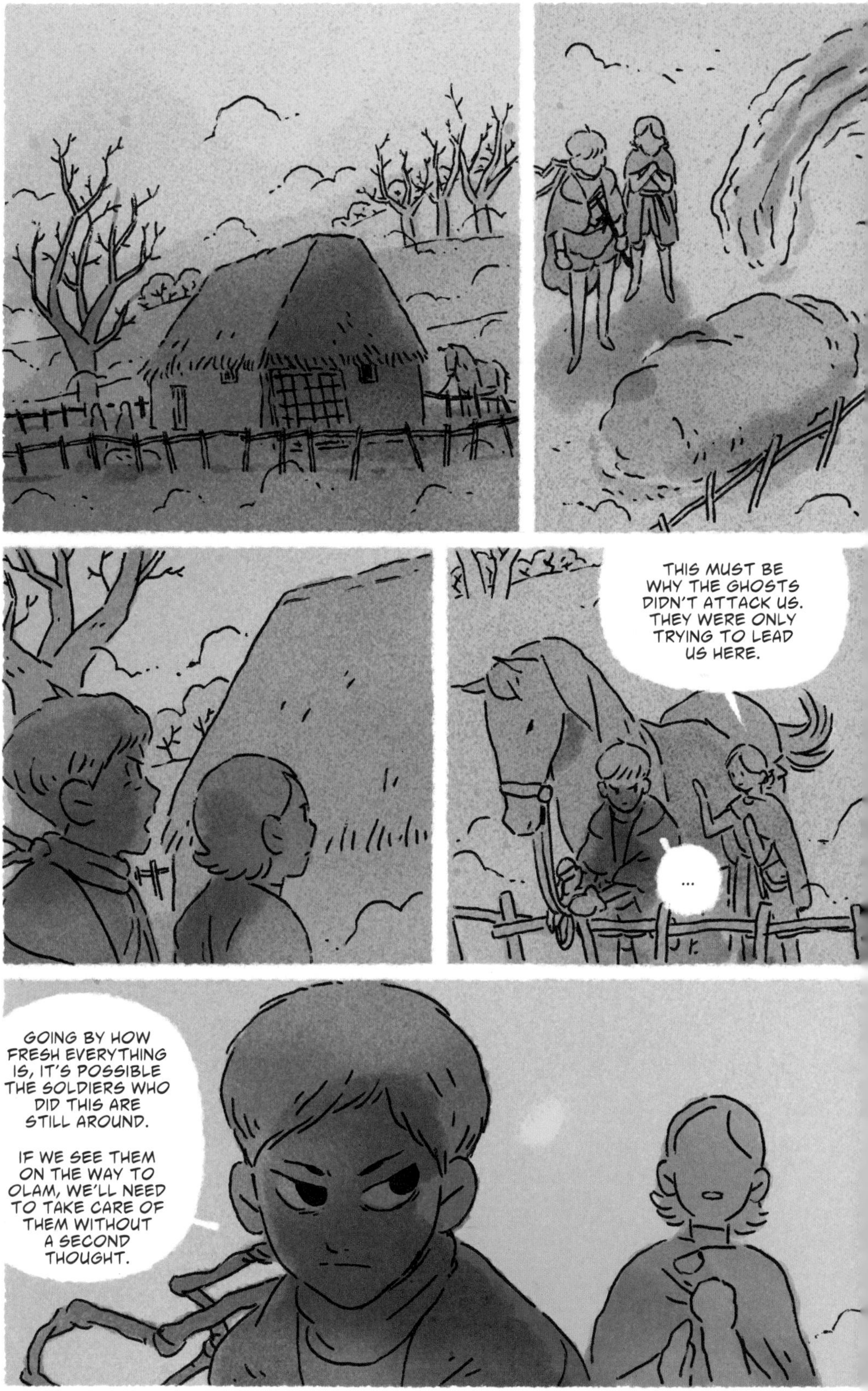
THIS MUST BE WHY THE GHOSTS DIDN'T ATTACK US. THEY WERE ONLY TRYING TO LEAD US HERE.
...
GOING BY HOW FRESH EVERYTHING IS, IT'S POSSIBLE THE SOLDIERS WHO DID THIS ARE STILL AROUND.
IF WE SEE THEM ON THE WAY TO OLAM, WE'LL NEED TO TAKE CARE OF THEM WITHOUT A SECOND THOUGHT.

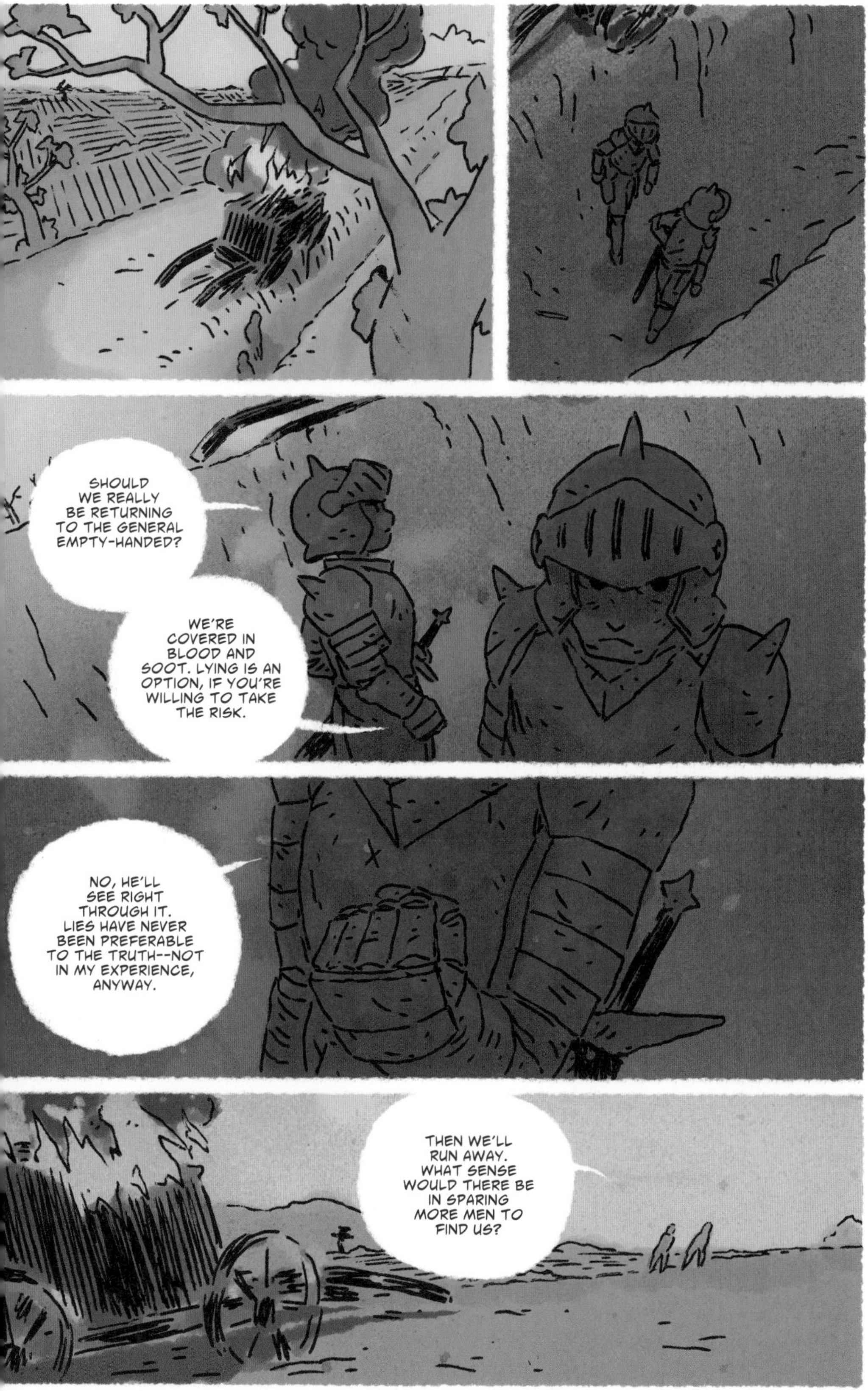
SHOULD WE REALLY BE RETURNING TO THE GENERAL EMPTY-HANDED?
WE'RE COVERED IN BLOOD AND SOOT. LYING IS AN OPTION, IF YOU'RE WILLING TO TAKE THE RISK.
NO, HE'LL SEE RIGHT THROUGH IT. LIES HAVE NEVER BEEN PREFERABLE TO THE TRUTH--NOT IN MY EXPERIENCE, ANYWAY.
THEN WE'LL RUN AWAY. WHAT SENSE WOULD THERE BE IN SPARING MORE MEN TO FIND US?

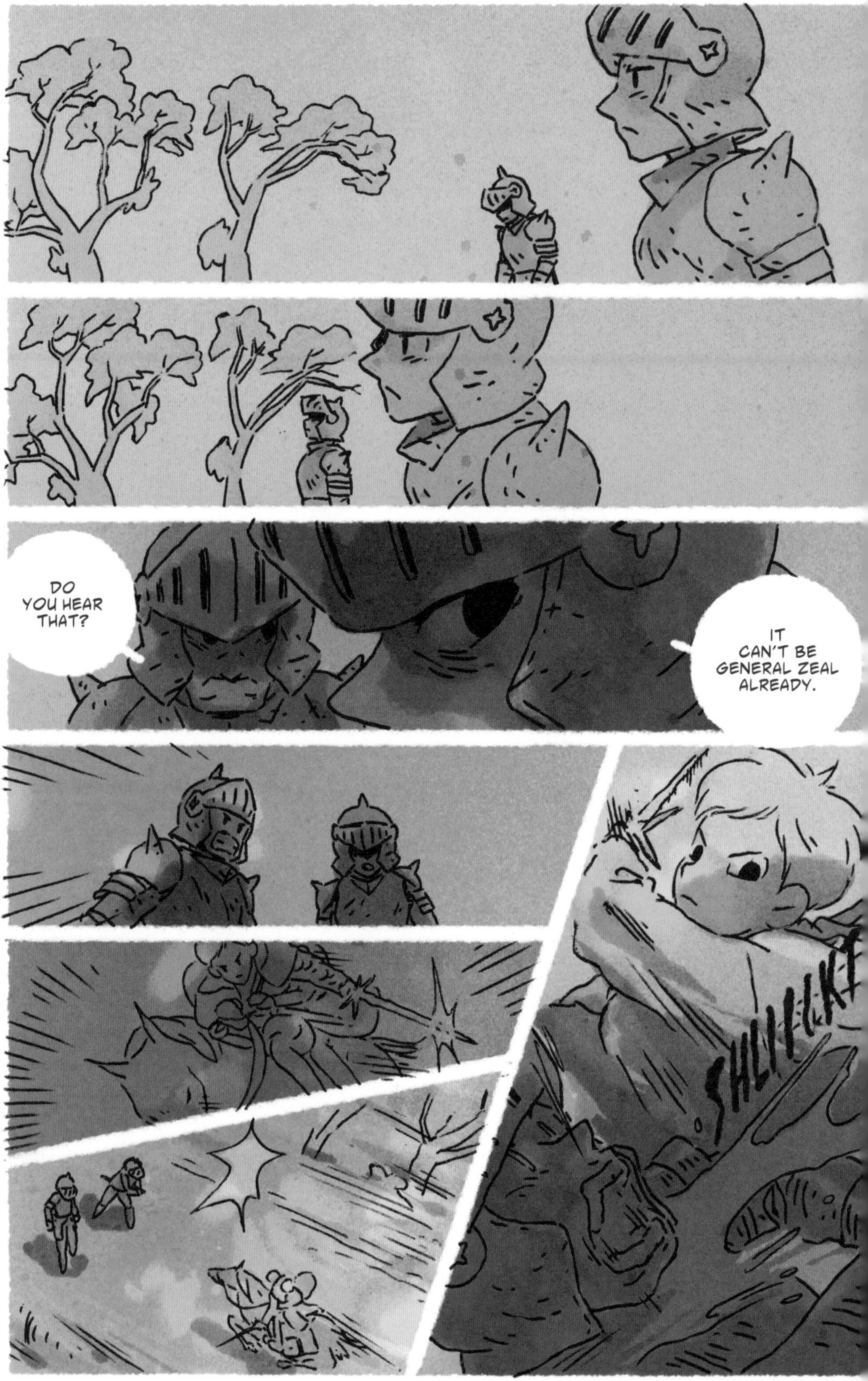
DO YOU HEAR THAT?
IT CAN'T BE GENERAL ZEAL ALREADY.
SHLIIICK!

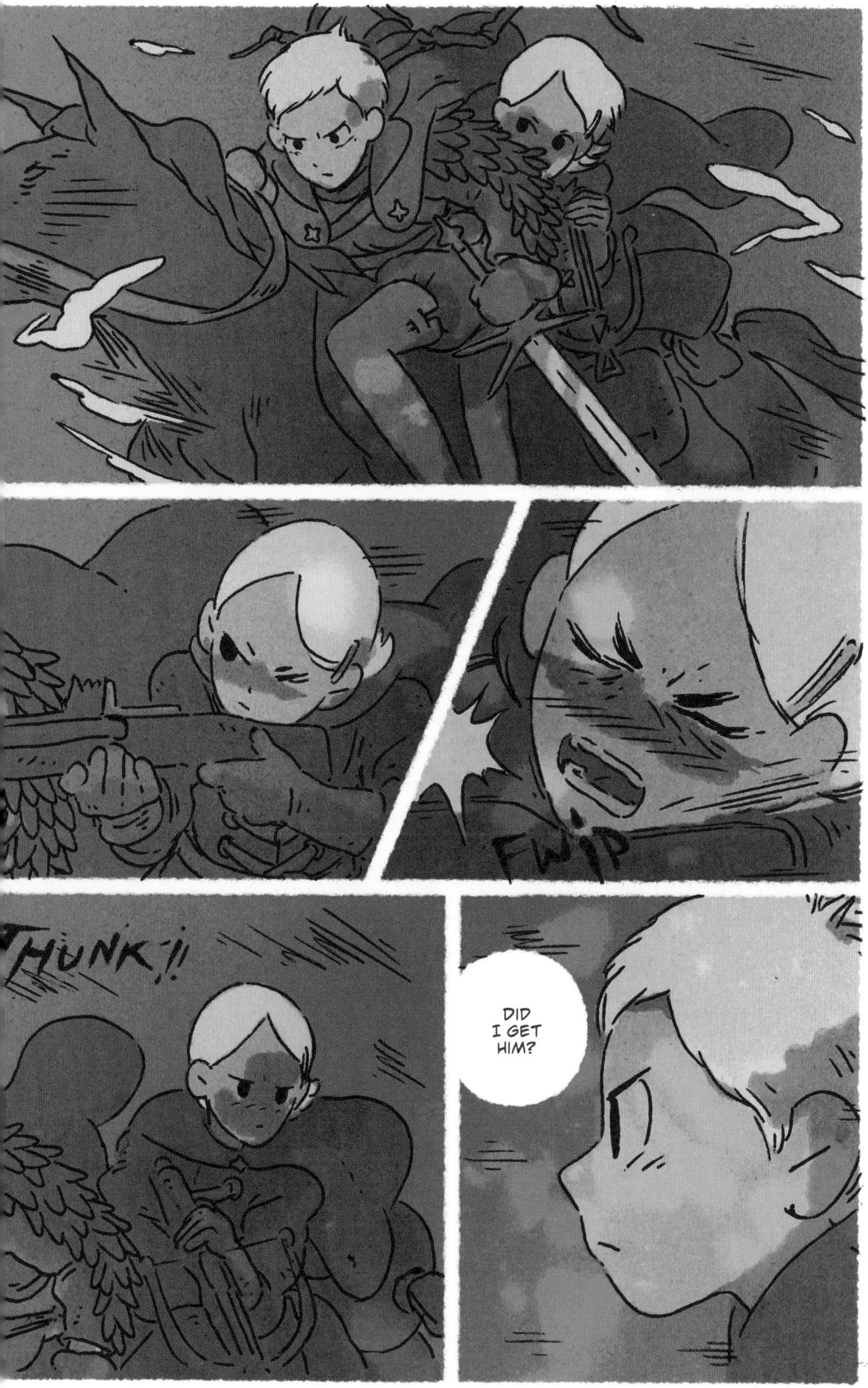
FWIP
THUNK!!
DID I GET HIM?

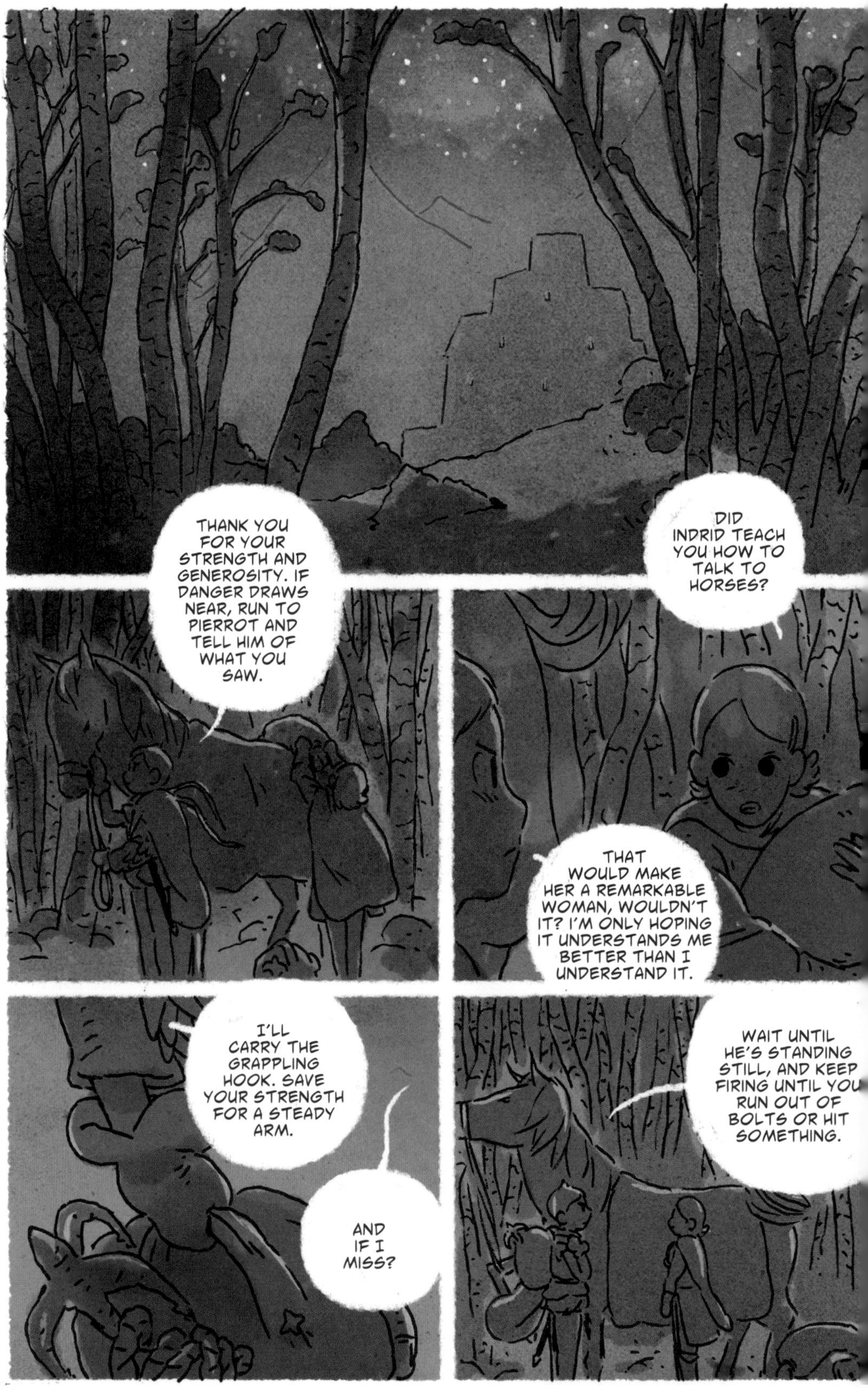
THANK YOU FOR YOUR STRENGTH AND GENEROSITY. IF DANGER DRAWS NEAR, RUN TO PIERROT AND TELL HIM OF WHAT YOU SAW.
DID INDRID TEACH YOU HOW TO TALK TO HORSES?
THAT WOULD MAKE HER A REMARKABLE WOMAN, WOULDN'T IT? I'M ONLY HOPING IT UNDERSTANDS ME BETTER THAN I UNDERSTAND IT.
I'LL CARRY THE GRAPPLING HOOK. SAVE YOUR STRENGTH FOR A STEADY ARM.
AND IF I MISS?
WAIT UNTIL HE'S STANDING STILL, AND KEEP FIRING UNTIL YOU RUN OUT OF BOLTS OR HIT SOMETHING.

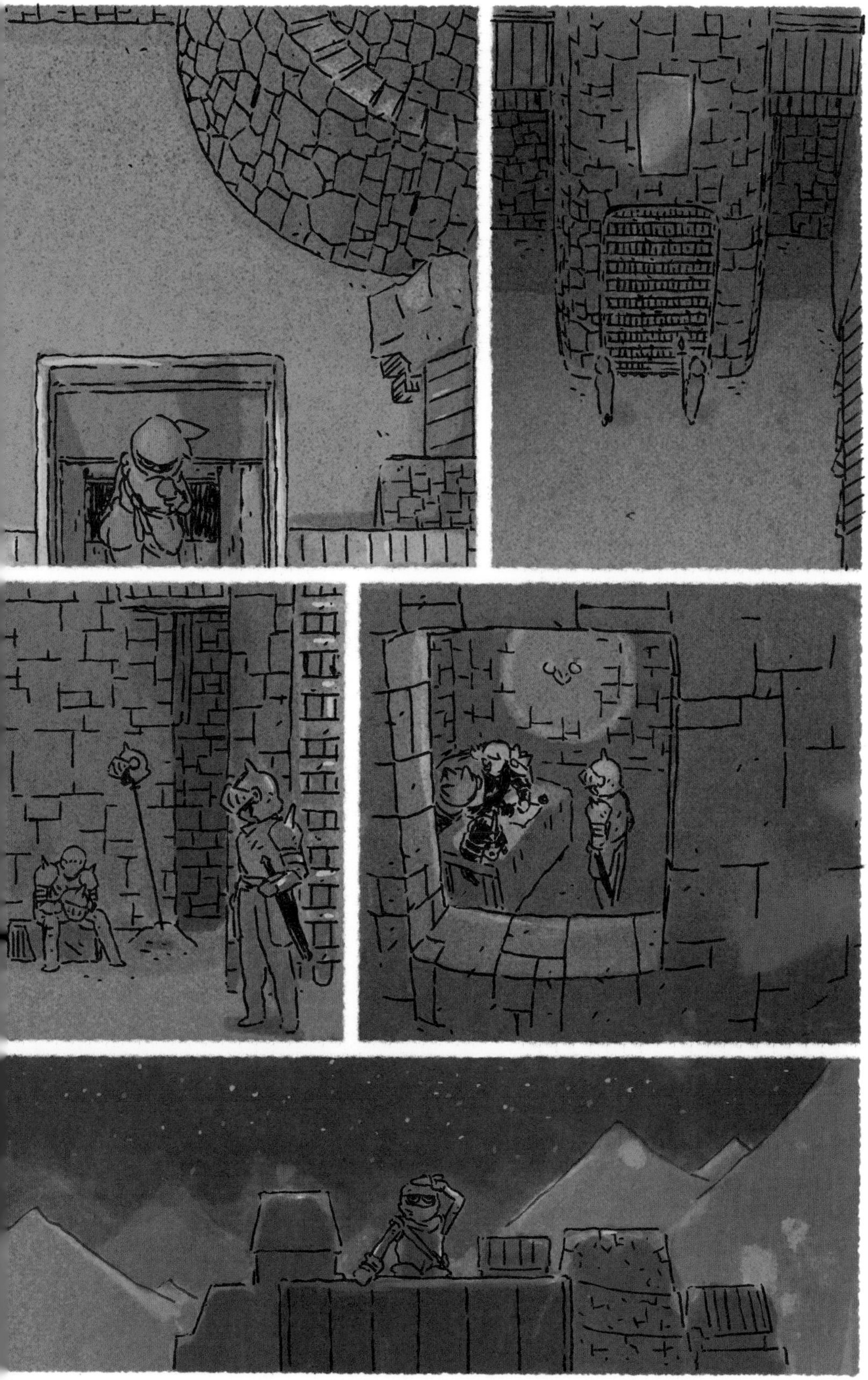

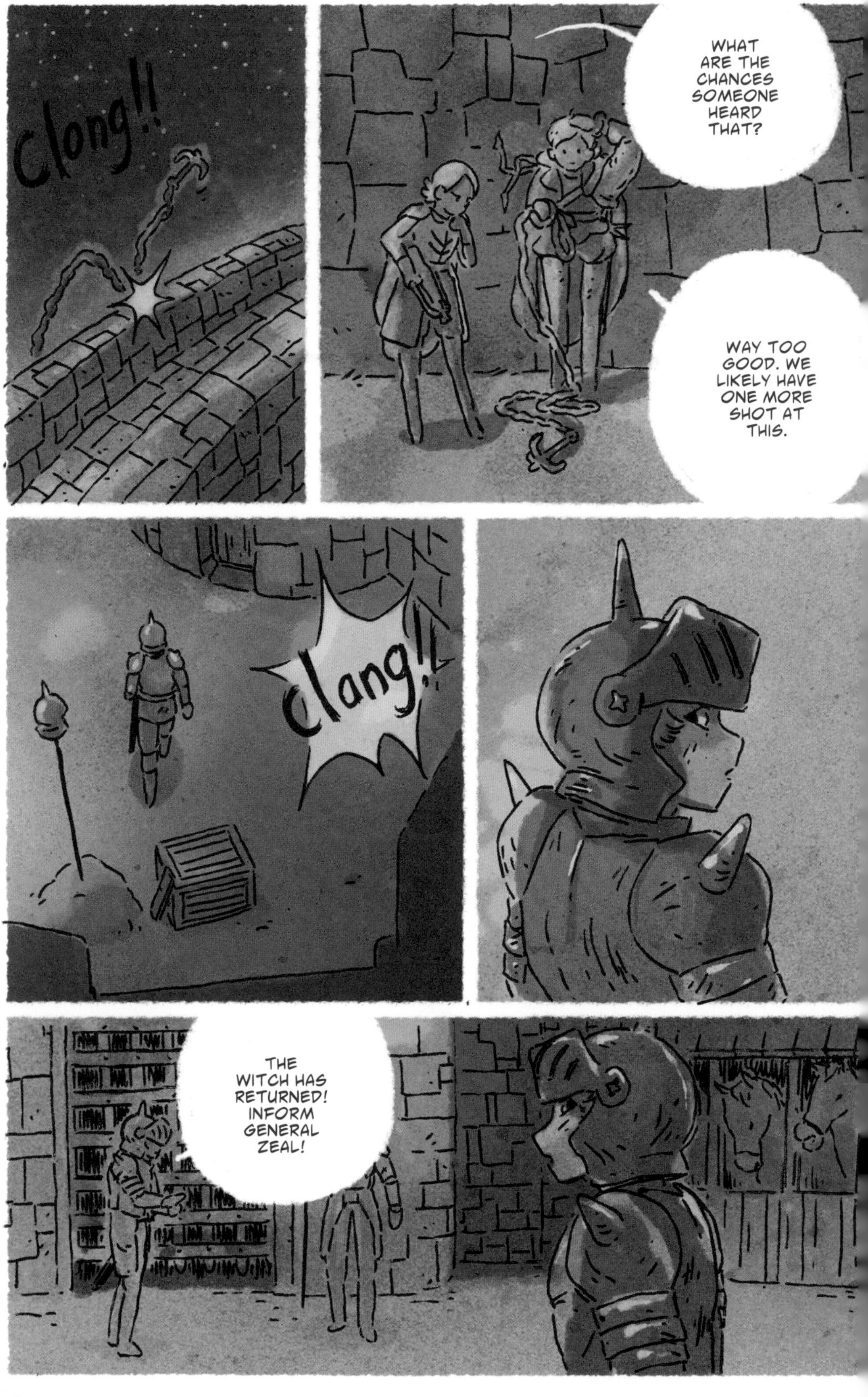
clong!!
WHAT ARE THE CHANCES SOMEONE HEARD THAT?
WAY TOO GOOD. WE LIKELY HAVE ONE MORE SHOT AT THIS.
clang!!
THE WITCH HAS RETURNED! INFORM GENERAL ZEAL!

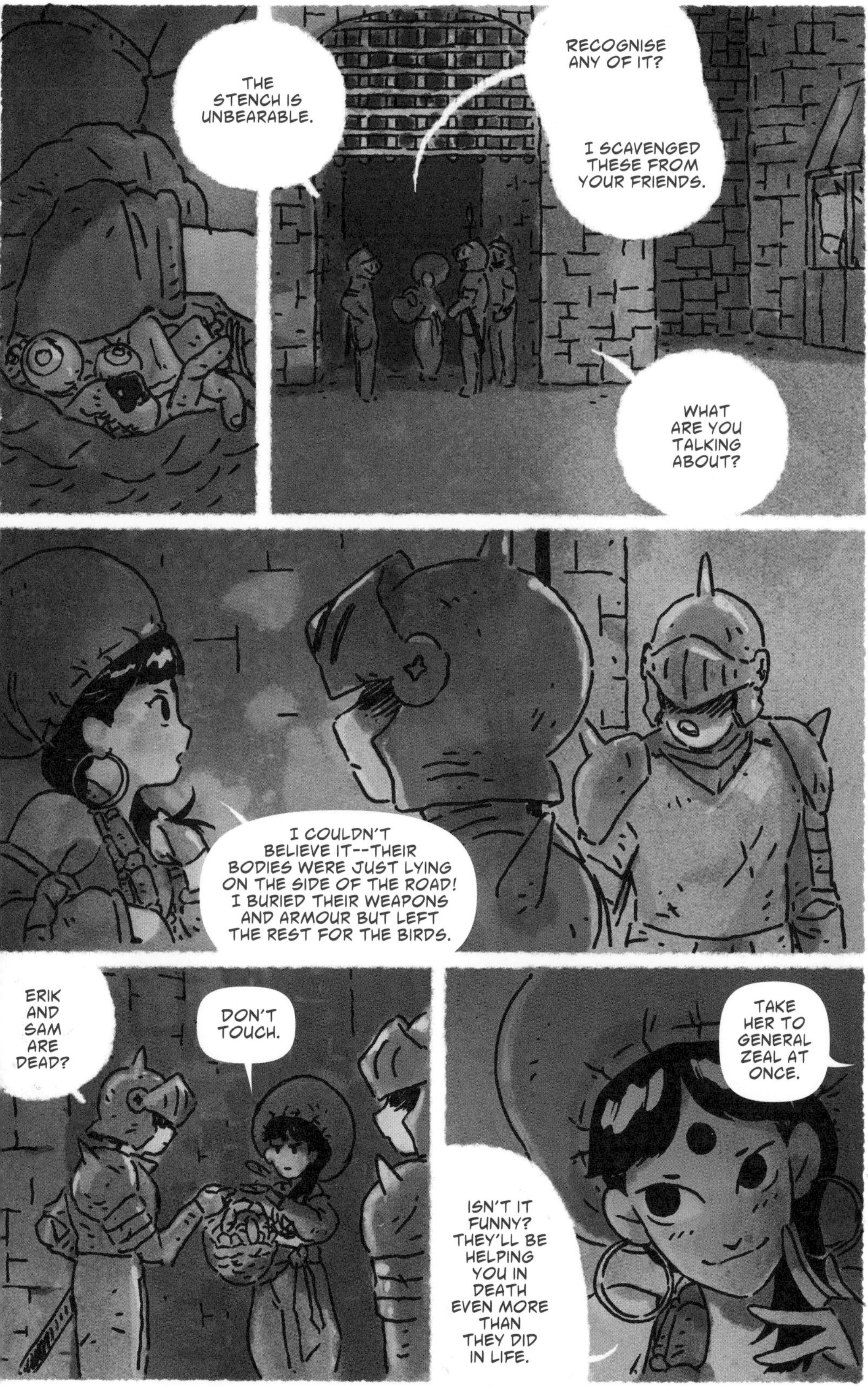
THE STENCH IS UNBEARABLE.
RECOGNISE ANY OF IT?
I SCAVENGED THESE FROM YOUR FRIENDS.
WHAT ARE YOU TALKING ABOUT?
I COULDN'T BELIEVE IT--THEIR BODIES WERE JUST LYING ON THE SIDE OF THE ROAD! I BURIED THEIR WEAPONS AND ARMOUR BUT LEFT THE REST FOR THE BIRDS.
ERIK AND SAM ARE DEAD?
DON'T TOUCH.
TAKE HER TO GENERAL ZEAL AT ONCE.
ISN'T IT FUNNY? THEY'LL BE HELPING YOU IN DEATH EVEN MORE THAN THEY DID IN LIFE.

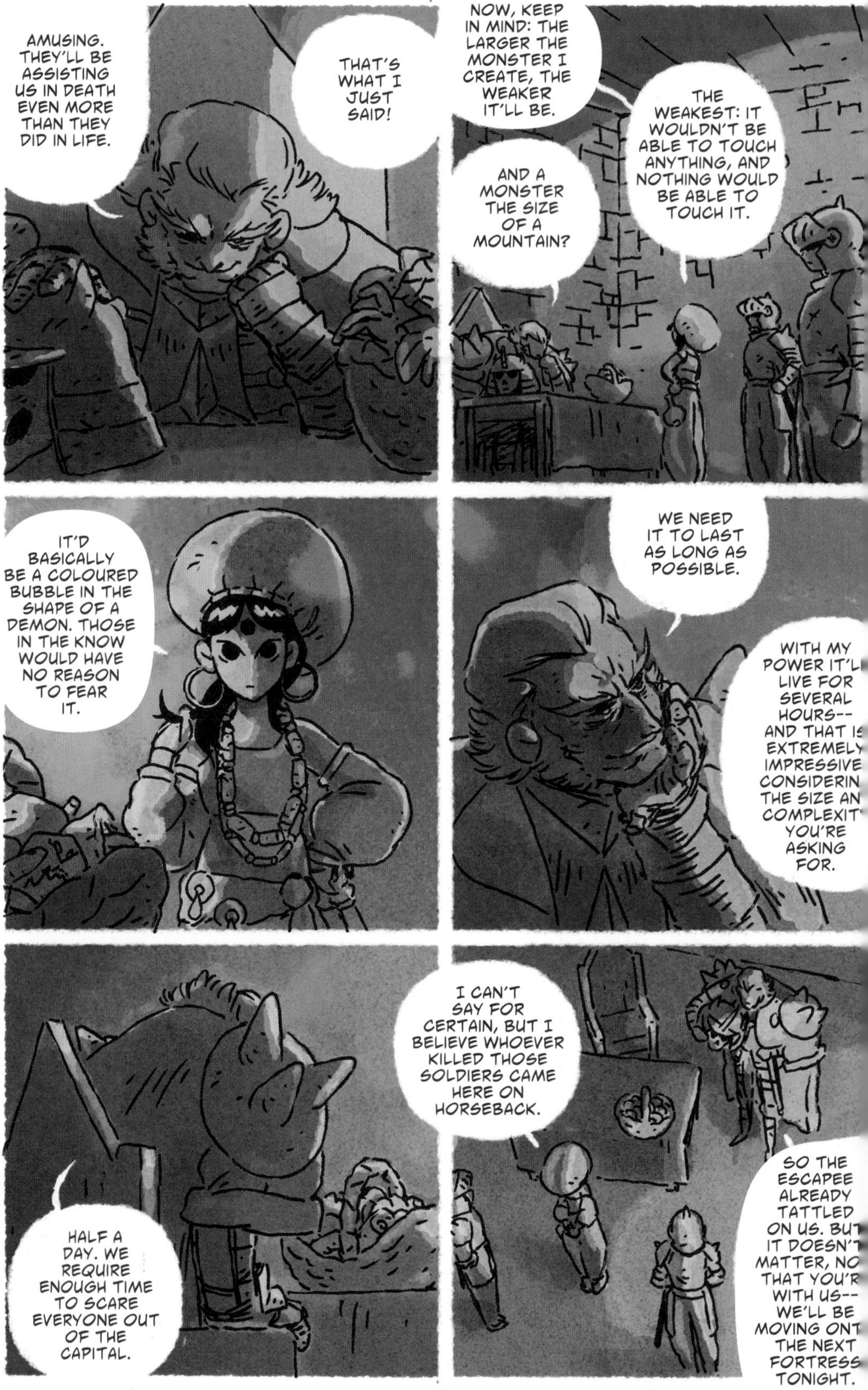
AMUSING. THEY'LL BE ASSISTING US IN DEATH EVEN MORE THAN THEY DID IN LIFE.
THAT'S WHAT I JUST SAID!
NOW, KEEP IN MIND: THE LARGER THE MONSTER I CREATE, THE WEAKER IT'LL BE.
AND A MONSTER THE SIZE OF A MOUNTAIN?
THE WEAKEST: IT WOULDN'T BE ABLE TO TOUCH ANYTHING, AND NOTHING WOULD BE ABLE TO TOUCH IT.
IT'D BASICALLY BE A COLOURED BUBBLE IN THE SHAPE OF A DEMON. THOSE IN THE KNOW WOULD HAVE NO REASON TO FEAR IT.
WE NEED IT TO LAST AS LONG AS POSSIBLE.
HALF A DAY. WE REQUIRE ENOUGH TIME TO SCARE EVERYONE OUT OF THE CAPITAL.
I CAN'T SAY FOR CERTAIN, BUT I BELIEVE WHOEVER KILLED THOSE SOLDIERS CAME HERE ON HORSEBACK.

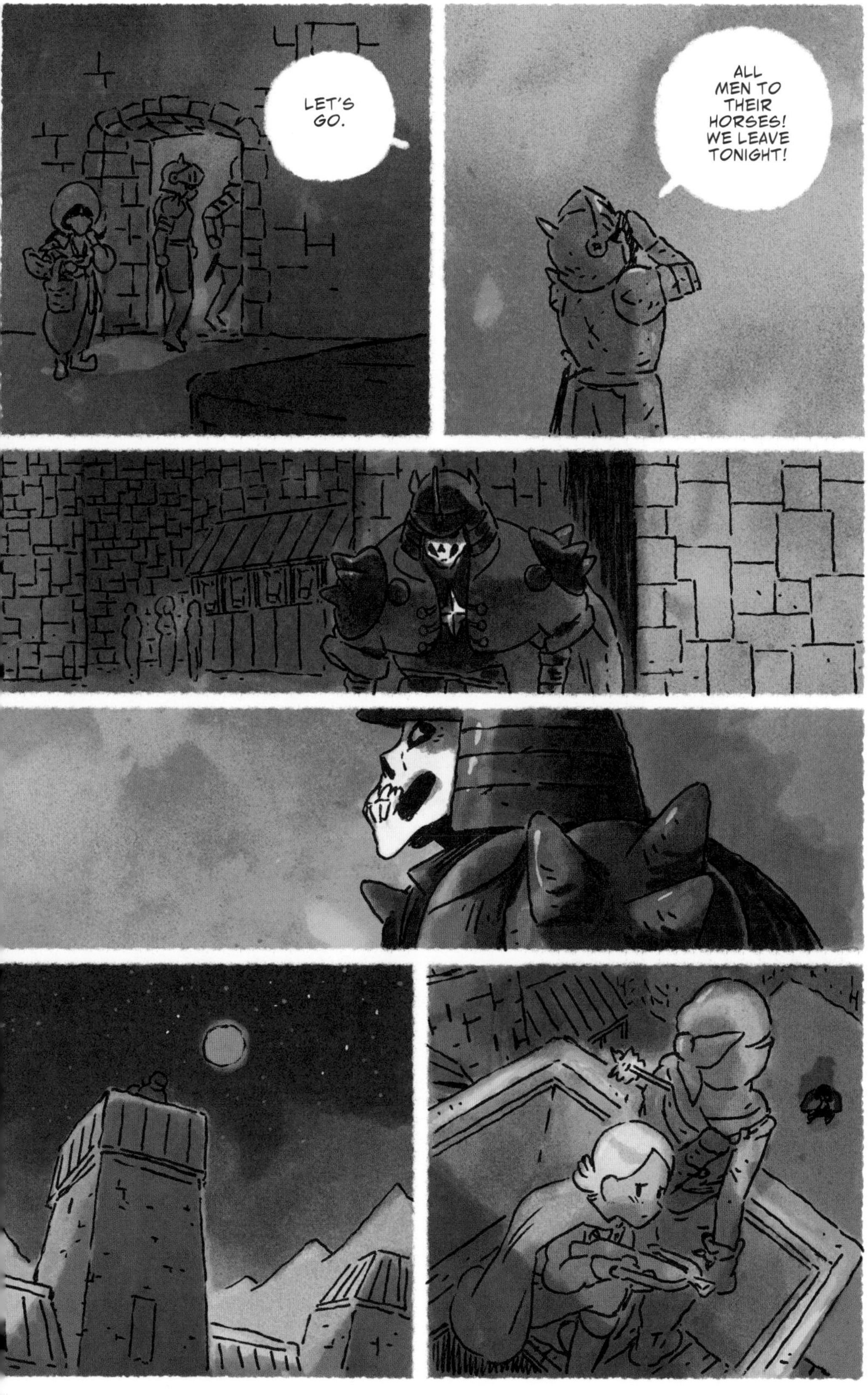
LET'S GO.
ALL MEN TO THEIR HORSES! WE LEAVE TONIGHT!

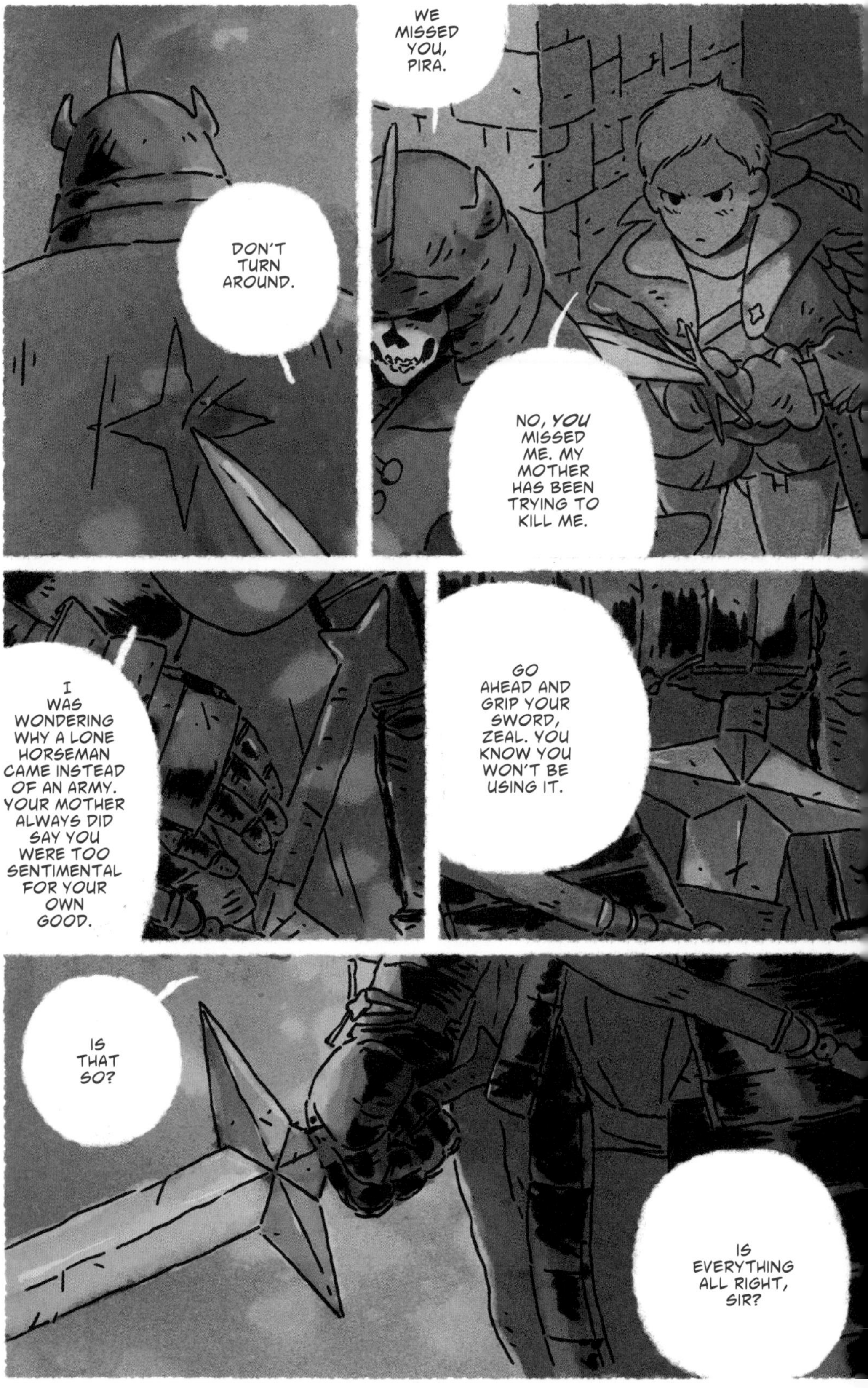
DON'T TURN AROUND.
WE MISSED YOU, PIRA.
NO, *YOU* MISSED ME. MY MOTHER HAS BEEN TRYING TO KILL ME.
I WAS WONDERING WHY A LONE HORSEMAN CAME INSTEAD OF AN ARMY. YOUR MOTHER ALWAYS DID SAY YOU WERE TOO SENTIMENTAL FOR YOUR OWN GOOD.
GO AHEAD AND GRIP YOUR SWORD, ZEAL. YOU KNOW YOU WON'T BE USING IT.
IS THAT SO?
IS EVERYTHING ALL RIGHT, SIR?

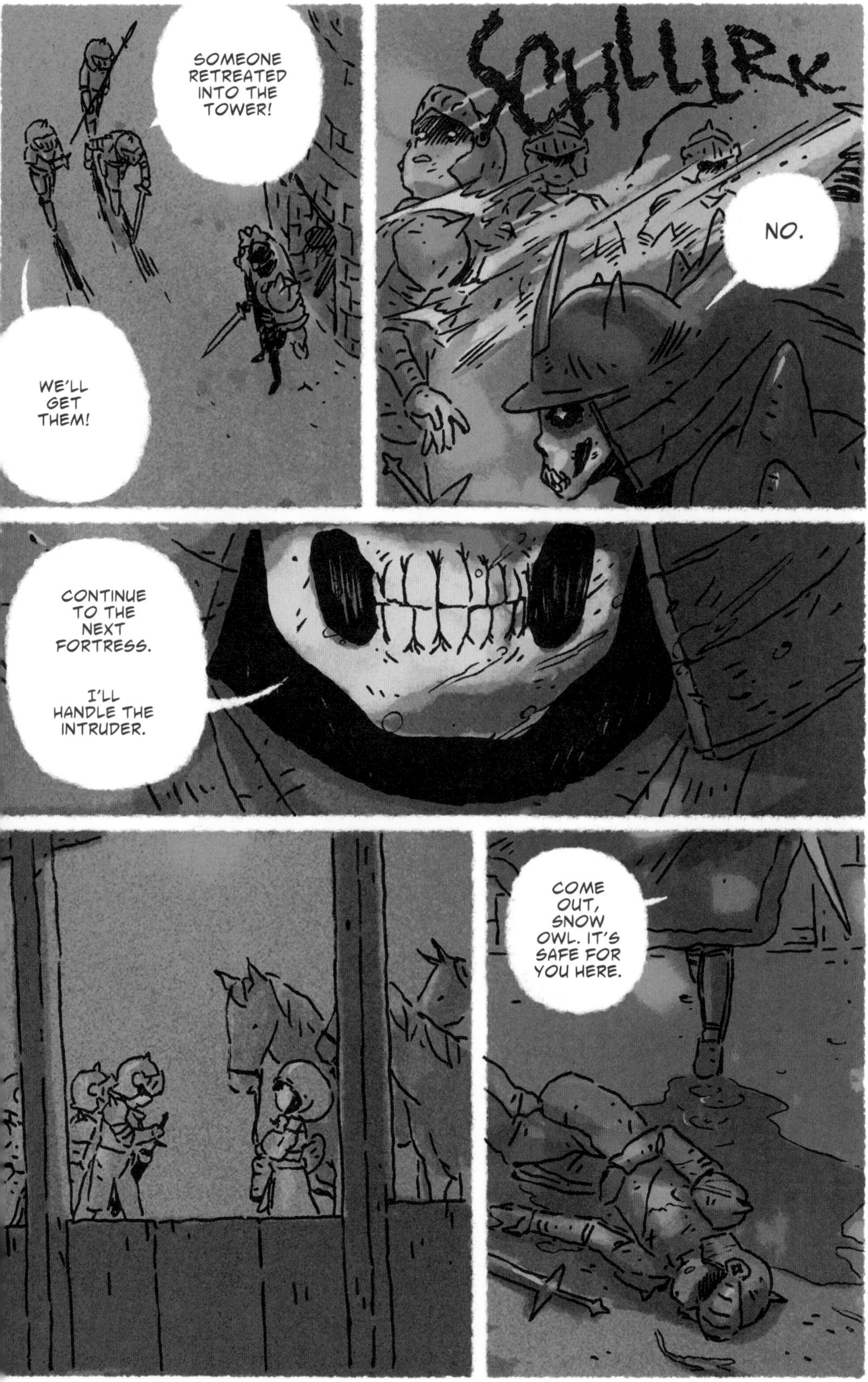
SOMEONE RETREATED INTO THE TOWER!
WE'LL GET THEM!
SCHLLRK
NO.
CONTINUE TO THE NEXT FORTRESS.
I'LL HANDLE THE INTRUDER.
COME OUT, SNOW OWL. IT'S SAFE FOR YOU HERE.

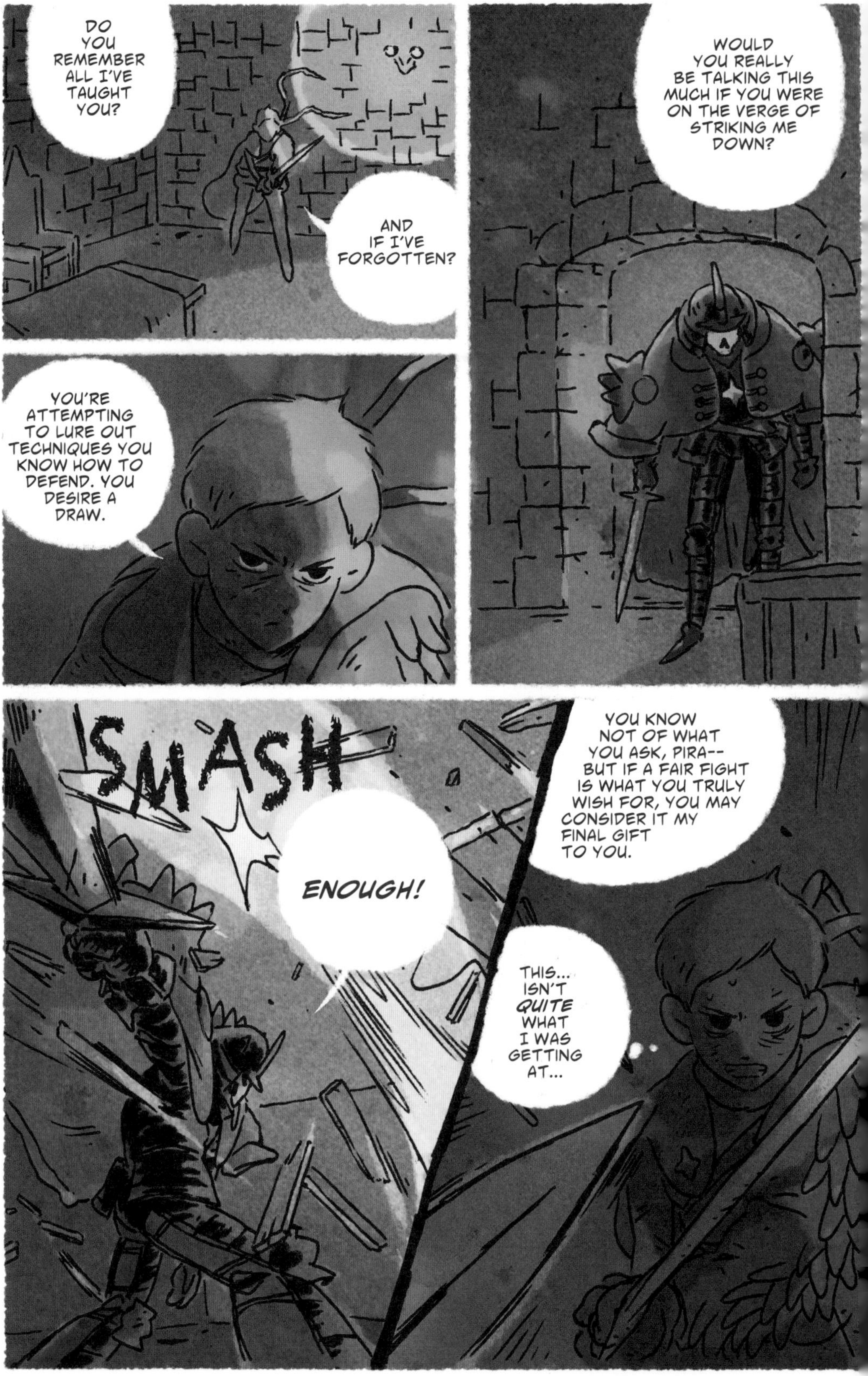
DO YOU REMEMBER ALL I'VE TAUGHT YOU?
AND IF I'VE FORGOTTEN?
WOULD YOU REALLY BE TALKING THIS MUCH IF YOU WERE ON THE VERGE OF STRIKING ME DOWN?
YOU'RE ATTEMPTING TO LURE OUT TECHNIQUES YOU KNOW HOW TO DEFEND. YOU DESIRE A DRAW.
YOU KNOW NOT OF WHAT YOU ASK, PIRA-- BUT IF A FAIR FIGHT IS WHAT YOU TRULY WISH FOR, YOU MAY CONSIDER IT MY FINAL GIFT TO YOU.
SMASH
ENOUGH!
THIS... ISN'T QUITE WHAT I WAS GETTING AT...

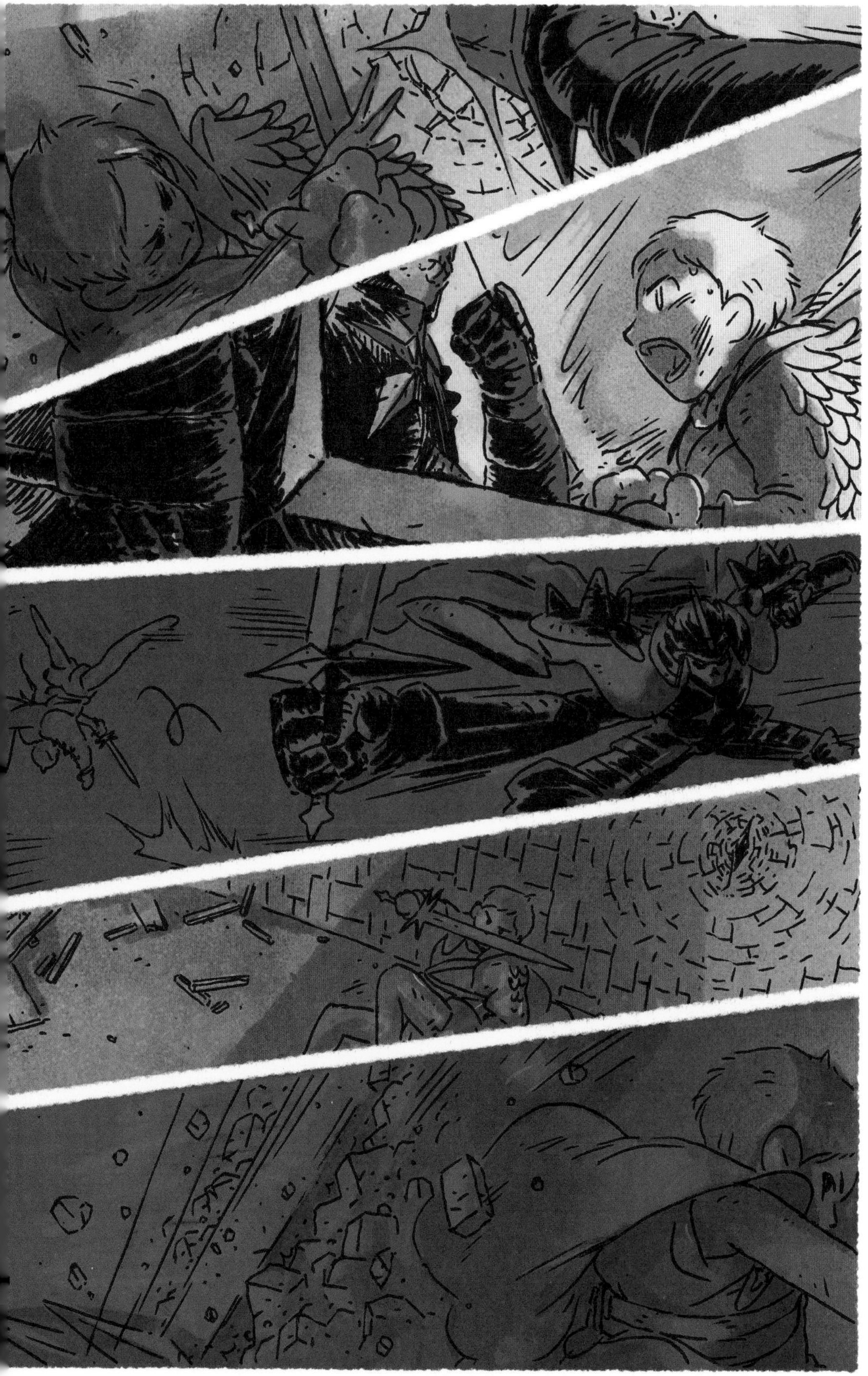

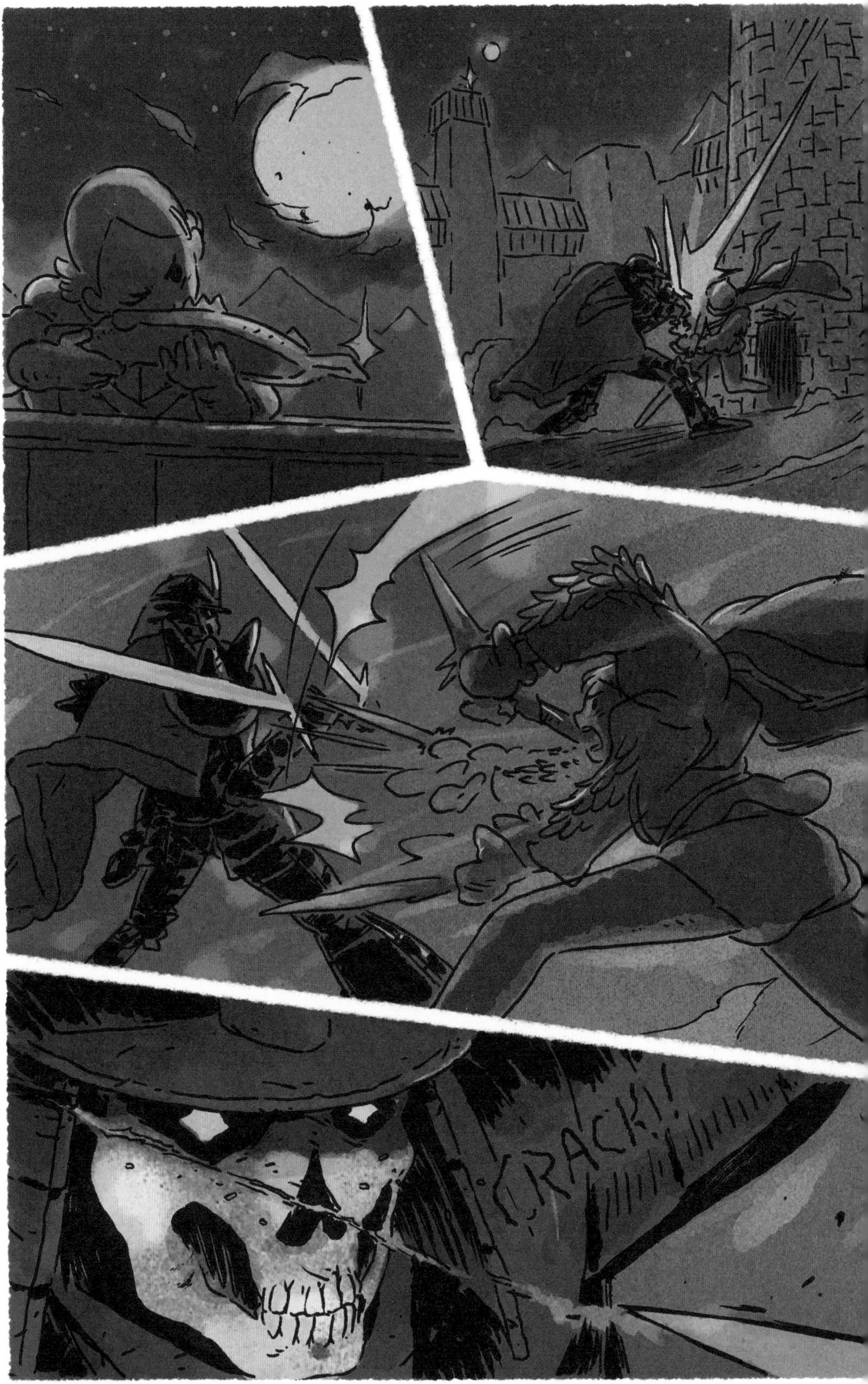
CRACK!

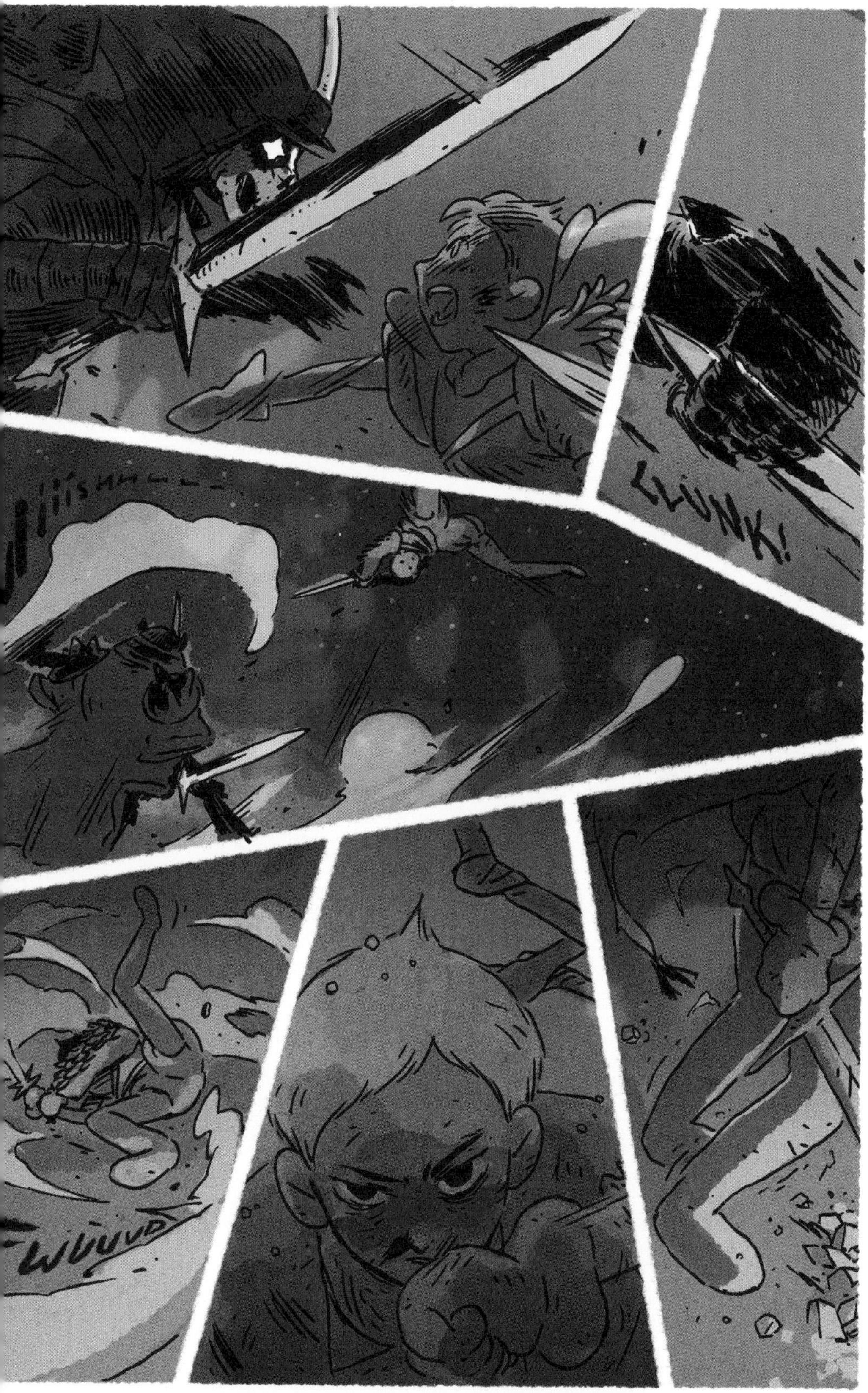
LLUNK!
IIISHH---
WUUUD

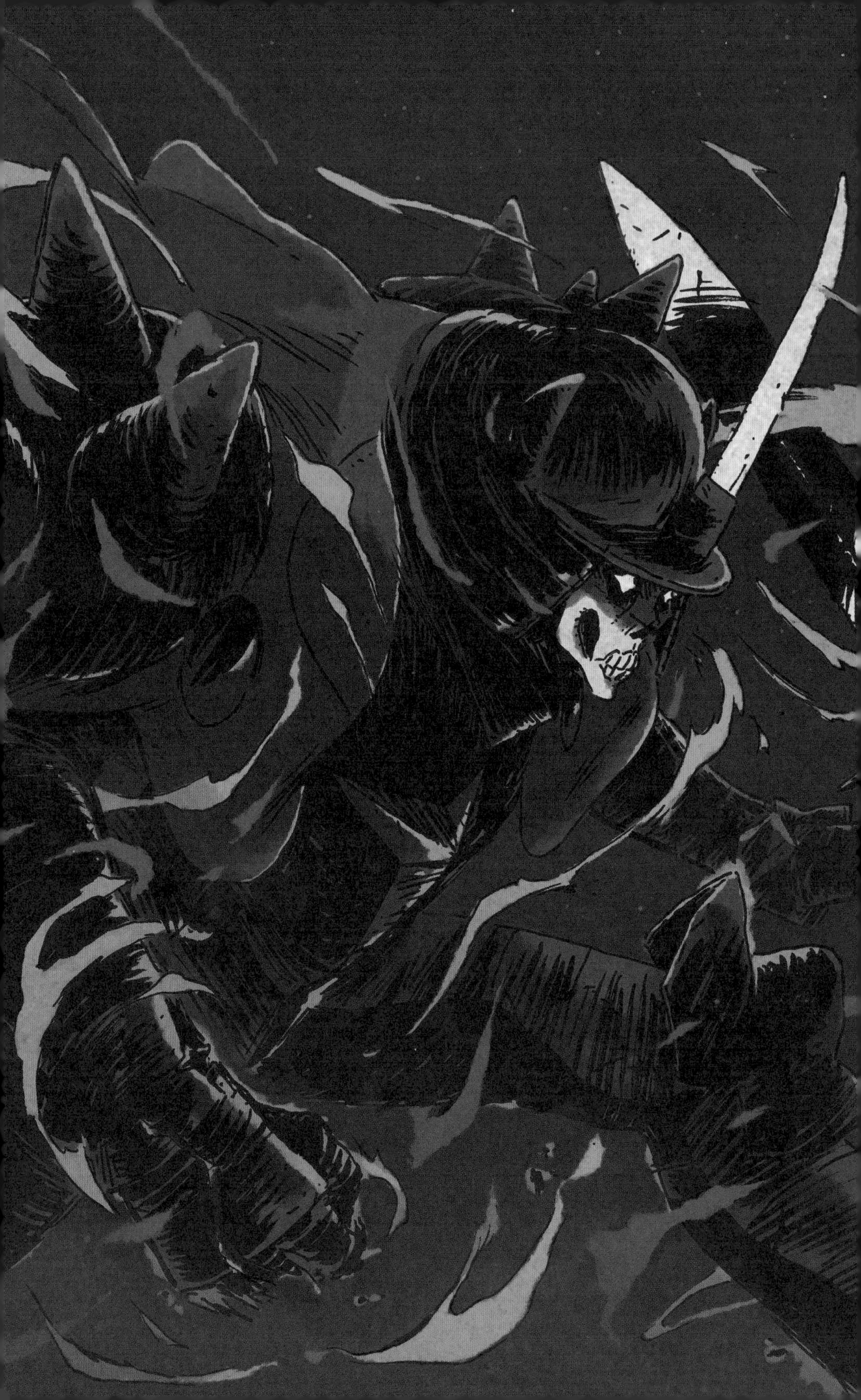

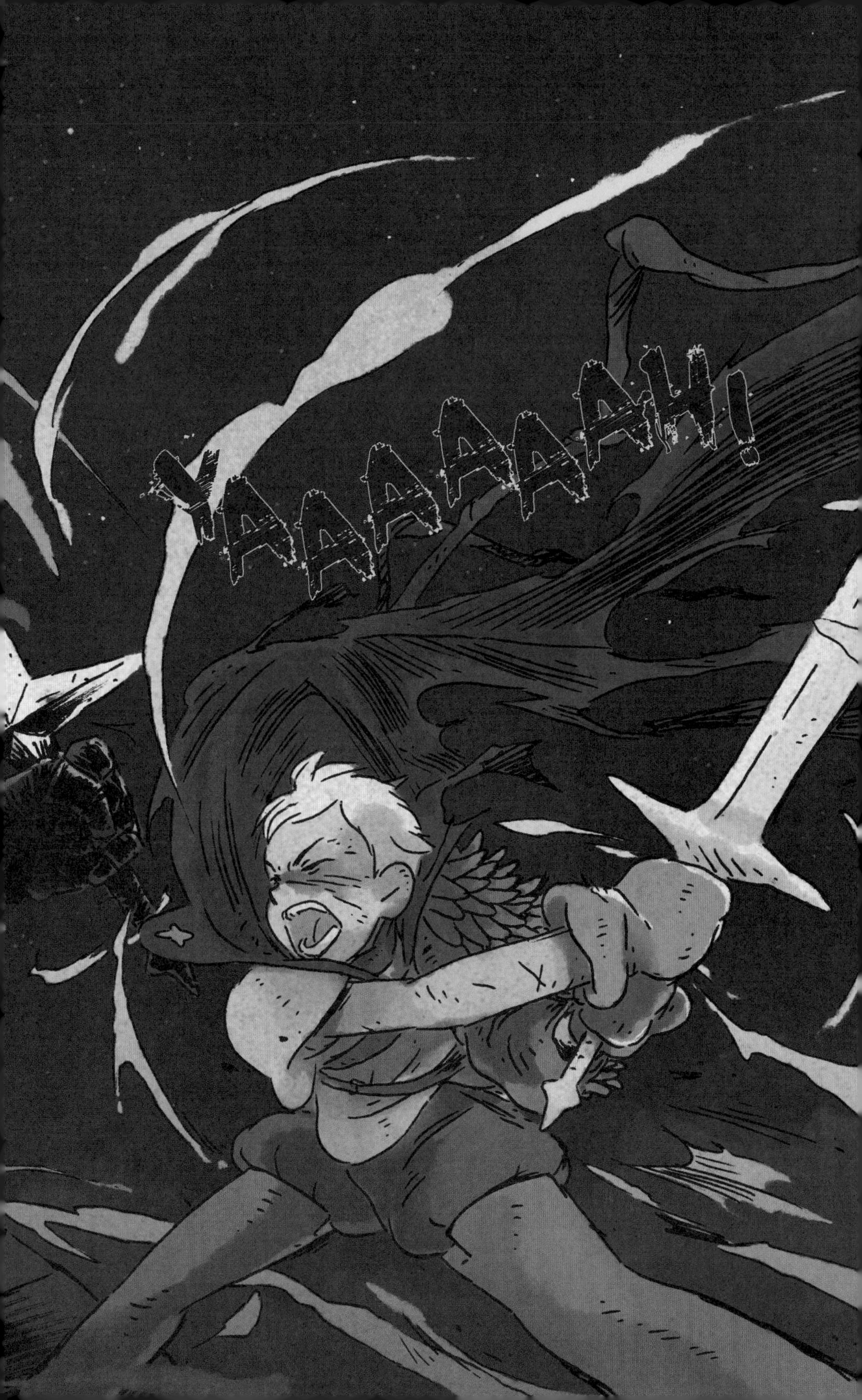
YAAAAAAH!

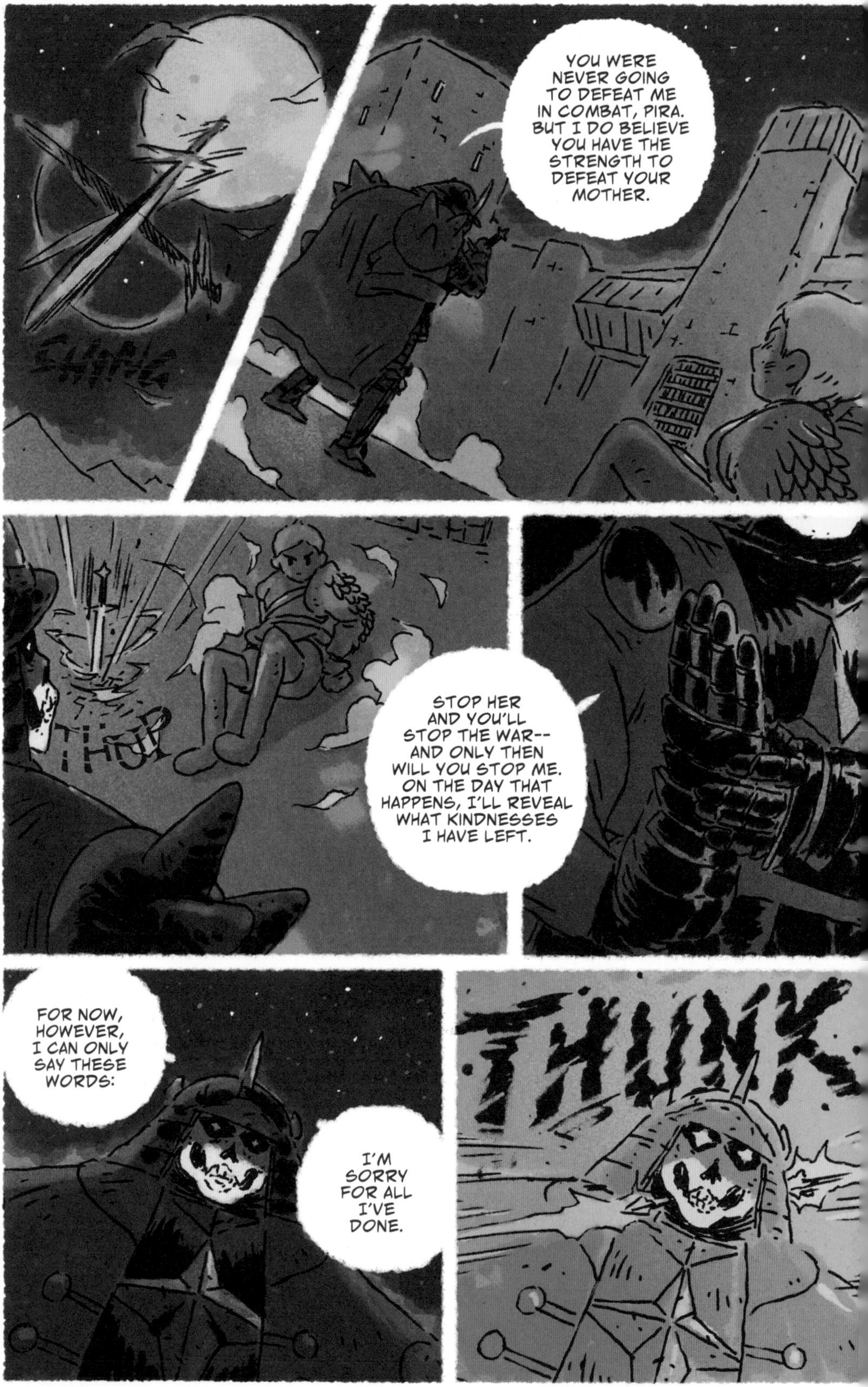
SHING
YOU WERE NEVER GOING TO DEFEAT ME IN COMBAT, PIRA. BUT I DO BELIEVE YOU HAVE THE STRENGTH TO DEFEAT YOUR MOTHER.
THUD
STOP HER AND YOU'LL STOP THE WAR-- AND ONLY THEN WILL YOU STOP ME. ON THE DAY THAT HAPPENS, I'LL REVEAL WHAT KINDNESSES I HAVE LEFT.
FOR NOW, HOWEVER, I CAN ONLY SAY THESE WORDS:
I'M SORRY FOR ALL I'VE DONE.
THUNK

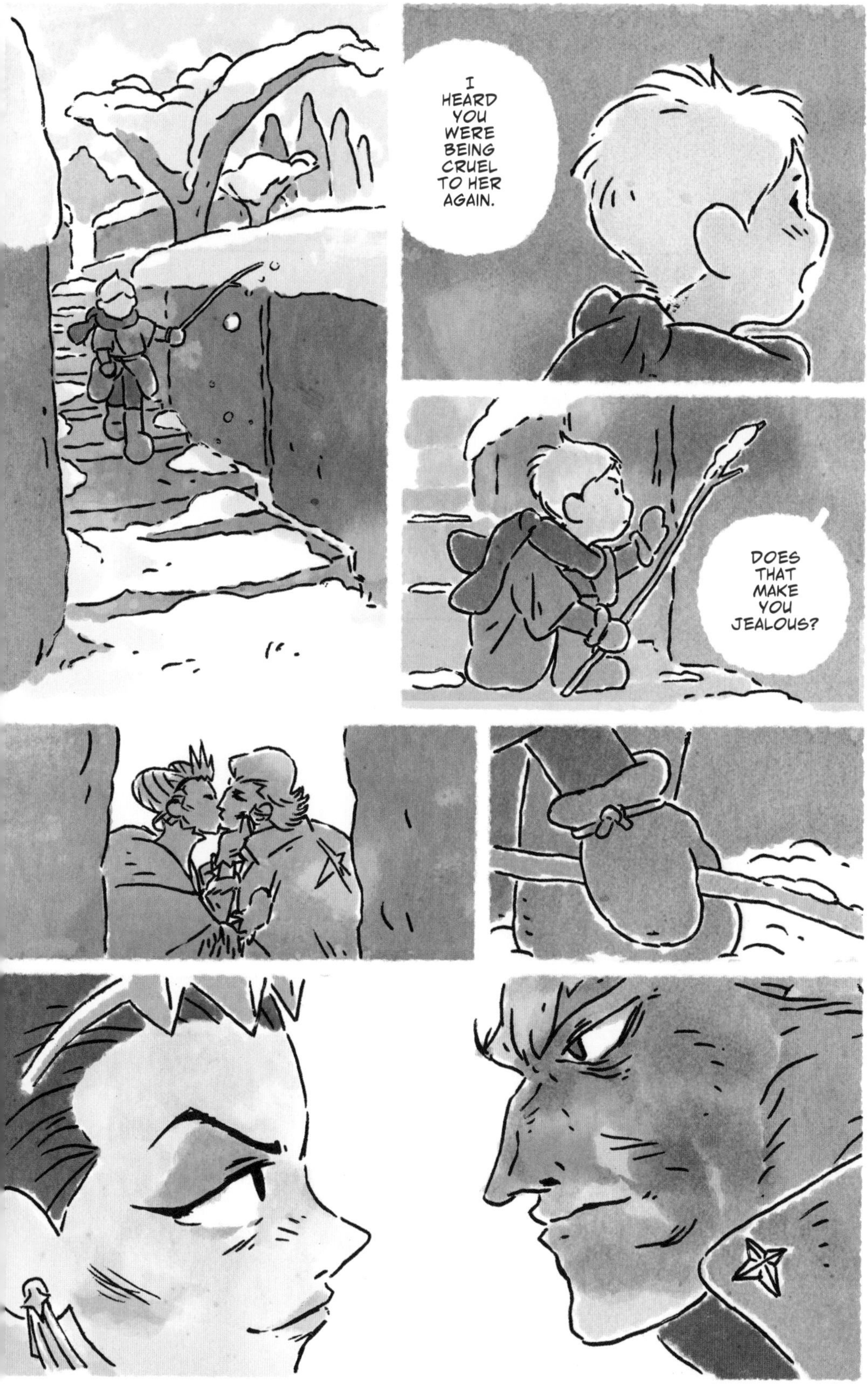
I HEARD YOU WERE BEING CRUEL TO HER AGAIN.
DOES THAT MAKE YOU JEALOUS?

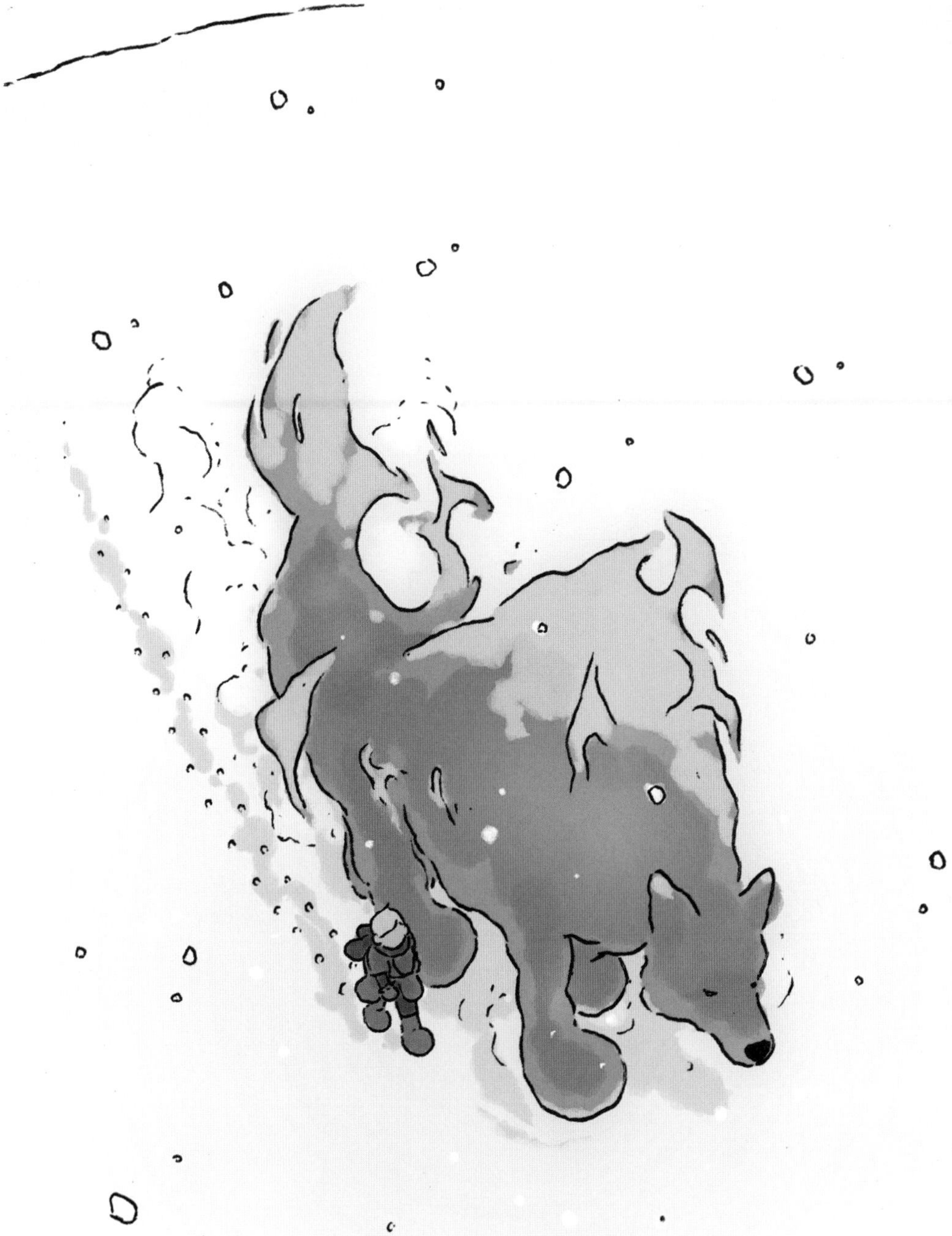

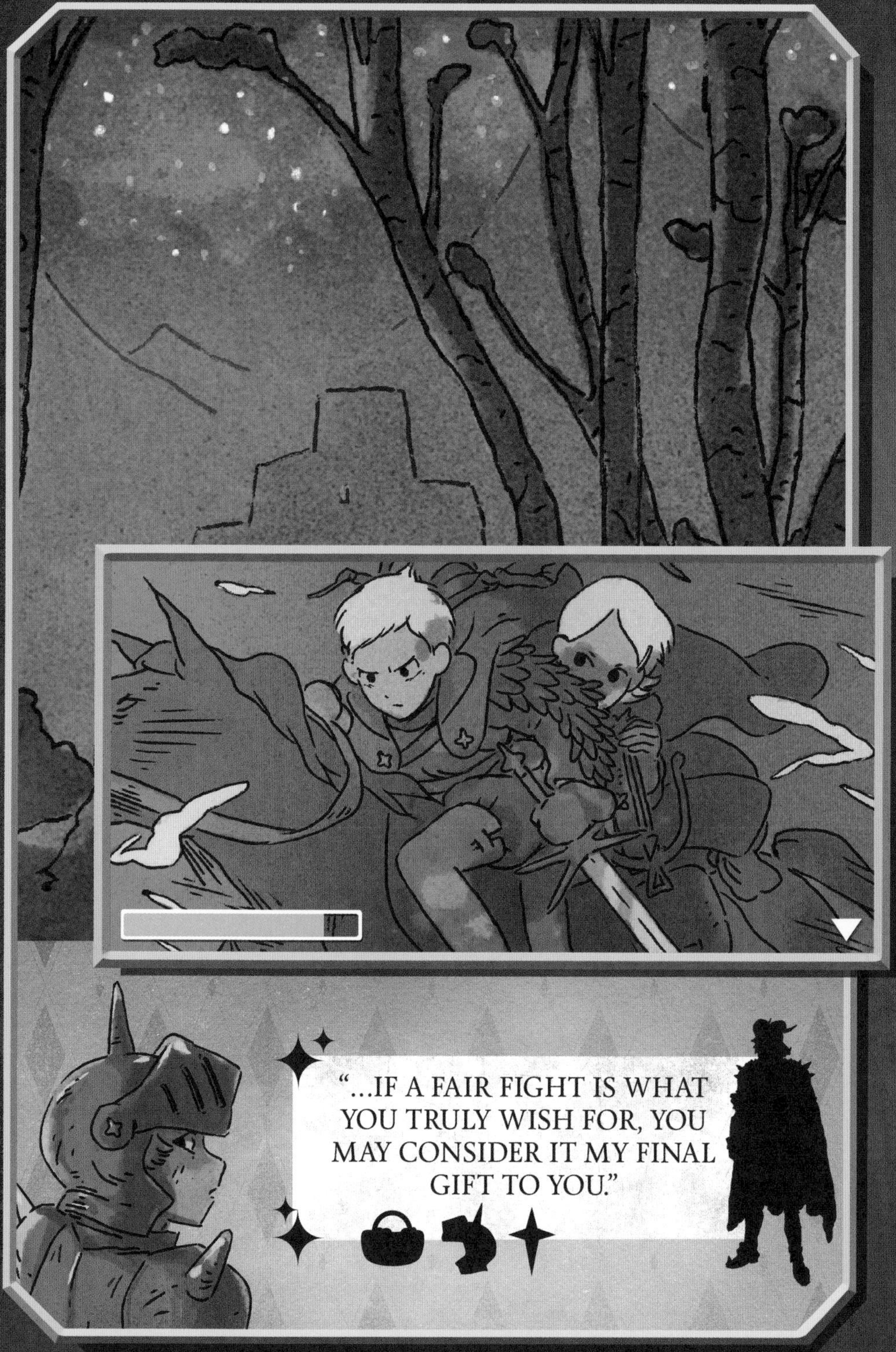
"...IF A FAIR FIGHT IS WHAT YOU TRULY WISH FOR, YOU MAY CONSIDER IT MY FINAL GIFT TO YOU."

SHORT STORIES
Table of Contents

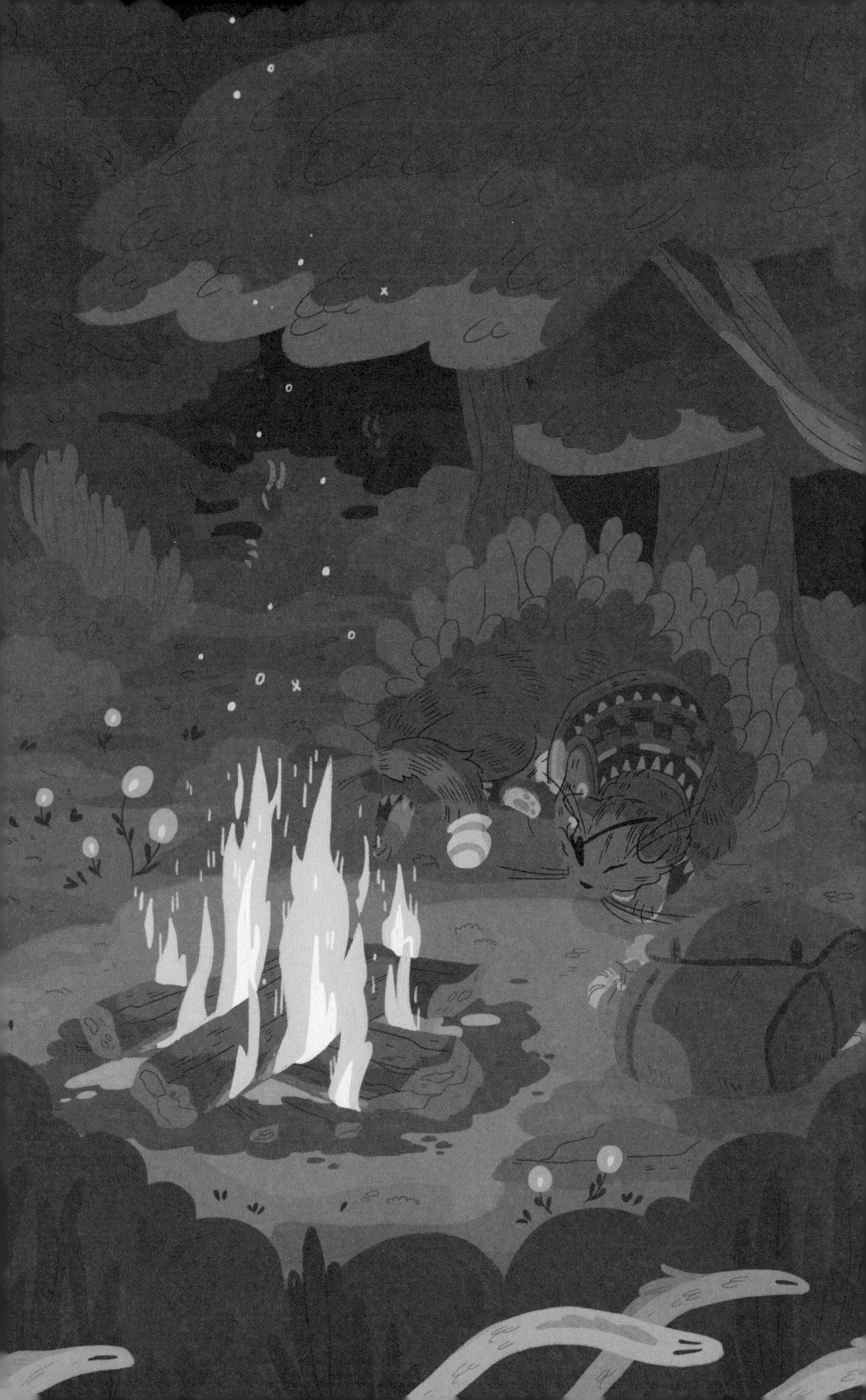

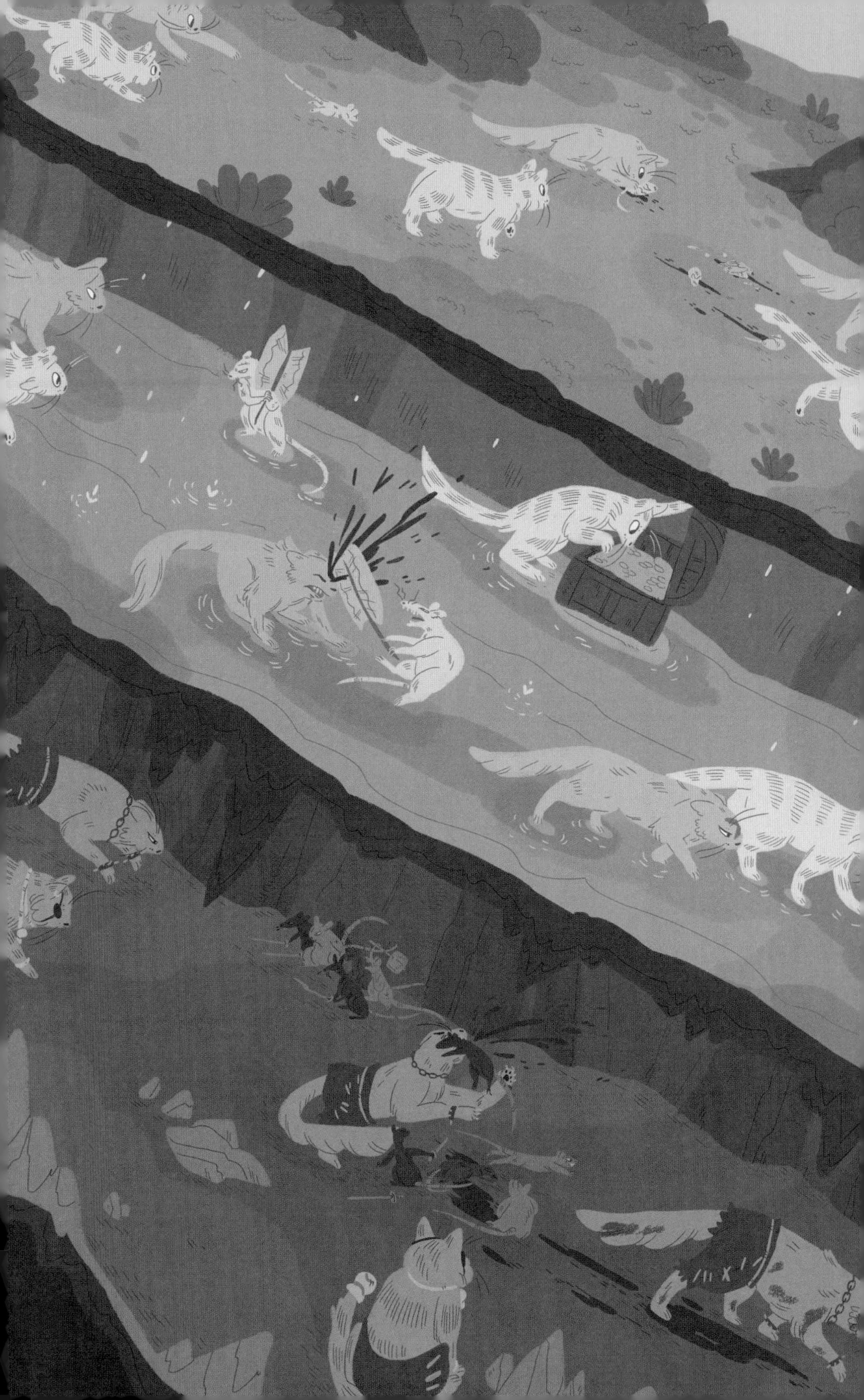

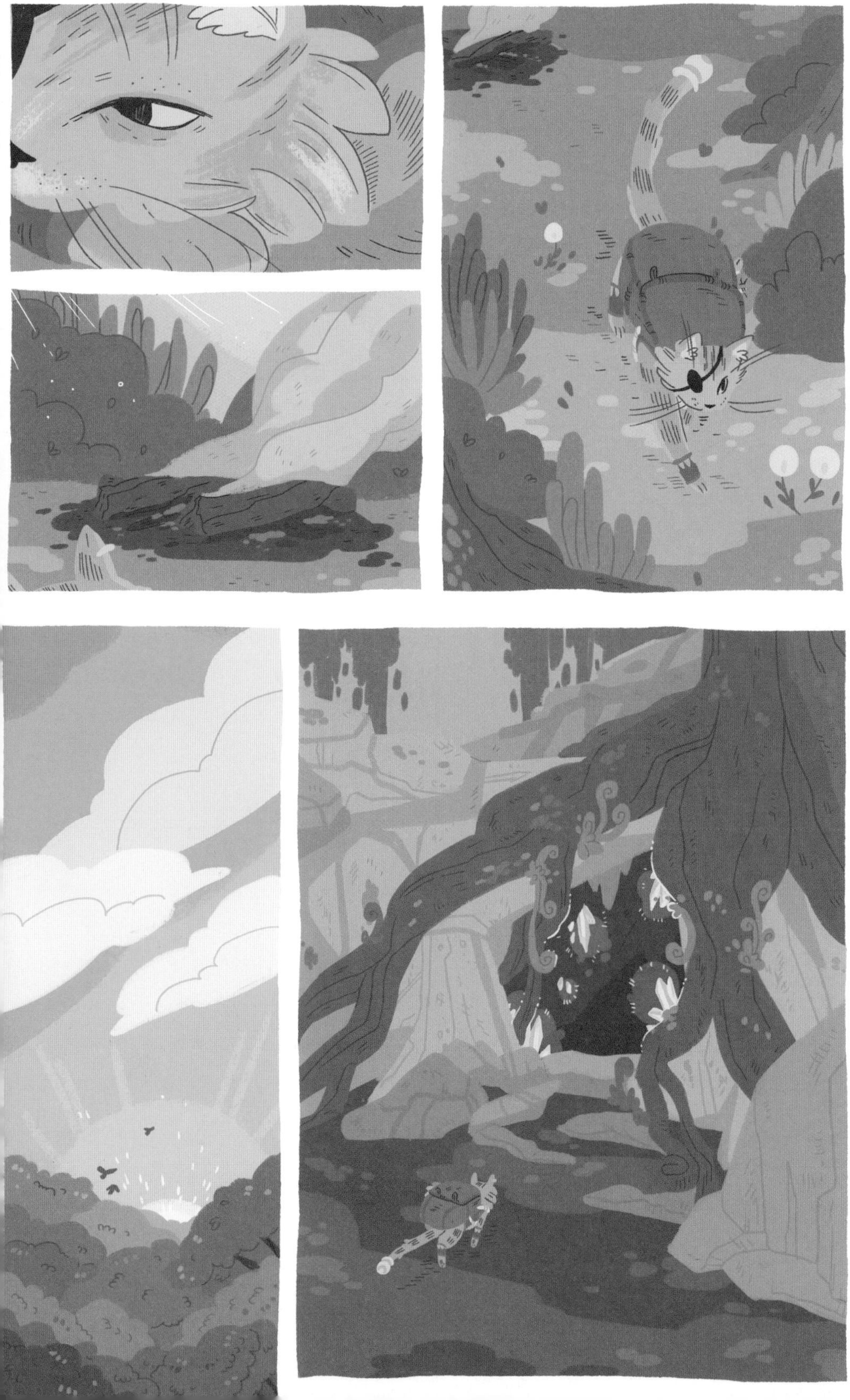

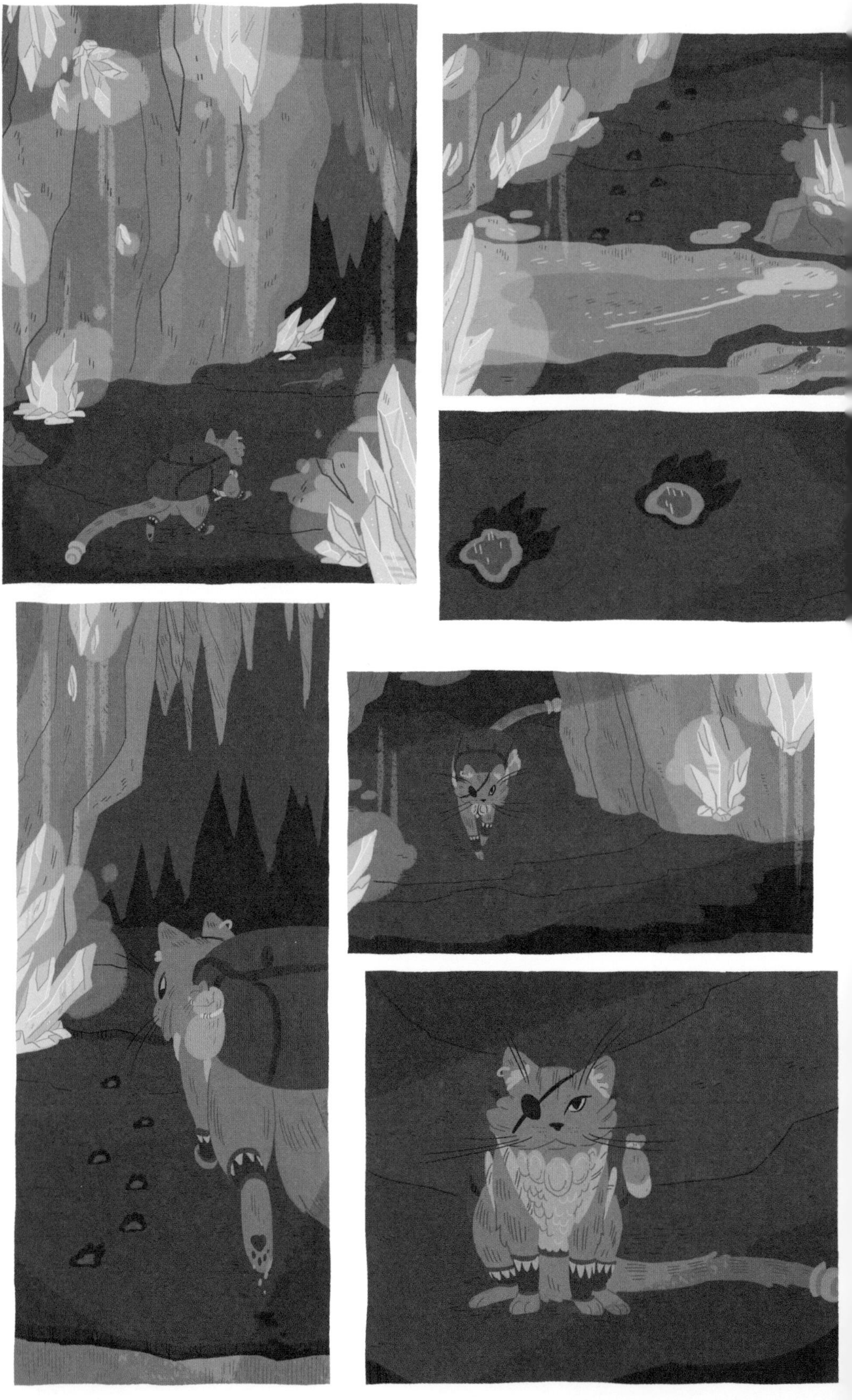

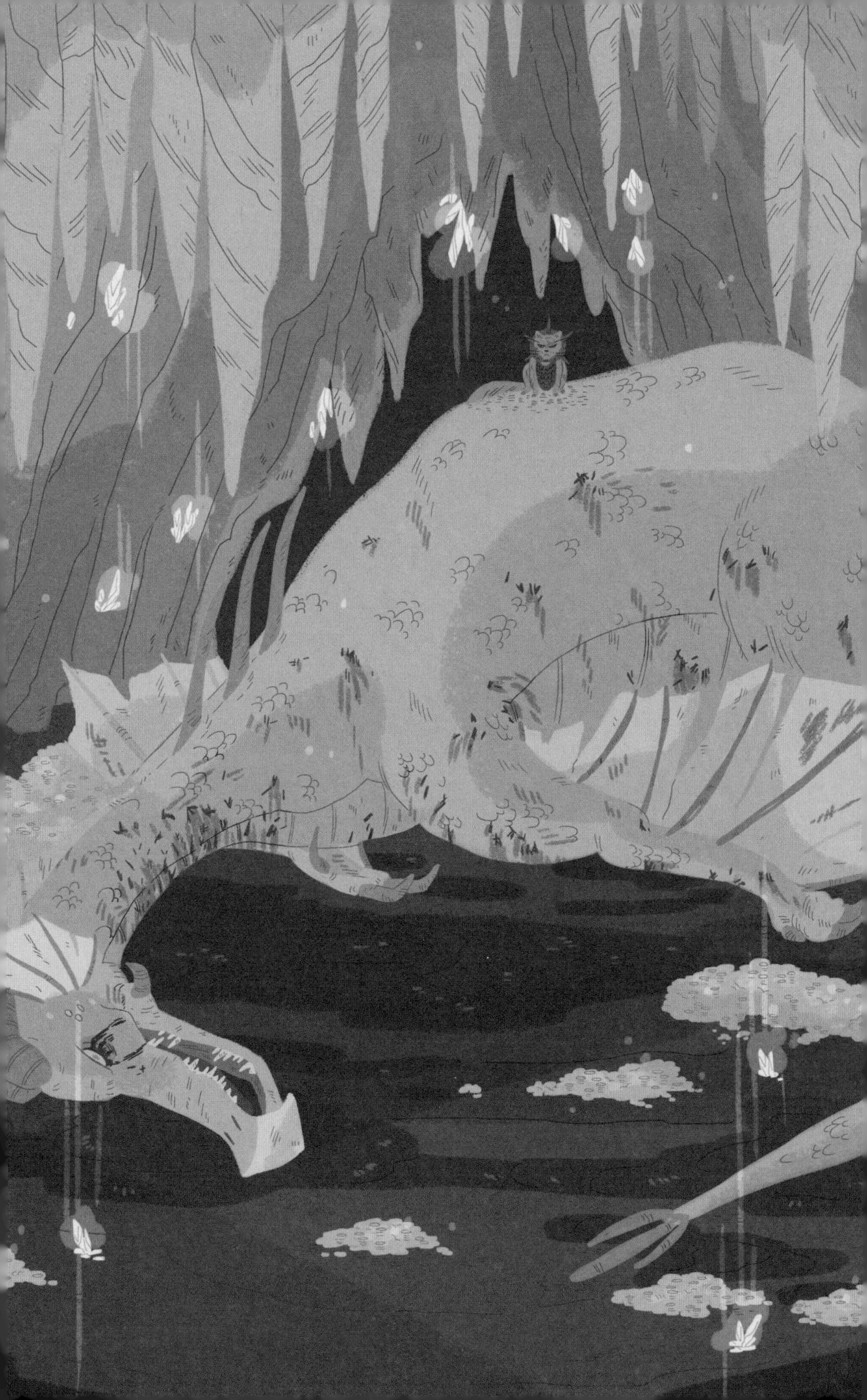

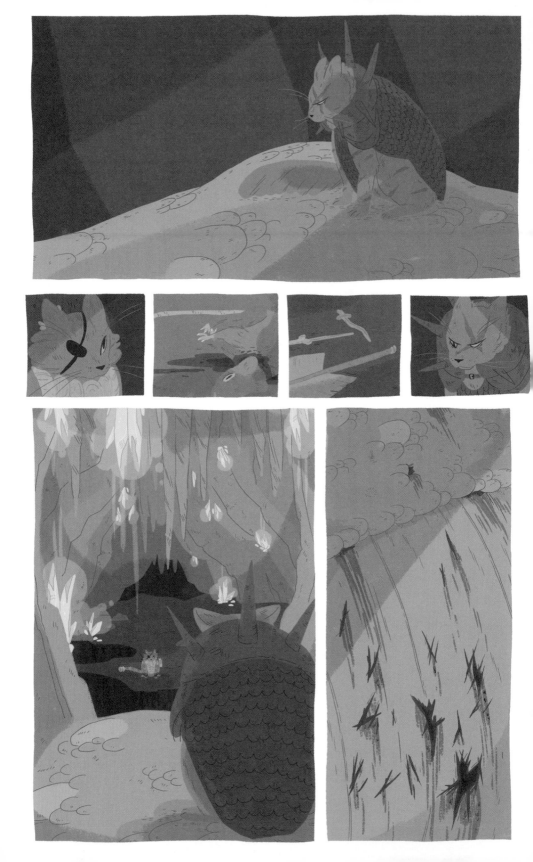

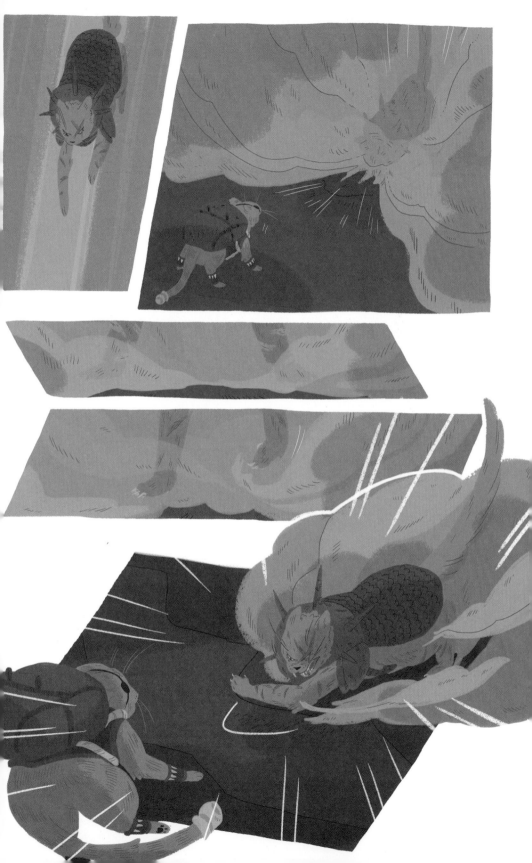

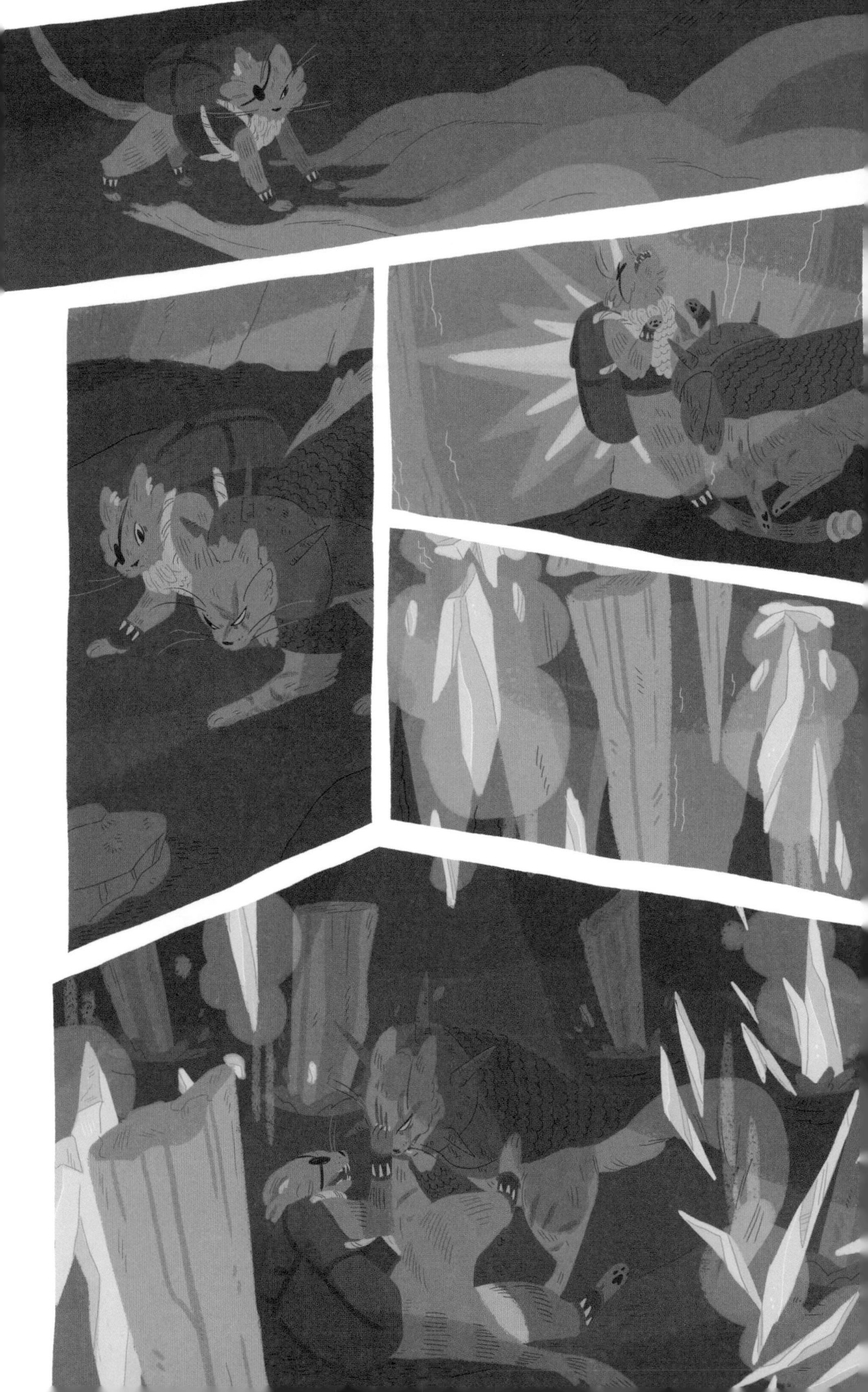

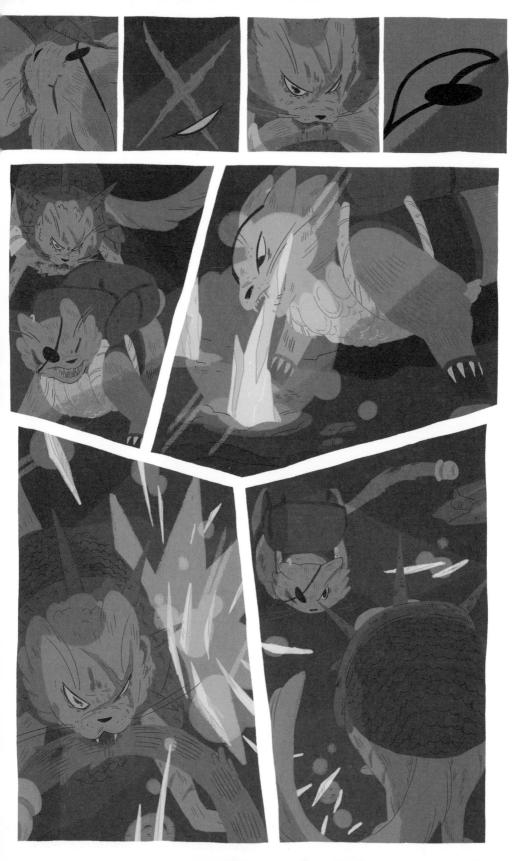

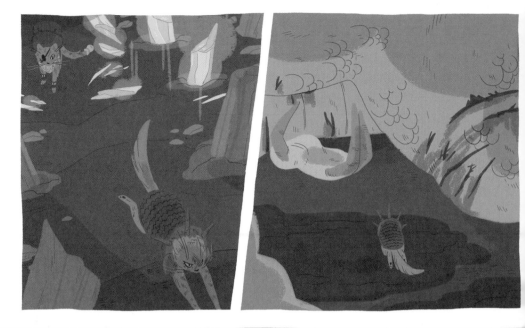

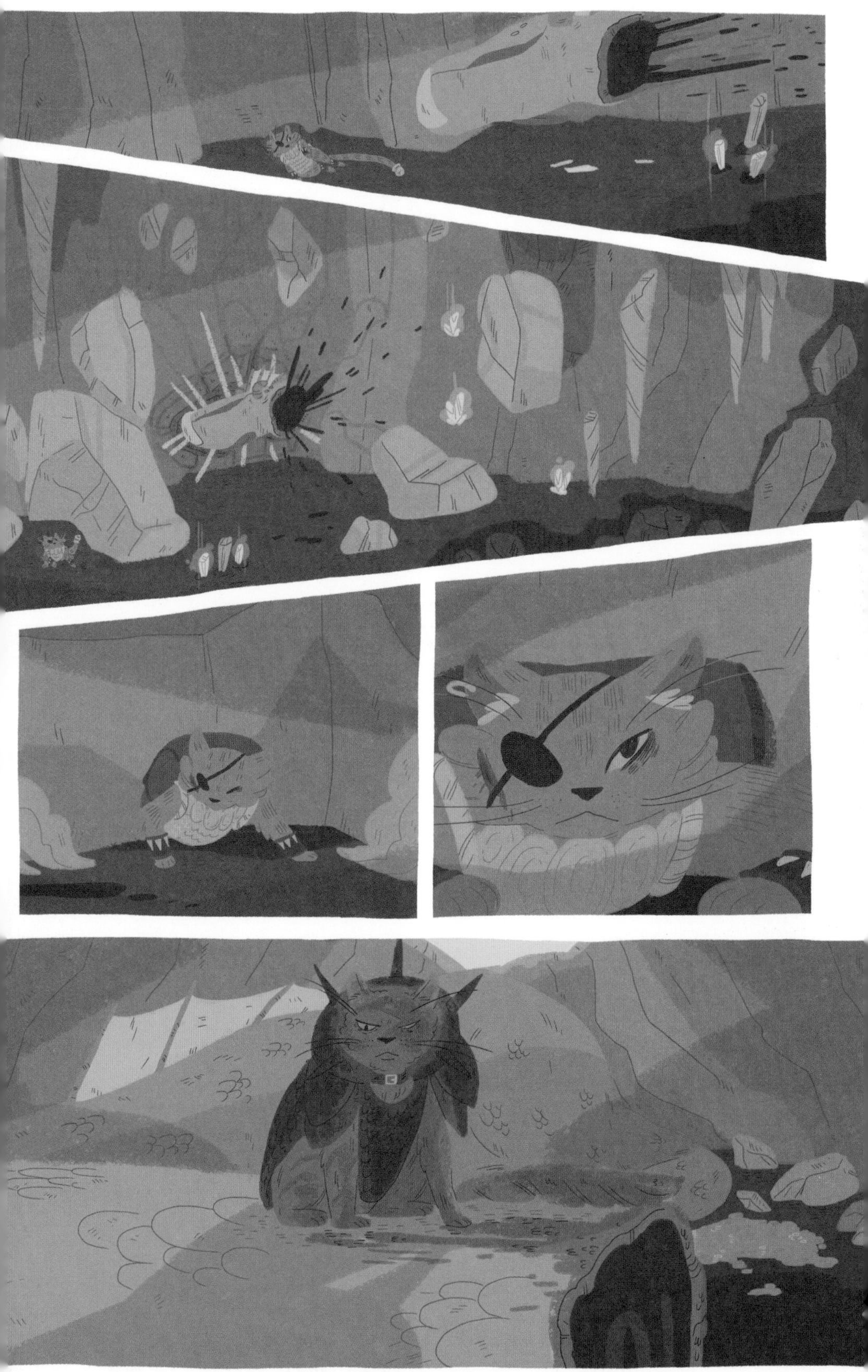

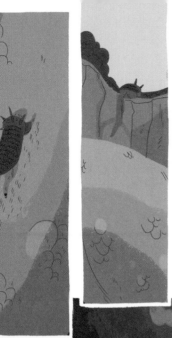

Zerk's Pu

ART by VICTORIA GRACE ELLIOTT
STORY by JOSH TIERNEY
ZERK DESIGN by SHELLY CHEN

continued in SPERA: ASCENSION of the STARLESS Vol. 2

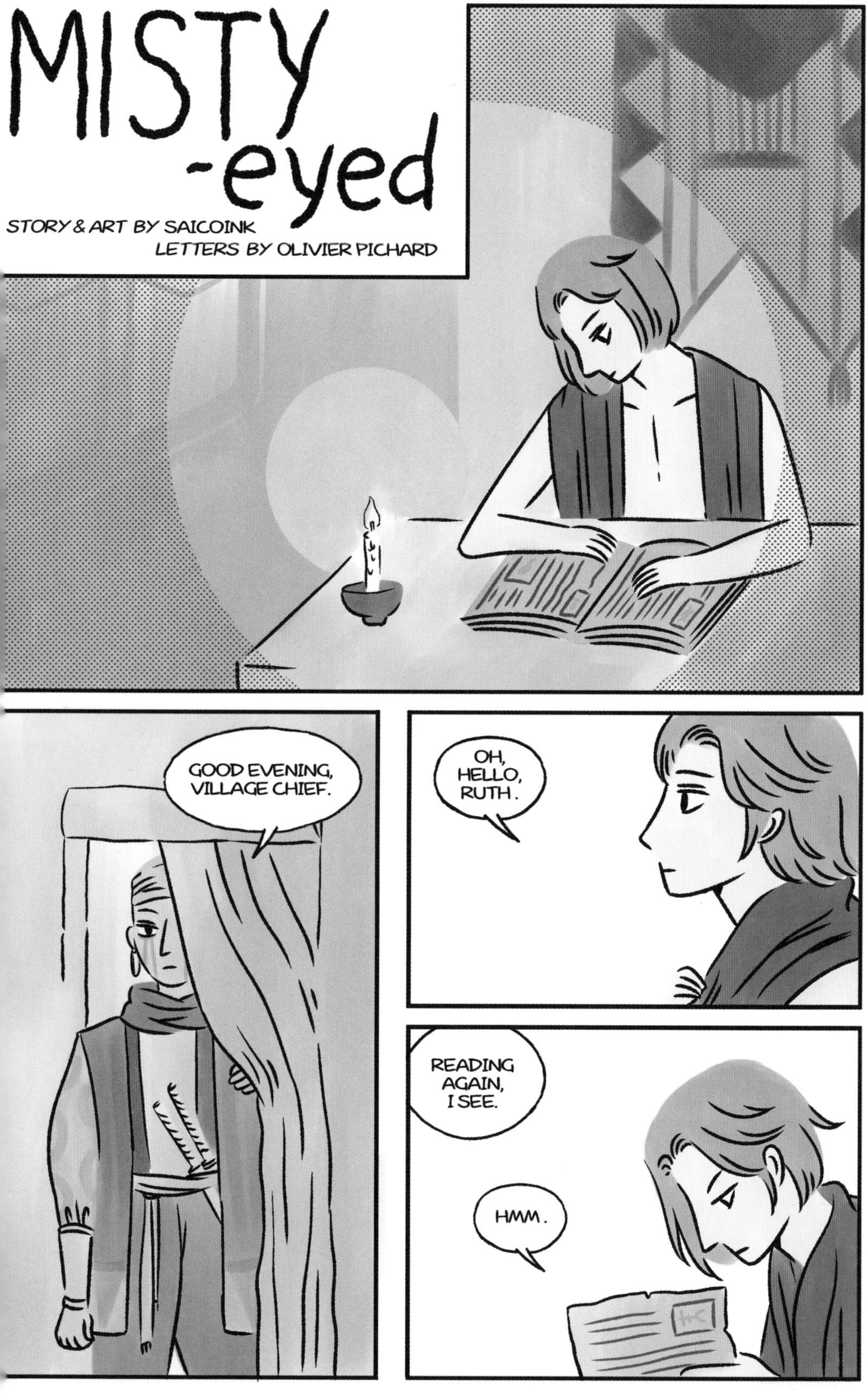
MISTY
-eyed
STORY & ART BY SAICOINK
LETTERS BY OLIVIER PICHARD
GOOD EVENING, VILLAGE CHIEF.
OH, HELLO, RUTH.
READING AGAIN, I SEE.
HMM.

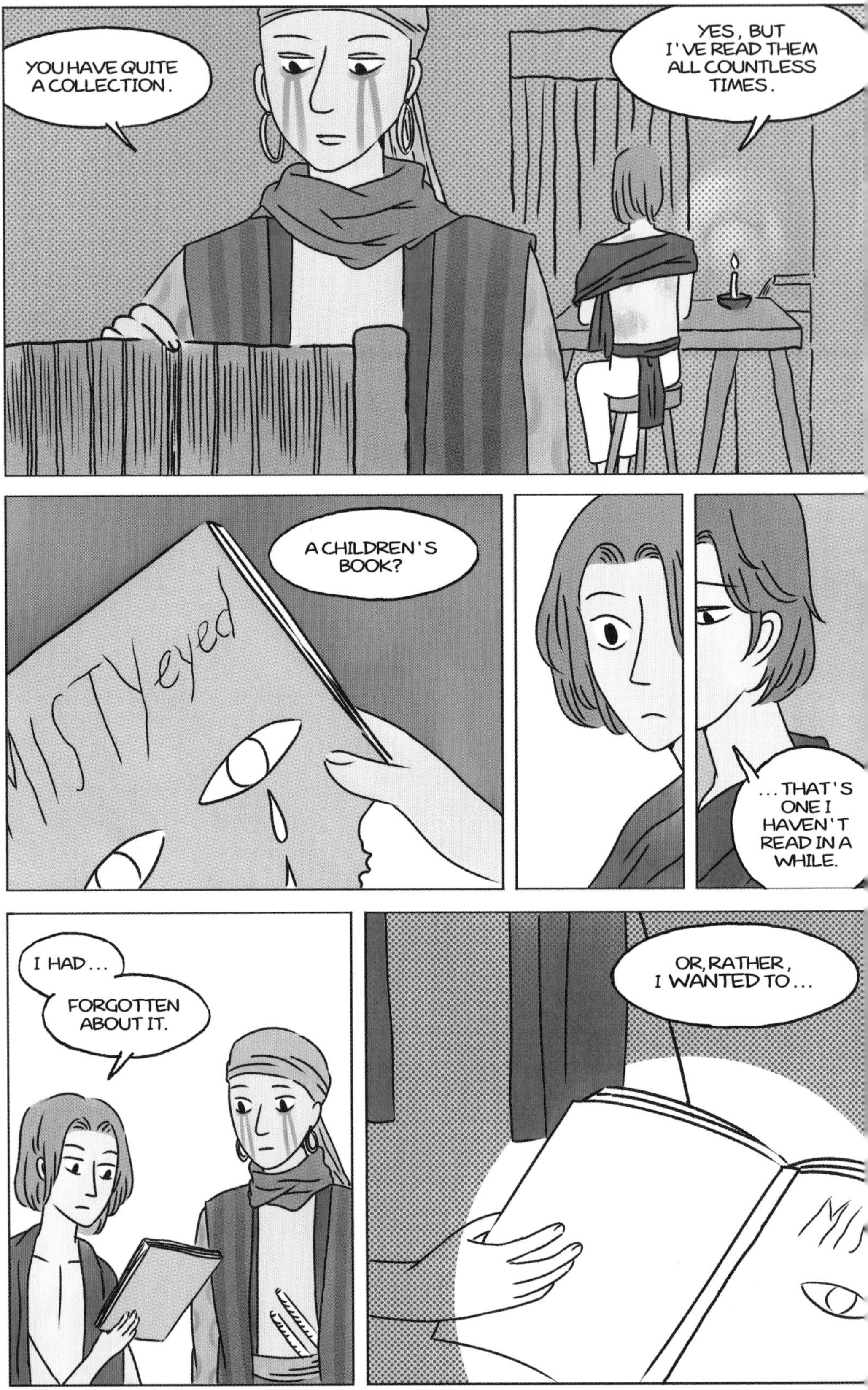
YOU HAVE QUITE A COLLECTION.
YES, BUT I'VE READ THEM ALL COUNTLESS TIMES.
A CHILDREN'S BOOK?
MISTY eyed
...THAT'S ONE I HAVEN'T READ IN A WHILE.
I HAD...
FORGOTTEN ABOUT IT.
OR, RATHER, I WANTED TO...

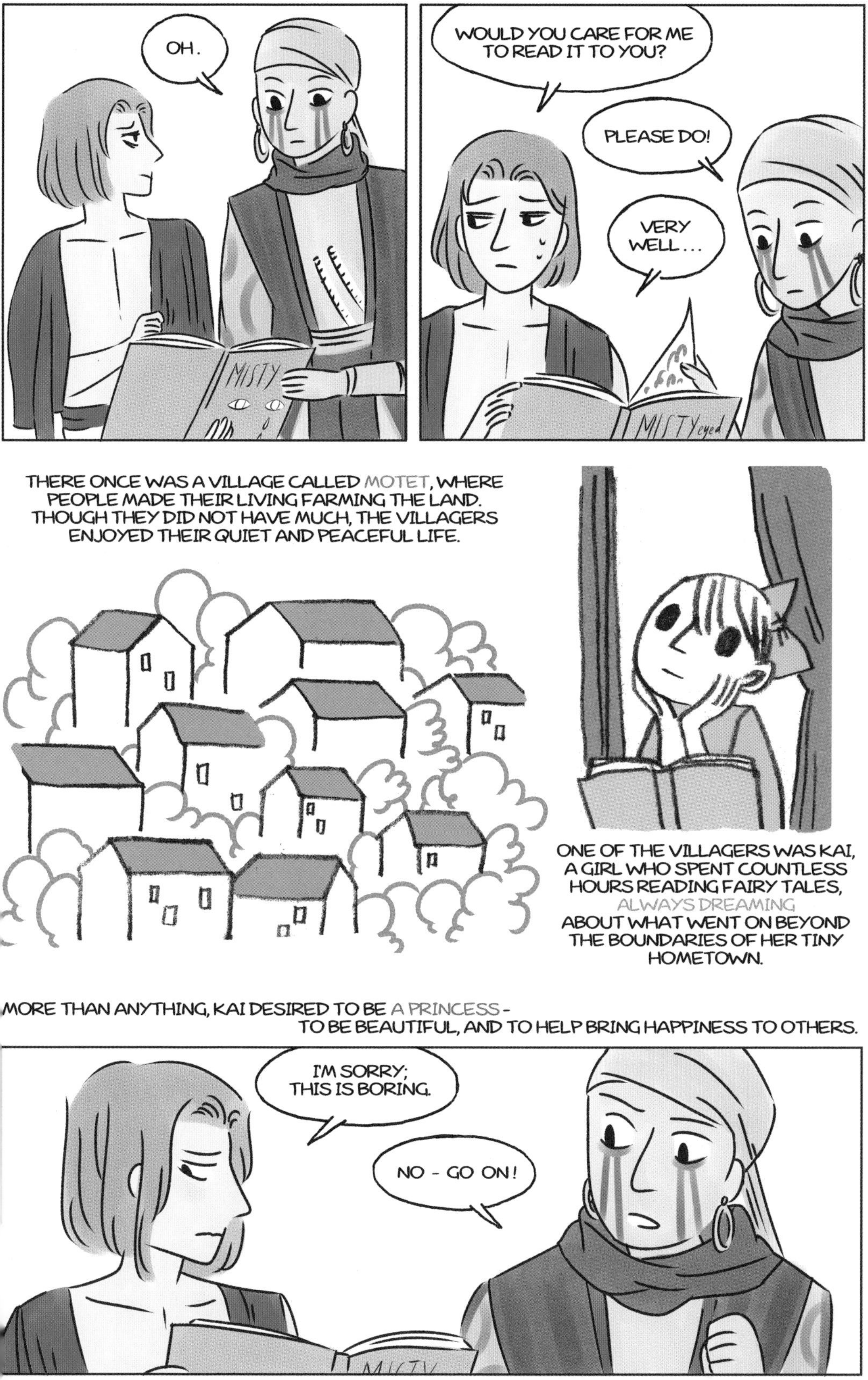
OH.
MISTY
WOULD YOU CARE FOR ME TO READ IT TO YOU?
PLEASE DO!
VERY WELL...
MISTY eyed
THERE ONCE WAS A VILLAGE CALLED MOTET, WHERE PEOPLE MADE THEIR LIVING FARMING THE LAND. THOUGH THEY DID NOT HAVE MUCH, THE VILLAGERS ENJOYED THEIR QUIET AND PEACEFUL LIFE.
ONE OF THE VILLAGERS WAS KAI, A GIRL WHO SPENT COUNTLESS HOURS READING FAIRY TALES, ALWAYS DREAMING ABOUT WHAT WENT ON BEYOND THE BOUNDARIES OF HER TINY HOMETOWN.
MORE THAN ANYTHING, KAI DESIRED TO BE A PRINCESS - TO BE BEAUTIFUL, AND TO HELP BRING HAPPINESS TO OTHERS.
I'M SORRY; THIS IS BORING.
NO - GO ON!

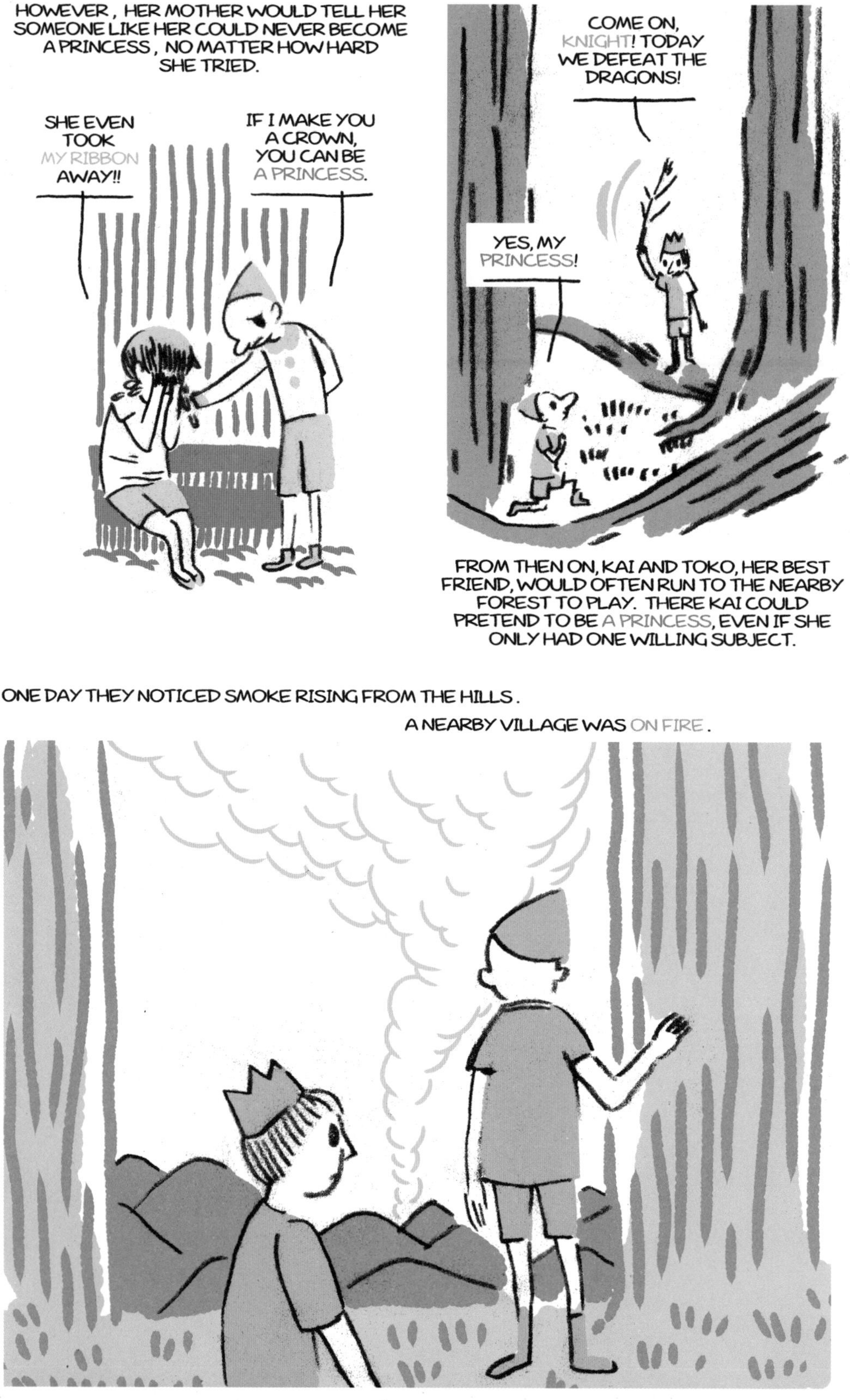
HOWEVER, HER MOTHER WOULD TELL HER SOMEONE LIKE HER COULD NEVER BECOME A PRINCESS, NO MATTER HOW HARD SHE TRIED.
SHE EVEN TOOK MY RIBBON AWAY!!
IF I MAKE YOU A CROWN, YOU CAN BE A PRINCESS.
COME ON, KNIGHT! TODAY WE DEFEAT THE DRAGONS!
YES, MY PRINCESS!
FROM THEN ON, KAI AND TOKO, HER BEST FRIEND, WOULD OFTEN RUN TO THE NEARBY FOREST TO PLAY. THERE KAI COULD PRETEND TO BE A PRINCESS, EVEN IF SHE ONLY HAD ONE WILLING SUBJECT.
ONE DAY THEY NOTICED SMOKE RISING FROM THE HILLS.
A NEARBY VILLAGE WAS ON FIRE.

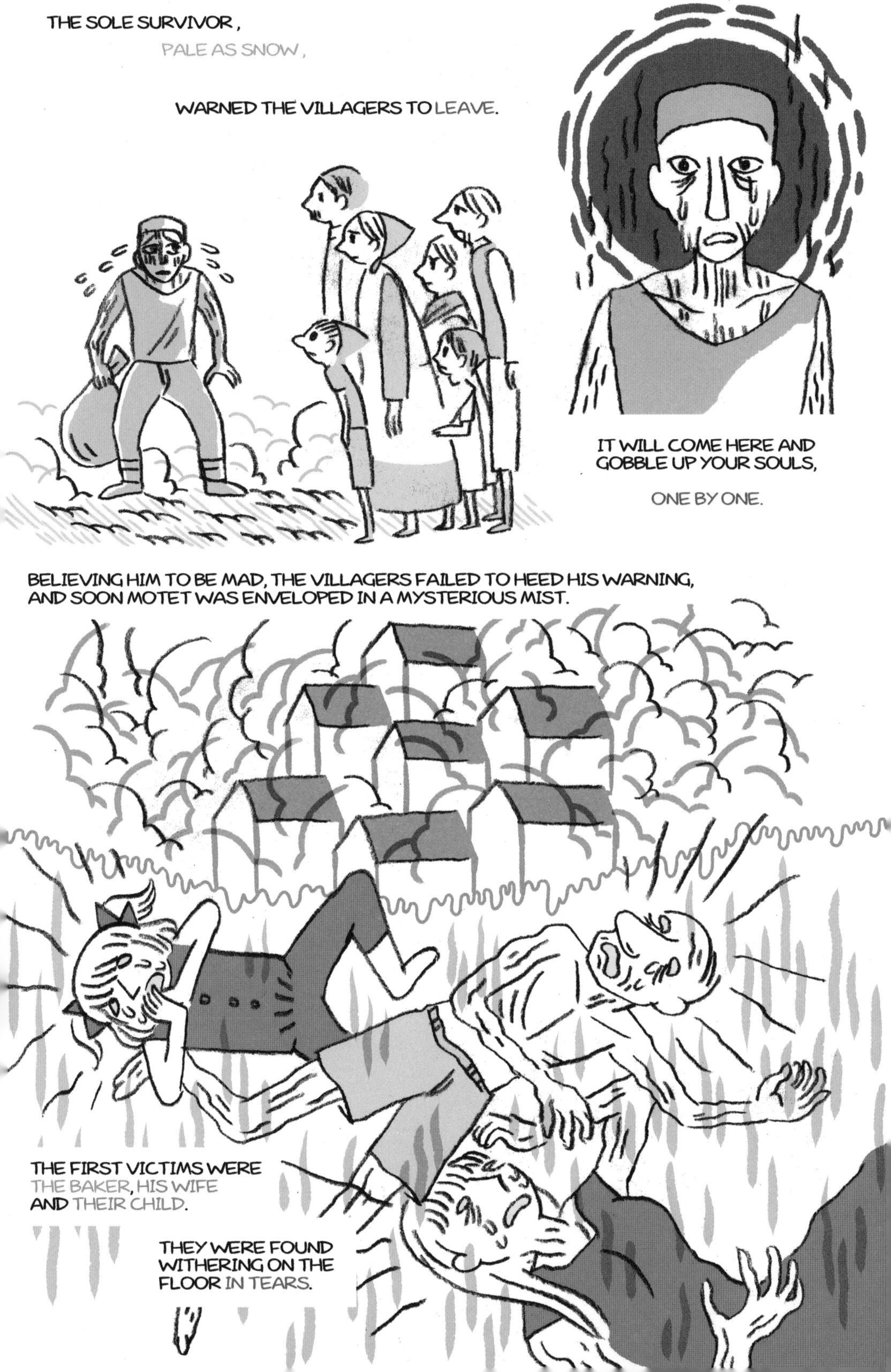
THE SOLE SURVIVOR,
PALE AS SNOW,
WARNED THE VILLAGERS TO LEAVE.
IT WILL COME HERE AND GOBBLE UP YOUR SOULS,
ONE BY ONE.
BELIEVING HIM TO BE MAD, THE VILLAGERS FAILED TO HEED HIS WARNING, AND SOON MOTET WAS ENVELOPED IN A MYSTERIOUS MIST.
THE FIRST VICTIMS WERE THE BAKER, HIS WIFE AND THEIR CHILD.
THEY WERE FOUND WITHERING ON THE FLOOR IN TEARS.

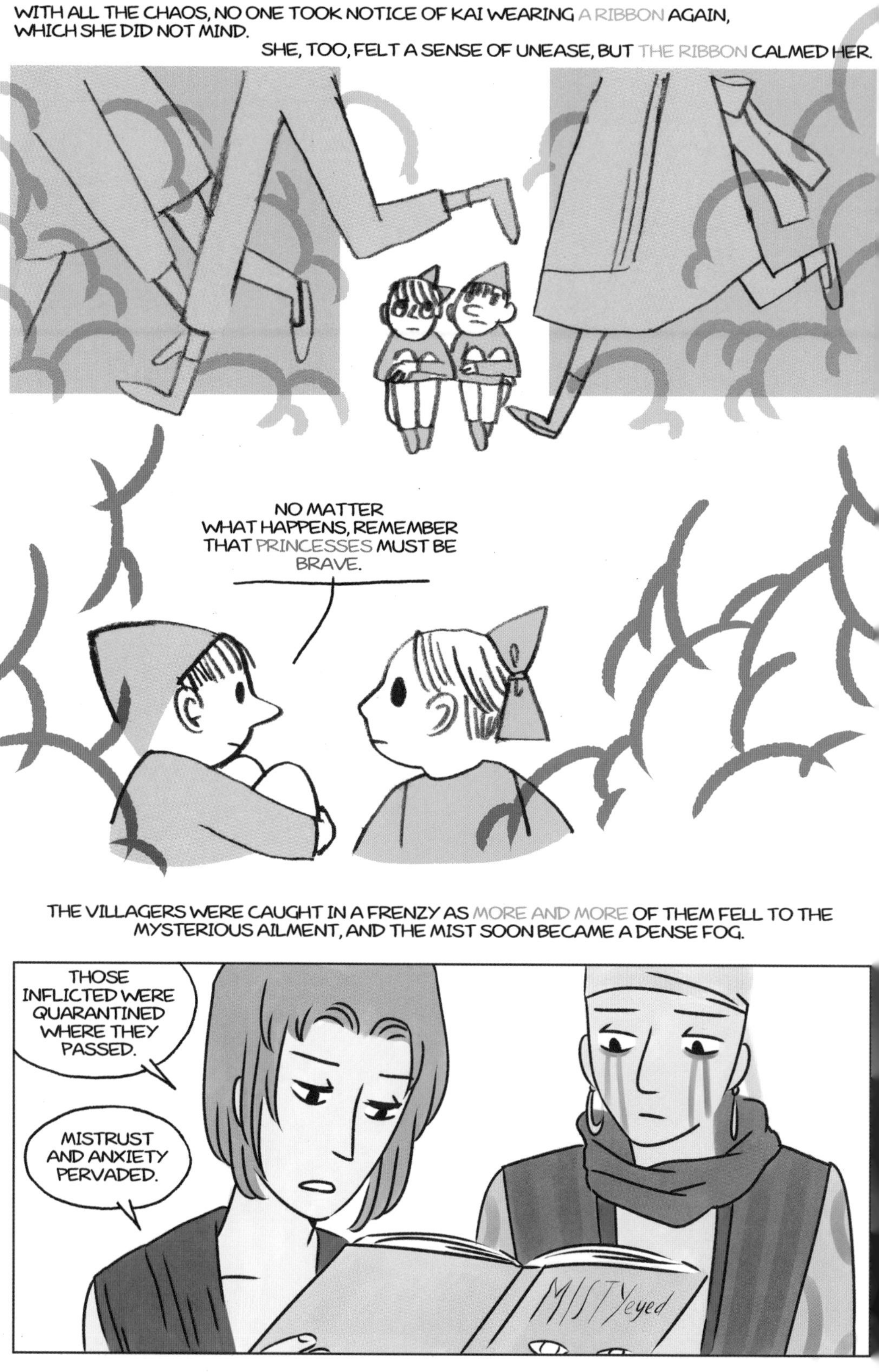
WITH ALL THE CHAOS, NO ONE TOOK NOTICE OF KAI WEARING A RIBBON AGAIN, WHICH SHE DID NOT MIND.
SHE, TOO, FELT A SENSE OF UNEASE, BUT THE RIBBON CALMED HER.
NO MATTER WHAT HAPPENS, REMEMBER THAT PRINCESSES MUST BE BRAVE.
THE VILLAGERS WERE CAUGHT IN A FRENZY AS MORE AND MORE OF THEM FELL TO THE MYSTERIOUS AILMENT, AND THE MIST SOON BECAME A DENSE FOG.
THOSE INFLICTED WERE QUARANTINED WHERE THEY PASSED.
MISTRUST AND ANXIETY PERVADED.
MISTYeyed

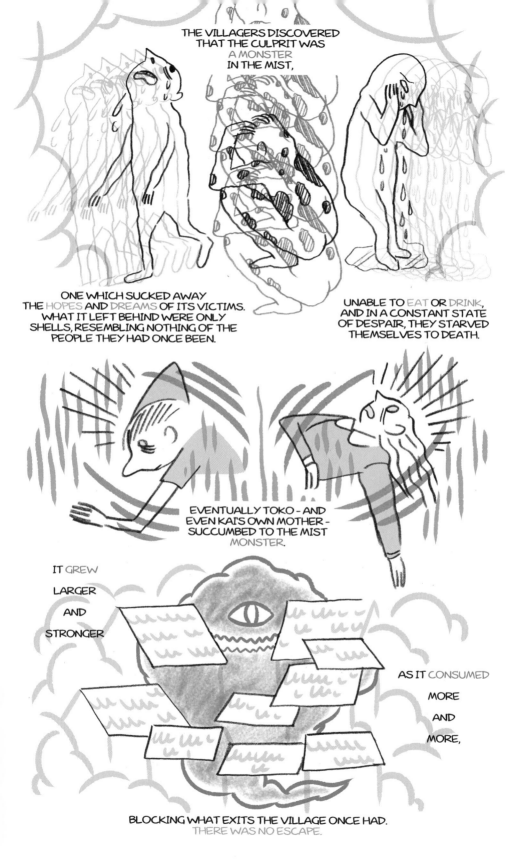

THE VILLAGERS DISCOVERED
THAT THE CULPRIT WAS
A MONSTER
IN THE MIST,

ONE WHICH SUCKED AWAY
THE HOPES AND DREAMS OF ITS VICTIMS.
WHAT IT LEFT BEHIND WERE ONLY
SHELLS, RESEMBLING NOTHING OF THE
PEOPLE THEY HAD ONCE BEEN.

UNABLE TO EAT OR DRINK,
AND IN A CONSTANT STATE
OF DESPAIR, THEY STARVED
THEMSELVES TO DEATH.

EVENTUALLY TOKO - AND
EVEN KAI'S OWN MOTHER -
SUCCUMBED TO THE MIST
MONSTER.

IT GREW

LARGER

AND

STRONGER

AS IT CONSUMED

MORE

AND

MORE,

BLOCKING WHAT EXITS THE VILLAGE ONCE HAD.
THERE WAS NO ESCAPE.

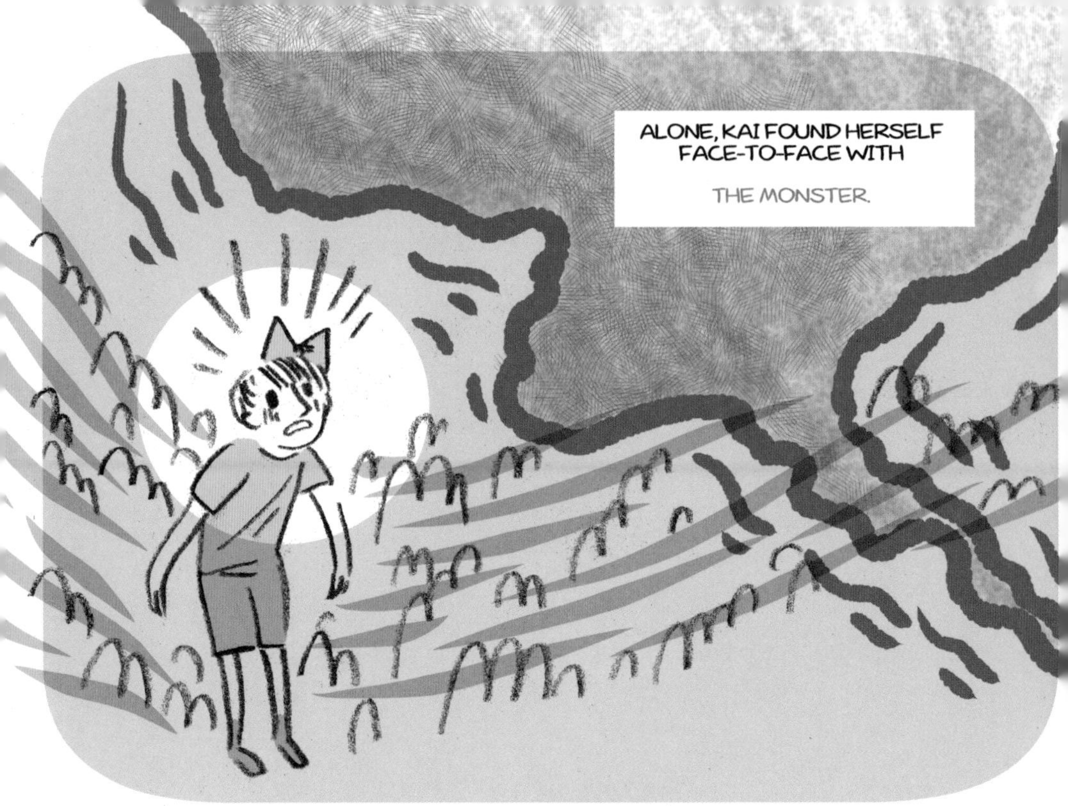
ALONE, KAI FOUND HERSELF FACE-TO-FACE WITH
THE MONSTER.

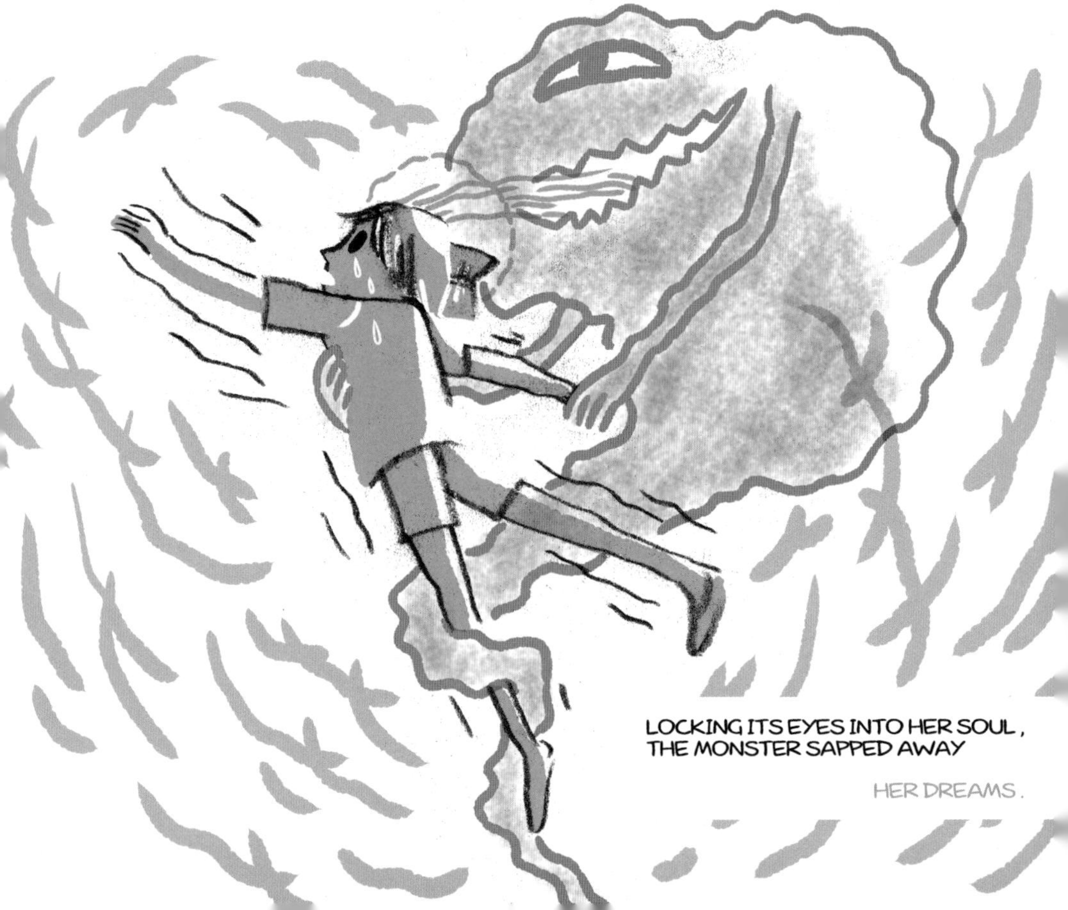
LOCKING ITS EYES INTO HER SOUL , THE MONSTER SAPPED AWAY
HER DREAMS .

KAI WATCHED

AS HER PRECIOUS DREAMS DISAPPEARED BEFORE HER,

ONE BY ONE.

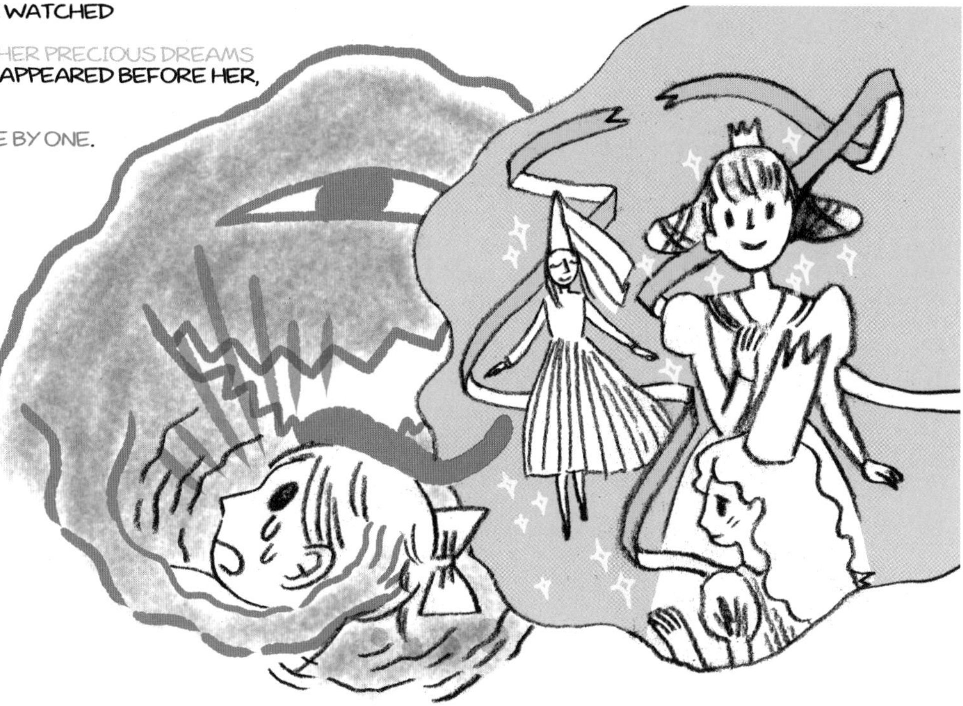

A PRINCESS IS BEAUTIFUL,
A PRINCESS IS LOVED BY EVERYONE,
A PRINCESS IS KIND -

BUT,
MOST OF ALL,
SHE IS
BRAVE!

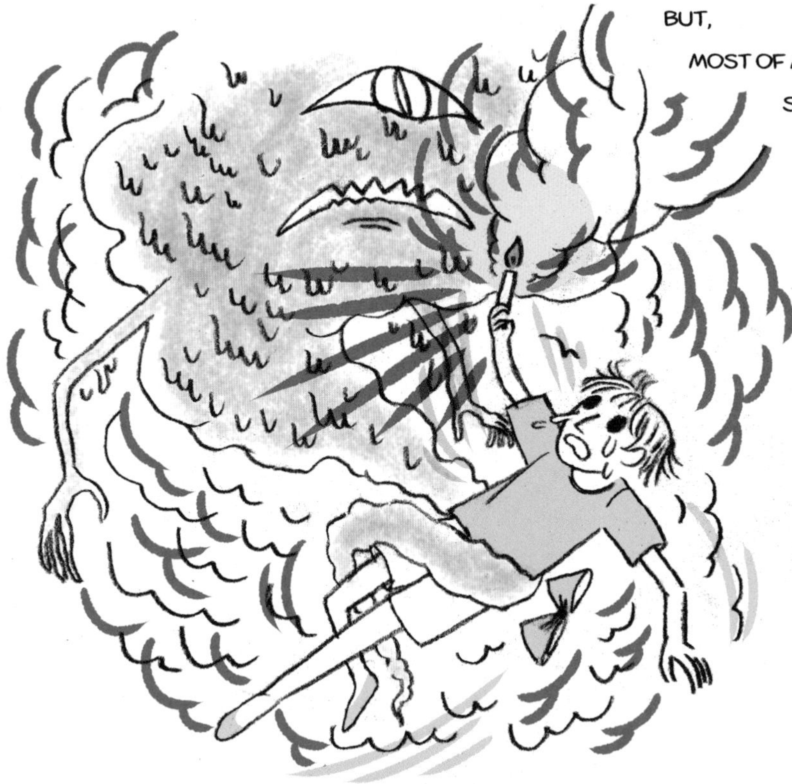

MUSTERING HER LAST OUNCE OF STRENGTH,
KAI PICKED UP A CANDLE AND LIT THE MONSTER ON FIRE.

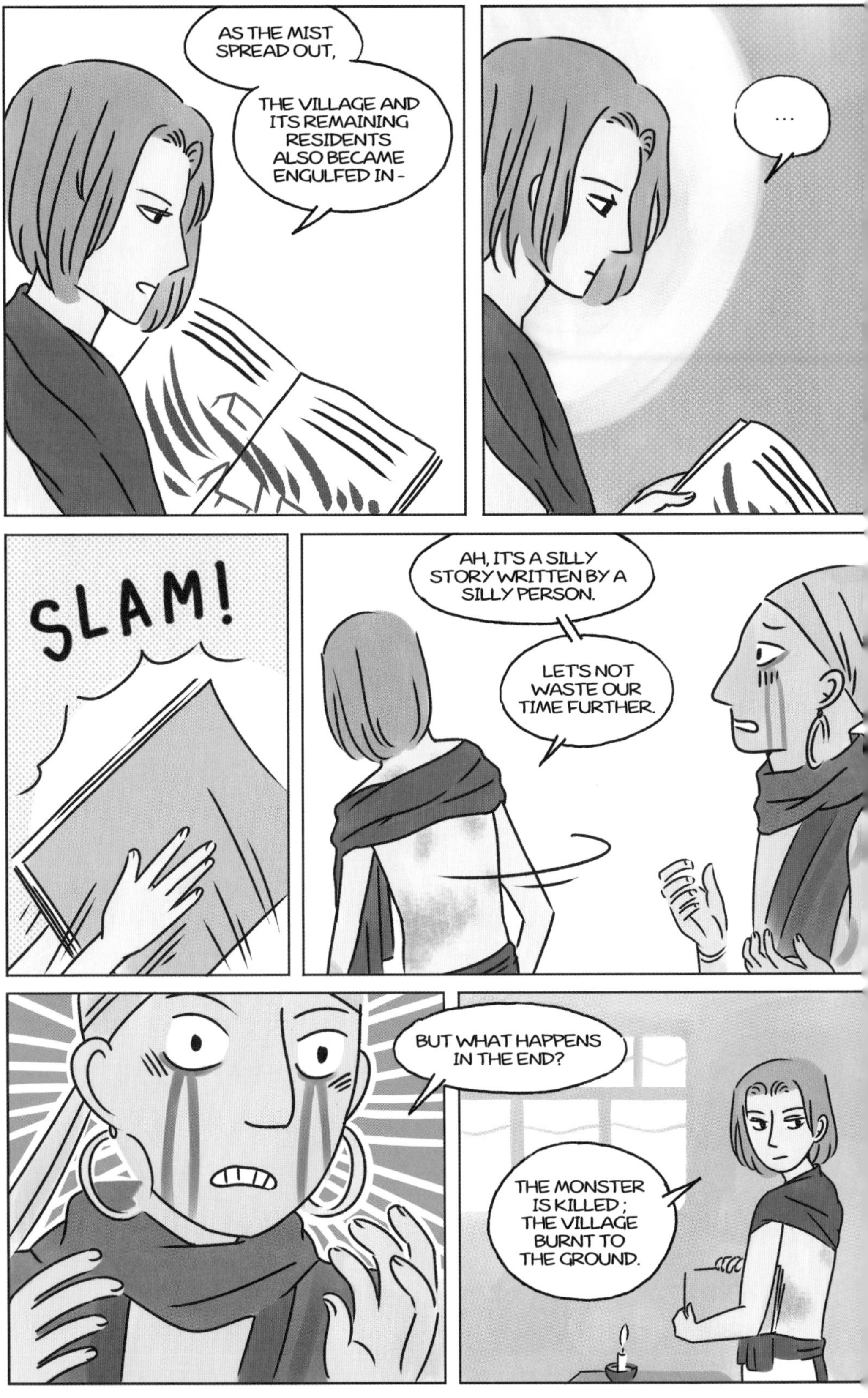
AS THE MIST SPREAD OUT,
THE VILLAGE AND ITS REMAINING RESIDENTS ALSO BECAME ENGULFED IN -
...
SLAM!
AH, IT'S A SILLY STORY WRITTEN BY A SILLY PERSON.
LET'S NOT WASTE OUR TIME FURTHER.
BUT WHAT HAPPENS IN THE END?
THE MONSTER IS KILLED; THE VILLAGE BURNT TO THE GROUND.

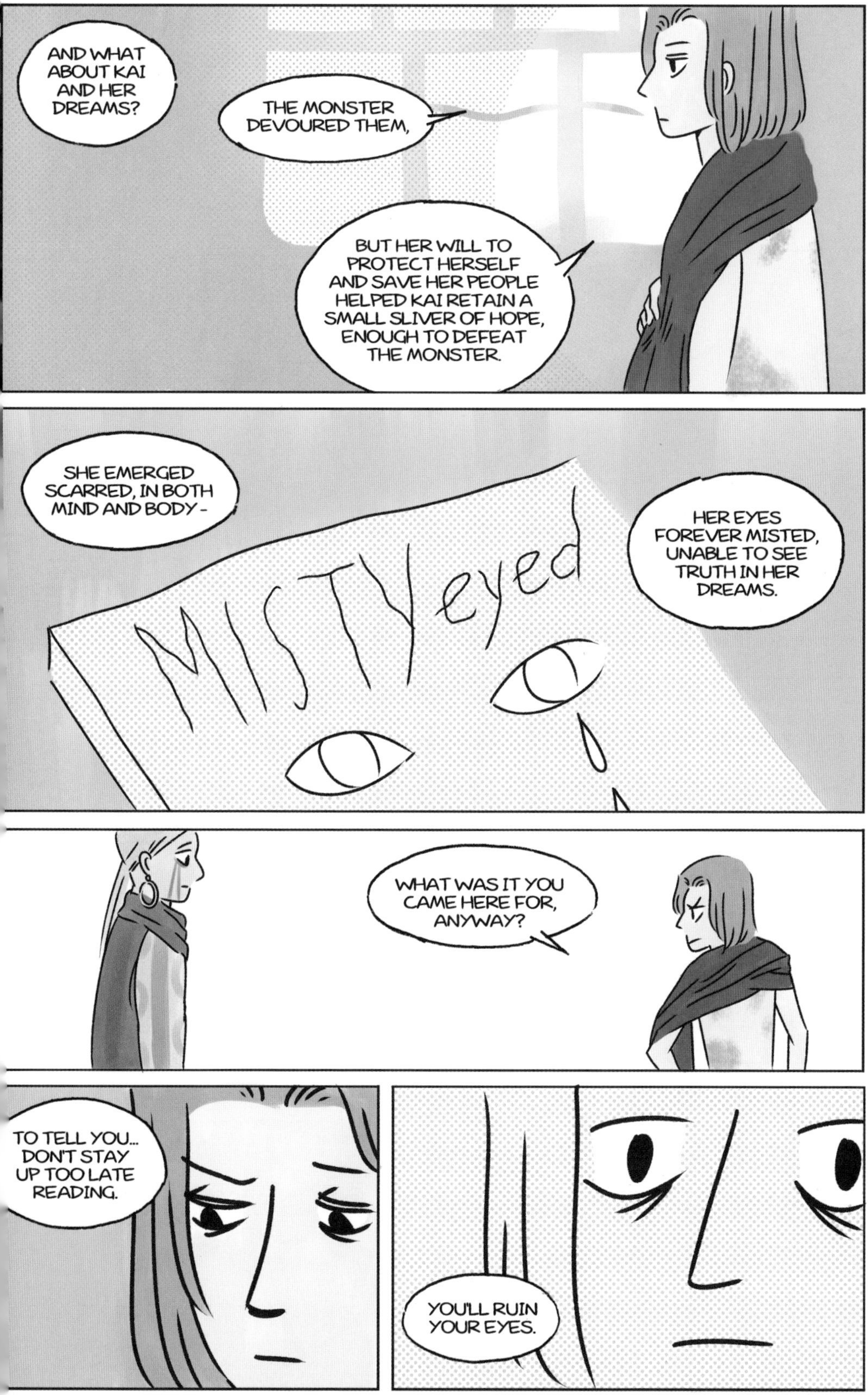
AND WHAT ABOUT KAI AND HER DREAMS?
THE MONSTER DEVOURED THEM,
BUT HER WILL TO PROTECT HERSELF AND SAVE HER PEOPLE HELPED KAI RETAIN A SMALL SLIVER OF HOPE, ENOUGH TO DEFEAT THE MONSTER.
SHE EMERGED SCARRED, IN BOTH MIND AND BODY -
MISTY eyed
HER EYES FOREVER MISTED, UNABLE TO SEE TRUTH IN HER DREAMS.
WHAT WAS IT YOU CAME HERE FOR, ANYWAY?
TO TELL YOU... DON'T STAY UP TOO LATE READING.
YOU'LL RUIN YOUR EYES.

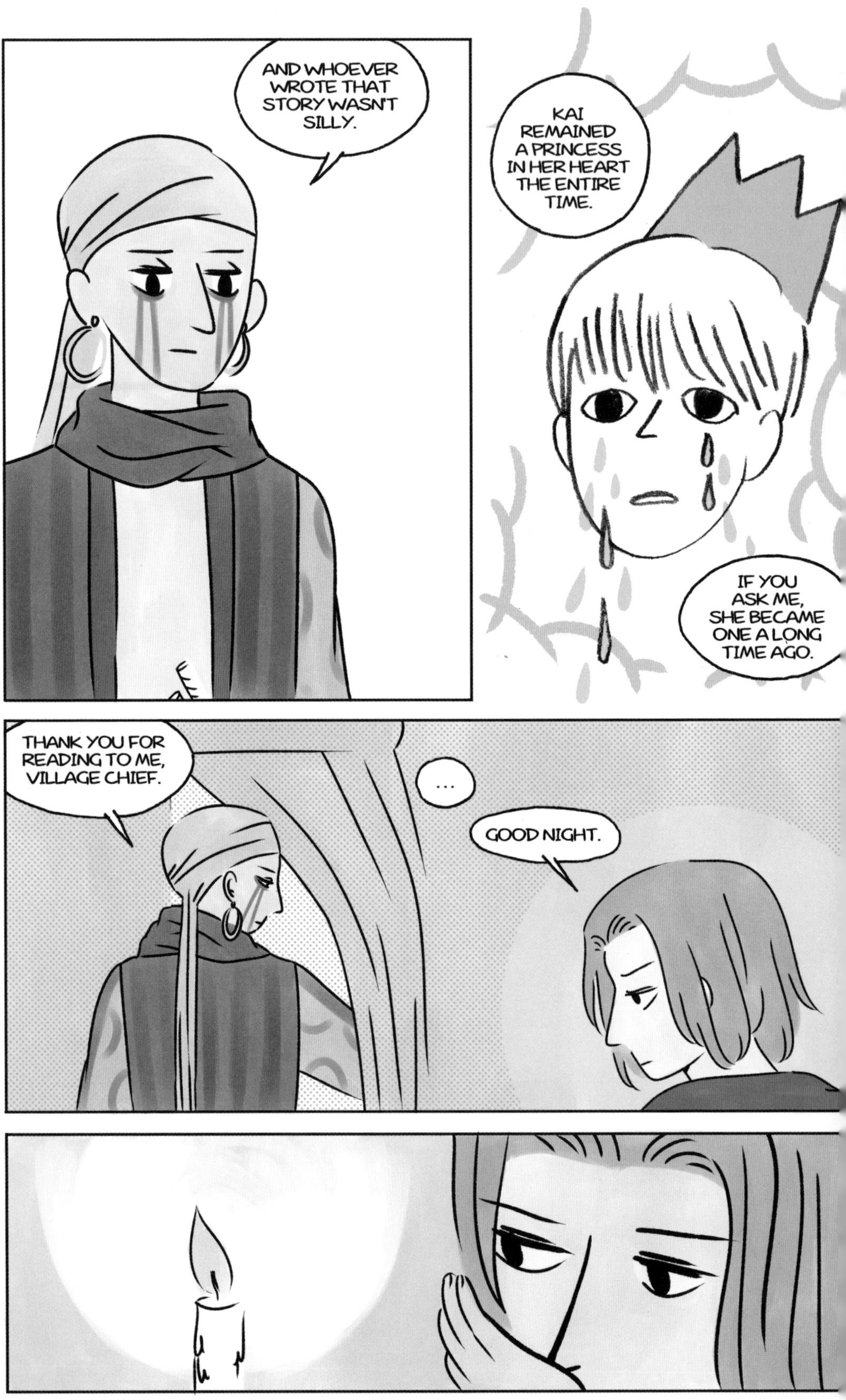
AND WHOEVER WROTE THAT STORY WASN'T SILLY.
KAI REMAINED A PRINCESS IN HER HEART THE ENTIRE TIME.
IF YOU ASK ME, SHE BECAME ONE A LONG TIME AGO.
THANK YOU FOR READING TO ME, VILLAGE CHIEF.
...
GOOD NIGHT.

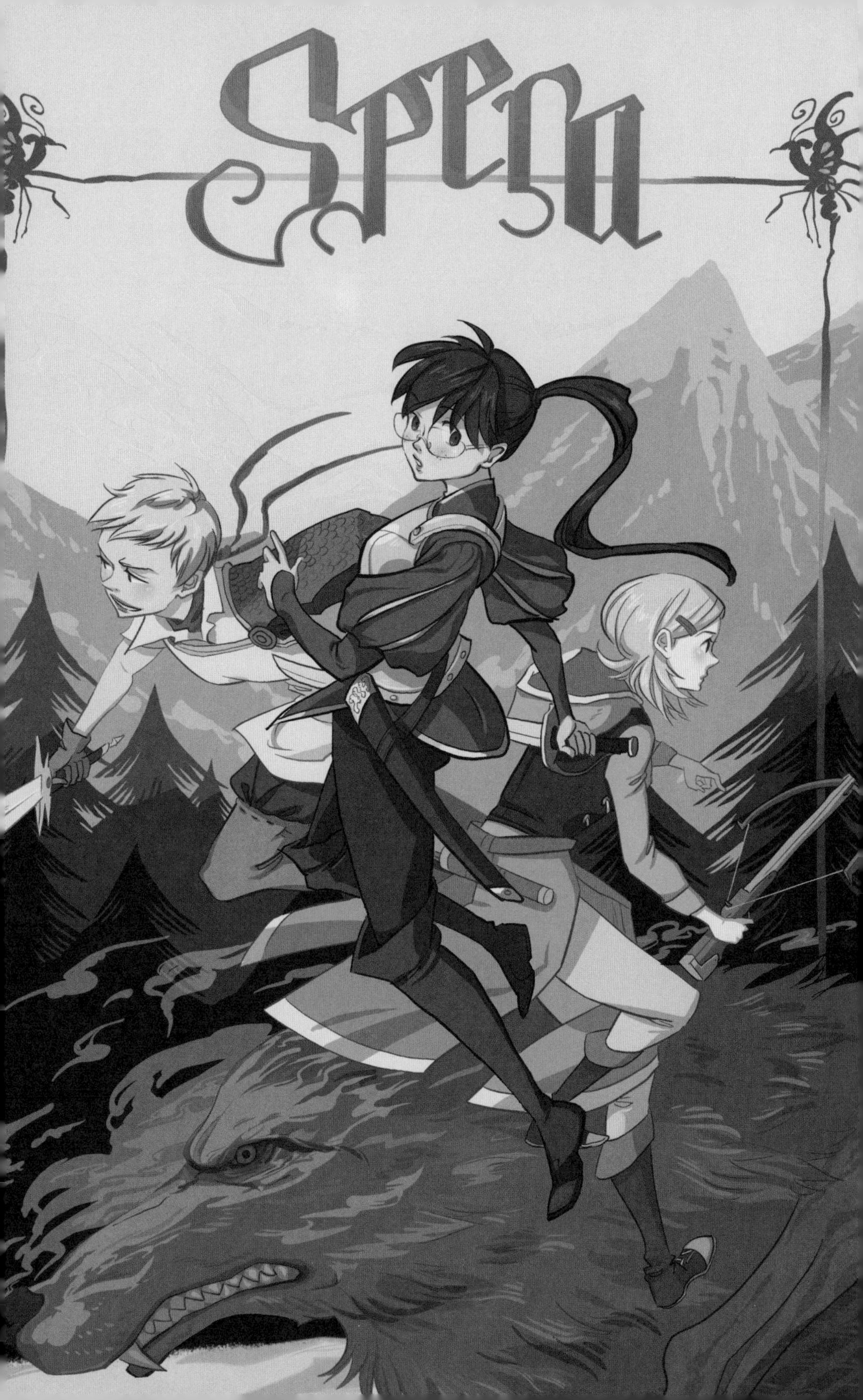
Spera

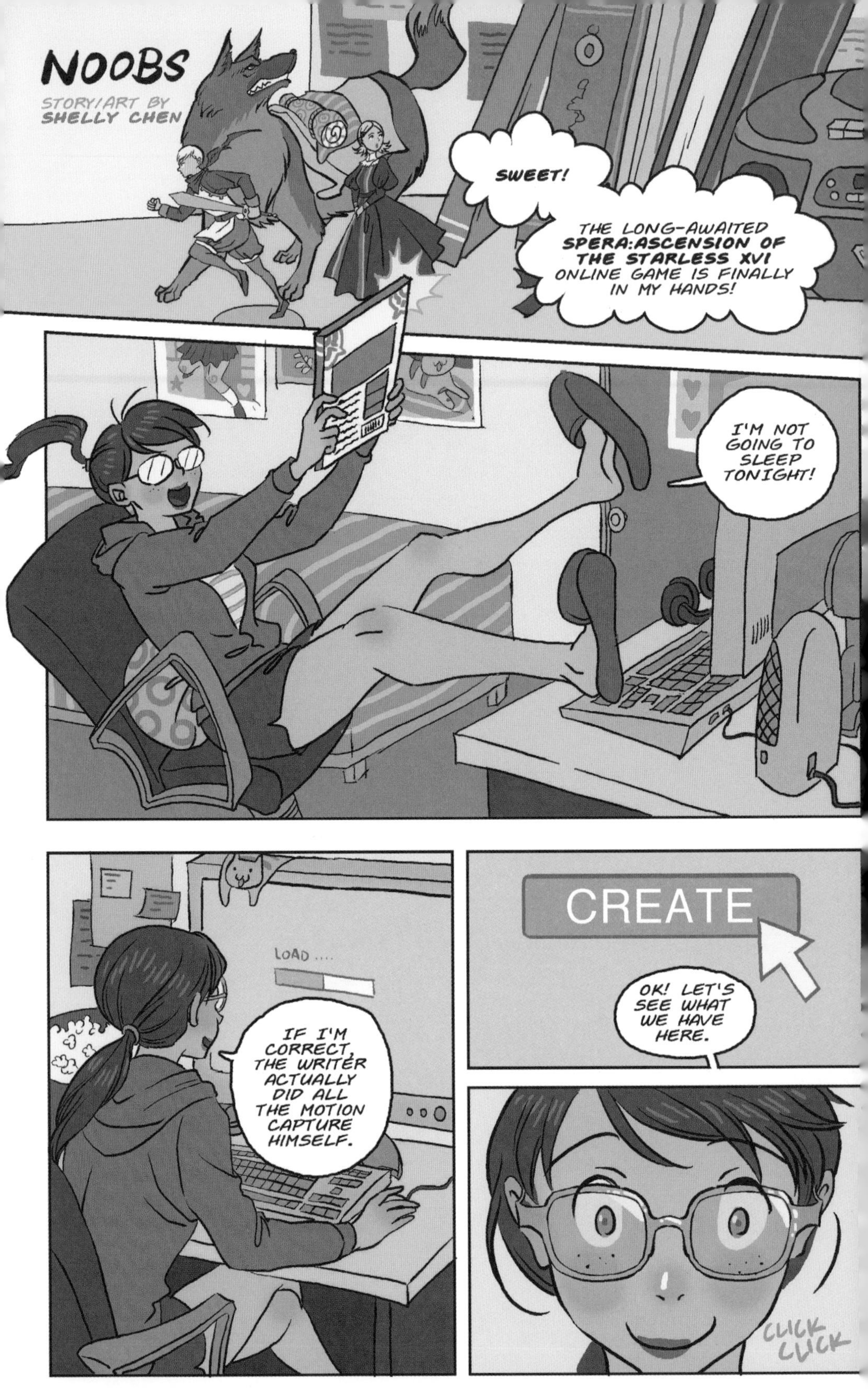
NOOBS
STORY/ART BY SHELLY CHEN
SWEET!
THE LONG-AWAITED SPERA:ASCENSION OF THE STARLESS XVI ONLINE GAME IS FINALLY IN MY HANDS!
I'M NOT GOING TO SLEEP TONIGHT!
LOAD ....
IF I'M CORRECT, THE WRITER ACTUALLY DID ALL THE MOTION CAPTURE HIMSELF.
CREATE
OK! LET'S SEE WHAT WE HAVE HERE.
CLICK CLICK

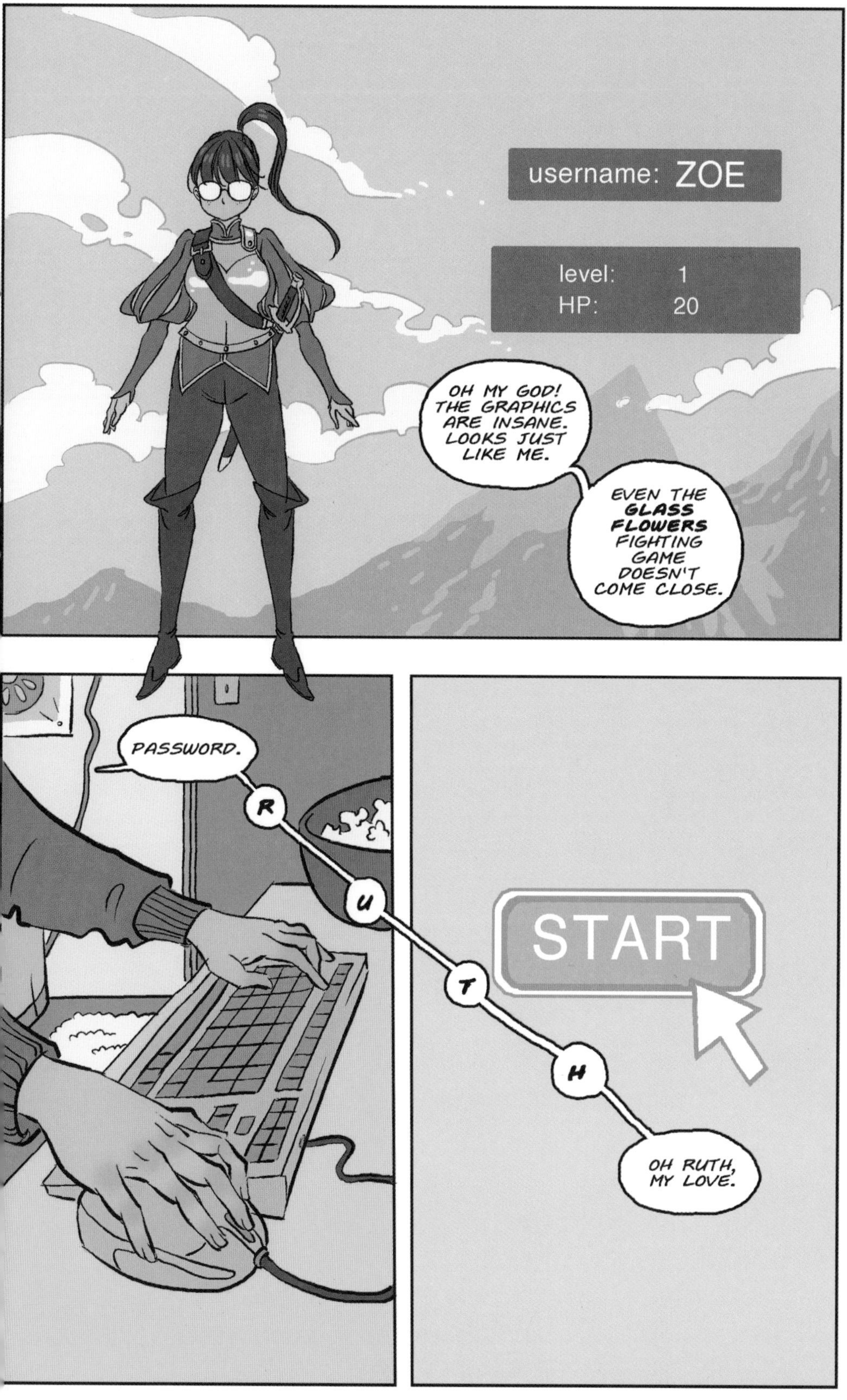
username: ZOE
level: 1
HP: 20
OH MY GOD! THE GRAPHICS ARE INSANE. LOOKS JUST LIKE ME.
EVEN THE **GLASS FLOWERS** FIGHTING GAME DOESN'T COME CLOSE.
PASSWORD.
R
U
T
H
OH RUTH, MY LOVE.
START

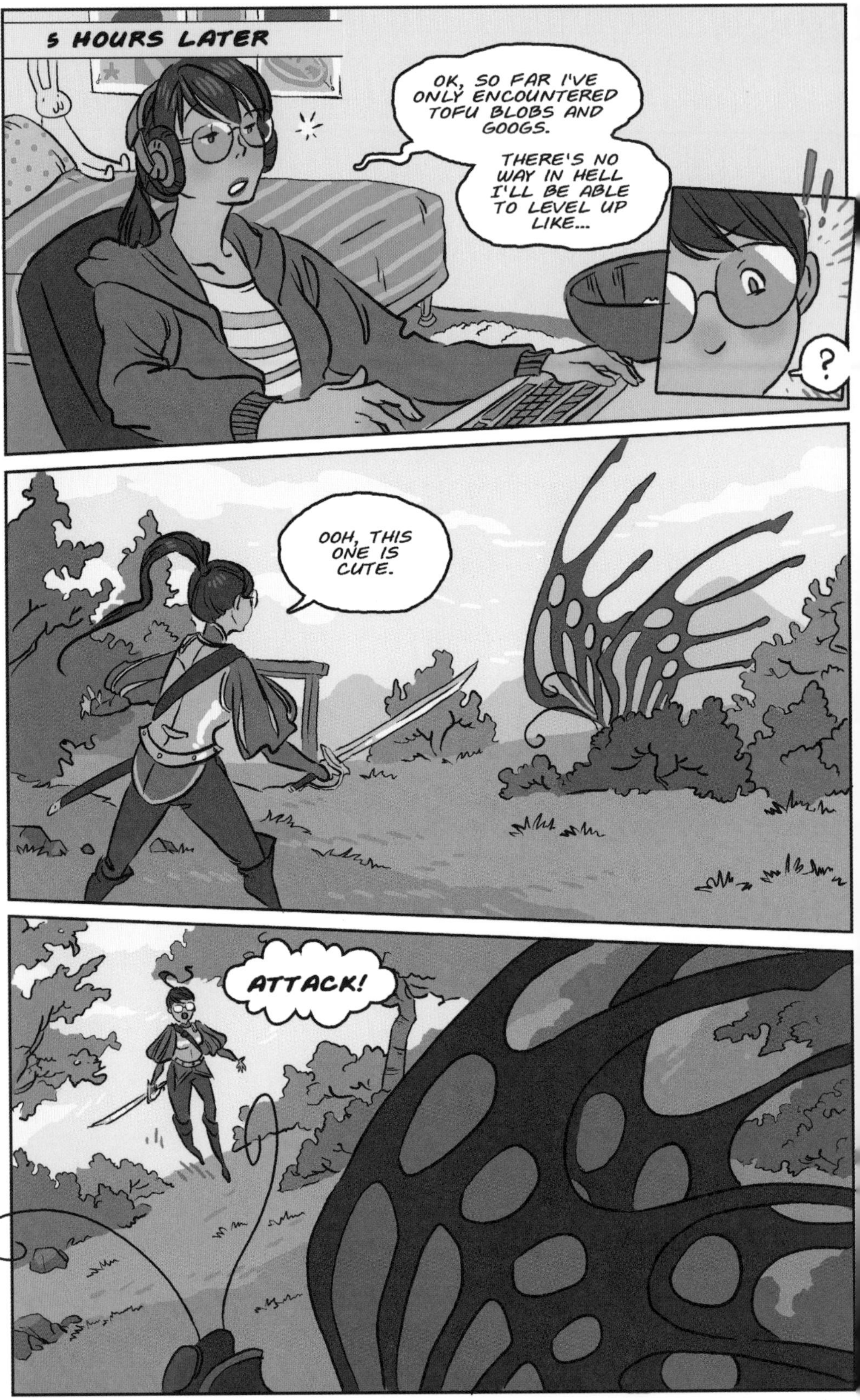
5 HOURS LATER
OK, SO FAR I'VE ONLY ENCOUNTERED TOFU BLOBS AND GOOGS.
THERE'S NO WAY IN HELL I'LL BE ABLE TO LEVEL UP LIKE...
!!
?
OOH, THIS ONE IS CUTE.
ATTACK!

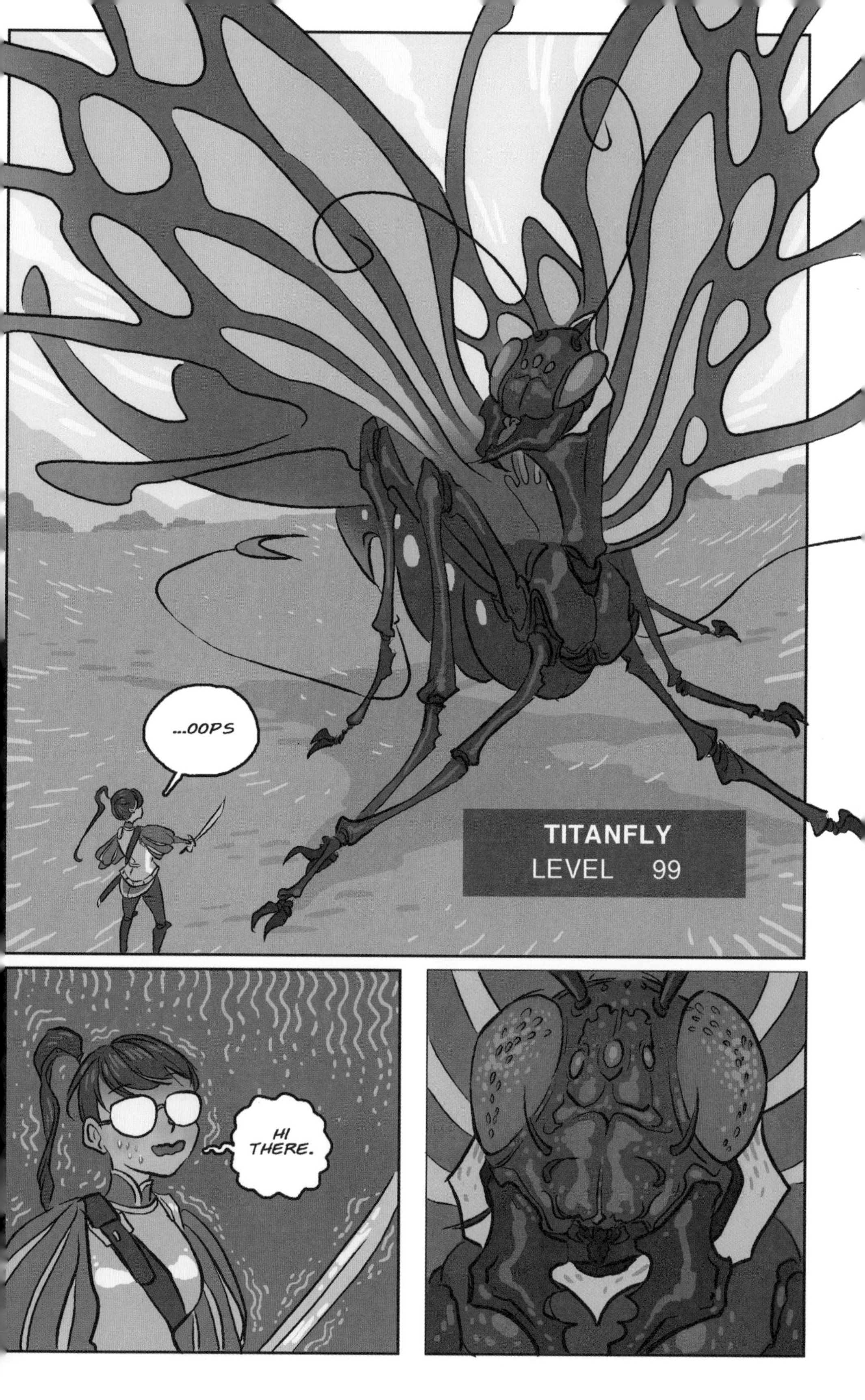
...OOPS
TITANFLY
LEVEL 99
HI THERE.

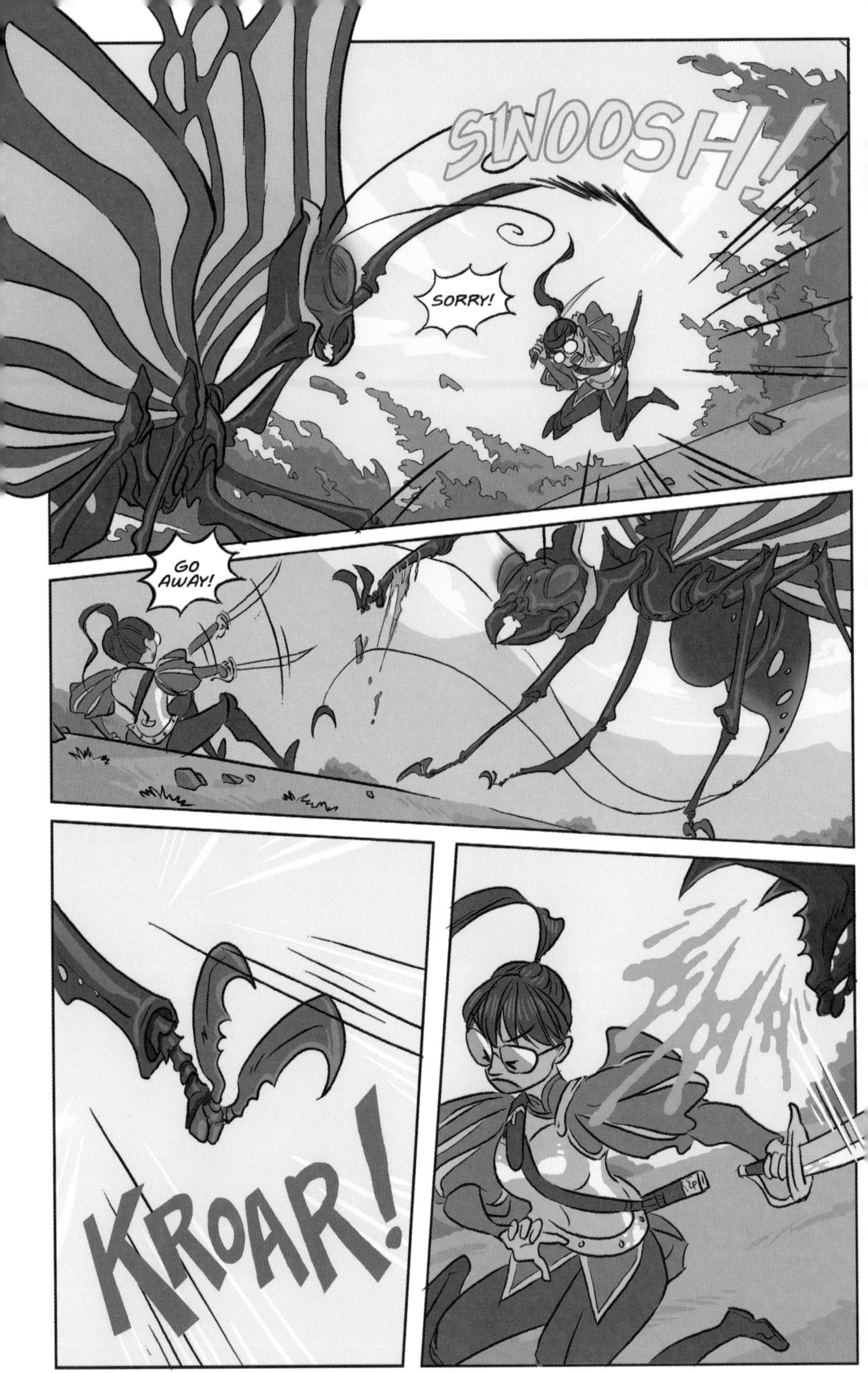
SWOOSH!
SORRY!
GO AWAY!
KROAR!

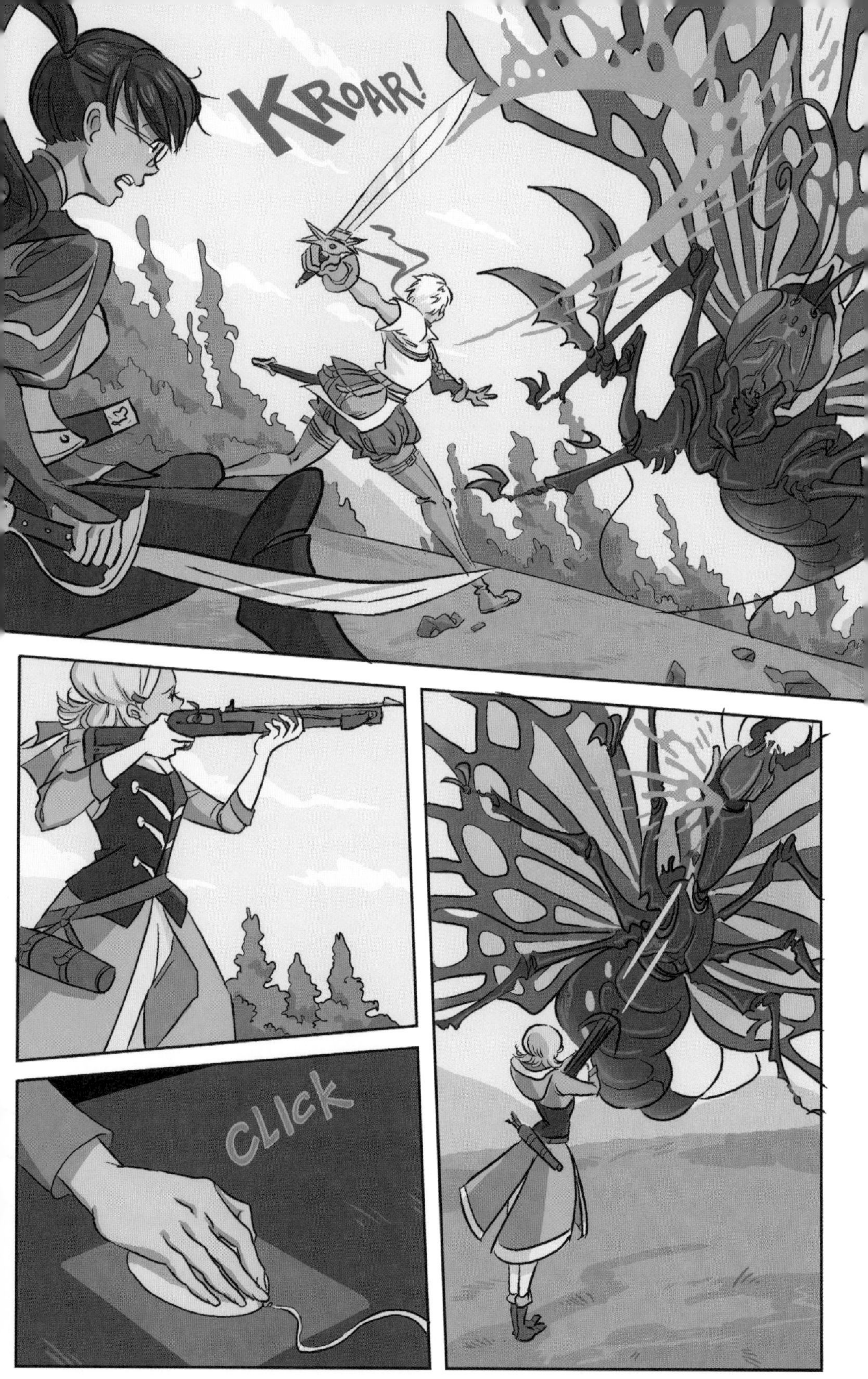
KROAR!
CLICK

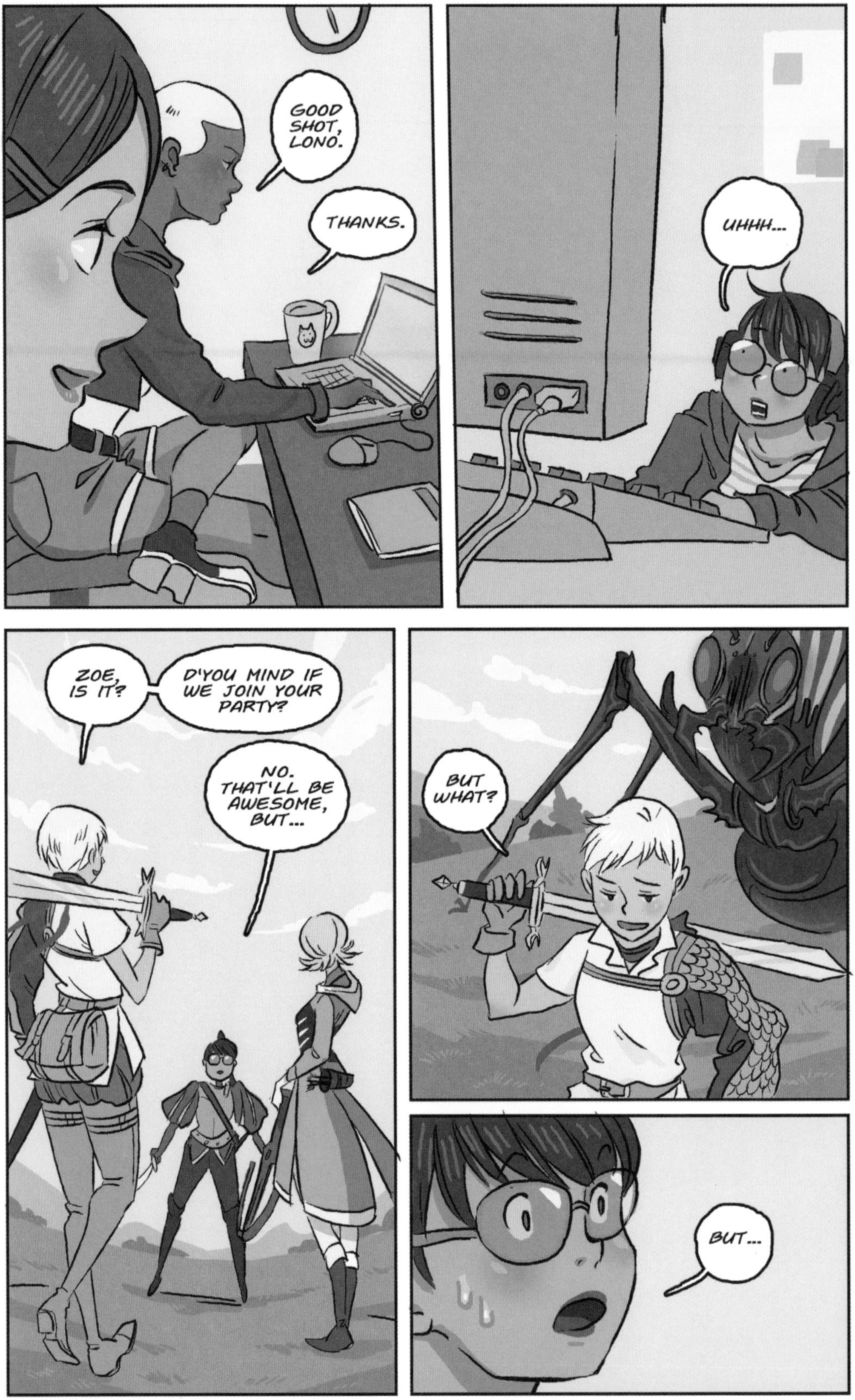
GOOD SHOT, LONO.
THANKS.
UHHH...
ZOE, IS IT?
D'YOU MIND IF WE JOIN YOUR PARTY?
NO. THAT'LL BE AWESOME, BUT...
BUT WHAT?
BUT...

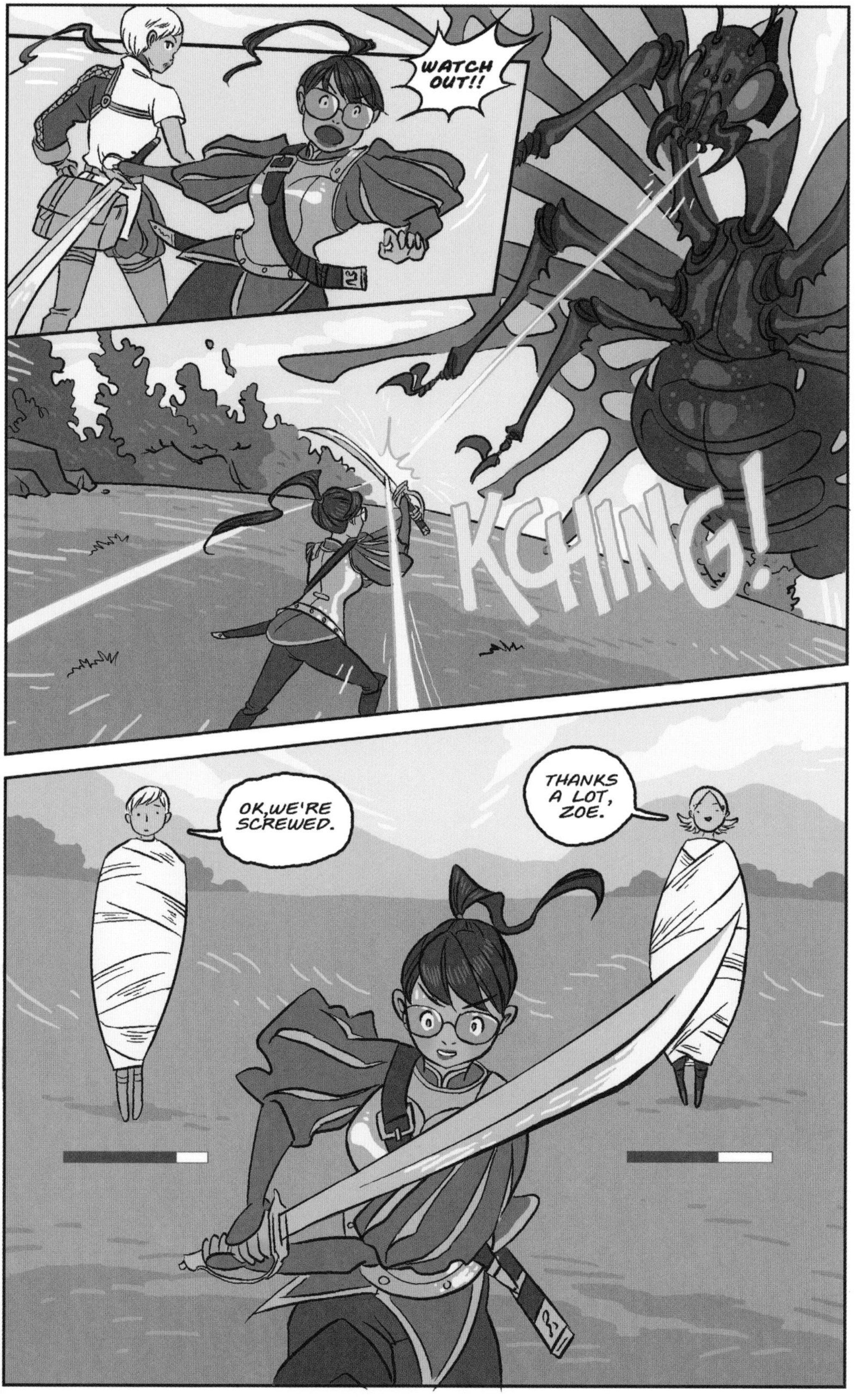
WATCH OUT!!
KCHING!
OK, WE'RE SCREWED.
THANKS A LOT, ZOE.

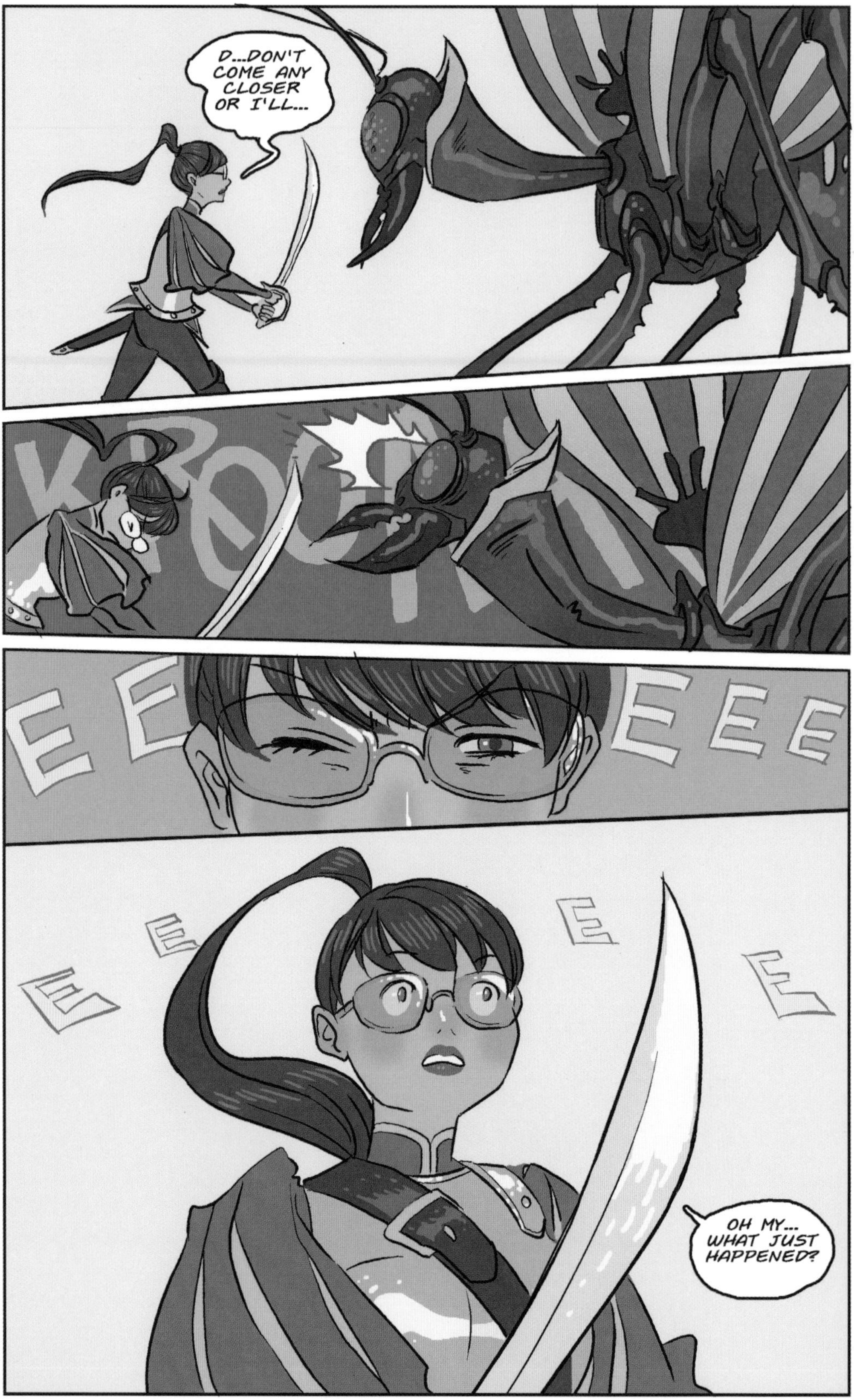
D...DON'T COME ANY CLOSER OR I'LL...
OH MY... WHAT JUST HAPPENED?

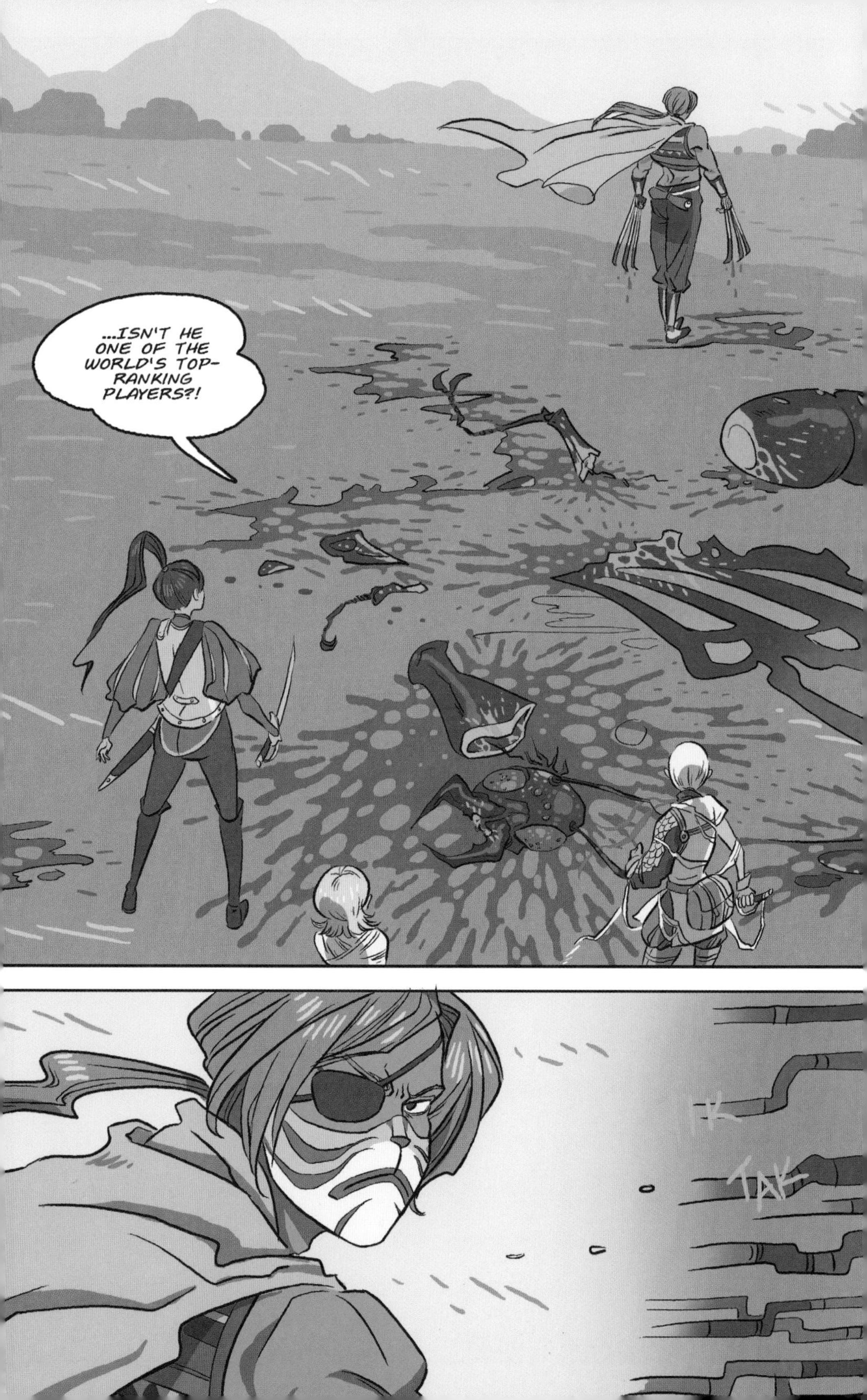
...ISN'T HE ONE OF THE WORLD'S TOP-RANKING PLAYERS?!
TAK

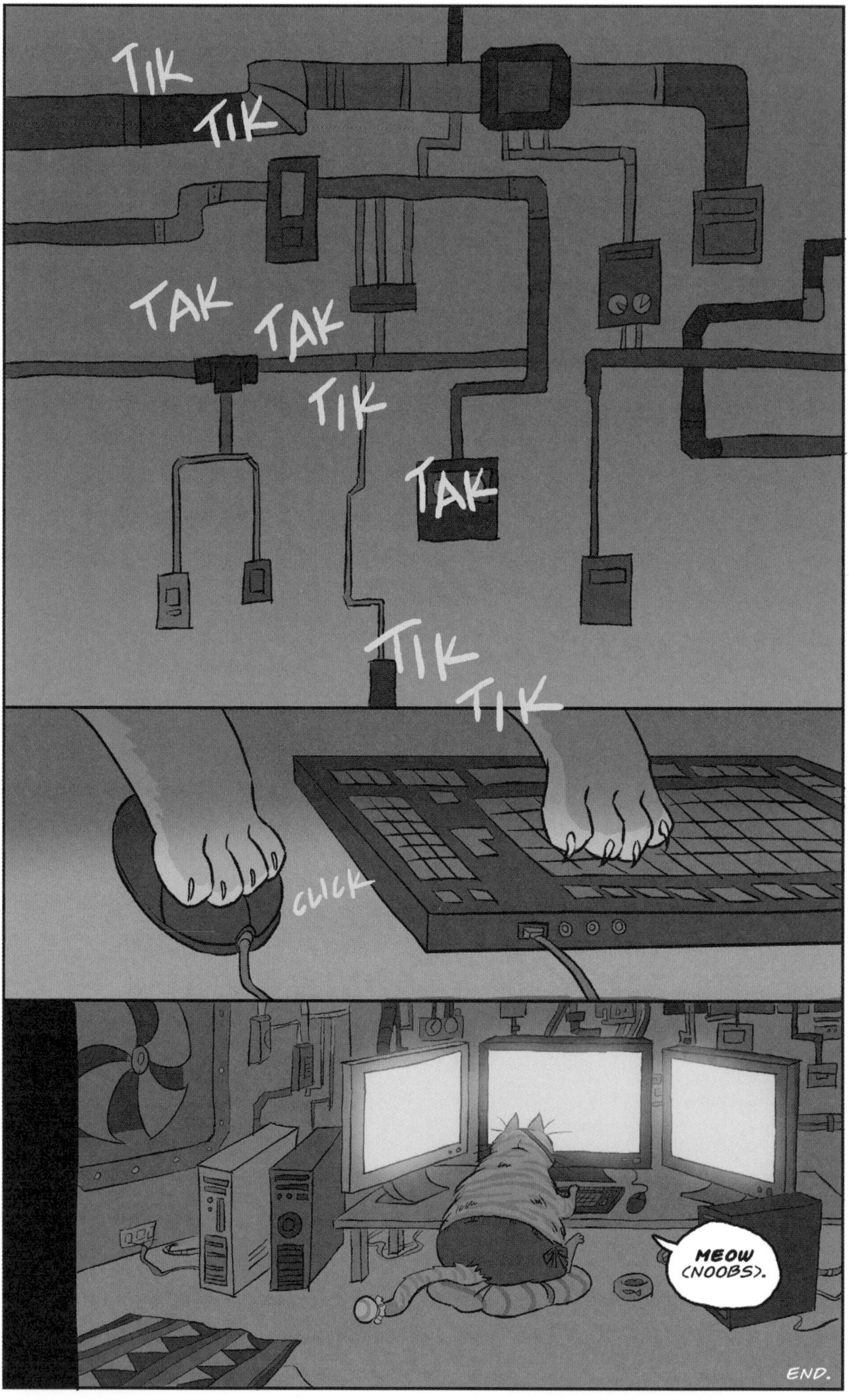
TIK
TIK
TAK
TAK
TIK
TAK
TIK
TIK
CLICK
MEOW (NOOBS).
END.

CHARACTER GALLERY

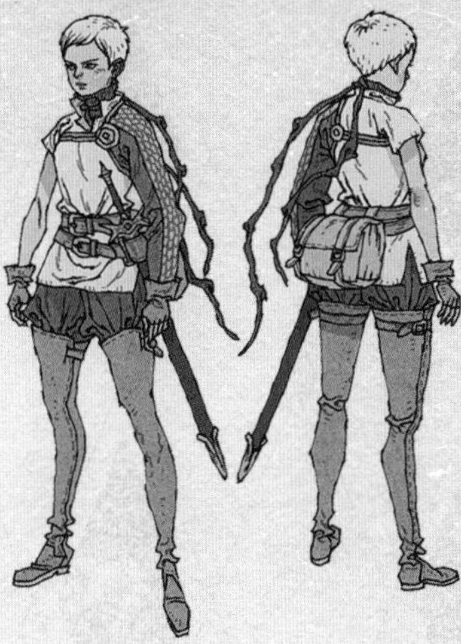

Pira

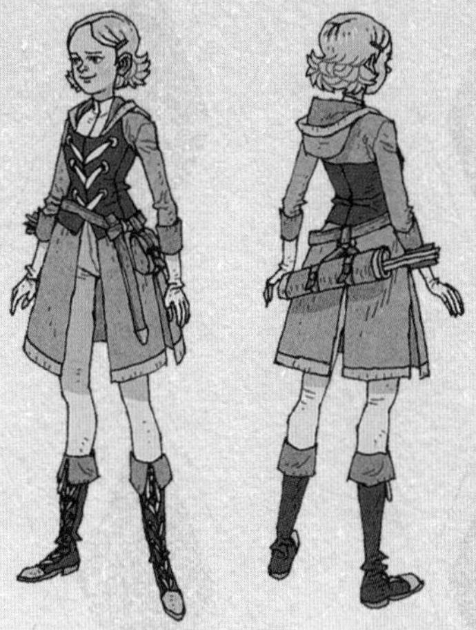

Lono

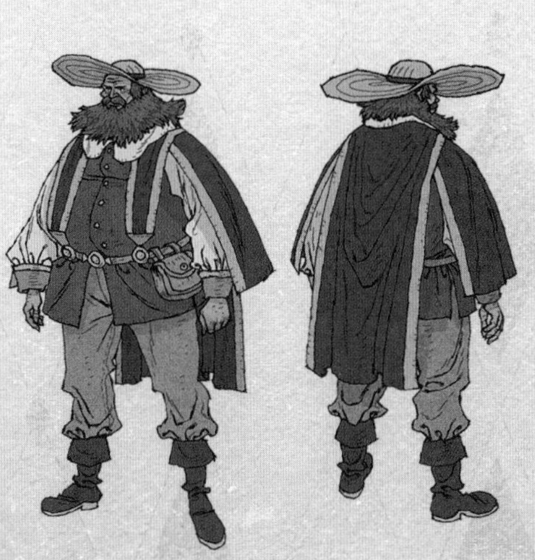

Yonder

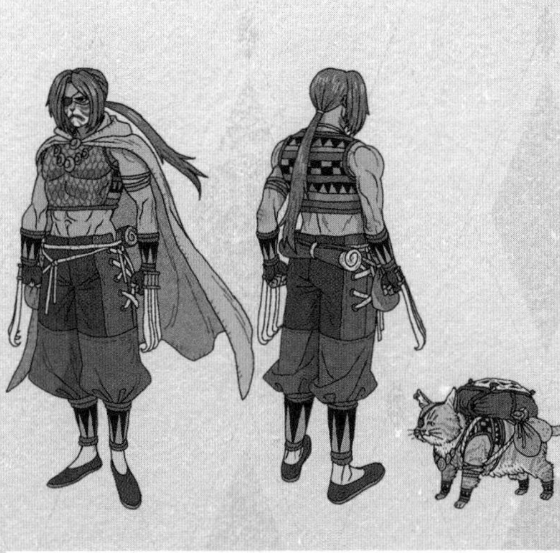

Chobo

Prince

King

Indrid

David

Sala

Ruth

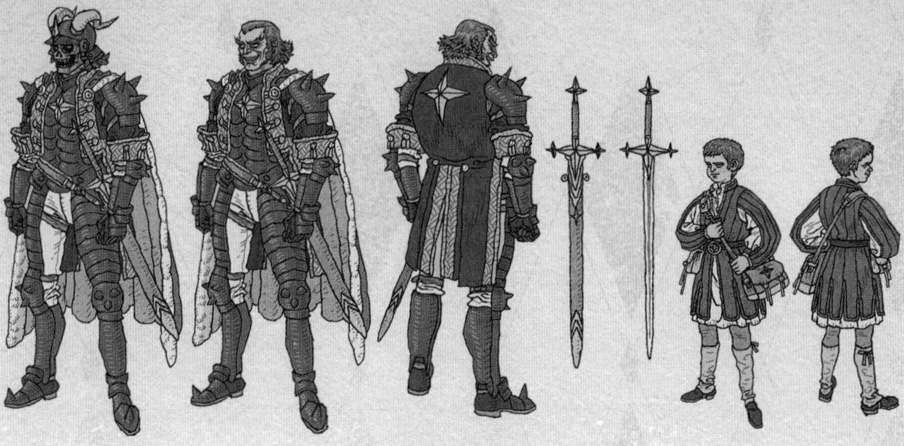

General Zeal

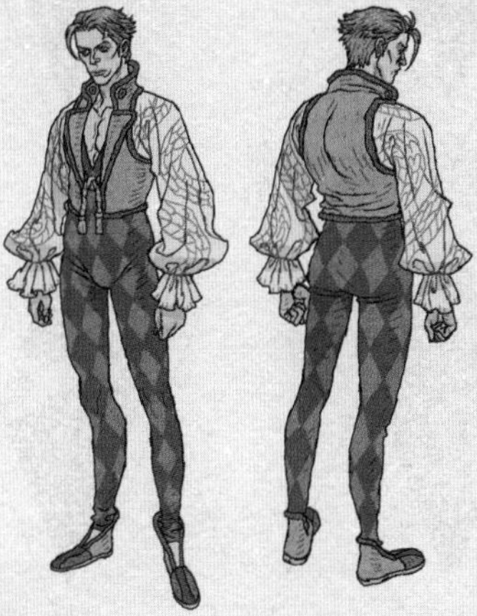

Pierrot

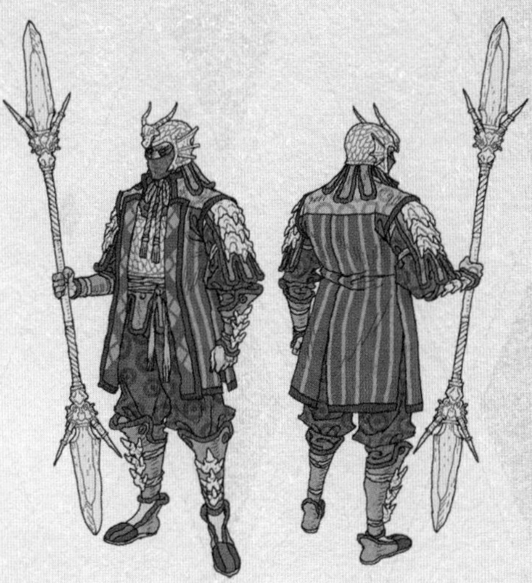

Elite Soldier

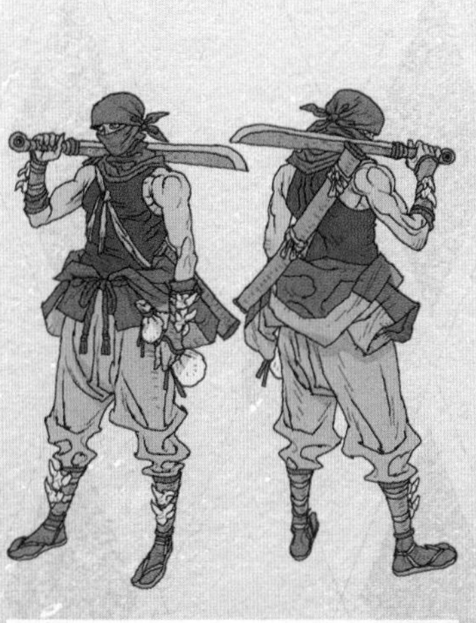

Speran Soldier

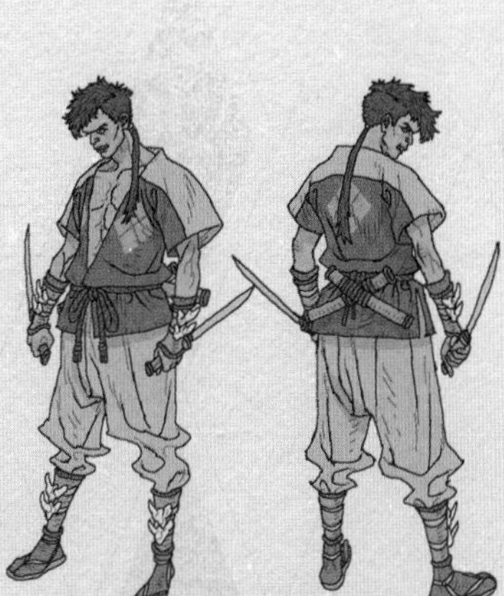

Speran Soldier

ABOUT THE AUTHORS

JOSH TIERNEY

resides in Ontario, Canada with his wife, daughter, and cat. In addition to writing and editing the *Spera* series of books for Archaia, Josh runs Spera-Comic.com with the help of Olivier Pichard.

AFU CHAN

is a freelance illustrator and comic artist. He also loves designing characters of all types and races, including monsters. To check out more of his work, visit www.afuchan.com.

GIANNIS MILONOGIANNIS

makes comic books on his own and with others. You can find his work in *Old City Blues* and *Spera* from Archaia and *Prophet* from Image Comics. Giannis' favourite things are coffee and samurai robots.

The **ATELIER SENTÔ** is a French duo (Cécile Brun and Olivier Pichard). They live in the mountains and are currently working on a watercolour video game set in Okinawa called *The Coral Cave*.

MINDY LEE is an artist living and working in Los Angeles, CA. She has worked for Sammy Studios, Warner Brothers, Pandemic Studios, Carbine Studios, and Six Point Harness. Her work can be seen on Mindydoodles.com and Mindyleedoodles.tumblr.com.

SOURYA SIHACHAKR

is a comic book artist living in Lyon, France. He is currently working on the *Rouge* series (Ankama) and *Spera* (Archaia). Besides drawing, Sourya also enjoys singing really loud when no one's around.

VALENTIN SEICHE

is a comic artist living in France. You can find him online at airfortress.tumblr.com.

VICTORIA GRACE ELLIOTT

is a witch hailing from the Kudzu Forests of the Deep South. She currently roams the Texas Hill Country in the company of a lone googtroll. She publishes *balderdash!* (balderdashcomic.com) and draws *House of Orr* (houseoforr.com).

SAICOINK

draws the mini-comic series *Open Spaces and Closed Places* and has contributed to *Electric Ant Zine, Love Love Hill,* and *Womanthology.* She lives near a river, perfect for walks in the spring and summer.

SHELLY CHEN

is a Taiwanese illustrator working in San Francisco. She specialises in watercolour painting, storytelling, and character design. To check out more of her work, please visit shellychenstudio.com.

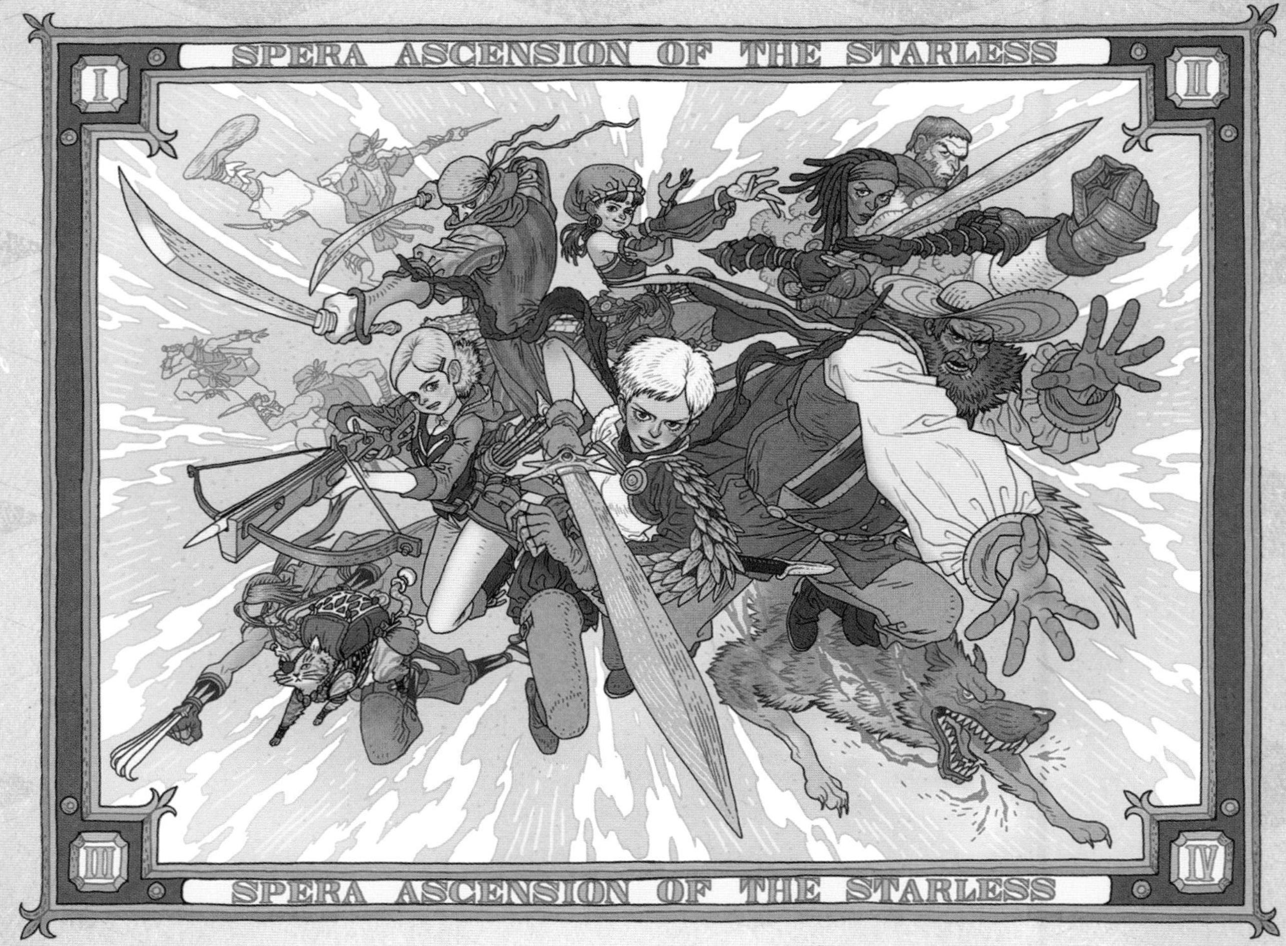
SPERA ASCENSION OF THE STARLESS
I
II
III
IV
SPERA ASCENSION OF THE STARLESS